DB2 PERFORMANCE AND DEVELOPMENT GUIDE

DB2 PERFORMANCE AND DEVELOPMENT GUIDE

Joseph R. Geller

VAN NOSTRAND REINHOLD
New York

Copyright © 1991 by Van Nostrand Reinhold

Library of Congress Catalog Card Number 90-24732
ISBN 0-442-00526-1

All rights reserved. No part of this work covered by the copyright hereon may be reproduced or used in any form or by any means—graphic, electronic, or mechanical, including photocopying, recording, taping, or information storage and retrieval systems—without written permission of the publisher.

Manufactured in the United States of America

Published by Van Nostrand Reinhold
115 Fifth Avenue
New York, New York 10003

Chapman and Hall
2-6 Boundary Row
London, SE1 8HN

Thomas Nelson Australia
102 Dodds Street
South Melbourne 3205
Victoria, Australia

Nelson Canada
1120 Birchmount Road
Scarborough, Ontario M1K 5G4, Canada

16 15 14 13 12 11 10 9 8 7 6 5 4 3 2 1

Library of Congress Cataloging-in-Publication Data

Geller, Joseph R.
    DB2 performance and development guide / Joseph R. Geller.
      p.   cm.
    Includes bibliographical references and index.
    ISBN 0-442-00526-1
    1. Data base management. 2. DB2 (Computer program)
I. Title.
QA76.9.D3G44   1991
005.25'65—dc20   90-24732
                                                        CIP

To my wife Audrey and my son Joshua

Contents

Preface		xi
PART 1 Design and Development		1
1: DB2 BASICS		3
1.1	DB2 Tables and SQL Coding	4
1.2	The DB2 Catalog	19
1.3	Authorization	21
1.4	Summary and Key Guidelines	25
2: DATABASE DESIGN AND CREATION		27
2.1	Logical Design	27
2.2	Table Design	40
2.3	Referential Integrity	49
2.4	Table Spaces	57
2.5	Indexes	74
2.6	Views	83
2.7	Summary and Key Guidelines	88
3: PROGRAM DEVELOPMENT		91
3.1	SQL in Programs	92
3.2	Synonyms, Secondary SQLIDs, and Aliases	112

3.3	Plans and DBRMs	116
3.4	Attachment Facilities	128
3.5	Dynamic SQL	132
3.6	DB2I—SPUFI	140
3.7	QMF—Query Management Facility	147
3.8	Summary and Key Guidelines	155

PART 2 Access Path Selection — 157

4: ACCESS PATHS—THE BASICS OF PERFORMANCE — 159

4.1	Access Paths to One Table	160
4.2	Access Paths to Multiple Tables—Joins and Subqueries	178
4.3	Clustered Indexes	191
4.4	Catalog Statistics	198
4.5	Predicates	213
4.6	Summary and Key Guidelines	218

5: EXPLAIN — 219

5.1	Why Everyone Should Use EXPLAIN	219
5.2	EXPLAIN Results—Interpreting the Plan_Table	222
5.3	Joins and Subqueries	245
5.4	Other EXPLAIN Data	254
5.5	Summary and Key Guidelines	258

PART 3 Tuning — 261

6: EFFICIENT PROGRAMMING AND PROGRAM TUNING — 263

6.1	Efficient Programming	264
6.2	Loading and Processing Large Volumes of Data	282
6.3	DB2 Locking and Concurrency	294

7: DATABASE TUNING — 303

7.1	Determining the Need for Tuning	303
7.2	Changing DB2 Catalog Statistics Manually	307
7.3	Table Space Reorganization	312
7.4	Adding and Dropping Indexes	319
7.5	Table Changes	329

7.6	Recovery	**342**
7.7	Archiving—Creating a History Table	**351**
7.8	Summary and Key Guidelines	**358**

8: SYSTEM TUNING **361**

8.1	Buffer Pools	**362**
8.2	Catalog Maintenance	**364**
8.3	Log Dataset Maintenance	**367**
8.4	Other System Parameters	**370**
8.5	Performance Monitors	**373**
8.6	Controlling SQL Usage. Resource Limit Facility (RLF) and the QMF Governor	**380**

9: APPLICATION INTERFACES **385**

9.1	Call Attachment Facility	**385**
9.2	CICS Interface	**387**
9.3	IMS Interface	**396**
9.4	Summary and Key Guidelines	**401**

APPENDICES

A: SAMPLE TABLES **403**

B: DASD CONSIDERATIONS **411**

C: REMOTE DATABASE ACCESS **413**

INDEX **419**

Preface

This book describes DB2 database design and programming, tuning, and performance. It is intended both for the experienced DB2 DBA or programmer and for the novice. It may seem like this is a lot to aim for in one book, but there are good reasons for it. There is a strong emphasis on the interplay between database design and programming. This is true in all regards, but especially for performance. The two tasks must go hand in hand. DBAs must understand SQL coding (and the application requirements), and how DB2 will process each statement. The programmer must know the design of the tables and indexes he/she will be using and how DB2 utilizes them.

DB2 is a rapidly growing market. Many companies are acquiring it and using it for most of their new development. It is a topic of great interest to DP professionals. Since it is being so heavily used for production systems, there is also much interest in the performance of the system. DB2 is very easy to use for access to any of the data in the database. The QMF query package brings this ease of use to the end-user. This means that there is going to be a very high usage of the system. Therefore, it is necessary to understand the considerations for good performance and how to achieve it.

Why is there such an emphasis on DB2 performance? It *is* being used widely for production and reporting, so naturally there is concern. But there are some other considerations. Early on, DB2 had a reputation for not performing well, and people are still afraid of that possibility. This reputation is partly due to early myths about relational systems in general, and partly based on the performance of DB2's first releases. The performance of DB2 today is much better than originally.

Many shops take existing application systems, convert them to DB2, and compare the results. Often, in these cases, DB2 does not perform as well as the old system. However, there are reasons for this other than DB2's capabilities. You can always find specific examples where one DBMS or file system will perform better than others, and other examples where it will perform worse. Also bear in mind that these applications (whether under IMS, VSAM, or other DBMS) were usually written a number of years ago and have been heavily tuned since. When first written, they might not have performed as well as they do today. The DP staff has also had several years of experience with the other DBMS. It is likely that their first try at a DB2 system will not be optimal. As the DP staff gains experience, they will find that DB2 can be made to perform very well.

DB2 and the SQL language are also very powerful tools. You can access any data field in any order and easily combine different data. Naturally, not all of these functions will perform well on all of the data. With IMS or VSAM you couldn't do many of the things that DB2 allows. Since these functions could not be done easily, they either weren't done at all or only in batch. DB2 users can get much more information out of the system. Since more can be gotten, and more easily, there will be much heavier access to the system. This is good. However, more system resources will be required (i.e., a faster CPU, more memory), and there will be a greater need for the system to perform well and for the programmers and DBAs to know how to use it well.

Tuning is normally something you expect mostly experienced DBAs or programmers to be concerned with. However, DB2 performance is rooted in the fundamentals of SQL calls and database design. It is not just an "after the fact" activity, but is integrated with the design and coding. That is why this is both a performance and development guide. It is important for even new programmers to understand these basics of DB2 performance. The rules and guidelines are fairly simple, but they are not always well-documented and obvious. These rules can be followed by the novice and are equally important for the experienced person.

Many people become DBAs without any knowledge of how to program for their databases. Likewise, many programmers are not taught much about database design and structure. To really utilize a DBMS (such as DB2) well, requires understanding both aspects. Therefore, introductory SQL chapters may be needed by senior DBAs, and introductory design chapters may be needed by senior programmers. These will lay the groundwork for the other material.

This book is also a practical guide. It describes the real tasks that are done by DB2 professionals. It does not describe every parameter that may be used to define a database or run a utility. Rather, it points the way to those features and utilities that are most useful, and discusses why you would use them. It is also task-oriented. It describes the common types of programming tasks and how best to accomplish them. The EXPLAIN function (which is fundamental to achieving good performance) is described with practical examples, showing what to look for, and in what order. Not all of the topics are directly performance-related. I chose those topics that are important to the effective use of DB2. In all cases I try to guide the reader (with practical examples) to the best way to do the tasks that are needed.

Performance issues cover the gamut from simple programming guidelines through MVS operating system parameters. However, 90% of the performance of a system is rooted in the basic programming and database design issues and their relationships. Therefore, my audience is not the systems programmer. It is the DBA (database administrator) and the programmer. It is not an introductory book for someone just starting out. However, it is also not primarily for the expert who already knows all about DB2 tuning. There is material in this book that might benefit them, but much of it they already know. However, the majority of programmers and DBAs do not know many of the basic performance issues. These groups are, therefore, the primary audience.

As mentioned above, DB2 today performs much better than the first releases. Every new release of DB2 has introduced new functions and has greatly improved performance. Some of the improvements are transparent to the DB2 user. Others require knowledge of how DB2 processes requests. Most of the material in this book is based on DB2 Version 2, Release 2 (hereafter referred to as Version 2.2). However, since many issues will change in the future, I have also tried to illustrate trends in performance improvements by showing examples of how data was accessed both in earlier releases and the current release. In fact, the next release (Version 2.3) has already been announced. (It is scheduled to be available in October, 1991.) This book includes information covering the new features of this release. The techniques that apply to Version 2.2 will generally still apply to Version 2.3. It is just as important for the reader to be aware of the types of things to look for as to know the specifics.

The DB2 manuals also change with each new release. All reference manuals use the titles of the Version 2.2 manuals. Other releases have similarly named manuals.

The book is divided into several parts. Part I covers general database design and programming guidelines and the performance aspects of each. It emphasizes the important parameters to use for all table design and program development.

Part II describes the DB2 access paths. How DB2 satisfies each type of SQL request is the most important topic for anyone interested in DB2 performance. Once you know what DB2 does in general, and how to find out what it is doing for a specific statement (through EXPLAIN), you will have the knowledge needed to guide you through database and program design.

Part III covers the various types of tuning—program, database, and system. Although tuning is often thought of as something to do when things are not efficient, these chapters provide guidelines for developing efficient systems in the first place.

The book is not divided into topics for programmers, topics for DBAs, and topics for systems programmers. Each of these groups *must* know and understand the other areas to most effectively use DB2.

I would like to thank the following people for the help they have provided in the preparation of this book: Dianne Littwin, my editor at VNR, Robert Gasperi (her assistant), the reviewers for their comments, and Laura Dann from IBM.

JOE GELLER
Hartsdale, New York

DB2 PERFORMANCE AND DEVELOPMENT GUIDE

part 1

Design and Development

1

DB2 Basics

DB2 is becoming a very widely used database management system for production applications as well as decision support systems. The development of good, efficient systems is of concern to all shops. Using a product efficiently (i.e., rapid, accurate development of the applications) and writing efficient programs are two tasks that are based on a good understanding of all aspects of the software products. This book will try to guide the reader to the simplest and best approaches to the use of DB2.

DB2 can be very efficient. However, because it is very easy to access any data in any order, it is also easy to use DB2 inefficiently. To develop efficient application systems there must be the proper combination of table design, choice of indexes, coding to take best advantage of the indexes and table structure, and testing and evaluation of the program performance. The programmer must have an understanding of how DB2 accesses data and how to code to get DB2 to do things efficiently. Tools are available (the EXPLAIN feature) to enable the programmer to find out DB2's choice of access path (see Section 5.1).

As described in the section on indexes (Section 2.5), there are misconceptions about DB2 as regards to what the programmer has to know. The assumption is that since SQL is easy to use and any data can be retrieved regardless of whether or not there are indexes, the programmer does not need to know the structure of the tables and indexes. Likewise, there is no need for the programmer to "navigate" through the database. It is true that you can write programs without any of this knowledge, but to write good efficient programs it is necessary to understand how *DB2* will navigate through the database and how to influence DB2 in its choice of access path.

It is true that such things as how well the operating system is tuned can affect DB2 performance. However, the most important factors are rooted in the basics of DB2 design and programming, and the interplay of these two processes. The DBA must know how to program in SQL and how *DB2* will process each SQL statement in order to most effectively design the databases and tune the system. While some of the material in this and other chapters may already be familiar to many readers, it may not be familiar to all, and it *is* important to all.

1.1 DB2 TABLES AND SQL CODING

When we talk about performance, the main thing we are concerned with is the performance of programs that access the database. This also includes queries and reports (e.g., as executed through QMF). Program performance is not just based on the individual statements, but also on the database design, database parameters, and system parameters. These are all interrelated. If a query is running too slowly, the DBA must first know exactly what the query is doing before he can determine whether it is the SQL statement or the tables and indexes that are the cause. Conversely, the programmers (and QMF end-users) must know something about the database and what indexes are available.

First, we must make a distinction between DB2 and SQL. DB2 is a relational database management system. It takes care of the storage and access of the data as well as the integrity and security of it. SQL is the language that programmers and users employ to access the DB2 database. It is possible for there to be other languages which could access a DB2 database, but SQL is the one which IBM has implemented. Actually, QMF provides several other languages for DB2 access. These are QBE and the prompted query, and now also SAA Language Access—a natural language query. These are discussed in Section 3.7. SQL is becoming a standard language for access to relational databases. Many other DBMSs are using it.

1.1.1 Tables

In DB2, a database is mainly a conceptual structure. It is a grouping of different tables of data. There is nothing inherent in DB2 that requires these tables to be related to each other or for all related tables to be in one database. You can have any number of databases. The actual basic unit within DB2 is the table. A table consists of rows and columns (Figure 1.1). There is a fixed set of columns. Each column represents a different data item (also known as a field or attribute). The columns are attributes of some entity type (a patient in this figure). There is one row for each occurrence of the entity. A row corresponds to a record or segment in other file systems.

A table contains one type of data. Different data is kept in different tables (Figure 1.2). This looks a bit like flat (sequential) files. There are some differ-

PATID	LASTNAME	FIRSTNAME	SEX	BIRTHDATE
030303030	JONES	PETER	M	1947-03-23
010101010	SMITH	MARY	F	1955-12-17
345678912	BAKER	BOB	M	1952-02-11
192837465	CLARK	KATHY	F	1959-09-07

Figure 1.1. The Layout of a DB2 Table.

PATID	ADMITDATE	DISDATE	CONDITION
030303030	1985-07-02	1985-08-03	9
010101010	1986-02-19	1986-02-20	7
345678912	1984-11-09	1985-04-12	7
192837465	1989-08-22	9999-12-31	
345678912	1986-05-12	1986-06-01	7

Figure 1.2. Different Data Is Stored in Different Tables.

ences. Let's look at some different types of file organizations and see how a relational database is different.

A sequential file is read one record at a time. There are no keys to the file and no direct access to a single record. There are no inherent relationships between different files. All relationships are completely under program control. Each program needs the same logic to ensure the consistency of the data.

A VSAM KSDS file is keyed. There is one (or a few) keys. Access can be sequential or can be direct by the keys that have been defined. Finding records with particular values in nonkey fields is sequential and under program control. All relationships between VSAM files is also under program control.

A database management system does many things for you. It provides backup and recovery functions. It logs updates so that the files can be recovered to the point of a failure. It allows you to define relationships between the data types. It also provides a processing language of some kind for the manipulation of the data.

1.1.2 What DB2 Does for You

1.1.2.1 Any Column Can Be Referenced

DB2 gives you the ability to reference data by column value for any column (Figure 1.3). Some other DBMSs do this, but many don't. They only allow lookup via key fields. Of course, even in DB2, performance is generally better when using columns that have indexes.

```
SELECT PATID,LASTNAME,FIRSTNAME
  FROM THSPATO
  WHERE BIRTHDATE BETWEEN '1952-01-01' AND '1952-06-30'
```
Figure 1.3. Any Column Can Be Used for Lookup.

1.1.2.2 Processing Sets of Data

Another major feature of relational databases is that a single statement can process a set of data. For example (Figure 1.4), you can update all rows with column = '......'. Most other DBMSs cannot process sets. A single statement will process a single data record. The ability to process a set of rows can simplify the application programs and improve performance.

These capabilities make DB2 a very powerful and easy to use system. They also create the requirement to more thoroughly understand the data and the processing requirements. A program statement may on one occasion update three rows, but another time have to access and update thousands of rows.

A feature of DB2 that takes a little getting used to is that there is no inherent order to the data rows. A table is a set of row occurrences. You can process a set (or subset) of rows. You can retrieve the rows in any order desired. However, if you don't *ask* for a specific order, there is no fixed order in which you will receive them.

1.1.2.3 Dynamic Relationships

Relationships between data entities are dynamic. They are defined by column value and are not fixed. The one exception to this is referential integrity rules (see Section 2.3). For example, patients have admissions. The basic patient data is in one table and the admission data is in a separate table. Both have the patient identification (PATID) as a field. To find the admissions for a patient, you select data from both tables where the rows have the same PATID (Figure 1.5). This is called a join of the two tables. Other DBMSs (such as IMS) require you to permanently define the relationships between entities. The admissions for a patient would either be stored physically near the patient data or there

```
-- For any patient who was discharged in 1985 and whose referral
-- was a 9, change the referral to an 8.

UPDATE THSDISO
  SET REFERRAL = 8
  WHERE YEAR(DISDATE)=1985 AND REFERRAL = 9
```
Figure 1.4. Sets of Rows Can Be Updated with One SQL Statement.

```
SELECT THSPAT0.PATID, LASTNAME, FIRSTNAME, ADMDATE, DISDATE
  FROM THSPAT0, THSADM0
  WHERE THSPAT0.PATID = THSADM0.PATID
```
Figure 1.5. Joining Two Tables.

would be pointers from one record type to the other. With DB2, the fact that a row from the patient table is related to some rows in the admission table can be based solely on their having the same PATID value.

An example showing the flexibility of DB2 is the relationship between services that a patient receives and the admission during which they occur. Figure 1.6 shows how to match these up. With another DBMS you might define the services as being dependent on the patient (rather than the admissions), since most access does not need to tie them to an admission. When they are needed by admission, a program would be required to find the matchups. With DB2, the SQL language provides that ability.

With DB2 you can combine several tables based on the values of any compatible columns. Compatible means they must have the same data type. This makes things much easier and much more flexible. There is, however, one drawback to this flexibility. It is also possible to join tables on columns that are not related to each other in any valid application sense. Two columns may both be numeric but may have nothing to do with each other.

The ability to do all of this is also not dependent on the existence of indexes. Any columns can be used for anything. Indexes can be defined for performance, but are not required for any other access (with a few exceptions, as described in Section 2.5).

All columns of a DB2 table are defined. This provides a great deal of data integrity and data independence. You could define a table as having one big character column. The individual fields could then be defined and manipulated by the programs. This is what you do with VSAM files and many IMS databases. However, this defeats the purpose and many of the benefits of DB2. When done this way, the integrity of the data placed in each column is in the hands of each program. This is much more error-prone. There have been many application systems developed where a single record type is used for several different sets of data. The columns are redefined for each set. This is a bad practice. Not only do the update programs need to distinguish the different data, but every retrieval

```
SELECT THSADM0.PATID,ADMDATE,SERVDATE,TYPE,CLINICIAN
  FROM THSADM0,THSSVC0
  WHERE THSADM0.PATID = THSSVC0.PATID AND
      SERVDATE >= ADMDATE AND SERVDATE <= DISDATE
```
Figure 1.6. Joining the Admissions and Services Tables.

program as well must have logic to decode the records and figure out which type of data is present in each part of the record layout.

Having only one type of data item for each column enables the creation of general-purpose programs such as QMF. The data is much easier to understand and use. SQL can reference any column for any type of access, so there is a general ease of use. For update, the data type (e.g., decimal, integer, character) is checked by the DBMS. This enhances data integrity. Also, SQL has a number of built-in functions for processing different types of data. For numeric columns you can get the sum, average, maximum, etc., of a column. This can work only if there is one type of data in that column. There are date arithmetic functions that work on date data-type columns. This is of tremendous benefit. Again, there must be date data in the column.

All of these benefits show why there is a big boost to productivity with a DBMS that enforces the definition and reference by column rather than by a chunk of data called a record.

1.1.3 The SQL Language

SQL is a language for accessing a relational database. It is used from within a program or a report writer. Generally, SQL has become a standard for relational access. In addition to DB2, it is also used with IBM's SQL/DS, the OS2 Data Manager for the PS2 personal computer, and ORACLE, which is available on many different computers.

SQL is divided into three types of statements—DML, DDL, and DCL:

> DML—Data Manipulation Language. These are the statements used for accessing the data. Therefore, they are the most commonly used part of SQL. The four basic types of DML statements are SELECT, INSERT, UPDATE, and DELETE. Each of these can operate on a set of data (i.e., multiple records) with a single statement.
>
> DDL—Data Definition Language. These statements define the data to DB2. Most of these start with the word CREATE. For example, CREATE DATABASE, CREATE TABLE, CREATE INDEX. DBAs certainly use these statements frequently, but programmers will also, for the creation of test tables. Sophisticated end-users may also be given the authority to create tables.
>
> DCL—Data Control Language. The previous paragraph used the word "authority." DB2 provides extensive features for the security and control of the data in the system. The ability to do anything in DB2 (creating and accessing objects) requires authority to do so. These authorities are GRANTed and REVOKEd with DCL statements. By default, any table can only be accessed by the creator of the table. To allow others to access it, they must be granted the appropriate authority.

1.1.4 SQL Performance

This section will illustrate the SQL DML statements and explain the basic performance issues of each. This topic is not only of interest to programmers, but should be of interest to all DBAs.

Retrieving data from DB2 tables can be viewed in simplified terms as consisting of the following steps:

- read each row from disk
- apply any selection criteria
- sort the selected data if required
- for statements that process several tables (e.g., joins), for each selected row in the first table, DB2 must find matching rows in the other tables.

Selection criteria identify which rows are to be returned or processed further. There is some CPU time involved in evaluating the criteria, but reducing the number of rows returned saves much time for data movement, sorting, joining with other tables, and applying functions to the selected columns.

This basic process of looking at every row is done with what is called a table space scan. DB2 will read every physical block in the table space and look at each row. For large tables this can involve a lot of IO. Having indexes on frequently used columns can substantially improve performance. An index is essentially a keyed file consisting of the indexed columns and the address of the data row.

To find rows with a particular value in an indexed column, DB2 can quickly find the entries in the index and then directly get the rest of the data. If many index entries match the criteria, then many data rows will be accessed. The data rows may or may not be in the same physical order as the index entries. If they are, then performance will be much better. This index would be considered clustered. Clustering is described in Sections 2.5 and 4.3.

If the data needs to be returned in a specific order, then generally, DB2 must sort the selected rows. However, if there is an index on the columns needed for the ordering, and if DB2 uses this index to read the rows, then the sort can be avoided.

This has been a very brief and cursory description of some of the performance factors. They will become clearer in later sections.

1.1.5 SELECT Statements

Each DB2 table consists of records (called rows). The table also has a set of columns. Every row has the same columns. Once data has been entered into a table, you can retrieve it with the SELECT statement. Figure 1.7 shows several SE-

```
SELECT PATID,LASTNAME
  FROM THSPAT0
(a)  Selecting several columns


SELECT *
  FROM THSPAT0
(b)  Selecting all columns


SELECT PATID,LASTNAME
  FROM THSPAT0
  WHERE BIRTHDATE = '1960-05-01'
(c)  Specifying selection criteria
```

Figure 1.7. Several Basic SELECT Statements.

LECT statements. The minimum requirement is for a list of columns to be selected (following the keyword SELECT) and a table from which to get them (following the keyword FROM). If you want to retrieve all of the columns of the table, * may be used instead of explicitly naming every column. This is very convenient for ad hoc query. For programs, it is better to list the columns that are needed (see Section 3.1). In this simplest form, every row of the table will be retrieved. Figure 1.7a retrieves the PATID and LASTNAME columns for every row of the THSPAT0 table.

Performance will be better if the select list only contains the columns that are needed. Each additional column requires some extra processing by DB2 to move the data. A few columns do not make much difference, but a hundred columns will. Any sorting that is needed will also be quicker with less data to be sorted. Furthermore, if the only columns that are asked for are in an index, then only the index will need to be accessed. This will save IOs.

Very often, you do not want every row, only those that meet certain selection criteria. This is specified with the WHERE clause (Figure 1.7c). This clause tells DB2 which rows it should access. In principle, this means that as DB2 gets each row of the table, it will evaluate the predicates in the WHERE clause and only return those that meet the criteria. In practice, DB2 will do this sometimes. However, it does not always have to retrieve each row and apply all of the predicates. If there are indexes on the columns that appear in the WHERE clause, DB2 may use those indexes to reduce the searching it must do. This can greatly reduce the number of rows that DB2 must examine. It also means a great reduction in the number of IOs necessary to process the SELECT. QMF users may sometimes select all rows and page through the rows, visually looking for the ones they are interested in. Performance will be better if they include WHERE clauses to limit the number of rows returned.

For small tables (a few thousand rows or less), scanning the entire table does not take long. For larger tables, the effective use of indexes can be important. When you use SQL, you do not tell DB2 whether or not to use an index. DB2 decides this for itself. It is important, however, to know what indexes exist and how best to take advantage of them. Chapter 4 discusses this in detail. As a basic guideline, DBAs should create indexes on columns that are frequently used in WHERE clauses. Programmers should understand how to code the SQL statements so that the indexes may be used.

Indexes affect performance, but remember, they do not have anything to do with which columns can be used as search criteria in a WHERE clause. Any column may be used.

1.1.5.1 Sorting

The rows of a table have no intrinsic order. Even if a primary key or other indexes are defined for a table, DB2 does not automatically order the data by any columns. If you do not ask for them in a specific order, then the order in which the rows are returned on a SELECT will depend on how the rows are physically stored at that point in time, and on whether or not DB2 chooses to use an index to satisfy the SELECT. The way you tell DB2 that you want the data in a certain order is with the ORDER BY clause. This is illustrated in Figure 1.8. You can name any number of sort columns, each of which can be ascending (the default) or descending. The ORDER BY columns have to be in the select list.

In order to present the rows in a particular order, DB2 has two choices. After retrieving all rows that meet the search criteria, it can sort them. Or, if there is an index in the desired order, DB2 can access the rows via the index. Then they will already be in the requested order and a sort can be avoided. DB2 will not necessarily do so, however. There may be a faster way to initially access the data and evaluate the full set of search criteria. If there are only going to be a few rows returned, then this alternative access, followed by a sort, may be preferable. If there are selection criteria on the high order columns of an index, and the ORDER BY clause is also on these same columns, then there is an increased chance that DB2 will use this index.

Sorting was greatly improved in DB2 Version 2, which can handle larger num-

```
SELECT PATID,LASTNAME,FIRSTNAME,SEX,BIRTHDATE
  FROM THSPAT0
  ORDER BY SEX,BIRTHDATE DESC
```
Figure 1.8. Asking for the Rows in a Specific Order.

```
SELECT EMPID, HOURS_WORKED * RATE + 10, YEAR(BIRTHDATE)
  FROM EMPLOYEE
```

Figure 1.9. Expressions and Functions in the Select List.

bers of rows fairly efficiently. However, generally speaking, large sorts should be avoided, whereas small ones are acceptable.

1.1.5.2 Expressions and Functions

The columns that are returned are not restricted to just the actual column values from the table. They can be any expression, including constants, expressions with one column, or expressions involving multiple columns. In Figure 1.9, we are asking DB2 to calculate the employees' wages as their hours worked times their rate, plus a $10 bonus. There are also built-in functions in SQL that operate on columns. This example has the YEAR function that takes a date column as its parameter and returns the year.

Expressions and functions can also be used in the WHERE clause, but doing so prevents DB2 from using an index on the columns involved. DB2 can use an index to find admissions in 1990 if the WHERE clause is written as:

WHERE ADMDATE BETWEEN '1990-01-01' AND '1990-12-31'

but it cannot use an index for:

WHERE YEAR(ADMDATE) = 1990

Using functions and expressions also adds to the CPU cost to process the statement.

1.1.5.3 Column Functions

There are also functions in SQL which operate on the set of selected rows. Figure 1.10 requests a count of the number of rows in THSPAT0 with a birthdate in 1960. The result of this SELECT is a single row with one value—the count of rows. The functions which operate on sets are:

COUNT
AVG—the average
MAX—the maximum value
MIN—the minimum value
SUM

These column functions can be used over the full set of (selected) rows. They are even more powerful when used with another clause of the SELECT state-

```
SELECT COUNT(*)
  FROM THSPAT0
  WHERE YEAR(BIRTHDATE) = 1960
```

Figure 1.10. Finding Out How Many Rows There Are.

ment. This is the GROUP BY clause (Figure 1.11). This clause tells DB2 to group the selected rows by one or more columns (which must be in the select list). This is similar to ordering, but groups are used in conjunction with the column functions. These are applied to each group of rows. In Figure 1.11, we are asking for the maximum and average weight of each active patient, grouped by sex. DB2 will select the active patients, sort them by sex, and then apply the functions to each group. Note that the select list can only contain column functions and the columns that are in the GROUP BY clause. One row is returned for each group. Therefore, it makes no sense, for example, to ask for the PATID column in this example, as there would be many such values for each group.

GROUP BY requires the data to be in order. As with the ORDER BY clause, this can be achieved either by sorting or with an appropriate index.

GROUP BY can be followed with a HAVING clause. This is similar to a WHERE, but is used as selection criteria for the groups. For example, you could find last names that occur for more than one patient:

GROUP BY LASTNAME HAVING COUNT(*) > 1

1.1.5.4 Joins

If you could only access one table at a time, DB2 would be severely limited. Part of its power is the ability to dynamically relate several tables based on the values of their columns. You can retrieve data from several tables in one SELECT statement. This is called a join. The basic format is shown in Figure 1.12. You tell DB2 that you are joining two tables by naming more than one in the FROM clause. In this example, we are joining the patient and admissions tables. The WHERE clause tells DB2 how to combine the rows of the two tables. We want to match up admissions with the respective patients. The WHERE clause, therefore, says PAT.PATID = ADM.PATID. This means that for every patient row,

```
SELECT SEX,MAX(WEIGHT),AVG(WEIGHT)
  FROM THSPAT0
  WHERE ACTIVEFLAG = 'Y'
  GROUP BY SEX
```

Figure 1.11. Grouping Rows Together.

```
SELECT PAT.PATID,LASTNAME,FIRSTNAME,ADMDATE
  FROM THSPAT0 PAT, THSADM0 ADM
  WHERE PAT.PATID = ADM.PATID AND
       LASTNAME LIKE 'SM%' AND
       ADMDATE BETWEEN '1987-01-01' AND '1987-12-31'
```

Figure 1.12. Joining Two Tables.

it should be joined with any admission rows that have the same PATID. There are a number of significant features in this example.

- There can be other search criteria in the WHERE clause other than the join criteria. In this example, we only want patients with a last name beginning with "SM" and only the admissions that fell in 1987. The more rows eliminated by other selection criteria, the less work DB2 has to do. This can be a significant factor in the performance of the join.
- The join criteria tell DB2 which rows to match up. Any columns with compatible data types can be used. If the columns do not have unique values, then each selected row of one table may match several rows of the other table. In Figure 1.12, PATID is unique in the patient table, but not in the admissions table. Therefore, each patient may match several admissions. In Figure 1.13, we are joining admissions and locations. PATID is not unique in either. Therefore, each admission may match several locations and each location may be matched with several admissions (even if they did not occur during those admissions).
- If there are no join criteria at all (i.e., there are no predicates with columns from both tables), then every row of the first table will be matched with every row of the second table! If each table has 1000 rows, the result will be 1,000,000 rows returned. Figure 1.14 has such a join. Every patient whose name starts with SM will be matched with every 1987 admission regardless of which patient the admission was for. Forgetting to give the join criteria is a very common error, espe-

```
SELECT *
  FROM THSADM0 ADM, THSLOC0 LOC
  WHERE ADM.PATID = LOC.PATID
```

Figure 1.13. If the Join Criteria Are Not Unique in Both Tables, Then Several Rows of Each Will Match Several Rows of the Other.

```
SELECT *
FROM THSPAT0 PAT, THSADM0 ADM
WHERE LASTNAME LIKE 'SM%'
    AND YEAR(ADMDATE) = 1987
```

Figure 1.14. If There Are No Join Criteria, Then Every Selected Row of One Table Will Match Every Selected Row of the Other.

cially when joining three or more tables. It will not only provide incorrect results, but is likely to also run for a long time. A join in which every row of one table is matched with all of the rows of the other table is known as a cartesian product.
- If you only refer to columns (either in the select list or WHERE clause) that have distinct names in the tables, then you do not have to specify which table they came from. If both tables have the same column name, then you must indicate which one you mean. You do this with a qualified reference. A qualified reference is essentially the table name followed by the column name (with a period in between). For example, THSPAT0.PATID. Since table names can be fairly long (my samples are 8 characters long, but they can be as much as 18 bytes), there is a shorthand alternative. In the FROM clause, you can assign a correlation name to the table name (e.g., PAT, ADM in these examples). This short correlation name can be used instead of the full table name when identifying the columns.
- The result of a join is the selected columns from each table. There is one row in the result for each matching pair of rows. If a row in either table does not match any rows in the other table, then it will not appear in the result. If a patient does not have any admissions, you do *not* get a returned row with patient data and blank admission data. You get no row returned. This type of request is sometimes called an outer join. However, you cannot use a join to find rows that do not match another table. Subqueries must be used instead.

1.1.5.5 Subqueries

Subqueries are used when the selection criteria is dependent on values in another table (or possibly other rows in the same table). There are several flavors of subqueries. Figure 1.15a has a basic one. It is finding the birthdates of patients who were admitted in January 1988. The subquery is part of the WHERE clause of the outer SELECT statement. For each patient in the outer table, the subquery looks for an admission record with a matching patient identification

```
SELECT PATID,LASTNAME,FIRSTNAME,BIRTHDATE
  FROM THSPATO PAT
  WHERE EXISTS
 (SELECT PATID FROM THSADMO ADM
    WHERE PAT.PATID = ADM.PATID AND
       ADMDATE BETWEEN '1988-01-01' AND '1988-01-31')
```
(a) A subquery

```
SELECT PAT.PATID,LASTNAME,FIRSTNAME,BIRTHDATE
  FROM THSPATO PAT, TSHADMO ADM
  WHERE PAT.PATID = ADM.PATID AND
       ADMDATE BETWEEN '1988-01-01' AND '1988-01-31'
```
(b) A join

Figure 1.15. Matching Patients and Admissions: (a) A Subquery; (b) A Join.

and an admit date in the requested range. If you think about this example for a minute, you will realize that the same result can be achieved with a join (Figure 1.15b). Some subqueries *can* be satisfied with a join.

There are cases, however, where the join is not quite equivalent to the subquery. In particular, this is true if the join columns are not unique. Each row of the outer select will only appear once in the result of a subquery. In a join, each row of both tables may appear multiple times in the result if the columns are not unique. You could use the DISTINCT keyword in the join to eliminate duplicates.

Not all subqueries match up rows as in a join. They can also be used to find rows in one table that do not match rows in another table. Figure 1.16 has a subquery to find patients who have not had any services in 1989.

These examples are just one kind of subquery. Subqueries are covered in more detail in Section 4.2, which describes DB2's access paths for processing them. Subqueries can often be very time-consuming. They must be used carefully—the choice of coding can directly affect the access path.

1.1.6 INSERT Statements

The INSERT statement is used to put new rows into a table. Figure 1.17a has an INSERT to add a patient row. You must have one value for each column of the table. When used in a program, the values can be in program variables.

```
SELECT PATID,LASTNAME,FIRSTNAME
  FROM THSPAT0
  WHERE PATID NOT IN
  (SELECT PATID FROM THSSVC0
     WHERE YEAR(SVCDATE) = 1989)
```

Figure 1.16. Using a Subselect to Find Rows That *Do Not* Meet Some Criteria.

```
INSERT INTO THSPAT0
  VALUES('123987456','JONES','ROBERT','M','1955-12-03','Y')
```
(a) All columns must have values supplied

```
INSERT INTO THSPAT0
  (PATID,LASTNAME,FIRSTNAME,SEX)
  VALUES('123987456','JONES','ROBERT','M')
```
(b) If you list the columns, you only need values for those columns

Figure 1.17. An INSERT Statement.

Figure 1.17b has an alternative coding. In this example, a list of columns is given. In this case, values only have to be supplied for the columns in the list, whereas in Figure 1.17a, every column must be given a value. If you omit some columns, they will be handled based on how they were defined in the CREATE TABLE statement (see Section 2.2). If they are defined as NOT NULL WITH DEFAULT, then they will get a default value (e.g., blank for a character column, 0 for a numeric column). If they are defined as allowing NULLs, then they will get a NULL value. If defined as NOT NULL, then you cannot leave them out. A value must be supplied. There is an advantage to explicitly naming columns. Often there are many columns in a table and you only have values for some of them. It takes a lot less typing to list those columns than to put in blank or zero values for all the other ones.

The basic INSERT statement differs from SELECT (and DELETE and UPDATE) in that it only inserts one row at a time, whereas the other statements operate on sets of rows. There is a format of INSERT that will insert a set of rows. This involves using a subquery to get values from another table to be inserted into this table. In Figure 1.18, we are selecting inactive patients and inserting them into another table that has some of the same fields as the patient table.

```
INSERT INTO THSPATX
   (PATID,LASTNAME,FIRSTNAME,BIRTHDATE)
   SELECT PATID,LASTNAME,FIRSTNAME,BIRTHDATE
     FROM THSPAT0
     WHERE ACTIVEFLAG ¬= 'Y'
```
Figure 1.18. Inserting into a Table Using a Subselect.

1.1.7 UPDATE Statements

Once data has been inserted into a table, it can be updated with the UPDATE statement (Figure 1.19). UPDATE also works on sets of rows at a time. The desired rows are identified with a WHERE clause. In this example, we are updating locations with a room number of '0253'. If there is no WHERE clause, then every row is updated. The columns that you want to update are identified with the SET clause. This clause gives the name of the column and a new value to assign it. Here we are setting WARD='1001' and ROOM='0332' for any row that had a room of '0253'. There may be no such row, or there may be many. DB2 will find them. Note that no rows are actually returned with the UPDATE statement. They are updated without being presented to you (you could always do a SELECT first if you want to see them). You do get back an indicator telling you how many rows were updated.

The performance of an UPDATE statement depends primarily on the selection criteria in the WHERE clause and the cost of finding the rows. However, if the columns being updated are in indexes, then the cost of updating the indexes can also be a factor.

1.1.8 DELETE Statements

Rows can be deleted with the DELETE statement (Figure 1.20). This, too, operates on sets of rows and can have a WHERE clause. If there is no WHERE, then every row of the table is deleted. The WHERE identifies which subset of rows to delete. As with UPDATE, no rows are returned to you, but the number of deleted

```
UPDATE THSLOC0
   SET WARD = '1001',
       ROOM = '0332'
   WHERE ROOM = '0253'
```
Figure 1.19. An UPDATE Statement.

```
DELETE FROM THSLOC0
  WHERE PATID = '555444333'
```
Figure 1.20. A DELETE Statement.

rows is. Furthermore, the more rows affected and the more indexes on the table, the greater the cost.

1.2 THE DB2 CATALOG

1.2.1 What the Catalog Contains

The catalog is an integral part of DB2. It is used both as a data dictionary and as part of the run-time environment. It contains all of the definitions of DB2 objects—databases, table spaces, tables, indexes, and columns. All authorizations for access to DB2 objects are also recorded there.

Programs require application plans (see Section 3.3) to execute. The catalog records the names of the plans, their dependencies (i.e., the tables and indexes they use), and the access paths that DB2 has decided to use for the plan.

An important part of DB2's choice of an access path is the size of the tables and indexes and various other statistics on the data. This information is also kept in the catalog.

All of this information is used when new objects are created or changed. It is also used at run-time to control the execution of the system.

The catalog itself is stored as DB2 tables which can be accessed in the same manner as any other table. This provides an easy way (standard SQL statements) to obtain the information contained there. DB2 Version 2.3 introduces an even easier way to see some of the data. Interactive panels can guide you through the catalog, looking at data for tables, table spaces, authorizations, as well as other catalog information.

1.2.2 How the Catalog Is Used

- It helps ensure the integrity of the system. The definitions of the tables and other objects are used at run-time. Each column is defined and must be given data of the correct data type. With other file systems, the record layout is defined in each program and there is no control to ensure that they all match.
- The development effort is enhanced. Programmers and DBAs can easily look things up in the catalog to verify the definition. If a programmer or user misspells a name, they will usually get back a message indicating that the object either doesn't exist or that they lack the

authority to use it. Existence of objects, their spelling, and the authorizations can all be checked.
- Performance and tuning are assisted by the statistics in the catalog. The DB2 optimizer determines the (hopefully) best access path to use for each SQL statement. The statistics are an important part of this process. The DBAs and programmers can look up these statistics to plan their tuning effort. They help them to understand DB2's access path choices, to plan for new indexes, the need for table space reorganizations, and just to monitor the growth of the application system.

Performance tuning requires a combination of using the EXPLAIN function (Chapter 5), knowing the database statistics, and knowing what indexes exist and what columns are in the indexes. Without using the catalog to obtain this information, tuning cannot be done properly.

Since the catalog is so important to the development effort, all DBAs and programmers should become familiar with it. The SQL reference manual (#SC26-4380) contains a list of all of the tables of the catalog, with a brief description of each column. You can set up some standard queries to select the important information of interest to you. Executing these and looking at the data help you to understand the structure of the catalog as well as many things about DB2. Section 4.4 of this book lists the columns and tables that are related to performance.

Listed here are some of the tables of the catalog. All of them have a creator ID of SYSIBM.

Table-related tables:
- SYSTABLES—a row for each table or view
- SYSTABLESPACE
- SYSINDEXES
- SYSKEYS—the columns which make up the indexes
- SYSCOLUMNS

Authorization-related tables:
- SYSTABAUTH—access to each table
- SYSPLANAUTH—use of each application plan
- SYSUSERAUTH—who can bind plans, create databases, etc.

This is just a subset of the tables. You should look at the SQL reference manual to see what the others are, and what is contained in each. Figures 1.21 and 1.22 are some sample queries to look at some of the data. The first one lists the columns of all tables created by GELLER. The second one finds the columns that make up each index for the THSPAT0 table created by GELLER.

```
SELECT TBNAME,NAME,COLNO,COLTYPE,LENGTH,SCALE,NULLS,COLCARD
  FROM SYSIBM.SYSCOLUMNS
  WHERE TBCREATOR = 'GELLER'
  ORDER BY TBNAME,COLNO
```
Figure 1.21. Finding the Columns of a Set of Tables.

```
SELECT IXNAME,COLNAME,COLSEQ,ORDERING
  FROM SYSIBM.SYSKEYS K, SYSIBM.SYSINDEXES I
  WHERE K.IXNAME = I.NAME AND K.IXCREATOR = I.TBCREATOR AND
        I.TBNAME = 'THSPAT0' AND I.TBCREATOR = 'GELLER'
  ORDER BY IXNAME,COLSEQ
```
Figure 1.22. Finding the Columns in Each Index.

1.3 AUTHORIZATION

DB2 was designed to have the security of the data built in to the database management system, rather than being strictly external to the DBMS software. Every activity to be done with DB2 requires authorization. These authorizations are handled by the SQL language. The statements which provide these functions are called DCL (data control language) statements. They include GRANT (to give authorization of some kind) and REVOKE (to remove the authorization).

1.3.1 Types of Authority

Authority is needed to access the data in a table (reading or updating), to create tables or other objects, to run utilities against the table spaces, and to execute the application plans that are needed by programs. There are many different privileges in DB2 and some are grouped in a hierarchy. For example, if someone has database administration authority for a particular database, he automatically has authority to create tables in that database, to access any of the tables in that database (regardless of who created them), and to run utilities against the table spaces in that database.

This book will not cover the full authorization scheme, just the basics that are needed for everyday development work. The DB2 SQL reference manual lists all of the privileges that may be GRANTed. The grouping of privileges is described in the DB2 Administration Guide (#SC26-4374).

Sometimes the set of authorizations are classified as privileges for:

- The System Administrator
- DBAs
- Programmers
- Users

However, in the DB2 development world, many of the functions will be needed by all of these groups. Programmers will often need, and will be given, the authority to create tables, table spaces, and indexes. So will advanced users who will be building some of their own tables for use with QMF. We will look at some of the tasks performed by different groups and see what functions are needed and what privileges must be granted to them.

1.3.2 Granting Authority

First, we must identify to whom privileges are granted. Every person using DB2 has a primary authorization ID. Under TSO, this is usually the person's TSO LOGON ID. Chapter 9 describes the possible authorization IDs for the CICS and IMS environments. It is also possible for a person to have a set of secondary IDs. This scheme is described in Section 3.2. For simplicity in this discussion, I will just talk about primary IDs.

Most DB2 privileges are granted to either individual authorization IDs, or to the special keyword PUBLIC. For example:

GRANT SELECT ON TABLE SYSIBM.SYSTABLES TO PUBLIC

gives every DB2 user the authority to select data from the SYSTABLES catalog table, and

GRANT CREATETAB ON DATABASE DHSHOS0 TO GELLER WITH GRANT OPTION;

allows GELLER to create tables in the DHSHOS0 database.

Obviously, only certain people are allowed to issue the GRANT statement for a particular privilege on a particular object. The WITH GRANT OPTION parameter of the GRANT statement will allow an individual to pass on the same authority to someone else. GELLER can give CREATETAB authority to someone else. If the above statement had been issued without the grant option, then he could not do so.

In general, the person who creates something has full authority over that object. The person who creates a table has access to the data. The programmer who binds a plan can execute the plan. As mentioned above, there is a hierarchy of authorities, whereby if an ID has a privilege it automatically has the subordinate privileges. For example, if you have DBADM (database administration) authority on a database, you also have full access to any of the objects in the database.

There is one special authorization called SYSADM (system administrator), which has full access to everything in the DB2 system. Initially, the SYSADM user ID has SYSADM authority and it may then be granted to other IDs. Typically, a few of the DBAs in the shop will have SYSADM. Sometimes a shop will grant SYSADM to all of the DBAs. The SYSADM IDs may retain control of the granting of authorizations to all of the programmers. Or they may grant some authorizations with the GRANT OPTION to the project leaders, who in turn can pass them on to the programmers.

Many shops require several people to have most of the functions of SYSADM but do not want them to have the ability to see the actual user data. Version 2.3 adds a new authority, called SYSCTL, which meets this need.

The following paragraphs will list the authorizations that are needed to perform the common development tasks (other sections of the book describe the actual tasks).

1.3.3 Authorizations Needed for Creating Tables

Tables are created by DBAs, by programmers, and sometimes by users. A table goes into a table space, which in turn is assigned to a database. There is a default database, and table spaces can be implicitly created when the table is created, otherwise they need to be created first.

To create a new database, you need CREATEDBA authority. If the database has already been created, then you need either DBADM authority, or CREATETAB to create a table within it.

To create a table space in a database, you either need CREATETS or DBADM authority on the database. If the table space already exists, then you need USE of the table space. To create a table space also requires a disk pack to place it on. This is done by assigning a STOGROUP (storage group). And, of course, you will need USE of that STOGROUP authority. Storage groups are set up by the system administrator, who then grants USE of the storage group. A buffer pool must also be assigned to the table space. The creator must have been granted USE of the buffer pool. The system administrator will usually assign this privilege to PUBLIC.

After a table space exists, the table can be created. Once created, the creator can access the data that is put into it—so can anyone with DBADM authority on the database. Anyone else will have to be granted access to the table.

1.3.4 Authorizations Needed by Programmers

Programmers write programs and bind plans (see Section 3.3). They and their programs access tables, they execute other peoples' programs, and they take over programs originally written by others. Obviously, they need to be granted access to the tables (access can be read only or insert, update or delete). An application plan is created at the same time as the program. To create this plan, the programmer must have BINDADD authority. BINDADD can only be granted by someone with SYSADM authority, unless they passed on the ability to the project leaders:

GRANT BINDADD TO project leader id WITH GRANT OPTION

The programmer who binds the plan owns it. He can execute the plan and bind it again. To allow anyone else to execute it, the programmer must grant EXECUTE authority on the plan. To allow someone else to bind the plan (i.e., if someone else is taking over the program), the original binder must grant BIND authority on the plan.

There is a new authorization in Version 2.3, called BINDAGENT. This authority allows someone to bind a plan without having access to the data in the tables. In many shops, the people responsible for putting programs and plans into production should not have the ability to look at the data. Previously, this was not possible. BINDAGENT provides this function.

Programmers often also use the LOAD utility to do much of their work (see Section 6.2). LOAD authority is on the database level, not the individual table space or table. DBADM authority automatically includes LOAD authority for that database. The database administrator can grant LOAD on the database to the programmers.

1.3.5 Authorization and Performance

There are a few ways in which the authorization scheme can affect performance. This is particularly true in the CICS environment. These issues are discussed in Section 9.2.

Authorization checking must be done for each execution of a DB2 plan and for each SQL statement issued through a program like QMF. DB2 will first check to see if access to the resource has been granted to PUBLIC. Then it will check to see if the individual person has been granted access. Obviously, the checking will be faster if PUBLIC has the authority. However, the overhead of doing the authorization checking is fairly small and should not be the most important factor in designing a security scheme.

The authorizations are stored in the DB2 catalog. Each time a GRANT statement is issued, a row will be entered in one of the catalog tables. This is true even if the same statement is issued repeatedly by the same person. This can clutter up the catalog, so you should not carelessly reissue the same GRANTs again and again.

1.3.6 Revoking Authority

Authorizations can be removed in two ways. Whenever an object is removed from the DB2 catalog, all authorizations are also automatically removed by DB2. For example, if a table is dropped, then all access to the table is also dropped. If the table is recreated, then the access must be regranted.

The other way to remove an authorization is through the REVOKE statement:

REVOKE SELECT ON TABLE THSPAT0 FROM JONES

The whole setup of DB2 security can sometimes get confusing. It is useful to know the basics so that it doesn't become a bottleneck to the development effort.

1.4 SUMMARY AND KEY GUIDELINES

- Programmers and DBAs must understand each other's tasks.
- Any column of a table can be used for selection criteria. Indexed columns will generally provide faster response time.
- DB2 allows sets of rows to be processed with one SQL statement. This can simplify the programming effort and improve performance.
- To guarantee retrieving data in a specific order, you must use the ORDER BY clause.
- Joins and Subselects are used to match rows from several tables.
- Reducing the number of IOs is the most important performance goal.
- Performance is improved by selecting only the columns that are needed, rather than selecting all columns.
- ORDER BY (and GROUP BY) do not require a sort if DB2 uses an index on the same columns as the ORDER BY.

2

Database Design and Creation

The design of any database (or any set of files) can be divided into two parts—logical design and physical design. The logical design concerns identifying and modeling the data and the relationships between the data. Physical design concerns how to represent and store the data and relationships with a particular DBMS or file system. The choice of a particular DBMS can have some impact on the logical design. This is due primarily to limitations within the DBMS. However, the majority of the logical representation is independent of the DBMS.

This chapter will look at the design and creation of DB2 databases. The first section will examine the issues of what makes a good design for any database, including the important topic of normalization. The remaining sections will move into the realm of DB2—table and index creation, data types, physical storage concerns, and referential integrity. The chapter will provide design guidelines as well as the specific DDL statements needed to create DB2 objects.

2.1 LOGICAL DESIGN

There are several different aspects to the process of logical database design. These include:

- Choosing a data model for representing the design.
- Identifying the goals of the design.
- Gathering the requirements for the system.

A data model is a means of representing the design in a way which can easily be communicated and understood by people. Storing and manipulating this model via a computer system is, of course, beneficial. However, the primary criteria is that the model can adequately represent the data. When initially designing the database it is best not to worry too much about the specific DBMS being used. This only clouds the picture. It is also unnecessary. A design using a good modeling system can fairly easily be translated into any of the major DBMS formats.

Before beginning the design, it is important to understand what are the goals of any database design. There are actually several different goals that must work together.

2.1.1 Database Design Goals

2.1.1.1 A Representation of the Data

Certainly the design must accurately portray the real world objects (also called entities) and their relationships. However, it is not always clear how to represent these objects. There is no one unique way to do so. Even something as simple as a person's address may be looked at in several ways. A person is an object. The address can be thought of as an attribute of the person. In this picture, the address is just a set of fields (street, city, etc.) in the person entity. Or, we can say that an address is itself an entity. There are still several ways to represent the relationship between the person and address entities. Is address a dependent of person? Or is address a separate entity with a many-to-many relationship between people and addresses? This model is a better representation of the world. Many people can live at the same address, and each person can have more than one address. This is especially true if we keep a history of a person's addresses. However, for most application systems, the first model is completely adequate and much simpler and easier for programmers to work with. This leads us to the second goal of any design.

2.1.1.2 Processing Requirements

A database does not sit by itself as a static picture of the world. It is processed by programs or query packages. In fact, the user usually does not directly "see" the database. He sees the output of a program. This is what is important to the user. In addition, users are not only concerned with the output of programs, but also with their efficiency (response time). They also want them written quickly. A database design must therefore make it easy for programmers to write the programs, and must enable efficient access to the data.

Relational databases, in general, are easier to use than other database models. Query packages such as QMF are being widely used by end-users. Therefore, it is important for the data to be easy to use by these people as well as the programs.

2.1.1.3 Cost

User management wants to save money. This means efficient processing of the data. It may also mean efficient DASD and tape utilization. Therefore, it is often important to consider storage space when designing the system.

2.1.1.4 Requirements

Requirements for a system include identifying all of the objects to be stored, and all of their attributes and relationships. It also means identifying all of the outputs required by the system and the inputs needed by the system. When examining the processing requirements, you should consider all of the transaction types. This includes transactions that add new data, update data, delete, and inquire. Both online inquiry and long-running reports are important. The order in which the data must be presented to the user is of great importance.

2.1.2 Data Models

There are a number of different models for representing data, and methodologies for developing the design. We will look at two of these methodologies in this section—the Entity/Relationship model and the Normalized Data Relations model. Very often a particular methodology is associated with a particular DBMS. However, that is not necessary. Most good models can easily be mapped into each of the major DBMSs. Normalized relations (as described below) are an obvious representation for a relational DBMS. But they can also be used to represent data that will eventually be handled by a network or hierarchical DBMS. Conversely, the Entity/Relationship model was initially associated with network structures. However, it can easily be mapped into relational tables.

2.1.2.1 Entity/Relationship Model

With this methodology, you start by identifying the data objects. Objects are also called entities. In relational terminology they are called relations. In DB2, they will be stored as tables. Examples of entities would include patients, admissions, services, drug orders, clinicians, and employees. For each of the entities, you then identify each of the attributes. Some examples are:

Patient	Admission	Service
patient ID	patient ID	patient ID
last name	admit date	service date
first name	discharge date	type
sex		clinician
birthdate		

Entities may be related in several ways. These are described as:

- one-to-one
- one-to-many
- many-to-many

The names are self-explanatory. Each patient has a set of characteristics. This is a one-to-one relationship. A pictorial representation of these entities is shown in Figure 2.1. Each entity is shown with its attributes. Lines connect the related entities. The "1" on each relationship line indicates the one-to-one relationship.

A patient has one or more admissions. This is a one-to-many relationship and is shown in Figure 2.2. The admission can be said to be dependent on the patient. Conversely, the patient is the parent of the admission entity. Entities may have relationships with more than one entity. In addition to being a dependent of patient, the admission entity is also the parent of discharge.

In a one-to-many relationship, each dependent (the many side) has one parent (i.e., each admission is for a single patient). In a many-to-many relationship, each occurrence of one entity may be related to several occurrences of the other, and vice versa. Patients and Clinicians are related in this way (Figure 2.3a). The many-to-many relationship is often best described (and pictured) with a relationship entity. This becomes necessary when there are data items which are applicable to the relationship occurrence, but not to the individual entities. An example of this is shown in Figure 2.3b. Services are provide by clinicians and are given to patients.

This diagram can be viewed in several ways. You can think of services as an entity with two parents—patient and clinician. Or you can look at services as representing the relationship between patients and clinicians—a patient is given services by a clinician. Besides identifying the patient and clinician, each occurrence of service has other data that are attributes of the particular occurrence. This includes service date and service type. These data items are often referred to as intersection data.

A simple example of a many-to-many relationship is the one between students and classes. Each student attends several classes and each class contains many students. Attributes of the class entity would include:

Class #—key
subject

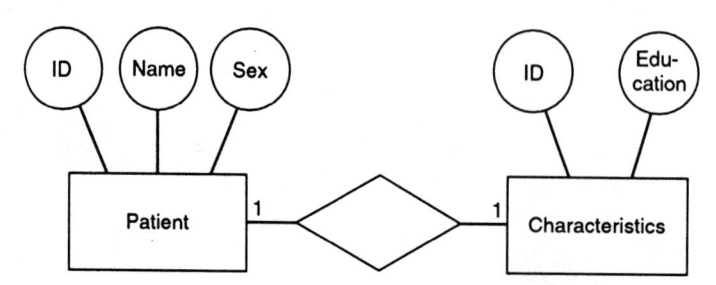

Figure 2.1. A One-to-One Relationship.

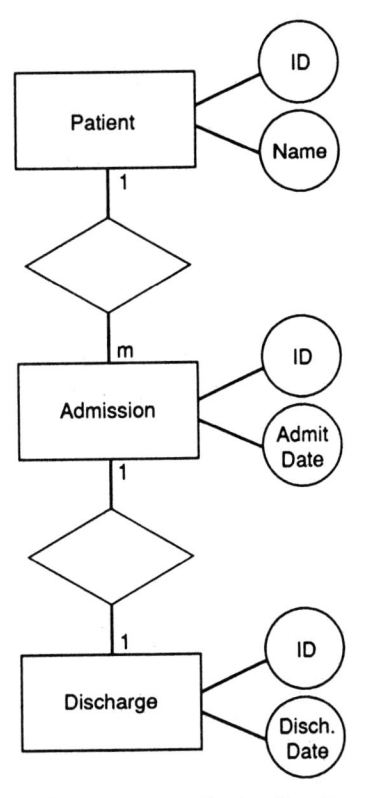

Figure 2.2. An Entity Can Be a Parent and a Dependent.

> room
> instructor

The attributes of the student entity would include:

> Student ID
> name

The relationship is represented by a relationship entity—Student_class. The intersection data would be the grade the student received in the class.

2.1.2.2 Normalized Data Relations Model

In this approach you start with a list of data items. For example, you might have the following list:

> patient ID
> last name
> first name

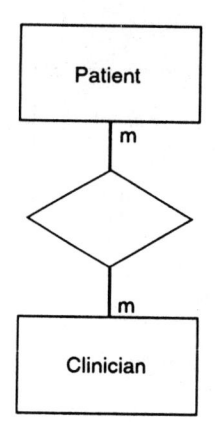

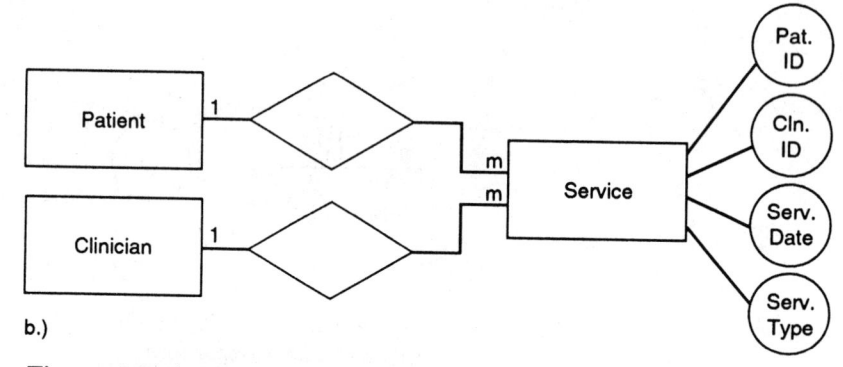

DESIGN AND DEVELOPMENT

a.)

b.)

Figure 2.3. A Many-to-Many Relationship: (a) Each Patient Receives Services from Several Clinicians; (b) Service Is the Relationship Entity.

    sex
    birthdate
    admit date
    discharge date
    service date
    service type
    clinician

You then group the items with other items to which they are related:

                  patient ID → last name
                                → first name
                                → sex
                                → birthdate
        patient ID, admit date → discharge date
      patient ID, service date → service type
                                  → clinician

This is a way of identifying and building up a set of objects (entities). Each of these groups is called a relation. Do not confuse this term with the term relationship as used above. Here the term relation deals with the *items* that are related to each other. Relation is, therefore, equivalent to the term entity.

From here we identify a primary key and then apply the rules of normalization to develop normalized relations. After we describe normalization, we will show how we could also map an Entity/Relationship model into normalized relations.

2.1.3 Primary Keys

Entities usually have a set of fields whose values uniquely identify each occurrence of the entity. This set of fields is called the primary key. It is not essential that every entity type have a primary key. However, in most cases, it proves useful to have one, even if program-generated sequence numbers are needed to make the occurrences unique.

Unique values for the primary key make certain programming functions easier. They also enhance the ability to relate two different entities to each other. Whether or not you do have a naturally occurring unique key, during the design stage you can usually identify one or more sets of fields that generally identify the occurrences. If there is more than one set of possibilities for the key, each set is called a candidate key.

DB2 Version 1 did not have any means of recording or using a primary key. This important piece of design information was lost when the logical design was implemented. With Version 2, you can identify a primary key for each table, but it is not required. We will discuss the benefits and drawbacks in Section 2.2.

2.1.4 Rules of Normalization

The process of normalization is a cornerstone of the relational database model. DB2 will support a design in which the tables are not normalized. However, a good relational design is based on normalized relations. There are five rules of normalization that have appeared in the literature. The first three are the ones most often referenced. This book will discuss these three.

2.1.4.1 First Rule of Normalization

A relation (hereafter called a table) is considered to be in First Normal Form if there are no repeating groups. A repeating group is like an array—a (fixed) set of similar values. The table below is not in first normal form because it has a repeating group—CHILD has five occurrences.

EMPLOYEE

EMPID   key
NAME
CHILD(5)
HIREDATE

To convert this table to first normal form involves creating a second table. You take the field CHILD out of this table and put it into the new table:

EMPLOYEE

EMPID   key
NAME
HIREDATE

EMPCHILD

EMPID   key
CHILD   key

The new table will have one occurrence for each child. The key of this table would be a compound key with the employee ID (which is the key of the employee table) and the child's name.

There are several problems with repeating groups.

- There are a fixed number of occurrences. If we allow up to five children for an employee, then the records for employees with fewer children will have wasted space. If any employee has more than five, then we cannot record that information.
- The SQL statements that would be needed to process a repeating group would be much more complicated, as described below.
- DB2 does not directly support a repeating group. There are no array data types. You would have to code five different columns CHILD1, CHILD2, CHILD3, CHILD4, CHILD5.

If you define five different columns, or even if DB2 allowed an array, the SQL would be cumbersome. To find out which employees have a child named Lucy you would need:

```
SELECT EMPID,NAME
  FROM EMPLOYEE
  WHERE CHILD1='LUCY' OR CHILD2='LUCY' OR CHILD3='LUCY' OR
        CHILD4='LUCY' OR CHILD5='LUCY'
```

If you had an array of 100, you can imagine the difficulties. With the tables in first normal form the SQL becomes much simpler:

```
SELECT EMPID,NAME
  FROM EMPLOYEE A, EMPCHILD B
  WHERE CHILD='LUCY' AND A.EMPID = B.EMPID
```

2.1.4.2 Second Rule of Normalization

A table is in Second Normal Form if it is in first normal form and if no nonkey field is a fact about a partial key. The following table violates this rule:

EMPPROJ

EMPID   key
PROJECT#   key
PROJSTART
EMPSTART
PERCENT_TIME

This table records the employees who are working on each project. PERCENT_TIME is the percentage of an employee's time that he is to spend on the project. EMPSTART is the date he starts on the project. Both are facts about the entire key. However, project start date is a fact only about the project. There are several problems with this design.

- PROJSTART will appear in every record for the project. If there are 10 people assigned to the project, then PROJSTART will be on all 10 records. This makes maintenance more difficult and can lead to inconsistencies in the data. Whenever the value changes, it must be changed in all of the records.
- If a project is defined but no one is assigned to it yet, then there will be no record of the project start date.

Tables can be put into second normal form by creating a new table whose key is the partial key of the original table. In this example we would now have the two tables:

EMPPROJ

EMPID   key
PROJECT#   key
EMPSTART
PERCENT_TIME

PROJECT

PROJECT#   key
PROJSTART

2.1.4.3 Third Rule of Normalization

A table is in third normal form if it is in second normal form and if no nonkey field is a fact about another nonkey field. The following table violates third normal form:

DIAGNOSIS

PATID   key
DIAGDATE   key
DIAGCODE
DIAGNAME

Every type of illness is assigned a diagnosis code (DIAGCODE). If the name of the illness (DIAGNAME) is stored along with the code, then the table violates third normal form. This table can be converted to third normal form by introducing a new table:

DIAGNOSIS		ILLNESS	
PATID	key	DIAGCODE	key
DIAGDATE	key	DIAGNAME	
DIAGCODE			

The problems with violating third normal form are similar to those for second normal form. If nobody has a particular illness, then there will be no record with the code and name of the illness. If it is decided to change the name, then it would have to be changed in every patient diagnosis record. A third problem is that if the name is much larger than the code, then there will be substantially more storage required to store it with every diagnosis record.

2.1.5 Mapping Entity/Relationships to Normalized Relations

As discussed earlier, it is common to have a fairly good idea of the entities of the system at the beginning of the design. If I do, I prefer to use the Entity/Relationship model as a starting point. I believe that it gives a good pictorial view of the data. This is good for understanding and communicating the design. If we are going to implement the database as a relational database (which, of course, in this book we are), then we must map these entities into normalized relations. This process is fairly straightforward.

The first step is that every entity becomes a table (relation). The identifying fields of the entity are the primary key of the relation. When you have a one-to-many relationship (i.e., parent/child), the key to the dependent entity is a compound key. The first part of the key is the primary key of the parent. For example, the key of the admission entity is the patient ID (which is the key of the patient entity), and the admission date. This was clear enough with the entity model. Nothing new is being introduced in mapping them into tables.

A dependent of admission (e.g., discharge) will have a key which starts with its parent's key. This will be the patient ID, the admission date, and the discharge date.

A many-to-many relationship requires the introduction of a relationship table. The key of this table will be the combination of keys from both of the two related tables. In the student/class example given earlier, the relationship table would be keyed by the student ID (key of the student table) and the class number (key of the class table).

2.1.5.1 One-to-One Relationships

When two entities have a one-to-one relationship, some people like to combine them into one entity. There are a number of drawbacks to doing so and I caution against it. An example of this relationship is that between a patient and his address. The address could be considered as an attribute of the person. By combining them into one DB2 table, you gain the benefit of obtaining both sets of data items with access to only one table. The problems, however, are:

- In this design, there is only one address per patient. At some later date we might decide to change the design to either allow several concurrent addresses or to keep a history of a patient's address over time. This cannot be easily accommodated if address is part of the patient table. It can more easily be handled if it is separate.
- Having address in the same table as the patient will speed up access to address when it is needed. However, most of the transactions in the system do not need address data. These are not benefited. Some access to the patient data will be slowed down. Each patient row would be much larger with the address data as part of it. This will reduce the number of rows that can fit in a physical block. Therefore, more IOs will be needed when accessing a set of patient records.

This example shows how physical design concerns (space requirements and IOs) can influence the logical design. It *is* worth considering at this point though, since it reenforces the argument that separate entities should stay separate and not be combined together just because they are one-to-one.

2.1.6 Denormalization

The topic of denormalization is one that receives a lot of discussion. It is primarily an issue of performance, but the performance impact is not always clearly understood. The premise is that by denormalizing some tables (i.e., violating some of the normalization rules), we can improve performance. There are some cases where that is true and some where it is false. Another tradeoff between normalized tables and denormalized is the type of SQL code needed to access the data for different queries. Denormalized tables will have some redundant data. To retrieve unique occurrences will require additional coding. On the other hand, with normalized tables, there is additional coding (i.e., more joins) needed to combine the different data.

Section 7.5 discusses these issues further, with some examples and a quantitative evaluation. Here we will discuss the design issues and basic tradeoffs.

First, I want to emphasize that you should always start with a design that is fully normalized. Then, only if you feel that performance might be a problem, should you consider denormalizing. There are several situations where you might consider it, but remember, there are always drawbacks. Some situations include the following.

Code Tables: Some data items are often stored in coded form. Sex is stored as M or F. Diagnosis is a coded number. So are service types, state codes, and drug codes. Each of these codes are shorter than the full name. This has the advantage of less storage space, less space on most reports, and easier to maintain consistency. There is less likelihood of a typing error. Associated with these codes, we are likely to have a table which has all of the codes and their translation. This table can be used for input verification and for expansion for reports.

The disadvantage of a code table is that if the expansion is needed for most transactions, then you will always need an access to that table in addition to the data table. Storing the full expansion value with the data will eliminate this access. However, if the expansion is only needed occasionally, then there is little performance benefit. This situation is similar to that for combining one-to-one relationships.

The same type of situation can occur with data other than code expansions. In our hospital database, the location table has the WARD field. If each ward number were unique across all of the buildings of the hospital, then the building number could be stored in a separate table keyed by WARD. However, if the building number is needed by most transactions that display the ward, then it would pay to redundantly store the building number on each location record.

Let's summarize the tradeoffs:

2.1.6.1 Advantages of Denormalized Tables

- Reduced cost if the data from the second table is needed most of the time when accessing the primary table.
- If the data is needed together, you do not need a join. This makes the SQL coding a little simpler. If the tables are only accessed by programs, then the reduction in coding effort is not too important. However, if it is frequently used by end-users, then easier coding is important.

2.1.6.2 Disadvantages of Denormalized Tables

- In describing the rules of normalization, we listed the reasons for them. Violating these rules can lead to inconsistency of data if the updating process is not carefully done.
- Denormalized tables have larger rows. Therefore, access to sets of rows in the primary table will take longer. If the expansion data is not needed most of the time, there will probably be an overall increase in cost.
- Some SQL queries will be much more difficult, unless you redundantly store the code, the expansion, and the code table. If you eliminate the code, then the queries must include the full expansion. Do you want to have to code:

SELECT * FROM THSSVC0
WHERE TYPE = 'PHYSICAL THERAPY—ARM SOCKET ROTATION'

Again, I want to emphasize that you should always first design and think normalized. Carefully weigh the need to denormalize and only do so when it will clearly be of benefit.

2.1.7 Other Design Considerations

Now that we have our tables normalized, we have a good relational database design—although not necessarily perfect. That depends on how well we did our requirements analysis. We are ready now for some other general design considerations.

2.1.7.1 Keeping a History

As we discussed earlier, some data is singly occurring (e.g., patient birthdate) and some is multiply occurring (e.g., admissions). Some data on the other hand, may initially be thought of as being singly occurring, only to be redesigned at a later date to handle a history of occurrences. You may only need a patient's current address for most processing. However, it might be useful to have a record of previous addresses. The patient's current set of physicians may be all that is needed for current processing, but the prior physicians might be needed to investigate past illnesses and treatment.

Even if there are no plans for any transactions to take advantage of prior data, it costs little (in storage space or processing time) to design the database to be able to handle a history. Multiple rows can be distinguished by having a date or sequence number as part of the key. If there is no natural date that would apply, then the processing date (or current timestamp) could be used as the key. The "current" row is the one with the most recent date. A sequence number could also be used, but this would require accessing the prior record to find the next number to assign. Access to the current data can be facilitated in DB2 by having an index include this date or sequence number column in descending order. This way the most recent can be retrieved first.

2.1.7.2 Archiving

Over time, there is an accumulation of data that is no longer active (in an application sense). Do you keep all of this data in the database forever? DASD storage space is not a serious concern for many installations (although it is for others). However, the performance of most DBMSs can be affected by the amount of storage needed. Sooner or later many systems have an archiving function added on to remove the older data. It is usually easier to design and code this archiving if it is planned for during the initial database design. This topic is covered in detail in Section 7.7.

2.1.7.3 Processing Date

I find it very useful to include in all tables a field which contains the date (or date and time) that the data was entered or last updated. This information can help both in problem-solving and in many application situations.

In many systems, the key of the entities includes the date on which the activity occurred (transaction date). However, sometimes the transaction does not get entered into the system in real time, and therefore does not always get entered on the same date. There are many functions (such as billing) which process all transactions that have been entered since the last run of the function. If transaction date is used as the trigger, then the data may not be accurately selected. Transactions entered late may be lost, or some may be processed twice. One solution would be to have a flag indicating that the record has been processed. However, this requires updating every record as it is selected. Alternatively, a timestamp stored when the transaction is entered can serve as an accurate marker for selection.

Processing date can also be useful for problem-solving. If a program with a bug is placed into production, invalid data may get stored in the database. Once the error is detected and corrected, the processing date may help in finding the affected records.

2.1.7.4 DB2 Design Concerns

All DBMSs place some restrictions on how data can be represented. Some of these are actual restrictions on the data model. Others are performance issues. While performance is not the primary concern of a logical database design, it is often of enough importance to warrant consideration even at the early stages of the design.

The logical design can be DBMS-independent. However, if you know which DBMS will be used, the logical model can be geared to this DBMS. The design can follow the naming conventions for entities and attributes and use the DBMS terminology for objects and relationships. This can help in the understanding and use of the data model. The rest of this chapter covers the DB2 design issues—some of which are physical design issues and some of which affect the logical design.

2.2 TABLE DESIGN

The design of the DB2 tables can be thought of as either an extension of the logical design, or the first part of the physical design. Assigning names to objects and elements and specifying their attributes is a formalization of the design and the prelude to the implementation. Some of these choices, however, are dependent on the environment in which the database will be used. Naming conventions and data types may partly depend on the primary programming language that will be used. There are also some storage and performance considerations.

2.2.1 Names of DB2 Objects

DB2 has naming requirements for tables, columns, and anything else you can define. The names for each of these are called identifiers. For some objects, DB2 allows long identifier names, and for others, short names. A long identifier can be up to 18 characters long and can include certain special characters such as an underscore (_). A short identifier can only be 8 characters long and cannot include underscores. Examples of each include:

Long identifiers
tables
columns
views
indexes

Short identifiers
creator IDs
databases
table spaces
plans

Some objects have a two-part name—a qualifier, followed by a period, followed by an identifier. For example, a qualified table name starts with the creator ID of the table:

GELLER.THSPAT0

To complicate matters, some objects are qualified by a creator ID and some are qualified by something else. Tables, indexes, and views are qualified by a creator ID. Table spaces are qualified by the database name:

DHSHOS0.SHSPAT0

This can get especially confusing when using some of the DB2 utilities which operate on table spaces or indexes.

In choosing names, it is always best to establish naming conventions for your installation. The purpose of standards is to make it easy to identify which objects are parts of the same system. It is, therefore, consistency of naming that is important, rather than any specific set of rules. In the examples in this book I have used the following rules.

While table names can be up to 18 characters, I have limited them to 8. Some programming languages cannot handle longer names and I find it preferable for the program variables to have similar names to the DB2 objects. I also want to establish a pattern for table names, and 8 is enough to work with. A third reason is that in the MVS operating system the names of members of partitioned datasets (i.e., libraries) can be up to 8 bytes long. Any DDL or control statements I produce related to a table will be stored in PDS members, and I like to be able to keep the names the same or similar.

On the other hand, the column names within a table should be as meaningful as possible. Therefore, I allow longer names for them, including underscores. I try to somewhat limit their length though, because shorter (but meaningful) names require less typing. However, when using a language such as IBM's Cross

System Product, which currently only allows 8 byte names, I might limit the length of the column names. I do *not* restrict the column names to anything silly, such as using the name to identify the data type. I know of shops that require character data columns to begin with a C, flags to start with an F, and numerics to start with an N or Q or something else. First of all, it is unnecessary. It is easy to find the data type definition for any column. Second, the data types of columns very often are changed during the development cycle. That means the names would have to change, too. And third, related fields will not have alphabetically similar names. Instead, all flags will be found near each other. All of this is more counterproductive than useful.

While I said I use the underscore, it should be mentioned that COBOL variables cannot use underscore. If you use the DB2 command DCLGEN to create COBOL structures, it will use a hyphen instead of underscore for these variables. This can be a little confusing since the column names in the SQL statements will have an underscore.

My basic naming structure for DB2 objects is:

AYYZZZNM

where

- A identifies the type of object; D for database, S for table space, T for table, X for index, V for view.
- YY identifies the application system. The hospital system in my examples uses HS for the application. Objects that are parts of particular applications are easily found this way.
- ZZZ identifies a particular entity within the application. PAT is for the patient table, table space, and indexes. ADM is for the admissions to the hospital.
- N is a version number for the entity. It is used for two purposes. I always prefer to have separate DB2 subsystems for production and test. Within each, the objects can have the same names. However, it is possible to mix production and test within one DB2 subsystem (even if you have separate production and test CICS regions). In this case, you must give different names to the tables. This byte can be used for that purpose. The other use is within the test system. It is common to have a table that is being actively used by the application developers, but that requires some changes. You can make additional versions of the table, with variations on the columns. Each one can exist at the same time if they have different names.
- M is used to allow multiple indexes or views for a table. The patient table is named THSPAT0. The indexes are XHSPAT01 and XHSPAT02.

This particular convention for names is one that I find useful. You need to know it in following the examples in this book. However, I'm sure that there are many other possible naming conventions that are equally useful.

2.2.2 Data Types

The basic data types allowable for DB2 columns are as follows.

Character columns:
- CHAR—a fixed length string up to 254 bytes.
- VARCHAR—a varying length string up to 254 bytes.
- LONG VARCHAR—a varying length string that can be up to the maximum available in a data page.

Numeric columns:
- DECIMAL (or NUMERIC, starting with Version 2.2)—packed decimal (called COMP-3 in COBOL, COMP-3 or PACKED DECIMAL in COBOL 2, or FIXED DECIMAL in PL/I).
- INTEGER—binary full word (called COMP in COBOL, COMP or BINARY in COBOL 2, or FIXED BINARY in PL/I).
- SMALL INTEGER—half word binary.
- FLOAT—floating point.

Date/Time columns:
- DATE—a representation of a date. There is no direct equivalent in any of the programming languages. It is represented as a 10-byte character string (described below) in these languages.
- TIME—a representation of a time.
- TIMESTAMP—the combination of a date and time, with greater precision for the time than with the TIME data type.

2.2.2.1 Choosing a Data Type

Most character strings are fixed-length and are shorter than 254 bytes. The CHAR data type, therefore, handles most of these fields. In general, fixed-length strings and variables are a little bit easier for programmers to work with. DB2 will also process rows more efficiently if all of the columns are fixed-length. If the row is always the same size, DB2 can quickly find particular columns of each row. If there is a varying length string in the middle, then DB2 must do a calculation to find the beginning of subsequent columns. Therefore, it is generally preferable not to use varying-length columns, but that does *not* mean you should always avoid VARCHAR.

VARCHAR is useful when the occurrences of the column will vary greatly in length. If the maximum you want to allow is 200 bytes, but most occurrences will be less than 10 bytes, the savings in storage space are well worth it. On the other hand, if the maximum is only 20 bytes, then there is no need to bother. Some people are afraid of using varying-length variables, but they are not really that difficult to work with. In COBOL, they are defined as a structure with a length field followed by a character field (Figure 2.4 has the COBOL definition of a varying-length field with a maximum of 100 bytes). The only extra work is for the programmer to set the length before inserting the row, and checking the length after selecting the row. In PL/I it is even easier. You can directly declare

```
COBOL:

01 TEXT-VAR.
    02 TEXT-L  PIC S9(4) COMP.
    02 TEXT    PIC X(100).

MOVE 'THIS TEXT IS 26 BYTES LONG' TO TEXT.
MOVE 26 TO TEXT-L.




PL/I:

DCL TEXT CHAR(100) VARYING;
TEXT = 'THIS TEXT IS 26 BYTES LONG';
```

Figure 2.4. Varying Length Variables in COBOL and PL/I.

a varying-length variable. The length will be set by PL/I when you assign a string to it.

Long string columns should be avoided except where they are being used for text data or other large strings that do not need too much manipulation. There are restrictions on what you can do with LONG VARCHAR columns. They cannot be fields in indexes, and they cannot be used in any type of operation that involves sorting. This includes ORDER BY and GROUP BY clauses, use of the DISTINCT keyword, or UNION (without the ALL option). In WHERE clauses you cannot use them with any operators other than LIKE. Thus, they can be of use, but not as much so as the other data types.

2.2.2.2 Numeric fields

Most numeric columns are defined as DECIMAL or INTEGER. Floating point is of importance to scientific work or other data that requires many calculations and high precision.

Note that there is no data type which is the equivalent to COBOL DISPLAY format. DISPLAY format (e.g., PIC '999') stores digits in character format. In COBOL or PL/I you can do arithmetic on these fields. DB2 does not have this data type. That leaves you with the choice of either using one of the numeric data types, or character. There are two drawbacks to using character.

- DB2 cannot do any arithmetic operations on a character column. You cannot add a number to it (e.g., GRADE + 3), or use an arithmetic function e.g., SUM(GRADE).
- When using the column in a WHERE clause, the value you are comparing it to must be enclosed in quotes (e.g., GRADE > '90').

If the numeric field is really an encoded value (i.e., 1-married, 2-single, 3-divorced), then character is a reasonable choice. The advantage of character for this type of field is that you are not restricted to numbers for the encoded values.

In most cases, however, you should use a numeric data type. Okay, now should you use INTEGER or DECIMAL? In some cases there is no choice. If the field can have a fraction, then it must be DECIMAL. The INTEGER data type only allows whole numbers. DECIMAL can be defined as allowing only integers, or allowing fractions. You specify the number of decimal digits that the field will have.

PRICE DECIMAL(7,2)

will define a column with a total of 7 digits—2 are after the decimal point. This leaves 5 digits before the decimal point. If a column is to only contain whole numbers, then you leave out the second number (or set it to zero):

EDUCATION DECIMAL(2)

For whole numbers, there is not that much difference in choosing between integer and decimal.

- Binary data can take up slightly less space than packed decimal. If SMALLINT is used, the space savings can be even more.
- Packed decimal is easier to read in a hexadecimal dump of the data fields. A programmer may on occasion need to do so.
- SPUFI will display a decimal point at the end of a decimal value, even if the column is defined without decimal places. This is a little sloppier to look at. However, end-users will be using QMF rather than SPUFI. QMF does not put in this extraneous decimal point.
- Binary data is slightly more efficient when used as an array index or when incremented as part of a loop. Database fields are rarely used for these purposes, and the performance difference is slight.

2.2.2.3 Date Fields

The DB2 date data type is an extremely useful innovation. It provides a consistent means of representing and manipulating dates. You no longer have to worry about whether one date field is YYMMDD and another is MMDDYY or

MM/DD/YY, and whether they are stored as display format, decimal, binary, or anything else. DB2 dates can be entered or displayed in several formats, but they are all stored the same way internally. Therefore, they can all be compared to each other.

The other good feature of this data type is the set of DB2 functions which can manipulate dates. You can subtract one date from another to get a duration, you can add a number of days to a date, and you can easily extract the parts of a date (month, day, and year).

The date data type is not perfect, however. There are a few things that programmers are not used to.

- All dates require a century. This is a good feature as we will soon be at a new one. The drawback, though, is that if you are converting data from an older system, you cannot directly input the old dates. YYMMDD is not valid to DB2.
- Not only is YYMMDD not a valid date, but neither is CCYYMMDD. There are several different allowable date formats, but each of them require a separator between the parts of the date. The default format is CCYY-MM-DD. This default can be changed by the installation. Another common format is MM/DD/CCYY. Note that the default is just the default way in which the date will be returned by a SELECT statement. It can be input in any of the valid formats. A shop can also define a LOCAL date format by writing an exit routine to recognize this format and translate it into one of the DB2 formats.
- A date column must have a valid date. It cannot be blank. Many people are used to using blanks to mean that there is no value for a date field. They can no longer do so. If the column is defined as allowing nulls, then NULL should be used. If not, then you must use a valid date as an indicator. 9999-12-31 seems to be the most logical choice.

2.2.3 Nulls and Defaults

Every column can be defined as either:

- requiring a value—NOT NULL
- allowing nulls—NULL means that there is no real value
- not requiring a value to be input, but using a default value instead of NULL—NOT NULL WITH DEFAULT

If a default is used, the value depends on the data type:

- Character data—blank
- Numeric data—zero
- Dates—the current date

There are important differences in the processing of nulls vs. default values. These are described in the DB2 Administration Guide. One important rule governing nulls is that primary keys cannot have nulls, whereas foreign keys can (see Section 2.3).

Occurrences of columns that have a null value still occupy the same amount of storage space as ones that have values. If you want to save space for strings with occurrences without values, you must use VARCHAR as the data type.

2.2.4 Column Order

The order in which the columns appear in a table is of little importance. The only performance factor is that it is better to have any varying length strings come at the end. This improves the access to the other columns. The columns that make up the primary key or other indexes do not have to come first, nor be consecutive. SELECT statements can return the columns in any order the programmer wishes.

2.2.5 Primary Key

Almost every entity has a primary key which identifies the occurrences. Sometimes, there are more than one candidate for the key. Both ID and name can identify a person. DB2 Version 1 did not have a means of specifying a primary key. You could define indexes, but they carried no semantic significance other than optionally assuring uniqueness. Starting with Version 2.1, you can define a primary key for a table, although it is not required. The main rule about primary keys is that they must have unique values and cannot be NULL. To ensure uniqueness, a unique index must be defined on the primary key columns.

Since the primary key must be unique, there are some restrictions on which candidate keys can be used as the primary key. Names are generally not unique and, therefore, cannot be used. IDs make a better choice.

Occasionally, the natural choice for the key does not intrinsically have unique values. The admissions entity has a key of patient ID and admit date. However, someone could be admitted and discharged more than once during a day. To make the key unique, we introduce a sequence number. Although it is not required to have a primary key defined for the table or to have any unique indexes, it is often useful to have unique values so that each individual row can be easily identified. This makes some application functions easier to code. Therefore, I try to make a unique key for every table whether or not I plan to define it as a primary key or use it in a referential constraint.

2.2.6 Redefining Fields and Using Arrays

DB2 tables are column-oriented. Each column has a particular data type and is used for a specific purpose. With other file systems it is easy to redefine a record and use it for several different purposes. You *can* do the same with DB2 to some degree, but it is not a good practice in general (it is not a good practice in other systems either). When a field is used for different data items, it is much easier to foul things up. Data manipulation is much harder. Every access, whether reading or updating, must reference a flag of some sort to ensure that it is only dealing with the right kinds of data.

The one exception I make to this rule is to have some general-purpose tables that can be used to record parameter information for a variety of programs. The records will have a key to identify the rows of each kind. The table is not used for three or four specific different functions, but rather for an unlimited number of possibilities. It is no different in concept than having control statements in a PDS member. However, by using a DB2 table, the parameters can be used in any environment batch, CICS, or TSO.

Similarly, while DB2 does not allow array columns, you could define separate columns for each occurrence of the array. The disadvantages of this were described in the previous section. The one case where it might be okay to do this is where each occurrence really represents a separate item and there are a fixed number of occurrences. If you have monthly sales totals, it might be useful to have 12 columns—one for each month. The processing of this design will be *more* difficult if you need to add the months, or have a general program that updates the current month. However, if they are almost always treated separately, you gain the benefit of only having one row for the year. It is a tradeoff that must be weighed closely.

2.2.7 FIELDPROCs, EDITPROCs, and VALIDPROCs

DB2 tables can have three types of user exits that are executed automatically when rows are processed by DML statements. By automatically, I mean that they will be invoked without any explicit calls from programs and for any access through QMF. These user exits serve different purposes. They must be written in assembler language, and they must be written very carefully. They run as part of the DB2 subsystem. If they have errors, they could cause all kinds of problems, including corrupting the database or causing a system crash.

2.2.7.1 FIELDPROCs

These are defined for an individual field and are used to encode a field value on insertion of a row, and decode the value on retrieval. They can only be defined for short string data columns (i.e., CHAR and VARCHAR). This means that they cannot serve as a general-purpose encoding mechanism. There is really not a whole lot of use for them. The one suggested use mentioned in the DB2 manuals is to change the collating sequence (i.e., sort order) for names. This way Macmillian can be sorted next to Mcmillian.

2.2.7.2 EDITPROCs

These exit routines are defined for the table. They can be used to encode the entire row. There are two obvious uses for this. One is encryption for highly sensitive data. The other is to compress the data. Section 7.5 discusses data compression in more detail. The idea behind it is that large character strings can often be compressed to take up less storage (other data can also be compressed). If the storage savings is substantial, then any processes that access the entire table space will run much faster. The compression (and expansion upon retrieval) of the row will use CPU cycles. However, overall there can be large savings in time and cost.

2.2.7.3 VALIDPROCs

These exits are also defined at the table level. They are used to automatically enforce validity checking on the values of one or more columns of the table. The exit is passed a parameter list by DB2. These parameters tell the routine where every column is located in the row, and what its attributes are. The routine can check any of the columns. It then sets a return code indicating whether or not the operation (insert or update) should continue. This mechanism is an extension to DB2's facilities for ensuring the integrity of the data. Programs (and QMF queries) could not be written which allow invalid values to be stored.

Each of these exit routine types require careful coding. In addition, once an EDITPROC or FIELDPROC is defined for a table, they cannot be dropped without dropping and recreating the table. Changing the routines requires careful planning. They will have encoded the data in some fashion. Any new version of the routine must be able to decode the existing rows. Some of the existing rows might conflict with the new rules. Overall, EDITPROCs and VALIDPROCs can be useful, but you must have personnel capable of developing them properly.

2.2.8 Summary

- The design of the tables is a relatively straightforward mapping from the logical design.
- Some consideration must be given to the data types to be used, as there is often a choice of data types that could be applicable.
- Use the data types that DB2 provides. While the DATE data type is not perfect, the functions available for processing dates are very powerful and worth any "rethinking" that is needed.
- Having unique keys for tables is generally a good idea. Defining them as a primary key is not as important unless the table will be a parent in a referential constraint.
- Do not be afraid of nulls and varying length strings
- Do not defeat the benefits of DB2 by using fields or columns for multiple purposes.

2.3 REFERENTIAL INTEGRITY

2.3.1 Fixed Relationships and Dynamic Relationships

When you develop a logical design, there are often relationships between different objects (entities). The various kinds of relationships are discussed in Section 2.1. How these relationships get implemented depends on the DBMS that you are using. For example, IMS, which is primarily a hierarchical database, is one in which the relationships are fixed. One entity is the parent and the other one is the child. A child cannot exist without a parent. An example of a relationship between two entities is that between the Patient and the Admission entities. An admission is for a patient. You should not have an admission without a corresponding patient. In IMS the patient would be the parent. The patient ID field would not be repeated in each admission record. Instead, the admissions are physically tied to their parent. If a patient is deleted, all admissions are also automatically deleted. If the PATID is changed, then in theory, it would be changed for all admissions (however, IMS does not allow a key to be changed).

In DB2, relationships do not *have* to be fixed. Prior to Version 2, there was no way to even specify that two entities (tables) were related. Relationships were based on value. In the above example, the PATID is repeated in each admission for the same patient. It is the value of the PATID field that identifies which admissions are for which patients.

This approach is very flexible. However, it means that all validation of relationships is under program control, not enforced by the DBMS. The program to enter an admission must verify that a corresponding PATIENT row exists. Programs that read admission data expect the existence of the patient row. A join between the tables will not work properly if the patient row is missing. In this case, the admission rows that have no corresponding patient row would not show up in the join result. Programs that delete a patient must also delete his admissions, locations, diagnoses, etc. Programs that change key values must also keep the rows of different tables in sync. Rules governing these relationships must be decided on and then coded into many different programs.

These types of rules can now be defined in the database. Then, the reading of other tables to validate the rules does not have to be explicitly coded. However, the program coding must still take the rules into consideration. They must now check the SQLCODE to see if any of the rules have been violated. The encoding of integrity rules into the database structure is called Referential Integrity and was introduced into DB2 with Version 2. We'll start by defining some terms and giving some basic rules.

- You do not have to use DB2's Referential Integrity. You may continue to relate tables by value and code any integrity checking.
- Referential Integrity defines the relationships between tables. If a row "belongs" to a row in another table, the owning row is called a parent row and the object is a dependent row. The table within which the parent row is held is called a parent table, and the dependent row is in a dependent table. The relationship between two tables is called a referential constraint. For example, in Figure 2.5, the patient with PATID = '123' has two admissions. The patient table is a parent table to the admissions table. The patient row with PATID='123' is the parent row of the two admissions rows that also have PATID='123'.
- Tables can be in more than one relationship. They can be parents in several and dependents in several. For example, PATIENT might be

```
Patient        Admission
PATID          PATID    ADMDATE


123            123      1990-03-15
               123      1990-06-31
```
Figure 2.5. Parent and Dependent Rows.

the parent table for ADMIT and for DISCHARGE, while ADMIT is also parent to DISCHARGE. The same table can be both the parent and dependent in a single relationship. There can also be a cycle (e.g., A is parent to B, B is parent to C, C is parent to A).

2.3.2 Primary Keys

In order for a row to be a parent, there must be a way to uniquely identify it. In some other DBMSs, dependents are physically tied to their parents by pointers (i.e., a parent points to its children). In some DBMSs, the child may in turn point to its parent. In DB2 there are no pointers; only column values are used to tie rows together. Therefore, any table which is going to be a parent in a relationship must have a primary key defined. A primary key is a column(s) with unique values. In our hospital database, the patient table is the parent to many other tables. It has a primary key of PATID. PATID does have unique values. The creation of unique index XHSPAT02 ensures that. However, in order to use THSPAT0 in a referential constraint, we must do a little more. A table may have several unique indexes, but it can only have one primary key. It is defined on the CREATE TABLE as in Figure 2.6. Once you have defined a primary key, you *must* create a unique index on these columns. Otherwise the table definition is incomplete.

Any table can have a primary key defined even if it does not take part in referential constraints. It is not mandatory to do so. As described in the previous section, there usually is a unique identifying key for most tables. If so, then explicitly defining it as such conveys useful information to the programmers. On the other hand, there are a few reasons why you might prefer not to bother defining a primary key:

- There are some restrictions on primary keys. They must be unique and no column in the key can have null values. This may or may not be a problem.
- There is a very slight increase in processing required at bind time for a delete or update. DB2 must check the catalog to see that there are no referential constraints defined in other tables, pointing to this primary key.
- You must define an index for a primary key. For small tables, indexes

```
CREATE TABLE GELLER.THSPAT0
   (PATID       CHAR(9)   NOT NULL WITH DEFAULT,
    LASTNAME    CHAR(15)  NOT NULL WITH DEFAULT,
    FIRSTNAME   CHAR(10)  NOT NULL WITH DEFAULT,
    SEX         CHAR(1)   NOT NULL WITH DEFAULT,
    BIRTHDATE   DATE      NOT NULL WITH DEFAULT,
    ACTIVEFLAG  CHAR(1)   NOT NULL WITH DEFAULT,
 PRIMARY KEY(PATID))
 IN DHSHOS0.SHSPAT0;
```

Figure 2.6. Defining a Primary Key.

are not needed for retrieval performance and you may prefer to not have any indexes on that particular table.

Choosing a primary key is usually easy. Most data has one or more identifying fields. People are identified by IDs, bank accounts by account number, services by date, and who received the service. Bear in mind that it must be unique. Name will not do. ID alone will suffice for the patient table, but not for the admissions. Using a sequence number to make a unique key is described in the previous section. I have already done this for several of the hospital tables, such as the admissions table. It is often useful in general to have unique keys. For admissions it is also important for the application system to identify the order of admissions on a day. The sequence number, therefore, serves two purposes.

2.3.3 Defining a Referential Constraint

Next we'll look at how a dependent and a relationship are defined. The column(s) in a table which are used to relate the table to (i.e., join it with) another table, is called a foreign key. The PATID column of THSADM0 is a foreign key. It is used to match up rows of THSADM0 with rows of THSPAT0 that have the same value in the corresponding field. A foreign key must have a data type that is compatible with the primary key of the table it refers to. To define the referential constraint, you code a FOREIGN KEY clause (Figure 2.7). In this example, the PATID field is defined as a foreign key in a relationship with the patient table. This relationship is given a name—PATADM. This name can be considered as both the foreign key name and the referential constraint name. You only have to mention the name of the parent table, but not the columns in the parent table. The relationship is implicitly with the primary key of THSPAT0.

The columns of the foreign key can be defined as nullable. If any column has a NULL value, then the foreign key is considered to be NULL. This means that the row does not have a parent.

```
CREATE TABLE GELLER.THSADM0
   (PATID       CHAR(9)         NOT NULL WITH DEFAULT,
    ADMDATE     DATE            NOT NULL WITH DEFAULT,
    ADMSEQ      SMALL INTEGER   NOT NULL WITH DEFAULT,
    DISDATE     DATE            NOT NULL WITH DEFAULT,
    DISSEQ      SMALL INTEGER   NOT NULL WITH DEFAULT,
    PROCESSED   TIMESTAMP       NOT NULL WITH DEFAULT,
   FOREIGN KEY PATADM (PATID) REFERENCES GELLER.THSPAT0
      ON DELETE CASCADE)
   IN DHSHOS0.SHSADM0;
```
Figure 2.7. Defining a Foreign Key.

2.3.4 Referential Integrity Rules

Saying that two tables are related doesn't really tell you anything in a practical sense unless you know what rules are followed for referential constraints. There are rules governing the insertion, updating, and deletion of data. You have several choices associated with each.

2.3.4.1 Uniqueness

This rule says that a dependent can only have one parent row for each referential constraint. Therefore, the primary key of the parent must be unique. To implement this rule, DB2 requires all primary keys to have unique values regardless of whether or not the table is a parent table in any referential constraint. The primary key columns must also be defined as NOT NULL. This rule is sometimes called Entity Integrity.

2.3.4.2 Insertion of Dependent Rows

The Existence rule. With one exception, dependent rows must have a parent row already in the parent table. That is, there must be a parent table row with a primary key with the same value as the foreign key of the dependent row. The one exception is if the foreign key has a NULL value. In this case, the new row does not have a parent.

2.3.4.3 Deletion of Parents

There are three choices. The DBA picks one based on the application requirements. This rule is defined for each referential constraint (i.e., when defining the dependent table).

- RESTRICT—a parent row cannot be deleted if any dependent rows exist. This is the default.
- CASCADE—when a parent row is deleted, all of its dependent rows are also deleted. If these dependents are also parents in some other referential constraint, DB2 will follow their delete rules also.
- SET NULL—when a parent row is deleted, the foreign key in any dependent is set to NULL. This option is probably of limited use in practice.

Figure 2.7 has the CREATE for a table with CASCADE for the delete rule of a referential constraint. The dependent table is for a patient's admissions. The parent table is the patient table. If a patient row is deleted, then all admission rows for that patient are automatically deleted by DB2. The programmer does not have to do anything to delete the admissions.

2.3.4.4 Update of a Parent's Primary Key

In theory, there should be the same three rules as for deletes. However, DB2 currently only implements one of the rules—RESTRICT. This means that if a parent has any dependents, then its primary key cannot be updated. If a particular parent row has no dependents, then its key can be updated. This is rather silly and is bound to confuse programmers. The idea behind this restriction is that a primary key identifies the entity occurrence (row) and, therefore, will not change. In practice, though, keys do change. The simplest case is that the data was keyed in incorrectly by the user. They now want to correct it. The CASCADE rule would make sense. If the primary key of the parent changes, change the foreign key of all dependents. However, you can't do it with DB2. Instead, you must insert a new parent with the new primary key, update all dependents to have the new value, and then delete the old parent. This is a step backward.

As I said, the DELETE rule is coded on the CREATE TABLE of the dependent row (as part of the FOREIGN KEY clause). The INSERT and UPDATE rules have only one option, so there is no coding necessary on the DDL statements.

2.3.4.5 Rules Related to DB2's Implementation

- In order to define a referential constraint, you must have ALTER authority on the parent table. This is necessary so that one person cannot arbitrarily create a constraint with tables that belong to someone else. If you use the RESTRICT rule for deletion, the processing of the parent table will be affected.
- Domain Integrity refers to being able to specify rules controlling the allowable values for a column. DB2 does not provide a direct mechanism for this area. There are two ways in which you can provide some control.
    - —Use a VALIDPROC exit routine. However, this is not a simple general-purpose mechanism. A routine is a program that must be written for a specific table.

—Use views with the WITH CHECK OPTION (described in Section 2.6). The view definition can have selection criteria that limit the values of each column. If update and insert authority are only granted for the views and not for the base table, then you have effectively prevented insertion of rows with invalid values. However, the view definition must be checked for each insert to ensure that the data values are acceptable. This will add to the processing time.

- Two tables can have more than one constraint between them. That is, two different foreign keys in one table can both point to the same parent table. The foreign keys cannot both be defined on the same set of columns in the dependent table.
- To create a cycle (i.e., A is parent of B, B is parent of C, C is parent of A) requires adding one of the constraints after the tables have been created (with the ALTER TABLE statement). In this example, the foreign key of A refers to the table C. This foreign key cannot be defined until C exists. However, C's foreign key cannot be created unless B exists and B's cannot be created until A exists.
- If a parent table is dropped, all constraints pointing to it are also dropped. They do not automatically come back if the parent table is created again. The DBA must explicitly add the constraint back (with ALTER TABLE).
- It is strongly recommended that an index be created for all foreign keys for performance reasons. Whenever a DELETE of a parent row (or UPDATE of the primary key) is issued, DB2 must check to see if any dependent rows exist. Without an index on the foreign key, this would require a scan of the entire dependent table.
- There are some DML restrictions, especially related to subqueries. These restrictions are based on the DB2 rule that the results of an SQL statement should not depend on the order in which DB2 accesses the rows. Since some deletes will depend on the existence of dependent rows, the order in which the statement is processed might produce different results. Therefore, DB2 does not allow any statement that *might* have a problem. The details of these restrictions can be found in some of the DB2 manuals, including the Referential Integrity Usage Guide (GG24-3312). This is one of the support center publications.

2.3.5 Benefits and Drawbacks

In theory, the same types of checking are done by DB2 for referential integrity as would be done by the programmers. The difference is that when DB2 does it, the checking is enforced and is automatic. When done by each program, it may not be done thoroughly.

Program coding becomes a little bit simpler. For example, there is no need to code a SELECT for the patient to see if it exists. However, after an INSERT of any dependent, the program must check for the SQLCODE that indicates that the parent is not present (-530). The same is true for the other rules. New ways of thinking about the program flow are needed.

In some cases there are tradeoffs, both in functionality and in performance, to using referential integrity. The tradeoffs depend on the specific application system and specific tables. Some of the considerations are list here.

2.3.5.1 Performance Issues

- Generally, the performance is very similar between DB2-enforced and program-enforced integrity.
- When DB2 does the checking, fewer SQL calls are needed. This saves some processing time.
- DB2 will do its checking every time. Knowledge of the data and the application may allow a program to skip some of the checking, thus saving much time. For example, the admission program checks for the existence of the patient and then inserts an admission row, a location, a characteristics, and an address. For each of those inserts, DB2 will check to see if the patient row exists. The program only has to do so once. A similar situation occurs if the program is inserting many dependents of one kind, each with the same foreign key value (e.g., 10 service rows for the same patient). DB2 will check the patient ID for each insert.
- As mentioned above, all foreign keys should have indexes defined on them. Otherwise the performance for deletes of the parent rows and udpates of primary keys will be very poor. This is true even if the integrity checking is being done by a program.
- When a parent is deleted, you cannot control the order in which DB2 will check for the existence of dependent rows. The programmer may "know" that there is more likely to be a row in a particular dependent table than in the others. The program could then check that table first.
- Primary keys cannot be updated if the row has any dependents. The process must therefore be:
    - Insert a new parent with the new primary key
    - Update all dependents to have the new value as their foreign key
    - Delete the old parent

  DB2 doesn't know that the program has already changed all of the foreign keys. Therefore, it must check all dependent tables to see if there are any dependent rows of the old parent.

2.3.5.2 Other Tradeoffs

- A big benefit of referential integrity is that it is *always* enforced. This prevents invalid processing through QMF or through incorrectly written programs.
- A disadvantage is that it is always enforced. Even test data must be more rigorously entered. On the other hand, that could be good.

- Deleting a parent *requires* the checking of all dependents. For some tables, you might want to validate the foreign key on input, but not care whether or not the parent row is later deleted or changed.
- The primary key cannot have any part of it be NULL. This may be a restriction that you do not want for a particular table.
- Primary keys cannot be updated if they have any dependent rows. This restriction is a little unnatural.
- The loading sequence for tables with referential constraints is more rigid. Parents must be loaded (inserted) before the dependents.
- The program flow must be different from what the programmers may have been used to. With program-enforced checking, the flow would be
    —read the parent table to see if the parent exists
    —if not (or any other error), put up an error screen
    —if everything is good, insert the dependent row
  With DB2-enforced checking, the flow becomes
    —check for other errors, putting up an error screen if needed
    —insert the dependent row
    —check the SQLCODE to see if there is a violation of a constraint
    —if there is an error, put up an error screen
  With this new flow, the DB2 insertions and updates no longer follow *all* data verification.

2.3.6 Summary

Each of the tradeoffs we have listed may be applicable in some situations. Overall, referential integrity can be a very useful feature to ensure the validity of the data. There may be some situations where you prefer not to use it. Performance wise, there is usually not too much difference either way.

2.4 TABLE SPACES

A table is really a logical collection of data of a given type. The physical collection is a table space. Table spaces can be thought of as the datasets that DB2 tables are stored in (a table space can actually consist of more than one VSAM dataset). There are three types of table spaces that can be defined with the CREATE TABLESPACE DDL statement.

- simple
- segmented (new with DB2 Version 2)
- partitioned

2.4.1 Simple Table Spaces

The most commonly used type is the simple table space, primarily because the segmented type was not introduced until Version 2. Both simple and segmented table spaces can contain one or more tables. For a simple table space, usually

```
CREATE TABLESPACE Saaxxxn IN Daaxxxn
   USING STOGROUP STG1 PRIQTY nnn SECQTY nnn
   CLOSE NO LOCKSIZE ANY
```
Figure 2.8. Creating a Simple Table Space.

only one table will be defined for the table space (mostly for performance reasons). When it is desirable to have more than one table in a table space, segmented table spaces should be used. Figure 2.8 has the CREATE statement to define a typical simple table space. The general syntax can be found in the DB2 SQL Reference manual. In my examples, I will use the parameters and values that are generally best. Later in this section, I will explain each of them.

There are several problems with having more than one table in a simple table space.

- The rows of the different tables are intermixed. Access to the rows of a table are either through an index, or through a scan of all of the rows when there is no appropriate index. Whenever a table space scan is needed to process an SQL request, it must scan the entire table space. The data from all of the tables must be passed over to read the rows of the table that is needed. This can greatly increase the number of IOs.
- If a table space lock is needed (see Section 6.3), the entire table space is locked—not just the one table. This can reduce concurrency. Users of other tables in the table space may also be locked out.
- A reorg of the table space will reload the data in the order of the clustering index of the table. It will only do so, however, if there is only one table in the table space.
- Finally, dropping a table or deleting all the rows of the table:

    DELETE FROM TAAXXXN

    will not reclaim the space. A reorg will be needed. This is true even if there is only one table in the simple table space. Other alternatives to emptying out a table are dropping the table space (which will reclaim the space) or LOAD REPLACE, which will replace *all* tables in the table space. Dropping a table or table space also drops all indexes, views, priveleges, and synonyms.

Before we see how these problems are solved by segmented table spaces, let's look at some reasons why we might want to store multiple tables in one table space.

- There is a limit on the number of files that can be open at one time to a DB2 subsytem. The default for Version 2.2 is 1000. The maximum number for MVS/XA is 3273. For MVS/ESA, the maximum can now be 10,000, either with Version 2.3 or with a modification to Version 2.2. Each table space and each index is a separate dataset. If they are

defined with CLOSE NO (which, for performance reasons, is the option usually used), then they will stay open while DB2 is up. For a small shop or one just starting to use DB2, this limit (even the lower limit) presents no problem. However, once there is a lot of development, it could be reached.
- For programmers, DBAs, and advanced users who are creating several (or many) small test tables, it pays to have these people put most of their tables in one table space to reduce the number of datasets needed. Backups (COPY utility) are done at the table space level. With one table space per programmer, fewer backups are needed.
- It is suggested in the DB2 manuals that small- or medium-sized tables that need coordinated recovery can be put into one table space so that they can always be backed up and recovered together. However, this is not essential if good operational procedures are put into place for production systems.
- QMF default table space. When a QMF user saves the results of a query with the SAVE DATA AS Tablename command, these results are stored in a table. If the table does not yet exist, it will be created. The QMF administrator decides where these tables are to be created. The default is for all tables to go into one table space.

2.4.2 Segmented Table Spaces

Because of the problems inherent in having more than one table in a simple table space, DB2 Version 2 introduced the segmented table space. In this type, the pages (physical blocks) of the table space are grouped into segments. A single segment will contain rows of only one table. They will not be intermixed with rows from other tables. Every table space has a space map which tells DB2 whether there is any available space on each page of the dataset. The space map for the segmented table space has been enhanced to record which segments are being used for each table. A segmented table space is created by using the SEGSIZE parameter when creating the table space (Figure 2.9). The segment size is a number from 4–64 and must be a multiple of 4.

Since the space map records which segments belong to each table, a table space scan does not need to read every page—only those for the table being accessed. This removes the performance problem of accessing the data. When a table is dropped or all rows are deleted, DB2 does not have to find each row and delete it (provided that the table is not a parent in a referential constraint). Instead, it

```
CREATE TABLESPACE Saaxxxn IN Daaxxxn
   USING STOGROUP STG1 PRIQTY nnn SECQTY nnn
   SEGSIZE n
   CLOSE NO LOCKSIZE ANY
```
Figure 2.9. Creating a Segmented Table Space.

only has to update the space map to indicate that the pages and segments are empty and available. This is also of benefit to table spaces with a single table. Deleting all rows is now fast and can be used instead of LOAD REPLACE or dropping the table. LOAD REPLACE will still replace all tables of a table space, and so is not useful for multiple tables even in a segmented table space. A reorg to recover the space is also not necessary after a table is dropped or its rows deleted from a segmented table space.

Segmented table spaces are, therefore, very useful for dynamic tables where all rows are frequently deleted, as well as for the situations listed above—programmers' test tables and especially the QMF default SAVE table space.

2.4.3 Partitioned Table Spaces

The third type of table space is the partitioned table space. A partitioned table space can contain one and only one table. The data in the table is physically separated into different datasets (partitions) by the values of a partitioning key. This key is made of the columns of the clustering index (also called the partitioning index). Clustering indexes are discussed more generally in Section 2.5. This index is required for a partitioned table space. Partitioning can be useful for large tables and has several benefits.

- Utilities can operate on each partition separately. This can lead to greater availability of the data. Backups can be run in parallel. If a recovery is needed for one partition, only that one needs to be restored. Reorgs can also be done on a single partition.
- Each partition can be placed on a different disk volume and even on different disk types. This separation can be useful for DASD performance.
- The LOAD utility can replace a single partition. For data that is cyclical and periodically purged (e.g., a year's worth of data is stored and each month the data from the previous year is deleted and replaced) the partitions can be by cycle period. LOAD REPLACE of a partition will delete all the data rows and clustering index entries quickly and easily with minimal actual delete or logging activity. Any other indexes, however, will still require each individual entry to be deleted and logged.

To create a partitioned table space, you must define the table space and the clustering index with a few parameters to indicate the partitions (Figure 2.10).

The NUMPARTS parameter tells DB2 that this is a partitioned table space and how many partitions there are. The number of partitions and the key value range for each partition is fixed. They can only be changed by dropping the table space (and all its dependencies) and recreating it. For the partitioning index, there is one PART clause for each partition. The VALUES clause gives the high end of the key range for that partition (the low end starts right after the previous partition). The value of the last partition is ignored. Any higher key value will go into the last partition. In this example, any row for which COL1 is less than

```
CREATE TABLESPACE Saaxxxn IN Daaxxxn
  USING STOGROUP STG1 PRIQTY nnn SECQTY nnn
  NUMPARTS n
  CLOSE NO LOCKSIZE ANY


CREATE INDEX creator.Xaaxxxn1 ON creator.Taaxxxn
  (COL1,COL2)
  CLUSTER
 (PART 1 VALUES('AAAAA',12345),
  PART 2 VALUES('AAAAA',66666),
  PART 3 VALUES('DDDDD',22222),
  etc.
 )
  USING STOGROUP STG1 PRIQTY nnn SECQTY nnn
  SUBPAGES 2 CLOSE NO
```
Figure 2.10. Creating a Partitioned Table Space.

'AAAAA' will go into the first partiton. So will any row for which COL1 equals 'AAAAA' and COL2 is less than or equal to 12345. Rows with COL1='AAAAA' and COL2 between 12346 and 66666 will go into the second partition.

The clustering index may have several columns. If it does, they do not all have to be involved in the partitioning. For example, in a multihospital database, if the columns are

HOSPID
PATID

the table space can be partitioned by HOSPID alone as in Figure 2.11.

If fewer values are provided than there are columns, high values are used for the remaining columns. In this example any row with a Hospital ID less than or equal to HSP111 with any Patient ID will go into the first partition. Any row with Hospital ID from HSP112 through HSP123 will go into the second partition. Any other row will go into the third partition. Obviously, this design is not ideal if new hospitals are likely to be added as dropping and recreating the table space is not something we want to do unless necessary.

The table space parameters are discussed below. The index parameters are discussed in Section 2.5.

```
CREATE INDEX creator.Xaaxxxn1 ON creator.Taaxxxn
  (HOSPID,
   PATID)
  CLUSTER
 (PART 1 VALUES('HSP111'),
  PART 2 VALUES('HSP123'),
  PART 3 VALUES('HSP259'))
  USING STOGROUP STG1 PRIQTY nnn SECQTY nnn
  SUBPAGES 4 CLOSE NO
```

Figure 2.11. Partitioning a Multiple Hospital Table Space.

2.4.4 Table Space Datasets

Table spaces are VSAM datasets. They can be allocated and managed by DB2, or the dataset can be allocated by the user with the IDCAMS DEFINE CLUSTER command. If you want DB2 to allocate the dataset for you, the STOGROUP parameter is used on the CREATE TABLESPACE statement. If you have done the allocation yourself, the VCAT parameter is used instead. VCAT will identify a VSAM catalog alias. STOGROUP is described below.

When DB2 allocates the dataset, it uses a VSAM Linear dataset. When it is done outside of DB2 it can be a Linear dataset or an ESDS (Entry Sequence Data Set). DB2 Version 1 used ESDSs. Linear datasets are a newer addition to VSAM. The original types of VSAM datasets were KSDS, ESDS, and RRDS. Linear datasets are similar to ESDSs in that they are unkeyed. Whereas an ESDS consists of a sequence of records, a Linear dataset consists of a continuous sequence of bytes (although it is broken up into physical blocks just like an ESDS). You really do not need to know more than that, as DB2 manages the space and storage of the data for you.

A simple or segmented table space will start off as one VSAM dataset up to a maximum of 2 gigabytes (2 billion bytes). If more space is requested and the 2 gigabytes are used up, then additional datasets (up to 32 datasets) can be allocated to the table space.

2.4.4.1 Table Space Dataset Names

The naming convention for the VSAM cluster is

node.DSNDBC.dbname.tsname.I000n.A000m

Node is the high order qualifier (VSAM catalog alias) defined for the storage group or by the VCAT parameter. I000n is a dataset number—n is 1 for the first VSAM dataset. If a second one is needed, it will have I0002, etc. The last node—

A000—is for partitioned table spaces (see below). Dbname is the name of the database. Tsname is the name of the table space.

Indexes are also VSAM datasets and generally have the index name as the 4th node instead of tsname. I say, "generally," because two different people (i.e., creator IDs) can create an index with the same name for different tables within a database. In this case, DB2 generates an internal name for the indexes to distinguish them. It would be this internal name which appears in the dataset name to make it unique.

VSAM clusters have a data component which for DB2 files has the same name as the cluster except for the 2nd node, which is DSNDBD.

You may be wondering why you need to know these dataset names since DB2 manages the datasets and you do not even need JCL DD statements for them. For the average user of DB2—programmer, end-user and most DBAs—there is no direct need. However, there are two situations where it can be useful. When you create a table space you specify how much space should be allocated for it. The amount you request is based on the size of the rows and an estimate of the number of rows that there will be. This estimate is often inaccurate or your arithmetic may be in error. Therefore, it is important to check on how much space is actually allocated and being used. There are also people assigned to monitor space utilization for the DASD packs as a whole—looking for wasted space or planning for growth needs.

One way to see how much space is being used by a table space is by running the STOSPACE utility which updates the SPACE column of the SYSTABLESPACE, SYSINDEX, and STOGROUP catalog tables. A query against these columns will show the space used. There are several problems with this approach. STOSPACE can only be run by someone with STOSPACE (or SYSADM) authority, and the catalog will only show statistics as of the last time STOSPACE was run. The space shown is also in bytes used, which still needs translation to tracks and cylinders. These are the DASD units which are usually looked at for overall space utilization.

A much quicker and up-to-the-minute way to check on space utilization is to simply look at the VTOC information for the disk pack. This can be done through TSO option 3.4. You can look at every dataset on a pack and see how much space is allocated, how many secondary extents have been used, and how much is available on the pack. In order to find the table spaces you are interested in, you obviously need to know their dataset names.

The other reason for knowing this naming convention is if you have chosen to allocate the dataset yourself first (with the IDCAMS DEFINE CLUSTER command) and then create the table space (using the VCAT parameter to indicate the appropriate VSAM catalog and high order node). If you define it yourself, then the name you give the VSAM dataset must match DB2's naming convention.

Is there any reason to do it yourself? Not usually. There are some VSAM options which cannot be specified when you use a storage group. There are also some very important parameters that, until DB2 Version 2, could not be changed once the table space was created. The most important of these is the space allocation. Once the table space has been created, an ALTER TABLESPACE statement can now change the primary and secondary space allocations; however, in DB2 Version 1 it could not (whereas a VSAM ALTER command could do so for a user-managed dataset). This was an important change with Version 2 and it eliminates the major use of user-defined datasets. A change in primary allocation will take effect with a RECOVER or REORG utility operation on the table space.

There is one place where a table space is usually allocated outside of DB2. The system administrator allocates temporary table spaces in database DSNDB07. These temporary table spaces are used by DB2 for intermediate results, such as needed by a sort operation or a create index. The sample job provided with DB2 for creating these table spaces, defines them with IDCAMS first.

2.4.5 Storage Groups

The USING block tells DB2 whether it should manage the datasets or the user should.

USING VCAT . . . indicates a user-defined dataset.
USING STOGROUP. . . PRIQTY . . . SECQTY . . . indicates a DB2-defined dataset

Leaving off the parameter will result in DB2 using the default storage group for the database.

What is a storage group? It is basically a list of disk volumes where DB2 may allocate datasets. It also has the high order node to be used for the dataset names. The system administrator decides which packs are to be used for DB2 table spaces. He then creates storage groups pointing to them, and grants use of the storage group to people who have authority to create table spaces. These people must have CREATETS (create table space) authority. People with DBADM (database administration) authority automatically have CREATETS authority for their databases. To create a storage group with name STG1 on packs DB2001, DB2002, and DB2003, you issue this DDL statement:

CREATE STOGROUP STG1 VOLUMES(DB2001,DB2002,DB2003) VCAT DB2T

The datasets which are created in STG1 will go to one of the three packs. They will go to DB2001 if it has enough room. They will only go to DB2002 or DB2003 (for a primary or secondary extent) if there is not enough room on DB2001. These datasets will all have names that start DB2T.DSNDBC.

If there are three packs available for datasets as in the above example and the system administrator wants to spread the datasets across all three, he can create three storage groups. Each one could have only one volume listed, or all three can be listed:

- STG1 could have DB2001,DB2002,DB2003.
- STG2 could have DB2002,DB2003,DB2001.
- STG3 could have DB2003,DB2001,DB2002.

This way each storage group would primarily use a different pack, but you have the added benefit of a cushion in case any one pack fills up. When a table space needs a new extent and there is no more room on any packs in its storage group, the task requesting the addition will fail and the table space will need recovery (with more room having to be made available). If the storage group has several packs and only the first pack fills up, space can be obtained on the next pack. This provides greater availability for the system.

You do not have to name a storage group on the CREATE TABLESPACE statement. There is a default storage group assigned to a database when it is created:

CREATE DATABASE DHSHOS0 STOGROUP STG1 BUFFERPOOL BP0

If the STOGROUP parameter is left off the CREATE DATABASE statement, a default storage group is assigned to the database. This default storage group is called SYSDEFLT and is set up when DB2 is installed. The database storage group does not put any restrictions on where table spaces can be placed. The create for the table space can name any storage group for which the creator of the table space has the USE privelege. The database storage group is simply a default. Note, though, that if the CREATE TABLESPACE does not name a storage group, it will not only use the database default storage group, but will also be restricted to the default space allocation.

2.4.6 Space Allocation

The default space allocation (see below) for a table space is adequate for small test tables. For larger tables it is important to be able to select the proper values for PRIQTY and SECQTY. These two quantities give the size of the primary space allocation for the dataset and the size of the secondary allocations. These values represent thousand byte chunks (actually 1024 bytes) rather than tracks or cylinders or even physical blocks. DB2 translates them into a number of pages. Pages are DB2's term. They are equivalent to a block or VSAM control interval (CI). VSAM then does the actual allocation in tracks.

2.4.6.1 Page sizes

There are two page sizes available with DB2—4K (4096 bytes) and 32K (32,768 bytes). You indirectly pick a page size when you specify the buffer pool on the CREATE TABLESPACE statement (see Figure 2.12) or the CREATE DATABASE statement. Buffer pools are areas of storage into which pages are read. They are described in more detail in Section 8.1. There are four buffer pools available—BP0, BP1, BP2, and BP32K. If BP32K is chosen, then a 32K page

```
CREATE TABLESPACE SHSPAT0 IN DHSPAT0
   USING STOGROUP STG1  PRIQTY 10000 SECQTY 2000  PCTFREE 10
BUFFERPOOL BP0
   CLOSE NO  LOCKSIZE ANY;
```
Figure 2.12. The Buffer Pool Determines the Page Size.

will be used. For the others, the page will be 4K. Many shops only use BP0, as one large buffer pool will usually perform better than three smaller ones.

Using a 32K page is much less efficient for system performance. More data at a time has to be transferred from disk, and the amount of memory needed for the buffer pool is much greater. Therefore, it is strongly recommended to only use a 32K page when the rows are too large to fit in 4K.

2.4.6.2 Calculating the Space

Calculating how much space is needed (or, conversely, how many tracks will be allocated for a given PRIQTY value) requires more than just adding up the field lengths. The things you need to take into consideration are:

- Length of each field as stored by DB2
- Overhead for varying length fields or fields with null values
- Overhead for each row
- Overhead for the page
- Freespace
- Number of rows
- Expected growth pattern

As a quick estimate to the space needed, you can just add up the field lengths. Multiplying the row size by the expected number of rows and dividing by 1000 will give a reasonable first guess to use for PRIQTY. Dividing the row size into 4000 will give an estimate of how many rows will fit per (4K) page. On a 3380 disk drive, there are 10 4K pages per track and 15 tracks per cylinder. Let's look at a simple example to see how these are all related.

- the columns add up to 100 bytes
- there are 10,000 rows
- the total space needed will be about 1 million bytes

A value of 1000 (1,000,000 bytes/1000) for PRIQTY will be approximately right (forgetting things like freespace and growth). At 100 bytes, 40 rows will fit in a 4K page (some space will be wasted in each page). Therefore, 10,000 rows will need 250 pages, which is 25 tracks or a little less than 2 cylinders.

$$250/10 = \text{no. of tracks} = 25$$
$$25/15 = \text{no. of cylinders} < 2$$

For a more exacting estimate, the following items are needed.

2.4.6.3 Storage Format

- Character fields are stored 1 byte per character
- Varying length character fields have a 2-byte length field
- Integers are 4 bytes
- Small integers are 2 bytes
- Decimal—stored as packed decimal—4 bits (1/2 byte) per digit with 1/2 byte for the sign
- Dates—4 bytes
- Times—3 bytes
- Timestamps—10 bytes
- Floating point—4 or 8 bytes
- Fields that can have null values have a 1-byte indicator (whether or not there is a null value for this occurrence)

2.4.6.4 Overhead

- There are 20 bytes of header and 2 bytes of trailer information for each page. That leaves 4074 bytes for rows. The largest individual row that can be defined is 4056 bytes. Any larger row would require a 32K page.
- Each row has 8 bytes of overhead. There is a 6-byte header. At the end of the page there is also an array of 2-byte pointers to the start of each row. The layout of a data page is shown in Figure 2.13.
- DB2 can store at most 127 rows in a page. For a 4K page, that means that if the row (counting the 8-byte overhead) is less than 32 bytes, there will be wasted space.
- If the row size is large, then there is also a good chance of wasted space in a page. For example, if the row is over 2037 bytes, only one row will fit in the page and the rest of the page will be unused. If a row is 900 bytes, four rows will fit, using 3600 bytes. 474 bytes (almost 12%) will not be used.

2.4.6.5 Freespace

When the table space is created, you specify freespace. This is space that is left unused by DB2 during an initial load (with the LOAD utility) or a reorganization. If either of these will be used, then the freespace must be taken into consideration when estimating storage needs. Freespace is useful when there will be insertions into the tables. DB2 will try to insert a row based on the clustering index. It will try to store rows near other rows with similar key values. This will help maintain clustering order and reduce IOs. If there is no space left free, then inserted rows will go to empty pages at the end of the table space. Freespace is described in more detail below.

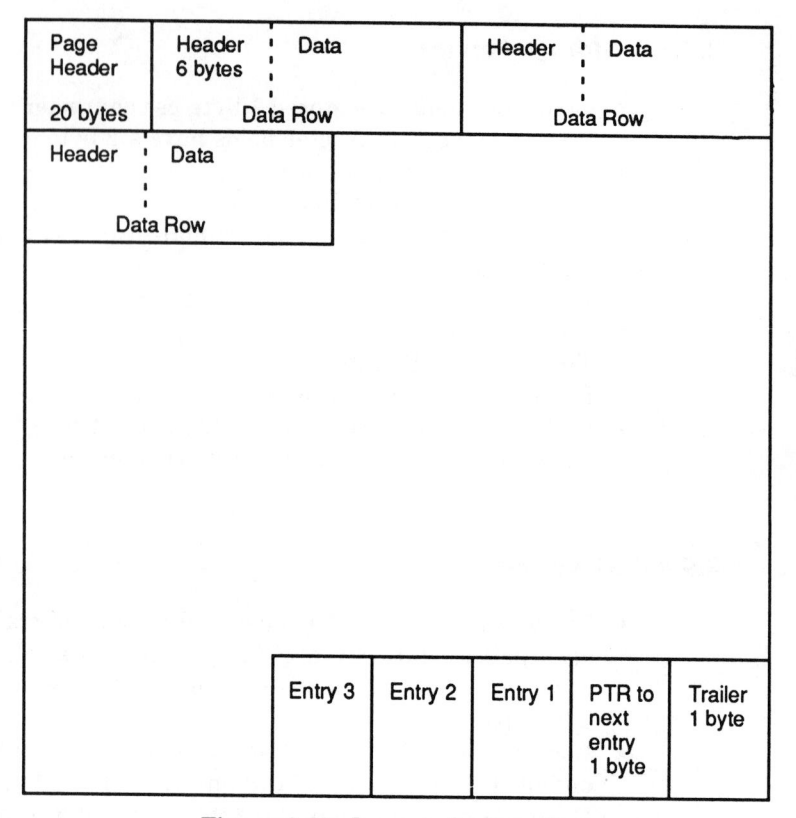

Figure 2.13. Layout of a Data Page.

2.4.6.6 Growth

Some table spaces are for read-only purposes or are refreshed periodically and therefore may not continually grow. Most data, though, does increase over time, and it is important to plan for it, both in terms of freespace and in total space allocation.

2.4.6.7 PRIQTY and SECQTY

There are two space parameters to use—PRIQTY and SECQTY. Initially, DB2 will allocate the primary quantity. When that space is used up, a secondary extent will be allocated. Up to 123 secondary extents can be allocated. At first glance, it appears that if you are worried about overallocating space, you can start small and just take secondary extents as needed. This is true and will work but will not be the most efficient approach. VSAM and DB2 will perform better if all of the data is in one primary extent. This way all of the pages (blocks) will be contiguous. Secondary extents will not necessarily be contiguous. It is often recommended in the manuals to make the primary extent big enough to store all the data. I tend not to worry about it that much. I try to make the primary big enough for the current data and expected growth, but if I underestimate and a couple of secondary extents are used, I don't get upset.

The secondary extents should also be fairly small compared to the primary extent because of the way DB2 allocates them. DB2 does not wait for an extent to fill up before asking for another secondary extent. Instead, when the amount of space left is less than one half of a secondary, it asks for the next secondary. For example, if the primary is 10 cylinders and the secondary is 6 cylinders, when there is less than 3 cylinders left in the current extent, a new secondary will be allocated. When the data is occupying just over 7 cylinders, the total space allocated will be 16 cylinders. If the secondary quantity is large, there may often be wasted space.

This scheme has a performance advantage in that the application does not have to sit and wait for space to be allocated. The next extent is always allocated before it is needed. However, it presents a conflict in trying to meet several design goals. Large secondary quantities will waste space, whereas small secondary quantities will result in many secondary extents if the primary is exceeded. This is bad for performance and increases the chance of running out of secondary extents. It is not easy to balance these requirements. The best situation is to pick a primary quantity that is large enough for the data (without overallocating too much), and not having too much growth (obviously, this is application-dependent and not something you can set). In practice, you should monitor the space utilization on a regular basis. If the primary is filling up, consider increasing it and doing a reorg of the table space.

As a rule of thumb, I generally make my secondaries somewhere between 10% and 33% the size of my primary. If my primary quantity is 6000 (10 cylinders), then I will make the secondary 600–2000. The choice will depend on whether the estimated number of rows and the expected growth are accurately known, or just a guess.

If you have very large tables exceeding two gigabytes, then provided the table space has not exceeded its 123 extents, DB2 will allocate a new VSAM dataset when the two gigabyte limit is reached.

For a partitioned table space, different PRIQTY and SECQTY values can be given to each partition (see Figure 2.14). If individual values are not assigned, then the values given in the general USING clause will be used for each partition. This is important to remember. The value is not divided evenly among the partitions, it is used for each one.

2.4.6.8 Default Space Allocation

If PRIQTY and SECQTY are left off, the default (and minimum) is three pages for each. VSAM will translate the number of pages requested by DB2 into tracks. The minimum is one track. For a 4K page, the minimum actually allocated is therefore 10 pages on a 3380 drive. The first two pages are for a header page and a space map. Therefore, there are eight data pages. This is quite enough for many tables, especially test ones. For a 100-byte row, 320 rows will fit on that first track. A 50-byte row can have 640 rows in the default primary extent. Sec-

```
CREATE TABLESPACE SHSDIA0 IN DHSDIA0
  NUMPARTS 4
   (PART 1
      USING STOGROUP STG1   PRIQTY 10000 SECQTY 2000   PCTFREE 10,
    PART 2
      USING STOGROUP STG1   PRIQTY  8000 SECQTY 2400   PCTFREE 5,
    PART 3
      USING STOGROUP STG1   PRIQTY 12000 SECQTY 2000,
    PART 4
      USING STOGROUP STG1   PRIQTY  6000 SECQTY 1500   PCTFREE 5)
  BUFFERPOOL BP0
  CLOSE NO   LOCKSIZE ANY;
```

Figure 2.14. CREATE TABLESPACE for Partitioned Table Space: Primary and Secondary Quantities Specified for Each Partition.

ondary extents can then handle many more rows (for test tables the impact of having secondary extents is not important).

2.4.7 Freespace

During a REORG or a LOAD, rows are stored consecutively in pages. The REORG will load the rows in order by the clustering index. The LOAD utility will store them in whatever order the input file is in. When loading the rows, each page will be filled up before the next page is used, except for any freespace that is specified for the table space. Freespace is specified with the PCTFREE and FREEPAGE clauses. PCTFREE nn leaves a percentage of each page free during the load. PCTFREE 20 would leave 20% unused. FREEPAGE represents whole pages to be left free. FREEPAGE 0 leaves no pages free. FREEPAGE 4 leaves every fifth page free—the 4 means after every 4 pages leave the next one free.

Freespace is useful for a table that will have much insert activity in between reorgs. When a row is inserted, DB2 will try to store it in the same page as the rows near it in clustering order. If there is no room in that page, it will have to go elsewhere. Therefore, a larger amount of freespace will enable the table to stay in good clustering order longer, thereby improving performance and reducing the frequency with which reorgs will be needed. The drawback with having too much freespace is that more space will be needed for the table. After the initial load and after reorgs, the rows will be spread out over more pages. This will not only use more space, but will result in longer data access (table space scans will have more pages to read). Tables with little insert activity should have little freespace specified. Tables that are read-only should have none.

The default values for a table space are FREEPAGE 0 and PCTFREE 5 (the defaults for indexes are different—see Section 2.5).

2.4.8 CLOSE

The CLOSE parameter is very important to understand because the default value is not a good choice for production online table spaces. The values are YES and NO, with YES being the default. This parameter controls whether or not the datasets should be closed or left open after being used by a transaction or query. YES means that the dataset should be closed. NO means that the dataset should be left open until DB2 comes down.

Opening a dataset takes a surprisingly long time. If a transaction requires several tables, each with a few indexes, transaction response time could be increased by three or four seconds. That's just for the file opens. Any table space (and the associated indexes) that are used frequently during the day in an online environment should have CLOSE NO.

Why is the default YES? As mentioned before, there is a limit to the number of datasets that can be open at one time to DB2. In addition, each open dataset requires some virtual storage set aside for it for VSAM control blocks. If every table space that were used even once in a day were left open, storage requirements would grow and the upper limit on datasets could be reached. Programmer test table spaces should be left with CLOSE YES as should table spaces that are only going to be used in batch. If QMF users are allowed to create their own table spaces, these too should probably be closed after each use (assuming they will not have frequent use).

Version 2.3 has an improvement which will make it more acceptable to define table spaces with CLOSE YES. These table spaces will no longer be physically closed when not in use. The actual closing will only occur if the open dataset limit is reached. This allows more datasets to be defined with CLOSE YES, but without the performance penalty in most situations.

2.4.9 Locksize

DB2 allows multiple users, programs, and jobs to access the same tables concurrently. In order to provide data integrity, DB2 will issue locks on pages or table spaces. Rows that are read will cause read (shared) locks. Rows that are updated will cause update (exclusive) locks. The locks can be on several different types of entities. The lowest level lock is on a page. The highest lock is on the table space. For a segmented table space, an individual table may be locked.

The lock level (i.e., page, table space) is specified on the CREATE TABLESPACE statement and can also be controlled with the LOCK DML statement. The choices for a table space are:

PAGE
TABLE (for segmented table spaces only)
TABLESPACE
ANY

Page locks provide greater concurrency. If the entire table space has an exclusive lock, then no other transaction can access the tables in it at all. The advantage of a table space lock is an improvement in performance when concurrency is not required. For example, a table that is only updated in batch, one job at a time, does not need the update concurrency that page locks would provide. The performance improvement is due to only one lock being required for the entire table space rather than for each page that is updated or read.

2.4.9.1 Limiting the Number of Locks—NUMLKUS, NUMLKTS

The meanings of LOCKSIZE PAGE and TABLESPACE are obvious. They indicate that either page locks or locks on the entire table space will be done. LOCKSIZE TABLE can be used for a segmented table space. The locks will be for an individual table rather than the entire table space.

LOCKSIZE ANY means that initially DB2 will take page locks for the table space until it reaches a limit (NUMLKTS—see below). At that point it will escalate the lock—a table space lock will be taken and the page locks will be released.

We are about to discuss DB2 locks and two installation parameters. You might think that these discussions belong in a later chapter. However, it is important for every DBA and programmer to understand the implications. The choice for the LOCKSIZE parameter on the CREATE TABLESPACE is based on this understanding. Therefore, this *is* a good place to discuss it.

Locks are maintained by the IRLM (IMS Resource Lock Manager), which runs in its own region. Each lock requires virtual storage. Allowing an unlimited number of page locks can increase the DB2 storage requirements in an unpredictable fashion. There are, therefore, limits set when DB2 is installed for the number of locks that can be held by a single unit of work (i.e., between commit points of a job or transaction). These two limits are called NUMLKTS and NUMLKUS. NUMLKTS sets a limit on the number of locks concurrently held for a table space by a unit of work before lock escalation occurs (provided that the table space has LOCKSIZE ANY). The default value is 1000 but this can be changed by the systems programmer who maintains DB2. NUMLKUS sets a limit on the *total* number of locks that may be held by the unit of work (default of 10,000). If this value is exceeded, then an error SQLCODE (-904) will be returned to the program.

LOCKSIZE PAGE means that the table space can have an unlimited number of page locks without lock escalation, although there is still the chance that NUMLKUS will be exceeded. LOCKSIZE ANY reduces the chance of exceeding NUMLKUS but does not eliminate it. NUMLKUS is usually set to 5 or more times NUMLKTS. In this way it would require the parallel updating of many tables to exceed NUMLKUS.

The programmer or DBA does not have any control of these limits. Therefore, it is usually best to use LOCKSIZE ANY. If PAGE is used, then the programmer can avoid exceeding NUMLKUS in one of two ways.

- LOCK TABLE statement. Any program can issue this LOCK statement to lock the entire table space for the run of the job. This is useful when you want to maintain high concurrency for most of the day, but have a stand-alone large update job for off hours. For a segmented table space, only the table is locked, not the table space.
- Issue COMMIT statements frequently. Locks are released at commit time (EXEC SQL COMMIT in batch or TSO, or when a CICS or IMS syncpoint is issued). Committing frequently for long-running batch jobs also has the advantage that if a failure occurs, the entire run will not get backed out and have to be rerun in its entirety. Of course, special rerun code may be necessary so that the program will know where to restart from. See Section 6.1 for more details.

LOCKSIZE ANY is usually the best choice. The programmers will usually not have to worry about exceeding the lock limits. However, it is important for the programmers to be aware of the implications of large update programs and their choices for committing and rerunning.

2.4.10 IN Clause

A table space is part of a database. This clause names that database. If the IN clause is left off, then the table space will be part of the default database DSNDB04. This may be acceptable for initial testing and one-time shots, but it is usually better to establish appropriate databases for ongoing work.

2.4.11 Summary and Key Guidelines

- Tables are physically stored in table spaces.
- You can have more than one table in a table space. You would do so for small test tables.
- Segmented table spaces are the best choice if you have more than one table in the table space.
- If you are going to use the LOAD utility with REPLACE to put data into a table, then you should only have that one table in its table space.
- Partitioned table spaces are good for very large tables.
- Use CLOSE NO for most of the table spaces—especially ones used by online transactions.
- LOCKSIZE ANY is usually the best choice.
- Storage groups should have more than one disk volume. This helps avoid the problems that occur when a disk pack fills up.

- For the best performance, PRIQTY should be large enough to fit the entire set of data pages. It is not all that critical, however. Too large a value for PRIQTY is also not ideal. It will waste space. For simple table spaces, it may also negatively affect DB2's choice of access path. This is because DB2 will use the allocated space to estimate the cost of a table space scan, rather than the size of the individual table within a simple table space.
- SECQTY should not be too large because it will result in wasted space. It should also not be too small or you run the risk of running out of secondary extents.

2.5 INDEXES

Creating indexes for a table is an important part of the design and tuning of a DB2 system. Before we discuss guidelines for using indexes, it is necessary to describe what they do and don't do. There is confusion about this, especially among new DB2 users. The main purpose of indexes is to help performance in the finding of DB2 rows. I use the word "find" rather than "select" because DB2 may use indexes to find rows for updating as well as for reading. This section covers the basics of index creation. Section 7.4 discusses guidelines for the design of indexes.

2.5.1 What Indexes Don't Do

The first basic rule about indexes is that:

> Indexes do *not* specify which columns can be used for selecting rows or in which order rows are returned.

The feature that sets DB2 apart from other DBMSs or VSAM files is that any column can be used in any search criteria (WHERE clause) and the rows can be presented in any order (ORDER BY clause). The SQL statement in Figure 2.15a will work the same regardless of whether or not there are any indexes. This has the nice feature that a programmer or end-user can issue a query without having to know whether or not there are indexes. This, of course, leads to a myth about DB2: Programmers do not need to know the structure of the database or about the existence of any indexes. Later we will see why this is a myth.

As I said, indexes do not explicitly control the order in which rows are retrieved—the ORDER BY clause does. However, if there is no ORDER BY, then the rows will be returned in an order based on how DB2 reads the data. If DB2 chooses to use an index to access the table, then the rows will usually be returned in the order of that index (an exception to this occurs if List Prefetch is used—see Section 4.3). If we have an index on THSADM0 with columns PATID and ADMDATE and issue the query in Figure 2.15a, the rows will be returned in PATID, ADMDATE order regardless of how DB2 reads the data. If we issue

```
SELECT * FROM THSADMO
  WHERE ADMDATE BETWEEN '1991-01-01' AND '1991-01-31'
  ORDER BY PATID, ADMDATE
(a) ORDER BY controls the sort order


SELECT * FROM THSADMO
  WHERE PATID BETWEEN '111100000' AND '111199999'
    AND ADMDATE BETWEEN '1991-01-01' AND '1991-01-31'
(b) Without ORDER BY, the order depends on the access path
```
Figure 2.15. Ordering the Selected Rows.

the SELECT in Figure 2.15b, the rows will be in PATID, ADMDATE order if DB2 uses the index, but not in that order otherwise.

You might be asking at this point why wouldn't DB2 use this index if there is one, especially if we want it to. The answer is the second basic rule:

> You cannot tell DB2 how to retrieve the rows of the table. DB2 will decide what it thinks is the best way. (We'll see later the various things that influence DB2's choice.)

This rule leads to a related myth. The programmer/end-user does not have to worry about "navigating" through the database. This is partially true. The programmer cannot tell DB2 how to access the data and, therefore, can retrieve whatever he wants without concern over indexes, number of rows, etc. However, for good performance, especially in online systems, a programmer does need to know these things. While he cannot *tell* DB2 what to do, he can code his SQL statements to try to *take advantage* of the indexes—to try to *influence* DB2 to use them. This represents the most critical aspect of DB2 performance. The DBA and programmer must work together to design and use indexes effectively. The choice of indexes must match the access requirements of the system, and the programmer must code his programs to take advantage of them.

2.5.2 What Indexes Do

We've discussed what indexes do not do. Now let's see some of the things that they can do. While the main purpose of indexes is for performance, there are several other uses that affect the content of the database.

2.5.2.1 Uniqueness

It is often necessary to ensure that duplicate values are not allowed for a field (or set of fields) in a table. An employee database would usually have a unique employee ID for each person. In DB2 this is controlled by using an index on the columns that have this requirement. An index can be defined as being unique or nonunique. The CREATE in Figure 2.16 creates a unique index on the EMPID column. DB2 will not allow a row to be inserted that has an EMPID equal to an existing row in the table. Without the keyword UNIQUE, duplicates would be allowed.

Uniqueness can be enforced on the combined value of several columns (Figure 2.17). This index will ensure that while an employee can be assigned to more than one project, he will only be assigned once to each project. A table can have any number of unique indexes and a column can appear in more than one index for a table.

2.5.2.2 Primary Keys

DB2 Version 2 implemented the concept of referential integrity (see Section 2.3). If a table is a parent table in a relationship, then it must have a primary key defined for it. This is done by using the keyword PRIMARY KEY in the CREATE TABLE statement, identifying the columns that are to make up the primary key. A unique index *must* be created on these columns. There can only be one primary key for a table.

```
CREATE UNIQUE INDEX XAAEMP01 ON creator.TAAEMP0
    (EMPID)
    USING STOGROUP STG1 PRIQTY _____ SECQTY _____ SUBPAGES 4
    CLOSE NO
```
Figure 2.16. Creating a Unique Index.

```
CREATE UNIQUE INDEX XAAPRJ01 ON TAAPRJ0
    (PROJID,
     EMPID)
    CLUSTER
    USING _____
```
Figure 2.17. Uniqueness Can Be Enforced for a Combination of Columns.

2.5.2.3 Clustering of Data

There is one more way in which an index can affect the data, but in this case it is just the physical placement of the rows—not their content. A table can have one index defined as a clustering index. This is done with the keyword CLUSTER. DB2 will try to insert rows approximately in order by the columns of the clustering index. However, if the rows are inserted in some other order, they will not get stored in exactly this clustering order. A REORG of the table (Section 7.3) will load the data exactly in the clustering order.

The advantage of clustering is that any request that asks for the rows to be sorted by these columns, or asks for a group of rows with similar values, will be processed much faster. Rows with similar values will be stored on the same page (or nearby) and can therefore be retrieved with fewer IOs. This is further discussed below.

It should be noted that rows are not inserted in clustering order when they are loaded with the LOAD utility with the REPLACE option. In this case, they are stored in the order in which they are presented to the LOAD utility.

2.5.3 Index Parameters

The various parameters of the CREATE INDEX are important to performance, and are described here.

2.5.3.1 CLOSE

The CLOSE parameter has the same meaning as in the CREATE TABLESPACE statement. Each index is a VSAM dataset. CLOSE YES means the file will be opened each time the index is used and closed at the end of the task that is using it. CLOSE NO will result in the index file being left open while the DB2 subsystem is running. Task refers to any batch job, CICS task, or QMF query. Opening files can take a long time, as described in the previous section. Each one can take as much as 1/2 second. The exact amount of time it takes is obviously related to the speed of the machine and disk drives. Therefore, for any frequently used table, you want to specify CLOSE NO for all indexes as well as the table space. NO is not the default—you must specify it. Tables that are only going to be accessed in batch or a couple of times a day can be left with the default.

2.5.3.2 Subpages

This parameter can have values 1–16. The default is 4. Each index page is 4K bytes. It is then divided into subpages. The subpage is the unit of locking (see Section 6.3 for a description of DB2 locking). When DB2 locks data (either shared or exclusive locks), it does not lock the individual row, but rather the data page and index subpage. Therefore, more subpages per page results in fewer index records being locked at a time and can lead to greater concurrency of access. On the other hand, requests that access many records are likely to span more subpages and will, therefore, result in greater locking activity. This can increase the CPU requirements of the transaction.

Concurrency is affected primarily by update transactions (which require exclusive locks). Therefore, a table that is updated at night in batch by one job at a time and only read by multiple users should have a low number of subpages (perhaps 1 subpage). Highly concurrent update activity will benefit from a higher number of subpages if sufficient freespace has been defined.

For high insert activity, if there is not enough freespace, it is better to have fewer subpages. Updates that change index column values result in index entries being deleted and inserted, so they too fit into this category. Index entries must be maintained in key order. Therefore, an index entry must always go in an exact spot based on its key value. If there is room in the subpage, then only the one subpage is locked. If there is no room, then the entries on the other subpages of the page are rearranged to try to make room. This will result in greater cost in maintaining the index.

Having more subpages will also result in more page splits. This can reduce concurrency. Whenever an index page is split, the page in the next higher index level gets updated and will be locked. This will effectively lock all index entries for all of the leaf pages under this nonleaf page. The reason that having more subpages increases page splits is that fewer index entries can fit on a page with 16 subpages than with only one or two subpages.

2.5.3.3 Index Storage Format

Each subpage has a header of 17 bytes (plus 4 more bytes in a subpage directory). An index page with 1 subpage will have about 170 bytes more space for index entries than a page with 8 subpages. Index entries cannot span subpages. If the size of each index entry does not divide evenly into the available space in a subpage, then there will be wasted space. The more subpages, the greater the chance of unused space in each one. With fewer index entries per page, page splits will occur more frequently.

Typically, I will use the default of 4 subpages for indexes with average update activity. If I expect much updating, but few new inserts, I will use 8 subpages. For a table with many inserts, I will use SUBPAGES 1 or 2. Figures 2.18 through 2.21 illustrate index pages and subpages and index entries. A page with only one subpage is sometimes called a nonsegmented index page, while one with more than one subpage is called segmented. Each nonsegmented page has 45 bytes of header information. A segmented one has a 28-byte header for the page, plus 21 bytes for each subpage.

An index entry for a unique index (Figure 2.20) consists of the indexed columns plus a 4-byte row identifier (RID), which contains the address of the data row. For a nonunique index, there is one entry for each different key value. The entry has a 6-byte header, the indexed columns, and the RIDs for each data row with the same key value.

The unique index XAAEMP01, which we defined earlier, uses 13 bytes per

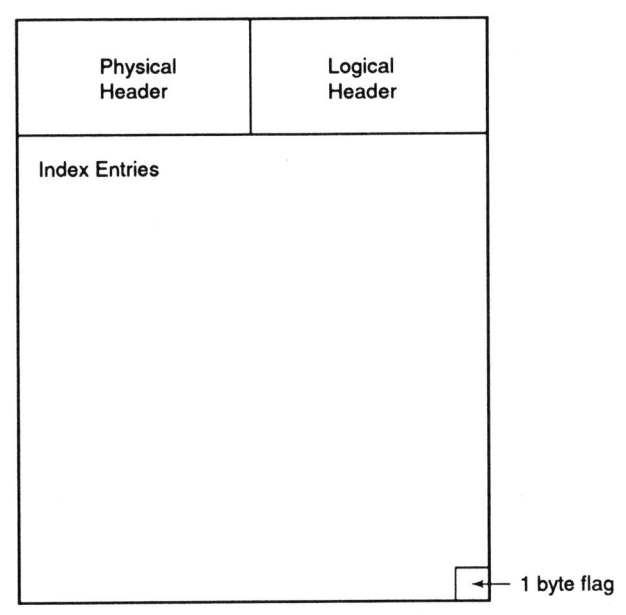

Figure 2.18. Nonsegmented Index Page (SUBPAGES = 1).

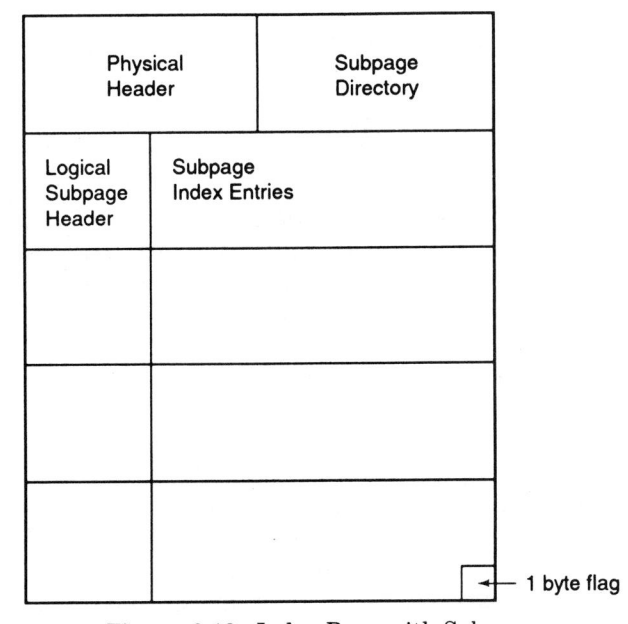

Figure 2.19. Index Page with Subpages.

Indexed columns value	RID

Figure 2.20. Index Entry for Unique Index.

Header	Indexed columns value	RID	RID	RID

Figure 2.21. Index Entry for Nonunique Index.

entry: 9 bytes for EMPID, plus the 4-byte RID. Therefore, you can fit over 300 entries in an index page. If there is only one subpage, then any lock taken on the page will lock all 300 entries. If there were four subpages, then only 75 entries would be locked with a page lock.

2.5.4 Creating Indexes

Indexes are created with the CREATE INDEX statement. They can be created either before there is any data in the table, or after there is data. Once indexes have been created, they get updated whenever data rows are inserted or updated. The indexes are also manipulated by utilities that reorganize or recover them.

2.5.4.1 Before There is Data

If CREATE INDEX is issued when the table is empty, then the index will be updated when data is entered into the table. This can happen with SQL DML statements (INSERT, UPDATE, DELETE) or with the LOAD utility.

When data is inserted into a table during normal processing, the data will usually be in random order. Over time, the index will become disorganized with many index pages physically out of sequence (the index entries are always logically in key sequence). A disorganized index takes up more space and is processed less efficiently by SQL queries. This is especially true if the index starts off empty and the inserts are random. Initially, the index will have just one leaf page. Early on, there will be widely separated key values in the one page. As it becomes full, it will be split and more pages will be created. Therefore, it may be necessary to periodically reorganize the index. The REORG utility is used for this purpose. After a reorg, the index entries will be in physical as well as logical order. If there is now a larger amount of data, these entries will be spread over many index pages. New inserts will be more evenly distributed, and it will take a little longer to become disorganized again.

When you start with a new system that has no initial data, all entries must come from new transactions. If instead, you are initially populating the table with data from another file, you have two choices. You can use a program that issues SQL INSERT statements, or you can use the LOAD utility.

When the LOAD utility is run on an empty table or with the REPLACE option (replacing all data), the indexes are built very efficiently. While loading the data, work records are written for each index. These are then sorted into the order of the index columns. The indexes are then built. This is an efficient process and the indexes are well organized at the end of the load. Well organized means that the indexes' records are physically in key sequence. No reorg will be needed at this time. The insert processing done with LOAD is so much better than INSERTs (see Section 6.2 for more information) that it almost always pays to use this approach when feasible.

2.5.4.2 Adding an Index

If a table already has data, then a CREATE INDEX will also build the index. How it does this depends on the version of DB2. In DB2 Version 1, CREATE INDEX unloaded records from the table (in the order of their physical layout) and inserted them one at a time into the index. This is similar to the processing done with SQL INSERT statements. The result was a very time-consuming process and a poorly organized index. For example, on one table with 900,000 rows, a create of one index took 3.5 hours on a 3090 150E. DB2 utility programs such as LOAD and RECOVER INDEX (to recover a damaged index) will use the operating system sort utility to sort the data before inserting the index records. They both took about 4 minutes to build this index.

With DB2 Version 2.1, the create process was improved immensely, but not as much as it should have been. It took 10 minutes to create this index. The new method involves sorting the unloaded data into index order and then building the index. This sounds like the method used by the LOAD utility (and also by the RECOVER INDEX utility). In fact, the process is similar but the implementation is different. CREATE now uses DB2's sorting mechanism to sort the data. This is the same process as when DB2 needs to sort data for an ORDER BY or GROUP BY clause of a SELECT statement. It uses the DB2 subsystem temporary table spaces to hold the intermediate results. There are two problems with this approach.

1. It does take longer than LOAD or RECOVER INDEX. Ten minutes is much better than 3.5 hours, but not as good as 4 minutes. For larger tables, there is a corresponding increase.
2. For a large table, there is a need for large temporary table spaces. The temporary table space is used by DB2 to produce result tables for certain queries—in particular, those needing sorting. The larger the amount of data selected by these queries, the bigger the temporary table spaces need to be (of course, a sort of a large table by non-indexed columns is not a good idea performance-wise, and should be avoided—there are alternative ways to get the data). CREATE IN-

DEX now also requires the temporary table space, and a large table will need a large amount of space. The formula is:

rows * (index size + 6 + 4) * 2.1 for a unique index

The index size is the sum of the length of the columns in the index. The 6 is for a prefix and the 4 is the RID of the data row. For this index that I was building, the columns were 14 bytes. Therefore, 45 megabytes of storage were needed. The temporary table spaces are initially created by the DB2 systems programmer when DB2 is installed. The default value is 16 megabytes of space. More space can be added later, but as you can see, much more may be needed than initially anticipated.

When a sort is done with the DB2 utilities, the work space can be temporary datasets, and it is released at the end of the job. The temporary table spaces remain. Allocating enough space for occasional use will result in wasted DASD space.

Hopefully, in the future, CREATE INDEX will be further modified to run as well as an index recovery.

This section provided the basics of defining and creating indexes. Chapter 4 (Access Paths) and Section 7.4 (Adding and Dropping Indexes) provide more information on how indexes are used by DB2, and how to decide which columns to create indexes for.

2.5.5 Summary and Key Guidelines

- Things indexes do:
  - are used for performance
  - enforce uniqueness
  - are required for a primary key
  - can be used to cluster the data rows
- Things indexes do not do:
  - affect the ordering of data
  - limit your access to columns
  - you cannot *tell* DB2 to use an index
- A column can appear in more than one index
- SUBPAGES
  - Fewer subpages are better when there is much insert activity, or there is no need for concurrent update
  - More subpages are good when there is much update activity for nonindexed columns
- Creating indexes
  - Indexes can be created either before data is loaded, or after
  - For a very large table, index create time can take a while and requires a large temporary table space

— If you are initially building a table with data from another source, the LOAD utility with the REPLACE option is your best choice for performance, especially for the building of the indexes

2.6 VIEWS

2.6.1 What Views Are

A table is a collection of data organized into rows and columns. If a user is granted access to the table, he can request any of the data in the table. If he only wants to see part of it, he can limit the request to specific columns (with the select list) and specific rows (with the WHERE clause). There is sometimes a need for a user to always see the same subset of data. To simplify and control this need, the DBA can define a view of the data. A view is a predefined way of looking at part of the data of a table, or a set of tables.

There are two main purposes to using views:

- Security—A view can be a subset of the rows of a table, based on data values. It can also contain a subset of the columns. Users can be granted access to the view, and not granted access to the underlying table(s). This will limit their access to the data that they are allowed to see.

    Figure 2.22 has the CREATE statement to define a view of the employee table. With this view, access is limited to those employees in department B13. It also limits access to only some of the columns of the table. Salary, for example, is not part of the view.
- Ease of programming and use—Users often need to see the same subset of data or join of several tables. Rather than having them code the same selection or join criteria in every query they issue, these criteria can be permanently coded into a view. This greatly simplifies their queries.

    In Figure 2.23 we are defining a view which includes data from the patient and drug order tables. It limits the rows to active patients. This view is useful for people who need to look at drug orders for active patients only. The ACTIVEFLAG column is needed to determine this status. Therefore, a join of patient and drug is always needed

```
CREATE VIEW VHSEMP01
    (EMPID,LASTNAME,FIRSTNAME,DEPT)
    AS SELECT EMPID,LASTNAME,FIRSTNAME,DEPT
        FROM THSEMP0
        WHERE DEPT = 'B13'
```
Figure 2.22. Creating a View.

```
CREATE VIEW VHSDRG01
  (PATID,LASTNAME,FIRSTNAME,DRUGCODE,DRUGDATE,DRUGSEQ)
  AS SELECT PATID,LASTNAME,FIRSTNAME,DRUGCODE,DRUGDATE,DRUGSEQ
     FROM THSPAT0 PAT,THSDRG0 DRG
     WHERE ACTIVEFLAG='Y' AND
           PAT.PATID = DRG.PATID
```

Figure 2.23. Views Can Join Tables.

```
SELECT PATID,LASTNAME,FIRSTNAME,DRUGDATE
  FROM VHSDRG01
  WHERE DRUGCODE='A11122200'
```

Figure 2.24. Finding Active Patients Using the View.

for these queries. With the view in place, a query to find active patients who have been given drug number A11122200 is done much more simply (Figure 2.24).

There is a third use of views that some people feel is important, but which is usually not done effectively. They feel that all programs should use views rather than going directly against the tables. This way they "isolate the programs from changes to the table definition." I have placed this in quotes because the way it is usually done does not accomplish its purpose.

The idea is that if a program uses SELECT *, or INSERT, without a column list, then if a column is added to a table, the program will no longer function correctly. This statement is true. In Section 3.1, I describe what the problems are. The best solution is always to use a column list.

If a view is used instead of the table, then the assumption is that the DBA can add a column to the table but leave the view alone. Then the program will still be pointing to its original set of columns. This will only work if there are separate views created for each program, each containing only those columns that the program needs. But how is that any different than the *program* using only the columns it needs?

Since it is too much maintanence for the DBAs to create a separate view for each program, they will often just create one general-purpose view which contains every column of the table. That way if they want to add a column, the view "can be left alone and not affect the programs." This, too, is in quotes because if the view is a general-purpose view with every column, then, initially, the DBA will not change it, but several weeks later it *will* get updated to reflect the new table definition. Then, the programs will be affected.

The point of this description is that while views *can* isolate programs from table changes, they can only do so if proper thought is given to how they are defined and used.

2.6.1.1 Alternative Look at a Table

A view is just another way to see the data in a table (or tables). There is no separate storage of the data in a view. The definition of a view is maintained in the DB2 catalog. Whenever an SQL statement is issued against a view, DB2 will use that definition to form the new way of looking at the data. If rows are inserted into a view, it is the base table that is updated.

2.6.2 Defining a View

Views are defined with the CREATE VIEW statement. In essence, you select columns from one or more tables, using a WHERE clause to limit the rows or to give join criteria (as in Figures 2.22 and 2.23 above). This is done with an ordinary subselect. Views can also use column functions and GROUP BY clauses. This can give a view which is a summary of the data in a table. In Figure 2.25, we have a view which gives the count of patients in each ward. To find out the number of people in wards 2000–2200, you now only need the simple query shown in Figure 2.26.

There are some limitations to what you can do with views. The view definition cannot have an ORDER BY clause. Views can be updated provided they are not read-only views. Any of the following in the view definition make the view read-only:

- Joins
- DISTINCT
- GROUP BY
- A column function such as COUNT or SUM

```
CREATE VIEW VHSLOC01
   (WARD,NUM_PEOPLE)
   AS SELECT WARD,COUNT(*)
        FROM THSLOC0
        GROUP BY WARD
```

Figure 2.25. Views Can Use Column Functions.

```
SELECT WARD,NUM_PEOPLE
   FROM VHSLOC01
   WHERE WARD BETWEEN '2000' AND '2200'
```

Figure 2.26. Using the View to Get Counts.

If any of those functions are used, then you can only issue SELECTs against the view. There are other restrictions that limit the type of updating:

- If any of the columns involve an expression (Figure 2.27), then you cannot insert into the view (but you can update one of the other columns).
- If the table has a column that does not have a default value and which does not appear in the view, then you cannot insert into the view.

Essentially, all of these restrictions say that you can only update a view where there is a direct simple mapping of each column of the view into a column of the underlying table.

2.6.2.1 With Check Option

A view definition can have a WHERE clause to limit the rows that will appear. What happens if you insert a row that has values that are not satisfied by the WHERE clause? That depends on whether or not the CREATE has the WITH CHECK OPTION clause (Figure 2.28). If it does *not* have the clause, then DB2 will allow the row to be inserted. Once inserted, you cannot retrieve that row through the view. If the CREATE *does* have the clause, then DB2 will prevent you from inserting a row that will not appear in the view.

```
CREATE VIEW VHSADM01
  (PATID,ADMDATE,DURATION)
  AS SELECT PATID,ADMDATE,DAYS(DISDATE) - DAYS(ADMDATE) + 1
      FROM THSADM0
      WHERE DISDATE NOT NULL
```
Figure 2.27. Expressions for a Column Cannot Be Updated or Inserted.

```
CRATE VIEW VHSEMP01
  (EMPID,LASTNAME,FIRSTNAME,DEPT)
  AS SELECT EMPID,LASTNAME,FIRSTNAME,DEPT
      FROM THSEMP0
      WHERE DEPT = 'B13'
  WITH CHECK OPTION
```
Figure 2.28. The WITH CHECK OPTION.

2.6.3 View Performance

Of course, it is important to know what impact, if any, a view has on performance. Conceptually, you can think of a SELECT against a view as though DB2 first creates the subset of data that is defined by the view, followed by applying the SELECT statement against this subset. This is only a conceptual picture. In reality, DB2 does not necessarily create the view subset first. Instead, it usually takes the view definition and combines it with the SELECT to make a composite SELECT against the underlying tables. It will then determine the best access path to satisfy this composite statement. There are some exceptions to this rule. There are cases where DB2 will materialize the view before processing the predicates of the SQL statement. These situations depend on the view definition and the SQL statement using the view. They involve views that were created with column functions, grouping or DISTINCT, and SELECTs on the view which include joins with other tables or column functions or grouping on the view. There is a good chance that in a future release of DB2, the processing of these situations will be improved.

In Figure 2.29, we are asking for the drug orders for patient 777888666 using the view created in Figure 2.23. This view was a join of active patients and drug orders. There are many active patients receiving medication. This SELECT is equivalent to the one in Figure 2.30, which goes against the patient and drug tables directly. The drug order table has an index whose high order column is patient ID. DB2 *will* use this index to quickly find this patient's drug orders. It will also read the patient row to verify that he is active. If he is not, then no rows will be returned.

From this example, it is clear that in most cases there is no negative impact of using a view for static SQL statements. However, there are other cases as listed above where there might be an impact. For dynamic SQL, such as through QMF, there is also the slight overhead of having to read the view definition from

```
SELECT * FROM VHSDRG01
   WHERE PATID = '777888666'
```

Figure 2.29. Select Drug Orders for an Active Patient.

```
SELECT *
   FROM THSPAT0 PAT, THSDRG0 DRG
   WHERE PATID = '777888666' AND
         ACTIVEFLAG='Y' AND
         PAT.PATID = DRG.PATID
```

Figure 2.30. The Same Select Against the Tables.

the catalog. There are, however, situations where views can improve performance. This is because the view is defined and tested out by (hopefully) experienced DBAs. The programmers and users using the view will not have to code the underlying join criteria and selection criteria. If the criteria are fairly complex (i.e., a join of several tables), then it is likely that users might not always code the equivalent statements as efficiently, or correctly. By simplifying the SQL needed to access the data, you improve both the performance and accurracy of user and programmer SQL statements.

2.6.4 Summary

- Views can be an effective way to simplify complex queries that are used repeatedly. They also provide a means of restricting access to subsets of the data.

2.7 SUMMARY AND KEY GUIDELINES

- Database design should start with an understanding of the data *and* the processing requirements. A data model must take both of these into consideration.
- Any design, whether for a relational DBMS or not, should go through the process of normalization. This process helps in the understanding of the data and relationships. You should always develop a set of tables that are in at least third normal form. Denormalization should not be considered as part of the initial design, it can always be done at the end, before development starts. It should only be considered when necessary.
- The order in which the columns are placed in a table is of no real significance (with the exception of placing varying length strings at the end). I suggest that fields that are closely related be placed near each other. This simplifies things for end-users and programmers. Alphabetical placement is of no real benefit unless the table has 100 columns. Tables with 100 columns probably have many fields that are rarely used together. Separating the table into several tables may be a better design anyway.
- Take advantage of the data types that DB2 provides. The DATE data type is not perfect, but the date manipulation functions are very useful.
- Referential Integrity is not a means of automatically achieving a perfect design and system. The programmers must understand the rules and how they are used. Programs must be written with these rules in mind. I find that in a well-controlled development effort with a small number of programs, program-coded integrity is just as easy to handle. However, when there are many programmers working on the same tables, it becomes harder to ensure that all of the programs will

be written with the same rules. DB2-enforced integrity is very helpful in this environment. It is not an all-or-nothing proposition. Referential constraints can be used for most relationships, but can be left off those where performance might be affected.

- The most important rule in creating table spaces and indexes for production use is to use the CLOSE NO parameter.
- Segmented table spaces should be used any time you expect to store more than one table in the table space.
- If many programmers will be issuing CREATE statements, it is better for them to each have their own database; otherwise, there will be contention on the catalog. In other regards, there is not that much difference whether each table space has its own database or many share the same one.
- The PRIQTY and SECQTY values are in 1000-byte units, not pages or 4K bytes. This can be a bit confusing in calculating appropriate values.
- LOCKSIZE ANY is usually the best choice for a table space.
- There can be one clustering index on a table. It does not have to be the index on the primary key.
- Indexes should be created on columns that are frequently used in WHERE and ORDER BY clauses.

3

Program Development

SQL is designed to be an easy-to-use language. Embedding it in an application program is relatively straightforward. There are, however, a number of considerations that the programmer must be aware of to use SQL in a program. There are also a number of things the programmer must know and use to be able to write efficient DB2 programs.

Understanding the development process is important for both programmers and DBAs. The programmer needs to know how embedded SQL differs from the SQL used with a tool like QMF. There are performance aspects to these differences as well as functional considerations. If the program is not written properly, it is likely to both produce the wrong results as well as run slowly. DBAs must be able to understand what a program is doing in order to be able to help solve problems. This chapter will cover the following:

- Embedding SQL in programs.
- Using synonyms to allow the same program source to be used for test and production tables.
- Application plans—what they are, what goes into them, how to structure them for CICS transactions, and what values to use for the BIND parameters.
- Attachment facilities—how to access DB2 from TSO, Batch, CICS, or IMS/DC.
- Dynamic SQL—how it is useful, and how it affects performance.
- SPUFI—how to use it well to aid the development process.
- QMF—report writer/query packages are an important part of the use

of a DB2 system. Many "programs" no longer need to be written in COBOL or PL/I. The programmer should know how to take advantage of this powerful tool.

3.1 SQL IN PROGRAMS

3.1.1 Static and Dynamic SQL

To access a DB2 table, a program must issue SQL statments. There are two modes of SQL—static and dynamic. Most application programs are written with static SQL. In this mode, the statements have a fixed format, but the particular values requested in WHERE clauses may vary. By fixed format, I mean that there is a statement type, list of columns, table(s), and perhaps a WHERE clause and an ORDER BY clause. Figure 3.1 is an example of a SELECT statement embedded in a PL/I program. The WHERE clause uses a program (host) variable so that at execution time the request can specify different values for the selection. Each time this statement is executed, though, it will always return the same three columns from table THSPAT0.

Dynamic SQL allows the statement format to be constructed at execution time by the program. Examples of programs that use dynamic SQL are SPUFI and QMF. These programs accept SQL statements from the programmer or user, verify their syntax, and build the necessary control structures for DB2 to execute them. In fact, SPUFI and QMF are two valuable tools for the programmer because they allow him/her to enter and test SQL statements without having to embed them in programs. Static SQL is very easy for a programmer to put into a program. Dynamic SQL is much more difficult. Section 3.5 will describe the basics of using dynamic SQL. In this section we will look at static SQL. The topics covered will be:

- embedding SQL statements in programs
- verifying the success of an SQL statement—using the SQLCA
- the SQL preprocessor
- using DCLGEN to describe the tables
- host variables
- cursor operations—selecting a set of rows
- specifying a list of columns rather than using SELECT *
- handling invalid data
- SQLCODEs—a description of the most common error codes, and their causes

3.1.2 Embedded SQL Statements

As you can see from Figure 3.1, the embedded statement looks very much like a nonembedded SQL statement. The differences are:

```
EXEC SQL SELECT PATID,LASTNAME,FIRSTNAME
   INTO :PATID, :LASTNAME, :FIRSTNAME
   FROM THSPATO
   WHERE PATID=:PATIENT;
```
Figure 3.1. Embedded SELECT Statement (PL/I).

- The statement starts with EXEC SQL.
- It ends with a ; (in PL/I). In COBOL it ends with END-EXEC.
- There is an INTO clause that names host variables (names that begin with a :). The data that is read from a table must be placed somewhere where the program can access it. The obvious place is into program variables.
- The WHERE clause can also use host variables for the comparison values in the relational expressions.

Using INSERT, DELETE, and UPDATE statements is as simple as that. SELECT statements that will always return at most one row can also be done in this fashion. However, SELECT statements that may return more than one row must be handled a little differently. Before we get to that, there are a few more elements of a program that we must go over.

3.1.3 Communicating with DB2—the SQLCA

The actual process of communicating with DB2 involves the program passing to DB2 a request, DB2 processing it, and DB2 passing back data in program variables and passing back information on the success or failure of the request. This information is passed to the program in special variables. The program defines these variables by including the data structure SQLCA. In PL/I or COBOL you use

```
EXEC SQL INCLUDE SQLCA;
```

The SQLCA is shown in Figure 3.2. The most important variable in SQLCA is SQLCODE. This variable should be checked after every DB2 statement. It contains a value to indicate the results of the statement. The most important values are described below. There are also fields in the SQLCA (SQLWARN 0–7) to indicate various warnings. These can be useful for program debugging. The field SQLERRD(3) returns a count of the number of rows that were updated, deleted, or inserted with a set operation. This may be useful information.

```
DCL 1 SQLCA,
      2 SQLCAID    CHAR(8),
      2 SQLCABC    BIN FIXED(31),
      2 SQLCODE    BIN FIXED(31),
      2 SQLERRM    CHAR(70) VAR,
      2 SQLERRP    CHAR(8),
      2 SQLERRD(6) BIN FIXED(31),
      2 SQLWARN,
        3 SQLWARN0 CHAR(1),
        3 SQLWARN1 CHAR(1),
        3 SQLWARN2 CHAR(1),
        3 SQLWARN3 CHAR(1),
        3 SQLWARN4 CHAR(1),
        3 SQLWARN5 CHAR(1),
        3 SQLWARN6 CHAR(1),
        3 SQLWARN7 CHAR(1),
      2 SQLEXT     CHAR(8);
```
Figure 3.2. The SQLCA.

3.1.4 The SQL Preprocessor

EXEC SQL statements are not actually understood by the programming language (COBOL, PL/I, or Assembler). First, the program goes through a translation step called the SQL Preprocessor, which translates each SQL statement into some structure declarations and a call statement to the DB2 interface. The preprocessor checks for valid syntax of the statement. This is a tremendous productivity improvement over coding call statements directly. Many errors are caught at compile time.

The preprocessor will also check that the tables and columns named in the statement are valid and that the host variables used have the right data type and length for the columns being accessed. The preprocessor does not actually connect to DB2, and so it cannot fully verify the accuracy of the columns. Instead, you can include in the program an SQL declaration for the table with EXEC SQL INCLUDE THSPAT0 (see Figure 3.3). The preprocessor will use this declaration for its checking. Obviously, the accuracy will depend on the accuracy of the table declaration. This can be easy to control. DB2 has a DCLGEN command which produces a table declaration as well as a structure of host variables

```
EXEC SQL DECLARE THSPAT0 TABLE
(PATID      CHAR(9),
LASTNAME    CHAR(15),
FIRSTNAME   CHAR(10),
SEX         CHAR(1),
BIRTHDATE   DATE,
ACTIVEFLAG  CHAR(1))


DCL 1 THSPAT,
      2 PATID      CHAR(9),
      2 LASTNAME   CHAR(15),
      2 FIRSTNAME  CHAR(10),
      2 SEX        CHAR(1),
      2 BIRTHDATE  CHAR(10),
      2 ACTIVEFLAG CHAR(1);
```

Figure 3.3. DCLGEN for the Patient Table.

(in the appropriate language) and stores it in a program library for inclusion in the program (with the EXEC SQL INCLUDE statements). If the DBA is in charge of generating this DCLGEN whenever the table definition changes, he or she can ensure that it is always accurate. Whenever a program is compiled, it should point to the current declaration for the table.

3.1.5 Host Variables

The host variables that the program uses can be the ones produced by the DCLGEN, but they do not have to be. It is only necessary that they be of the correct data type. The Application Programming and SQL Guide (#SC26-4377) lists the data types needed for variables in each of the programming languages. Figure 3.4 shows a simple program with the basic elements of DB2 access. Host variables are identified with a leading colon (:). There are times when the colon is not required—basically, when there is no chance of ambiguity (i.e., when a column name could not appear in that part of the statement). They are not needed in the INTO clause (because only host variables can be used there) or in a WHERE clause following LIKE or IN (because a column cannot be used in these cases). They are also not required when qualified by a host structure.

Host variables can be elementary variables or elements of structures but not

```
        EXEC SQL INLCUDE SQLCA;    /* DECLARATION FOR THE SQLCA */
        EXEC SQL INCLUDE THSPAT0;  /* THE PATIENT TABLE */


        /* SQL STATEMENT */
        EXEC SQL SELECT PATID,LASTNAME,FIRSTNAME
            INTO :PATID, :LASTNAME, :FIRSTNAME
            FROM THSPAT0
            WHERE PATID='223344556';
        IF SQLCODE = 0  /* CHECK THE RETURN CODE FROM THE CALL */
            THEN DO;
                /* PROCESS THE ROW */
                END;
            ELSE
        IF SQLCODE = 100
            THEN DO;
                /* NO ROW FOUND */
                END;
            ELSE DO; /* NEITHER 0 OR 100 */
                /* SOME ERROR ACTION */
                END;
```

Figure 3.4. The Basic Elements of a Program.

elements of arrays. If they are parts of structures, then they must be qualified with one level of qualification. Figure 3.5 shows some examples. PATID is a level 3 variable. In PL/I, it can be referred to as OUTPUT__RECORD.PATID, OUTPUT__RECORD.PATIENT__DATA.PATID, or PATIENT__DATA.PATID. The COBOL equivalent would be PATID of PATIENT-DATA. However, in the SQL statement, it must be PATIENT__DATA.PATID regardless of the language. This can be confusing at first.

Column names usually can be unqualified. They may need to be qualified by the table name when the same column name occurs in two tables that are being joined. In this case, you must tell DB2 which one you want for the select list or the WHERE clause. In Figure 3.6, we show two ways of qualifying a column

```
DCL 1 OUTPUT_RECORD,
     2 PATIENT_DATA,
        3 PATID    CHAR(9),
        3 LASTNAME CHAR(15),
        3 ....,
           .
           .
           .
     2 ADMIT_DATA,
        3 .....,
          . .....;
```

Figure 3.5. Host Variable Structure with More Than Two Levels.

```
SELECT THSPAT0.PATID, LASTNAME, FIRSTNAME, ADMDATE
   INTO :DCLPAT.PATID, :DCLPAT.LASTNAME,
        :DCLPAT.FIRSTNAME, :DCLADM.ADMDATE
   FROM THSPAT0, THSADM0 ADM
   WHERE THSPAT0.PATID = ADM.PATID;
```

Figure 3.6. Join of Two Tables — Column Names Must Be Qualified.

name. You can use the table name itself (e.g., THSPAT0.PATID). Or you can give a correlation name to the table (e.g., ADM for THSADM0) and use this correlation name to qualify the column reference. Correlation names are required if the same table appears more than once in the SELECT.

The names of the host variables can be the same as column names. In a WHERE clause, either a column or host variable can be used. If a colon is used, DB2 knows it is a host variable. If no colon is used, the rules depend on whether or not it is a qualified reference. For an unqualified name, if there is no colon, DB2 will assume that it is a column name. However, if it is a qualified name (i.e., OUTPUT_RECORD.PATID), DB2 will assume that it is a *host variable*. In Figure 3.6, we used THSPAT0.PATID and ADM.PATID to mean columns from the tables. If there were host structures with these names too, DB2 would assume we meant the host variables. The join would not work as intended. Therefore, it is important not to use any host structures that match a correlation name (e.g., ADM) or the table name. The DCLGEN is usually created by the DBA for use by all programmers. The DCLGEN also should not use a host structure name that matches the table name (e.g., THSPAT0).

3.1.5.1 Indicator Variables

Some columns can have null values. Null is not a value that program variables normally can have (PL/I pointer variables are an exception, but these do not correspond to DB2 data types). In order for a program to deal with null values, it uses indicator variables. These are halfword integer (2 bytes) variables. In PL/I, they are declared

DCL I1 FIXED BIN(15);

In COBOL, it is

01 I1 PIC S9(4) COMP.

In the SQL statement, you use them as :VAR1:IND1, where VAR1 is the host variable and IND1 is the indicator variable. To insert or update a column with a null value, you first set the indicator to a negative value and then issue the SQL statement. If the indicator is 0 or positive, then the value will be taken from VAR1. On a SELECT, if the column has a null value, IND1 is set to -1 and VAR1 is not changed. If the column is not null, IND1 is set to 0. You *must* use indicator variables if you select a column that has a null value. Otherwise, an error SQLCODE will be returned.

An indicator variable has another use besides representing NULLs. When selecting character columns, if the host variable is too short for the character string and the value is truncated, then IND1 is set to the original length of the data.

3.1.6 Cursors—Set Operations for SELECTs

One of the reasons that relational databases and SQL are so powerful and easy to use is that they can process sets of data rather than just one record at a time. Any of the DML statements (INSERT, UPDATE, DELETE, and SELECT) can process a set of rows. The first three, however, do not return any data to the program. A SELECT statement, however, returns as many rows as meet the criteria.

When a SELECT is issued through SPUFI or QMF, these programs take care of receiving the rows and presenting them to the user. A program that you write must do the same.

In some cases, you know that there will only be one row returned (as in Figure 3.1). Many tables have unique indexes—a set of columns that can only have one occurrence for each value of the index. If the WHERE clause asks for a row for a specific value of this index (e.g., each column with an = operator), then only one row (or none) will be returned. In this case, there is no problem with having a normal SELECT statement with an INTO clause. This is simple to code, although you must be careful. This type of SELECT cannot be used if more than one row meets the criteria. If there is more than one row, then DB2 will return an SQLCODE of −811.

There is no direct means for DB2 to return a set of rows all at once to the program. There are a few reasons why that would be difficult or undesirable. A SELECT may return an unknown number of rows. There may be no rows that fit the criteria, there may be 100, or there may be 100,000. DB2 does not currently allow arrays to be used for the host variables, so there is no way to specify where to put a set of rows. Even if arrays were allowed, a program might not always want to receive all of the rows at once. It may want to process them one at a time and stop after some limit or other condition. An online program may want to only read in one screen's worth at a time. For an online program, reading in all the rows at once may take too long. Also, the amount of program storage required to hold the rows may be too large. For example, 10,000 rows of 200 bytes each would require 2 megabytes of storage for the data. If the rows are longer, or if the number of rows returned is larger, the storage requirements would be even more. If most of the time fewer rows are returned, but the program is written to handle up to 1 million rows, then the storage space will be wasted.

What all this means is that for most SELECT statements, a program must do some extra work. It uses what is called a cursor to define the SELECT statement and to process the rows. Figure 3.7 illustrates the process. First, you declare a cursor for the SELECT statement. The cursor is given a name (PAT1 in this example). Note that the SELECT does not have an INTO clause. This declaration defines what is being selected but does not specify where the data will be placed.

The cursor is then opened. After that, the rows are fetched into the program variables, one row at a time. The program issues a FETCH statement for each row that it wants to read in. The variable SQLCODE indicates when there are no more rows. When the program is done fetching, it closes the cursor. The program can do this either when there are no more rows (SQLCODE = 100) or at any time previously, if it does not want to read in all the rows. If the program wants to reissue the SELECT (perhaps with different values in the host variables in the WHERE clause), it may do so by reissuing the sequence of OPEN, FETCH, and CLOSE. The DECLARE CURSOR does not have to be reissued. Actually, the DECLARE CURSOR does not result in any executable code being issued. It is used by the SQL Preprocessor to set up parameters for the subsequent OPEN statement. In COBOL, the DECLARE CURSOR can be coded in either the Data Division or the Procedure Division.

Note that it is the FETCH statement that has the INTO clause because this is where the rows are actually brought in to the program. There can be different FETCH statements within the loop, using different host variables (i.e., the first FETCH could read the data into one set of variables and subsequent fetches could use a different set of variables).

There is a very important performance question related to cursors. If 100,000

```
EXEC SQL DECLARE PAT1 CURSOR FOR
    SELECT LASTNAME,FIRSTNAME
      FROM THSPAT0
      WHERE SEX = 'F';


EXEC SQL OPEN PAT1;   /* OPEN THE CURSOR */
IF SQLCODE ¬= 0
   THEN error


EXEC SQL FETCH PAT1   /* GET THE FIRST ROW */
     INTO :LASTNAME, :FIRSTNAME;
IF SQLCODE = 100
   THEN no rows
   ELSE
IF SQLCODE ¬= 0
   THEN error


DO WHILE (SQLCODE = 0);  /*LOOP WHILE THERE ARE STILL MORE ROWS*/
   process the row just fetched
   EXEC SQL FETCH PAT1   /* GET THE NEXT ROW */
        INTO :LASTNAME, :FIRSTNAME;
   END;
IF SQLCODE = 100
   THEN no more rows
   ELSE error


EXEC SQL CLOSE PAT1;  /* CLOSE THE CURSOR */
IF SQLCODE ¬= 0
   THEN error
```

Figure 3.7. A Cursor Is Needed for a SELECT That Will Return a Set of Rows.

rows meet the search criteria, but the program only wants to read in 15 of them, will DB2 still go out to the table, find all 100,000 rows, and get them ready? If it does, then it might take quite a lot of time to process, even though only 15 are actually going to be used by the program.

The DB2 manuals are unclear about this point. They say that the OPEN statement processes the SELECT and you can *think* about it as though DB2 will produce a results table with all 100,000 rows and that the results table is then fetched one row at a time. In reality, this sometimes happens, but not always. DB2 will produce an intermediate results table if it has to, but, otherwise, the OPEN will not read all of the rows. They will be read from the table one at a time with each FETCH.

When will DB2 need to produce a results table? The answer is fairly simple. If the SELECT cannot be satisfied without first reading in every row, then DB2 will read the rows first. The simplest case of this is if DB2 has to do a sort. Figure 3.8 has a SELECT with an ORDER BY clause. If there is no index on column DISDATE, or if DB2 decides not to use the index, then a sort is necessary to return the rows in the order requested. Obviously, in order to do the sort, all the rows must first be read in and the sort performed, before any rows can be returned to the program. On the other hand, if DB2 decides to use an index that matches the columns of the ORDER BY, then it does not have to read any rows ahead of time. For each FETCH, it will go to the index to find the next row, apply any WHERE clause criteria, and so on. Since it is looking at the rows in the order desired, there is no need to sort. Therefore, there is no need to read the rows ahead of time. Each FETCH will cause one requested row to be read. If there is no ORDER BY clause, the program is not asking for the rows in any particular order. In this case, too, the rows will only be read one at a time with each FETCH.

Knowing how this works is very important for online programs. It is very common for an online program to want the data in a particular order, but to not want to fetch in every row. The programmer and database designer must work together to understand the processing requirements. An index should be created in the desired order and the program should be written to take advantage of the index. We'll look at some examples of this and other online programming considerations in Chapter 6.

3.1.6.1 Page Locking During Cursor Operations

As described in Section 6.3, DB2 allows concurrent access of tables by protecting records as they are accessed. When a row is updated, its data page is locked until a commit point is reached. When rows are read, their pages receive share locks. A SELECT done with a cursor, is a set operation. It is important to know how long the fetched rows are protected. There are two choices (controlled by the programmer when he binds the application plan). With the repeatable read (RR) option, all the pages are locked until the cursor is closed. With cursor stability (CS), the page of each fetched row is locked until a row on a different page is

```
EXEC SQL DECLARE ADM1 CURSOR FOR
    SELECT PATID,ADMDATE,DISDATE
      FROM THSADM0
      WHERE DISDATE BETWEEN '1989-02-01' AND '1989-20-28'
      ORDER BY DISDATE,PATID;
```
Figure 3.8. Cursor SELECT That Requires a Sort.

fetched, or until the cursor is closed or a commit is issued. The lock on the previous one is then released. Each of these options is useful for different situations.

A commit closes all cursors, and positioning within the cursor is lost. This means that if a program wants to commit before it has finished fetching in all of the rows, it must then reopen the cursor and reposition to the next row. Section 6.1 describes this process. It would be nice to be able to commit updates periodically without losing position. DB2 Version 2.3 introduces a new cursor hold option for the TSO or batch environment which will allow this.

When a page has a read lock, no other task can update or delete any row on that page. If the program must read several rows through the cursor before following some action, it may be important for none of the rows to be updated until the entire process is complete. Repeatable read will ensure this. On the other hand, the majority of programs do not have this requirement. They only need to deal with one row at a time. In this case, holding on to the locks of all the pages will reduce concurrency. None of the fetched rows (or other rows on those pages) will be available for updating by other programs until the cursor is closed. Therefore, CS is the preferred option in most cases. RR should only be used when it is necessary for the application requirements. Unfortunately, RR is the default for the BIND operation (see Section 3.3). Don't forget to specify CS on your binds. When you use SPUFI you also specify CS or RR (on the SPUFI defaults panel). SPUFI is primarily used for testing, and it is rare that you would need repeatable read. It is, therefore, important for all programmers to change their default to CS before using SPUFI the first time.

3.1.6.2 Row Access During a Cursor Operation

While you are fetching in rows with a cursor, there are no restrictions on what else your program may be doing. It cannot only issue SQL statements against other tables, but can also issue SQL statements against the same table and against the same rows. You can even have two cursors open at the same time, processing the same set of rows. However, you cannot open the same cursor twice at the same time. A cursor must be closed before it can be opened again.

After you have fetched a row, it can be updated or deleted in one of two ways (Figures 3.9 and 3.10). You can issue a normal DELETE or UPDATE statement, using values returned with the FETCH to identify the row(s) to update (Figure

```
EXEC SQL DECLARE PAT1 CURSOR FOR
    SELECT PATID,ACTIVEFLAG
      FROM THSPAT0;

EXEC SQL OPEN PAT1;   /* OPEN THE CURSOR */
IF SQLCODE ¬= 0
   THEN error

EXEC SQL FETCH PAT1
     INTO :PATID,:ACTIVEFLAG;
IF SQLCODE .....
   THEN .....
IF ........
   THEN DO;
        EXEC SQL UPDATE THSADM0
             SET DISDATE = NULL,
                 DISSEQ = NULL
             WHERE PATID = :PATID;
```

Figure 3.9. Update Based on a Fetched Row.

3.9). Alternatively, you can use the WHERE CURRENT OF cursor name clause (Figure 3.10) to indicate that only the current row (the one just fetched) should be deleted or updated. For an update, the columns that are being updated must be identified in the DECLARE CURSOR statement with the FOR UDPATE OF clause. The advantage of this means of updating is that you can pinpoint a specific row when there is no unique index that can be used.

3.1.7 SELECT * vs. SELECT Column List

A SELECT statement can list the columns that you want returned:

SELECT EMPNO,EMPNAME,DEPT FROM EMPTABLE

or can ask for all columns:

```
EXEC SQL DECLARE SVC1 CURSOR FOR
       SELECT PATID,SVCDATE,SVCSEQ
         FROM THSSVC0
         WHERE SVCDATE < :ARCHIVE_DATE;


EXEC SQL OPEN SVC1;   /* OPEN THE CURSOR */
IF SQLCODE ¬= 0
   THEN error
/* LOOP WHILE SQLCODE = 0 */
EXEC SQL FETCH SVC1
         INTO :PATID,:SVCDATE,:SVCSEQ;
IF SQLCODE = 0
   THEN DO;
      /* program code - archive the record */
         EXEC SQL DELETE THSSVC0
               WHERE CURRENT OF SVC1;
      END;
/* END LOOP */
```
Figure 3.10. Delete the Row Just Fetched.

SELECT * FROM EMPTABLE

SELECT * is very useful when using SPUFI or QMF. It is easier to type and does not require remembering the column names. However, it is not a good idea to use * in a program. In a program, the SELECT (or FETCH) lists program variables where the data is to be placed. The list is fixed at compile time. The application plan in the DB2 catalog will however, still say *—all columns. It does not contain the names of the specific columns that were originally wanted. If there are 10 host variables to receive the columns, then DB2 will try to return the first 10 columns. If the table is subsequently changed to contain more columns, then, at execution time, the first 10 columns may no longer be the same 10 columns the program was expecting. This will, of course, have invalid results. Unfortunately, the results are not even always the same or immediately indicative of the problem. Figure 3.11 shows several examples.

The SELECT * in this figure actually tells DB2 to return the first two columns of the table (there only being two columns). If a third column is added, at exe-

```
CREATE TABLE GELLER.TXXTST0

(AAA   CHAR(4),

 BBB   DECIMAL(5,0))

IN DXXTST0.SXXTST0;
```
(a) create the table

```
EXEC SQL SELECT * INTO :AAA, :BBB   FROM TXXTST0;
```
(b) SELECT * returns two fields - one char, the other decimal

```
DROP TABLE GELLER.TXXTST0;

CREATE TABLE GELLER.TXXTST0

(AAA   CHAR(4),

 CCC   CHAR(5),

 BBB   DECIMAL(5,0))

IN DXXTST0.SXXTST0;
```
(c) drop and recreate the table

Figure 3.11. SELECT * Causes Problems If the Table Changes.

cution time DB2 will still return the first two columns. If the new columns were added at the end, then the original two will be returned and the program may still work. If the new column is added as the first or second column, then if the data types of the (new) first two columns match the original two, the program will get back a good SQLCODE (0) but the data will not be the two columns that were asked for. If the new column is of a different data type (e.g., DECIMAL vs. CHAR as in the example) then an error SQLCODE will be returned to indicate that the host variable is not compatible with the column (−303 on a SELECT, −301 on an INSERT). If there are now fewer columns (e.g., only one column in this example), then only the first host variable will be filled in with anything (possibly) meaningful. This variety of results can be really confusing. To solve the problem after it is diagnosed, the program will have to be changed and recompiled (possibly only recompiled if the INTO uses the structure from the DCLGEN and the DCLGEN has been rerun after the columns were added).

One of the benefits of DB2 is data independence. Programs only have to know about the columns they need. If other columns are added, changed, or deleted, a program does not need any changes, *provided* that they do not reference those other fields in any way (including SELECT *). That is why it is always better to explicitly list the columns to be selected.

Some people feel that using a view will insulate the program from changes, and that it is okay to use SELECT * from a view. This is only true if the view is used just by the one program. Any other view is just as likely to be changed as the table itself. A view that contains all fields does no good. The DBA may initially leave the view unchanged so that programs will not be affected by the adding of columns; however, in this case, sooner or later the DBA will update the view to reflect the altered table.

INSERT statements have the same problem. Two formats for INSERT are shown in Figure 3.12. Not listing the columns means that all columns must have values given in the value-list. The value-list could be a structure of variables (perhaps from the DCLGEN); however, once again, if the table structure is changed, the program will have to be changed. If all of the columns are declared as NOT NULL, then all columns must be in the list and the program would have to be changed anyway, so the first format is okay. However, if some of the columns allow nulls or have NOT NULL WITH DEFAULT, then the program with a list of columns would not have to be changed when a new column is added. It would, therefore, be better to only include those columns for which the program must supply values.

3.1.7.1 Performance Issues

Selecting more columns than needed also affects performance.

- Each column has to be moved by DB2 to the program variables individually. There is less data movement if fewer columns are selected.
- If the only columns that are needed are in an index, then it may not be necessary to access the data rows at all. The index alone can satisfy the request.
- If a sort is necessary, DB2 sorts the selected columns. The larger the data to be sorted, the longer it takes to do the sort.

```
EXEC SQL INSERT INTO THSADM0
    VALUES (:THSADM); /*THSADM IS A STRUCTURE MATCHING THE TABLE*/
(a) With no columns listed


EXEC SQL INSERT (PATID,ADMDATE,ADMSEQ) INTO THSADM0
    VALUES (:THSADM.PATID,:THSADM.ADMDATE,:THSADM.ADMSEQ);
    /* THE OTHER COLUMNS WILL GET DEFAULT VALUES */
(b) With columns listed
```
Figure 3.12. INSERT statements.

There is another pragmatic reason for only specifying the columns that are needed. The preprocessor translates each SQL statement into calls to DB2, along with structure declarations for parameters used in the calls. Variables are generated for each column referenced. SELECT * really means select all columns. The size of the structures, therefore, grow with each additional column. The resulting compiler listing can also get very large and bulky. Each SQL statement may take several pages (for a table with many columns) in the compile listing. This makes it more clumsy and difficult to work with.

3.1.8 Handling Invalid Data

One of the nice features of DB2 is that if you try to use an invalid host variable data type, DB2 will let you know in a nice way. If you have a DECLARE TABLE (from the DCLGEN), these errors will be caught by the preprocessor at compile time. In other cases it may be caught at execution time (with an error SQLCODE returned).

However, there is a very common type of programming error, which until Version 2.2, DB2 did not handle nicely. If the host variable did not have a valid value for the DB2 data type, the program would abend rather than return an error code (starting with Version 2.2 you get a −302 SQLCODE). The most common case is for decimal columns. If you are inserting a row or updating a column and you have not given a valid value to a decimal variable, the program will abend with a 0E4 abend (with a reason code of 00E7000D). As 0E4 is the abend code that you get with almost any DB2 problem, this can be very confusing, especially to a new programmer. For a CICS transaction, the transaction abends with an error in the interface module.

An INSERT without a column list is the type of code that most often results in this problem. Columns that are defined to allow nulls or are NOT NULL WITH DEFAULT do not need to be listed in the INSERT statement. If they are not, then an appropriate default will be given to them. However, if they are listed (e.g., INSERT without a list of columns means all columns), a value *must* be supplied. Columns defined as NOT NULL (without default) must be listed. It is very common for programmers to fill in those variables for which they have values and to forget to fill in a default for the others. If you forget to fill a value into a variable, it contains whatever was in storage at that spot. For character and binary (integer) fields, anything is valid for that data type (but not necessarily for the application). For decimal fields, it is unlikely that the storage contains a valid packed decimal number. Unfortunately, DB2 did not catch the invalid data for you, but instead abended.

The first step in avoiding this problem is to be aware of it, so that if the abend occurs, you have an idea what to look for. Prevention is even better, however. Only list the columns you need, and make sure that you initialize any columns that are listed in the SQL statement. This is still the best way to code—rather than having DB2 catch your errors for you.

3.1.9 SQLCODEs

After every SQL executable statement (i.e., not a DECLARE TABLE or DECLARE CURSOR), DB2 fills in several fields in the SQLCA. The most important of these is SQLCODE. SQLCODE contains an integer value which indicates the success or failure of the call. It is very important for the program to check this code after every call. Sometimes the program needs to check it to find out if there are any rows returned or if none matched the selection criteria. Other times there is only one code that is expected. However, even in these cases, SQLCODE should be checked for any error conditions. Checking logic may look somewhat like the code in Figure 3.13. First, the program checks for the expected codes. Then it checks for any other code. If there is one, it displays the SQLCODE, the table being accessed and the function being executed. The declaration of SQLCODE in PL/I and COBOL is shown in Figure 3.14.

```
EXEC SQL SELECT .... INTO ....    FROM ....
    WHERE .....;


IF SQLCODE = 100 /* NOT FOUND */
    THEN DO;
        some logic
        END;
    ELSE
IF SQLCODE = 0 /* FOUND */
    THEN DO;
        some other logic
        END;
    ELSE DO;
        error routine - display sqlcode and table
        END;
```

Figure 3.13. Checking the SQLCODE.

```
COBOL - PIC S9(9) COMPUTATIONAL

PL/I  - FIXED BIN(31)
```

Figure 3.14. SQLCODE Declaration in COBOL and PL/I.

There is another way to check for an error code. The SQL WHENEVER statement can be placed in a program. There are three variations:

EXEC SQL WHENEVER SQLERROR GO TO label;
EXEC SQL WHENEVER NOT FOUND GO TO label;
EXEC SQL WHENEVER SQLWARNING GO TO label;

The first one is for a negative SQLCODE. The second is for the not found condition (SQLCODE=100). The third one is for warning codes (SQLCODE > 0 but not 100, or the SQLWARN0 flag is set). Notice, however, that the only action is to branch to a label. In COBOL, this is a section or paragraph name. There is no CALL option. This is not very conducive to writing well-structured code. Therefore, it is better to do the checking yourself after each SQL statement.

The following section will list the most common codes returned to programs, both the "normal" codes as well as some common error codes. It goes without saying that you should have the DB2 Messages and Codes manual (#SC26-4379) handy to look up any others that your program might get.

3.1.9.1 SQLCODE Values

- 0: Successful execution—actually, successful as far as DB2 is concerned. If the programmer made a mistake in the statement, it might not return the data that was intended.
- 100: No record found—this is returned on a SELECT that found no rows, and on a FETCH after the last row has been returned. During cursor operations, you would normally keep fetching while the SQLCODE = 0. When it is 100, then you are done. An UPDATE or DELETE statement for which no rows met the criteria in the WHERE clause will also return a 100. Depending on the application, this may be valid. Figure 3.15 shows an example. Both 0 and 100 are valid responses for this program.

There are a few other positive SQLCODEs, but most of the error codes have negative values.

```
EXEC SQL UPDATE THSLOC0
         SET ROOM = '2222'
         WHERE ROOM = '2221';
IF SQLCODE = 0 | SQLCODE = 100
   THEN;
   ELSE error
```

Figure 3.15. An SQLCODE of 100 May Be Okay.

- −530: A foreign key value does not have a matching parent row. When referential integrity is being used, a parent row must exist with a primary key equal to the foreign keys being inserted (unless the foreign key is NULL).
- −803: A record is being inserted or a column updated such that there will be a duplicate value for a unique index. Not every table has unique indexes, but if there is one, then duplicates are not allowed. A program might be written to first do a SELECT to see if there is already an existing row with these values. Alternatively, the program may just do the INSERT and check for −803 after the SQL statement. This is a valid approach when there will usually not be a duplicate.
- −805: The plan being used does not contain the DBRM for the program being executed. See Section 3.3 for a description of DBRMs and Plans.
- −811: A noncursor SELECT can only be used when at most one row will be returned. If there are more than one, than −811 will be returned. Sometimes a program needs to know if there are any rows and doesn't care how many or what the data are. Doing the SELECT and checking for 0 or −811 is one way. The other way would be to use a cursor and only fetch in one row. This is a little more coding, but is a cleaner approach.
- −818: The timestamp of the load module does not match the timestamp of the DBRM in the plan. DB2 tries to ensure that plans and programs are in sync (i.e., created at the same time). If they are not, −818 is returned. See Section 3.3.
- −904: Unavailable resource. If a table space or other resource is unavailable (perhaps in need of recovery or stopped by the DBA), then −904 is returned. The resource and reason are identified in the SQLERRM field of SQLCA and on the system console log. −904 is also returned when a program exceeds the limit on the number of locks that can be held by a program. This limit is set by the person who installs DB2. See Section 2.4 for more information on this subject.
- −922: Connection to DB2 failed. The most common reason for this is that you are not authorized to execute the plan. For a batch or TSO program, if *you* did not bind the plan, then the person who did must grant you execute authority for it. For a CICS transaction, the DB2 administrator decides on one of several authorization schemes (see Section 9.2). Under most schemes, the authorization ID is not the same as your user ID. Therefore, it is necessary to grant execute authority to the appropriate authorization ID. In many cases, there will be CICS or application security being used to control transaction access and execute authority can be granted to PUBLIC. A −922 also results if the DB2 subsystem name used to execute the program is invalid. The

default subsystem name is DSN, but many shops use different subsystem names.
- −923: Connection not established. You can get this for a number of reasons. Most common are DB2 not being up or a problem with the application plan. If you mispelled the plan name and used one that does not exist, you get −923. You also get it if the plan is inoperative. This can happen if a change was made to the tables or indexes that the plan is dependent on (e.g., if a column was removed from the table and the program referenced that column). If an index is dropped, you will not necessarily get an error. DB2 will do an automatic rebind when the plan is next executed. However, if the rebind is not successful (perhaps the plan owner is no longer authorized for the tables), then the plan becomes inoperative and −923 will be returned to the program.

For some of these error codes, the messages manual lists several possible reasons. They all sound cryptic. Knowing the usual causes for each of these can save you a lot of time in figuring out your problem.

3.1.10 SQLWARN Values

There are several "warning" conditions that DB2 reports on through flags in the SQLCA. These are usually not severe errors that a program must catch. They are of most benefit in catching programming errors in the development phase. There are seven flags, SQLWARN1–SQLWARN7. If any of these are set (to 'W'), then the field SQLWARN0 will also be set to 'W'. Since these types of conditions are more likely to occur in programs that have not been fully tested yet, you might consider using the SQL WHENEVER SQLWARNING statement during early development and remove it later. The more common warnings are:

SQLWARN1—truncation of a string column. If the host variable is shorter than the column, the data will be truncated and this flag will be set.

SQLWARN2—when using a function on a column, some occurrences had a NULL value and were eliminated from the result. For example, AVG(SALARY) will compute the average of the SALARY column for those rows where SALARY is not NULL. This warning might be useful information, telling you that not all rows went into the result.

SQLWARN3—there are more columns than there are host variables to receive them. This is especially useful for debugging.

SQLWARN4—a dynamic SQL UPDATE or DELETE was issued without a WHERE clause. This lets you know that every row of the table was affected.

3.2 SYNONYMS, SECONDARY SQLIDS, AND ALIASES (Table Names in Programs)

As we have seen, DB2's naming convention for tables is creator.TABLENAME. If the person using the table is the creator, then it can be referenced as just TABLENAME. Referencing tables in this manner works fine in SPUFI or QMF for ad hoc queries, but presents some problems when used in a program. Let's examine why.

3.2.1 Table Names in Programs

When you create a program that uses SQL, you must also create a DB2 plan. The plan is created with the BIND command (described in Section 3.3). It is the BIND which checks the DB2 catalog to verify that all of the tables and columns referenced in the program are valid and that the binder of the plan has authority to access them.

In Figure 3.16, the programmer, GELLER, was the creator of the table and he does not use his ID in the reference. When he binds the plan, DB2 knows his ID and knows to use table GELLER.THSPAT0. Now, programmer JONES takes over this program. At bind time, DB2 will think the program is accessing JONES.THSPAT0, which in this case does not exist.

As an alternative, the programmer uses the fully qualified table name (Figure 3.17). This will solve the problem of someone else binding the plan, but still has problems. Most shops have test systems (maybe more than one) and production systems. Even if they only have one DB2 subsystem, they probably have test and production tables. The production tables probably have a different creator than do the test ones. They may also have slightly different names (if one DB2 subsystem is used, different table names distinguish the test and production tables). There may also be several versions of the test tables with different sets of test data. The program in Figure 3.17 always references table GELLER.THSPAT0. It cannot reference any other. A separate version of the program would be needed to reference the production patient table or a different test table.

3.2.2 Synonyms

There are two solutions for this problem. The first involves the use of synonyms. The second utilizes secondary SQLIDs (introduced with DB2 Version 2.1). Version 2.2 introduced a new object called an alias. These are particularly useful

```
EXEC SQL SELECT cols INTO :vars FROM THSPAT0;
```
Figure 3.16. An Unqualified Table Reference Uses the Plan Owner ID as the Qualifier.

```
EXEC SQL SELECT cols INTO :vars FROM GELLER.THSPAT0;
```
Figure 3.17. Selecting from the Qualified Name Limits the Program to One Table Only.

with distributed databases, but can also be used for local tables. Version 2.3 introduces another solution involving a new BIND parameter—QUALIFIER. This will be discussed in Section 3.3.

A synonym is exactly what it sounds like. A programmer (or user) defines for himself a synonym for a DB2 object. The SQL statement:

CREATE SYNONYM HSPAT FOR GELLER.THSPAT0

will equate HSPAT with GELLER.THSPAT0. Each person who is going to use this synonym will have to create it for himself. If Jones issued this CREATE statement, it would create the synonym JONES.HSPAT. Whenever Jones uses HSPAT in a program (or QMF), DB2 interprets it as GELLER.THSPAT0. The programs can all be written using HSPAT. Whoever binds the plan must first have a synonym for the appropriate table. If the creator of the production tables is PROD, then the person who binds the production plans will need a synonym HSPAT for PROD.THSPAT0. If Geller wants to run the program against another test table, SMITH.THSPAT1, he needs to drop his synonym HSPAT and recreate it pointing to the other table. Then he can rebind the plan. It will now access SMITH.THSPAT1.

Although this scheme works very well, there is one drawback. Whenever any DB2 object is dropped, all dependent objects are also dropped. If a table needs changing and the DBA drops the table, all indexes and views are also dropped and the DBA must recreate them. All access authorizations are also dropped and must be regranted. All synonyms for the table or view are also dropped. All the programmers (and QMF users with synonyms) must recreate their own synonyms for the table. There is, therefore, a problem of coordination between the DBA and the programmers whenever a table is dropped and recreated. There is also a timing problem for the recreation of the synonyms. Certainly, the programmers must recreate their synonyms before binding any plan that uses the table. However, it is important for them to do it quickly. Whenever a table is dropped, DB2 marks all plans that reference the table as being invalid (if the table does not exist, the plan can't access it). When the plan is next executed, DB2 will do an automatic rebind. Normally, this is fine and the plan is back in shape. However, if any resources are no longer accessible, then the automatic rebind will fail and someone will have to do an explicit rebind of the plan. Some of the things that might not exist are:

- the plan is accessed before the DBA recreates the table
- the owner of the plan no longer has authority to access the table (the DBA forgot to regrant the authorities)
- the owner of the plan has not recreated his own synonym

The last of these is the one that is not in the DBA's control. If the plan owner is on vacation, it is quite possible for there to be a lag in this process. When the program is executed by another programmer, the plan will be made inoperative and must be rebound by someone else (who must have been granted bind authority for the plan by the original owner). This problem is most likely to occur in a test environment; as for production, it is likely that only one user ID will be used for all plans.

3.2.3 Secondary SQLIDs

Another alternative to synonyms became available with DB2 Version 2. Whenever someone connects to DB2 (e.g., through SPUFI, QMF, executing a program, binding a plan), they connect with a primary authorization ID. Through TSO or batch programs (using the TSO batch interface), this primary ID is usually the TSO user ID. This ID is used as the default qualifier for table names (i.e., THSPAT0 is GELLER.THSPAT0). It is the also the default for table references during the bind of a plan. In addition to the primary ID, there is now also the possiblity of a list of secondary authorization IDs.

Before secondary IDs can be used, the system administrator must decide if the shop wants to use them. Then, a DB2 exit must be used to enable them. DB2 comes with a sample exit that can be used in conjunction with RACF (IBM's security system), using the RACF group IDs associated with the user, as the secondary IDs. If the shop does not use RACF or wants to use a different scheme, they must write their own exit routine.

How are secondary SQLIDs used? There are several aspects to their use. The first one involves the granting of privileges. Instead of individual people (i.e., user IDs) being granted access to tables, the authority can be granted to the group they belong to. This can reduce the effort to maintain table authorizations. If a new person (user or programmer) is assigned to a function, they will probably be added to the appropriate RACF groups. They will not need to be granted DB2 access to the tables they need, as the group will already have access. Conversely, when a person leaves (or changes his job function), they do not need privileges revoked from their ID, they just need to be removed from the group.

When a person accesses a table (through QMF or when binding a plan), his privileges are the composite of the privileges of each of his secondary SQLIDs, as well as his primary SQLID.

When creating an object (i.e., a table, a view, a synonym), the creator ID is no longer restricted to the primary authorization ID. Instead, it is the CURRENT SQLID. This is initially the primary ID (user ID) but can be reset during a session (e.g., SPUFI or QMF) with the SET CURRENT SQLID statement. It can be set to any of the person's secondary IDs. When binding a plan, the programmer can use the OWNER parameter on the bind to specify a different ID to be the owner of the plan. This ID will be used by DB2 to identify the tables. This provides a means of writing programs with flexible table names.

All programmers on a project can be assigned to a group for that project. The DBA who creates the tables and views will use the group ID as the creator ID of the tables. For example, the programmers for the hospital system could be in group HOSPTEST. The test patient table will be created as HOSPTEST.THSPAT0. The programmers would all use OWNER(HOSPTEST) in their binds, and in their programs they will use THSPAT0. For production, the plans will be owned by PROD and the table will be PROD.THSPAT0. The programs will be fine for production and test.

There are several nice features of this approach. Without the use of secondary IDs, anybody could use a different creator name when creating a table, but a view can only be created with a different creator ID, by someone with SYSADM authority (most DBAs will not have SYSADM). Now, a programmer or DBA can create a view with any of his secondary IDs as the creator. The other nice feature is that the individual programmer IDs do not have to be granted access to each table (only HOSPTEST has to be granted access in this example). The programmers in this group will then automatically have the authority. This means less maintenance effort for the DBA. Programmers would also not need synonyms, thus eliminating that headache.

There is, however, one shortcoming. This scheme works fine provided that there is only one table name used for the table. Shops that use different names for different versions (e.g., test vs. production) would still need synonyms to distinguish them. To use secondary IDs also requires that a shop be set up to properly maintain the use and assignment of groups. Some places are very careful with their use of RACF and security, others are not. The system administrator should work with the security department, DBAs, and project leaders to determine whether secondary IDs can be useful for their shops.

3.2.4 Aliases

Until recently, DB2 tables had two-part names—creator.tablename. Version 2.2 introduced the first DB2 implementation of distributed database processing. This allows programs connected to one DB2 subsystem to access tables in another subsystem. These are considered remote tables. This release allows a distributed unit of work, whereby tables from several DB2 subsystems can be accessed within the same unit of work. Version 2.3 introduces additional distributed database capabilities. There are some more powerful functions, but only implemented as a remote unit of work, whereby only one remote system (either DB2 or SQL/DS) can be accessed with a single unit of work. Both of these capabilities are described in Appendix C.

Under Version 2.2, remote tables require three-part names—location.creator.tablename. Tables in the local subsystem (called local tables) also now have three-part names. If a two-part name is used, the default is the location of the connected DB2 subsystem (therefore, all current programs will still work). To achieve location independence (i.e., to allow programs to remain unchanged even if a table is moved to a new location), there is a new object called an alias. An alias is similar in some ways to a synonym in that it is an alternate name for a table. However, whereas synonyms are created and used by individual IDs, aliases can be used by anyone. The statement:

CREATE ALIAS HOSPTEST.THSPAT0 FOR GELLER.THSPAT0

will create an alias for the patient table created by GELLER on the local DB2. Anyone can use HOSPTEST.THSPAT0 as a reference for GELLER.THSPAT0. Since aliases still have creator names, to use them directly in a program they are most effective if used in conjunction with either secondary SQLIDs or synonyms. You can create a synonym on an alias (or vice versa). So, HSPAT could be a synonym used for the alias HOSPTEST.THSPAT0. The programs could use HSPAT. Aliases are most beneficial for use with distributed databases where a three-part name would be required.

The remote unit of work of Version 2.3 does not require the use of three-part names. Since only one subsystem can be accessed at a time, the location does not have to be identified with each SQL statement. When the program connects (with the CONNECT SQL statement) to another subsystem, it identifies that location. Alternatively, if the program will only be accessing one subsystem, that location can be identified with a new BIND parameter (see Section 3.3).

3.3 PLANS AND DBRMS

3.3.1 Plans

Before DB2 can execute any program or SQL statement, it must figure out the best way to do so. It does this by identifying which tables and columns are being accessed, looking at the catalog statistics for the tables, seeing what indexes are available, and calculating what it thinks will be the most efficient approach. For dynamic SQL (such as entered through SPUFI, QMF, or a user-written program that employs dynamic SQL), it does this for each statement before executing it. All of this takes time. For static SQL (as used by most programs), the form of the statements (i.e., tables, selected columns, and ORDER BY clauses) does not change from one run to the next. Therefore, it is possible for DB2 to decide on the access paths once, and save this information for use at execution time. This saved plan of access is called an application plan. It is saved in the DB2 catalog. DB2 Version 2.3 introduces some important new concepts in the organization of plans. Most of this section is geared to the options of Version 2.2, but mention will be made of the new functions.

The process of producing a plan involves the following steps:

- The program with SQL statements goes through the DB2 Preprocessor. This program translates the SQL into calls to DB2. It also produces an output file called a DBRM (Data Base Request Module). There is one DBRM produced for each separately compiled program.
- The program is then compiled and link-edited to produce a load module.
- The BIND command is executed to produce the plan. The input to the BIND is the DBRMs for all program modules that will be executed by the same task. For a batch or TSO program, this is all modules link-edited together (i.e., the main routine and any subroutines it calls). CICS programs and their plans are discussed below.

Up through Version 2.2, the DBRMs of all program modules of the task were combined into a plan. The BIND processed them all at once. Under Version 2.3, there is a new object called a package. A package is a miniplan for a single program module (i.e., only the one DBRM is input to the BIND). Each package is stored separately in the DB2 catalog. The application plan will now point to each of the packages that are required for the full plan. This new feature is an option. Plans may continue to contain all of the DBRMs, or they may be mixed—some of the DBRMS can be stored as part of the plan and some can be stored separately as packages.

With the use of packages, the BIND process is faster. And, if the same program is part of several load modules, its package can be used by each of several plans, without having to bind those plans whenever the program is changed.

Figure 3.18 shows the BIND process. Figure 3.19 shows some sample JCL for compiling and binding a program to run under TSO. The BIND parameters are described below. The output of the BIND (the plan or package) is stored in the DB2 catalog. Information about it can be found in the catalog tables (for Version 2.2):

- SYSIBM.SYSPLAN—the basic plan information, including the values from the BIND command.
- SYSIBM.SYSDBRM—information about each DBRM of each plan, including the timestamp of when the DBRM was created.

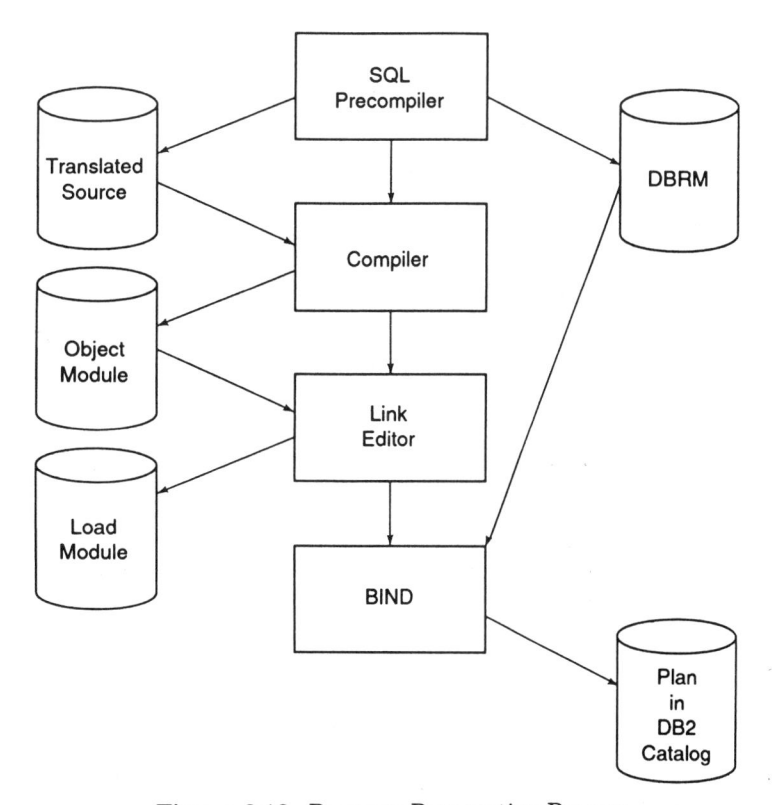

Figure 3.18. Program Preparation Process.

```
//* PRECOMPILE - CREATE THE DBRM
//PC EXEC PGM=DSNHPC,REGION=2000K
//STEPLIB DD DSN=DSN220.DSNLOAD,DISP=SHR    DB2 load modules
//DBRMLIB DD DSN=DB2T.DEV.DBRM(&MEM),DISP=SHR    DBRM goes here
//SYSCIN  DD DSN=&DSHNOUT,....   output of precompiler
//* syslib has modules to be copied in, including DCLGEN output
//SYSLIB  DD DSN=DB2T.DEV.INCLUDE,DISP=SHR
//SYSIN DD DSN=DB2T.DEV.SOURCE(&MEM),DISP=SHR    program source
//* COMPILE THE PROGRAM
//COMP EXEC PGM=the compiler
//.... DD cards for steplib and work datasets
//SYSIN DD DSN=&DSNHOUT,DISP=(OLD,PASS)   the output from PC step
//SYSLIB DD ...    libraries with modules to be copied in
//SYSLIN DD DSN=&&LOADSET,.....   object module
//* LKED THE PROGRAM
//LKED EXEC PGM=IEWL...
//   DD CARDS FOR THE LINKAGE EDITTOR
//SYSLIN DD DSN=&&LOADSET,DISP=(OLD,DELETE)    object module
//       DD DSNAME=SYSIN    for control cards
//SYSLIB DD ....   subroutine library
//SYSLMOD DD DSN=DB2T.DEV.LOADBAT(&MEM),DISP=SHR   load module
//* the control cards list modules to be included into the load
//* module.
//*   DSNELI is the DB2 TSO interface module
//*   for CICS it is DSNCLI
//*   for call attach it is DSNALI
//*   for IMS you use the IMS interface module - DFSLI000
//SYSIN DD *
 INCLUDE DSNELI
/*
//* BIND THE PLAN
```
Figure 3.19. JCL to Compile and Bind a Program.

```
//BIND     EXEC PGM=IKJEFT01    the TSO monitor program
//...      DD CARDS for TSO and BIND
//DBRMLIB  DD DSN=DB2T.DEV.DBRM,DISP=SHR    the DBRM library
//* SYSTSIN has the input to TSO - the DSN and BIND commands
//SYSTSIN  DD DSN=DB2T.DEV.BINDCARD(DSN),DISP=SHR   the subsystem
//         DD DSN=DB2T.DEV.BINDCARD(&MEM),DISP=SHR  bind command for plan
```

Figure 3.19. (*Continued*)

- SYSIBM.SYSSTMT—the text of each SQL statement for each DBRM of each plan.
- SYSIBM.SYSPLANDEP—the names and types of all objects (e.g., tables, indexes, synonyms) that the plan is dependent on.
- SYSIBM.SYSPLANAUTH—who has privileges to execute or bind the plan.

Whenever you want to execute a program that uses DB2, you must name the plan to be used, as well as the program. Figure 3.20 has the control statements to execute a TSO program. To run a batch program, most often it is run using the TSO interface. The JCL to run one is shown in Figure 3.21. IKJEFT01 is the TSO terminal monitor program. The application program is executed by issuing the same TSO commands as is done to run a program directly under TSO.

```
DSN SYSTEM(DB2T)
RUN PROGRAM(HSPAT01) LIB('DB2T.DEV.LOADBAT') PLAN(HSPAT01)
END
```

Figure 3.20. Executing a Program Under TSO.

```
// EXEC PGM=IKJEFT01,REGION=1M
//STEPLIB  DD DSN=DSN220.DSNLOAD    DB2 load library
//SYSPRINT DD SYSOUT=*
//SYSTSPRT DD SYSOUT=*
//SYSTSIN  DD *
DSN SYSTEM(DB2T)
RUN PROGRAM(HSPAT01) LIB('DB2.DEV.LOADBAT') PLAN(HSPAT01)
/*
```

Figure 3.21. JCL for Executing a Batch DB2 Program.

There are two commands needed. The DSN command tells TSO to connect to DB2. The SYSTEM parameter identifies the DB2 subsystem with which to connect (there may be several subsystems running). The RUN command identifies the application program, the load module library where it is located, and the name of the plan to be used with the program.

There are some important relationships between the program(s) being compiled and the plan(s) produced. DB2 tries to ensure that a valid plan is used with a program. It does this in several ways. When the preprocessor translates the statements and produces the DBRM, it creates a number of parameters for the DB2 call in addition to the tables and columns to be accessed. One is the name of the DBRM (i.e., the program) issuing the call. If the plan being invoked does not include the DBRM of the executing program, then an error SQLCODE is returned to the program (−805). A timestamp is also included as a parameter, and this timestamp is made part of the DBRM. When the program is executed, if the timestamp for this DBRM (as found in the plan) is earlier than the timestamp in the program, a −818 SQLCODE is returned. In other words, every time you recompile a program, you *must* do a BIND on all plans that use that DBRM. Obviously, if you made any changes to the SQL statements in the program, the plan would have to be bound again as the access is now different. However, even if no changes are made to the SQL (or even if no changes are made at all), a recompile requires you to bind the plans again.

The above rule applies for Verion 2.2 and prior releases. It still applies for Version 2.3 unless packages are used. With packages, each plan names the packages that it contains. Whenever a program is recompiled and its package is bound, the new version of the package is immediately used by all plans that contain it.

Note that I am being very careful to avoid the use of the word "rebind." There is some confusion in the terminology used by DB2. There are several bind processes. BIND (Figure 3.22) can be done with the parameter ADD (the first time you bind) or the parameter REPLACE (the first or subsequent time you bind). There is also a REBIND command (Figure 3.23). REBIND is not a full bind. It is used if there is a change to the database that may affect the choice of access path. For example, a new index was added or new statistics have been collected for the table and you want DB2 to take advantage of them. It cannot be used for

```
BIND PLAN(HSPAT01) MEMBER(HSPAT01,HSPAT02) ACT(REPLACE) -
ISOLATION(CS) RETAIN EXPLAIN(NO) VALIDATE(BIND)
```

Figure 3.22. BIND Command.

```
REBIND PLAN(HSPAT01)
```

Figure 3.23. REBIND Command—Using the Same Parameters as the Last BIND.

a change in the SQL statements of the program. When the program is recompiled, you must do a BIND with REPLACE, not a REBIND.

There is no problem having more than one plan for the same load module as long as they are produced after the compilations. The same program may be part of several different load modules (i.e., the same subroutine called by different main routines). If the load modules have different sets of subroutines, they may need different plans. You might also want several plans for one load module if you want to try out different BIND parameters. A more likely reason for having several plans is that one plan can access one specific set of tables. If you have several sets of test tables or a production and test table, you clearly need separate plans for each set. This is very important. The plan that is created to access the test tables cannot be used for the production tables. If the production tables are in the same DB2 subsystem, then the table names must be different. If they are in a different DB2 subsystem, then the plan would not be known to the production subsystem (each subsystem has its own set of catalog tables).

I said that you could just BIND a separate plan for the production tables. This is true if you use one load module library for test and production (or just copy the load module from one library to the other). Many shops also recompile the programs when they go to production. They must also bind the plans at that time.

Another new feature of Version 2.3 is the ability to assign a version number to a package. A new parameter is used at precompile time. The version number is stored as part of the package and as part of the load module. This enables the programmer to create several versions of the program to test out different functions or to access different tables. When a particular version of the program is executed, DB2 will select the correct version of the package. This way the programmer can alternate executions of different versions of the program without having to bind the plan in between.

3.3.2 Plans for CICS Transactions

For batch and TSO programs, the plan must include all DBRMs for any called subroutine. For CICS programs, there are more requirements and the situation can be a bit confusing. Essentially, the plan must have all DBRMs for programs that are executed as part of the same CICS task. This includes called subroutines. It also includes modules that are reached via CICS LINK or CICS XCTL. These are compiled and link-edited separately and are invoked dynamically. There are several ways to organize the flow of a CICS application, and it is important to understand the flow structure in order to know which DBRMs go into a plan. There are now (starting with DB2 Version 2) two ways to organize the plans. Under the original scheme, each CICS transaction code could have only one plan associated with it, no matter how many different paths (i.e., programs linked to) the transaction might have. Under the new scheme (called dynamic plan selection), it is possible to associate different plans with one transaction. To use this option, a user exit must be written to determine which plan to use each time. We will first examine the basic structure with one plan per transaction code.

As mentioned above, there are several ways to structure the program flow in CICS. The first distinction we need to make is between conversational and pseudo-conversational transactions. Most CICS systems are written pseudo-conversationally as it provides better overall use of system resources. CICS is an online transaction processing system. The typical function involves sending a screen to the terminal, the user enters some data, a program processes the data (including reading and writing to some files), and a screen is sent back to the user. In a conversational program, after sending each screen, the program sits and waits for the user to respond and then reads in the screen. All the time that the user is thinking and typing, the program is still in storage and the task is still active. This wastes a lot of system memory and other resources. In a pseudo-conversational program, after sending a screen, the program returns to CICS and ends the task. However, it tells CICS what to do (i.e., which transaction and program to invoke) when the user responds. CICS will then start that transaction (which could be the same as the one before) and this program will read in the screen, do some processing, and send the next screen. While the user is thinking, there is no active task.

The pseudo-conversational scheme has a lot of implications for record-locking and consistency. We will look at this in Section 6.1. Here we will look at the program flow as it impacts the creation of DB2 plans.

3.3.2.1 Transaction Flow

Figure 3.24 has one typical flow. There are other good ways to organize the system. In this example, the programs are designed so that each screen is handled by one program. Each program must use a flag to keep track of where it is in the transaction flow. The first time a program is invoked it will put up an initial screen and return to CICS. When the user sends the screen back, the same program will be invoked. This time it will know (via its flag) that the screen will have data filled in or updated by the user. After processing the data (if it is valid), the program will transfer control (XCTL) to the next program in the sequence. This program will be in its initial state and will put up its first screen and go away.

3.3.2.2 The DBRMs Needed for Each Plan

In this example, there are three transactions. MENU invokes the MENU01 program, which sends the menu screen and ends. MENU is invoked again, MENU01 reads the screen and transfers (XCTL) to the selected program (i.e., PGM01). PGM01 puts up its screen and returns to CICS. As we can see at this point, the MENU transaction may invoke only program MENU01, it may invoke MENU01 and PGM01, it may invoke MENU01 and PGM02, etc.

When PGM01 returns to CICS, it tells CICS to invoke transaction PG01 when the user transmits the screen. PG01 will start with program PGM01, which after

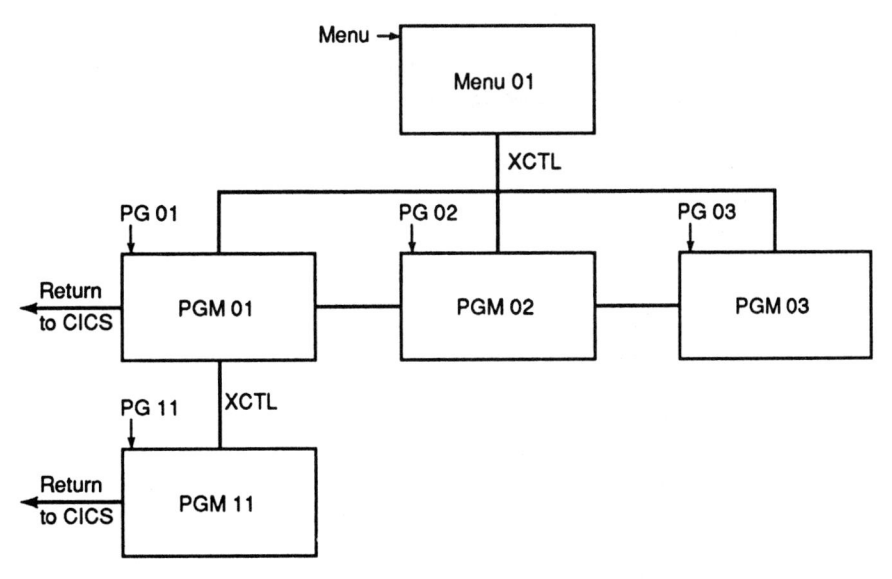

Figure 3.24. CICS Transaction Flow.

reading the screen and processing the files will XCTL to PGM11. PGM11 will put up a screen and return to CICS. The next transaction to be invoked will be PG11, which will start with program PGM11. Transaction PG01 will execute either just PGM01 or PGM01 and PGM11.

As I said, in the basic scheme, each transaction code can only have one plan associated with it. This plan must have all DBRMs that may get executed. I haven't mentioned which of these programs use DB2, but let's assume that they all do, each time they are invoked. Therefore, we need plans that include:

Transaction	DBRMs
MENU	MENU01, PGM01, PGM02, PGM03
PG01	PGM01, PGM11
PG02	PGM02, . . .
PG03	PGM03, . . .
PG11	PGM11, . . .

So, basically, we need five plans, one for each transaction. The PGM01 DBRM will be in plans for MENU and PG01. The PGM11 DBRM will be in plans for PG01 and PG11. This list assumed that each program does some DB2 work each time it is invoked. If any of them do not do any DB2 or do not do any on the first time in, then obviously the plans may not need all of the DBRMs. For example, if the menu program does no DB2 access and PGM02 does not do any the first time in, then the plan for the MENU transaction will only need DBRMs for PGM01 and PGM03.

Figuring out and keeping track of which DBRMs are needed for which plans can be a little confusing. It is also important to bind all necessary plans when a program is recompiled. If PGM01 is recompiled, the MENU and PG01 plans should be bound. This is because of the timestamp checking. With a called subroutine that is link-edited in, a recompilation of the subroutine will not be used by all load modules unless they are all relink-edited. However, with a program that is reached by CICS LINK or XCTL, the newly compiled program will be used by all programs that invoke it. Version 2.3's packages simplify the process. Only the DBRM of the modified program needs to be rebound. The plans that use that package will automatically pick up the new one.

There is also another timing problem when recompiling a CICS/DB2 program. The BIND goes into the DB2 catalog as soon as it is done. The compiled program, however, is not accessed until a CICS command is issued to tell CICS that there is a new version. If the program is invoked in between, then a -818 (timestamp error) will result. This is mostly a problem for a production environment where there is heavy transaction usage and you don't want users to experience a problem. Therefore, it is best to do the compiles and binds on off hours for this environment (most shops do so anyway). If you can't wait for off hours, but don't want any errors, you can first quiesce all transactions that use this program, preventing further access. Then, after the BIND and the CICS new copy command for the program are issued, the transactions can be made available again.

3.3.2.3 Large Combined Plans

Some people use an alternative to these separate plans. A plan must have all DBRMs that it needs, but may contain others that it doesn't need for a particular execution. Therefore, some people combine all DBRMs for an application system into one big plan. All transactions are then associated with this one plan. There are some drawbacks to this approach. In the first release of DB2, there was a performance penalty of having plans much larger than needed. A large plan took up more system memory for each active task. However, this is not as much of a problem now because DB2 will only bring in those parts of the plan that are needed for the task.

A problem that still exists is that with this scheme the plan can get very large and the time it takes to bind the plan can be become excessive. The large plan will have to be bound each time any program is recompiled. The bind time will be long and it will lock part of the DB2 catalog, interfering with other groups' work. It can be cumbersome to work with. Generally, I find it much better to keep things to manageable chunks. Plans should have what they need, and no more. Version 2.3's packages will certainly speed up the bind process, as only one package at a time will need to be bound. However, I still prefer smaller plans that contain only the packages that they require.

3.3.2.4 Dynamic Plan Selection

There is a new option (as of Version 2.1) called dynamic plan selection, which involves associating a transaction with an exit program rather than a specific plan. This exit program is invoked at the first DB2 call of the task. It is also called after a CICS syncpoint, which commits all updates, and a LINK or XCTL to another module. The exit will decide which plan should be used. To decide this, it will be passed the name of the DBRM of the first SQL statement that is executed. If it needs additional information to decide on the course of action, the program must establish its own control mechanism. Dynamic plan selection can be very useful if a transaction has many branches. For example, if the menu has a dozen choices, each of which does some DB2 work first time in, then the menu plan would need all dozen DBRMs. If the menu itself did not do any DB2, then separate plans for each branch could be created, with the DBRM of the invoked program identifying which branch was taken.

3.3.3 BIND Parameters

Figure 3.25 has a sample control statement to bind a plan. The JCL for running the BIND command is in Figure 3.19. BIND can also be run interactively using the DB2I panels. The main advantage of running it in batch is that the control statement can be placed and saved in a library. This way, all the necessary parameters for the plan are readily accessible and it is easy to rerun. You can always look up the BIND parameters for a plan in the DB2 catalog (table SYSIBM.SYSPLAN). However, it is quicker to just browse a dataset, and it is easier to rerun the BIND this way.

Some of the parameters are straightforward. PLAN is the name of the plan. It does not have to match either the program name or the transactions it is used with, but it should be meaningful. For IMS/DC transactions, the default is for plan names to be the same as program names. MEMBER lists the DBRMs that are to be included in the plan. The names of the DBRMs are the member names in the DBRM library. They do not have to match their programs but they should. LIBRARY names the libraries that contain the DBRMs. Instead of using this parameter, you could code a DD statement in the JCL. The DDname is DBRMLIB.

If a package is to be included as part of the plan, it is identified with the PKLIST parameter. The binding of the package itself is done with the BIND PACKAGE command (rather than BIND PLAN). Packages can also be grouped into a collection. The name of a package is actually Location.Collection.Package.Version. The PKLIST parameter can name specific packages, or a collection. If a collection is named, then a new package (for a new program) can be bound and put in the collection, and will automatically be part of the existing plan.

The owner of a plan is normally the primary authorization ID (user ID) of the

```
BIND PLAN(HSPAT01) MEMBER(HSPAT01,HSPAT02) ACT(REPLACE) -
LIBRARY('DB2T.DEV.DBRM') OWNER(HOSPTEST) -
ISOLATION(CS) RETAIN EXPLAIN(NO) VALIDATE(BIND) -
ACQUIRE(USE) RELEASE(COMMIT)
```

Figure 3.25. BIND Command.

binder. The owner can grant EXECUTE authority to allow other users to execute the plan, and can grant BIND authority to allow other people to BIND the plan in the future. The OWNER parameter can be used to make somebody else the owner. This can only be done if the binder has SYSADM authority, or if secondary SQLIDs are being used. In this case, the value must be one of the binder's secondary IDs.

With the bind of a package, there is a new parameter called QUALIFIER. Normally, the owner ID of the plan is used to qualify any unqualified names in the program. Instead, each package (or version of a package) can specify a different qualifier to be used. This can enable testing with different sets of tables. It could also be used instead of synonyms for allowing several programmers to bind the same plan, or for moving programs to production. One version of the package could use the test tables, while the production version could use the production tables.

ACTION is either REPLACE or ADD. ADD can only be used for a new plan. REPLACE can be used for an existing plan, but can also be used instead of ADD for a new plan. Therefore, there is not much point in coding ADD.

When a plan is replaced, all execute privileges are revoked unless RETAIN is coded. It is not very likely that you want to automatically revoke execute authority just because you are binding the plan again, so always code RETAIN (it is not the default).

VALIDATE tells DB2 when to check on the validity of the SQL statements. This checking includes verifying that the tables that are referenced exist, and that the binder has authority to access the tables. The default is VALIDATE(RUN), which means that the checking is done each time the plan is executed. This is time-consuming and usually unnecessary. VALIDATE(BIND) should usually be used. The checking will be done at BIND time only.

ISOLATION can be either RR (the default) or CS. These were described when we discussed cursor operations. RR (repeatable read) will retain page locks for records that are read, until commit time. CS (cursor stability) will release read locks when a row on another page is read. CS should always be used unless there is an application requirement for repeatable read.

3.3.3.1 ACQUIRE and RELEASE Parameters

These two parameters control when certain resources are obtained and released. The choices for ACQUIRE are USE (the default) and ALLOCATE. The choices for RELEASE are COMMIT (the default) and DEALLOCATE. The resources being obtained are table space locks, opening of datasets if they are not already open, and the loading of the database descriptors and application plan skeletons (SKCTs) if they are not already in the EDM pool. ACQUIRE(USE) and RELEASE(COMMIT) provide the greatest concurrency and hold onto the resources for the shortest period of time. USE means acquiring each resource when it is first referenced. COMMIT means all resources will be released at a commit point. ACQUIRE(ALLOCATE) will get all resources at the beginning of the thread (connection to DB2). DEALLOCATE will hold them until the end of the thread (the end of the transaction).

If a plan has many resources but each execution only references some of them, then the defaults are probably better as only the resources needed by this execution will be acquired. If all resources are used for each execution, then ALLOCATE, DEALLOCATE will acquire the resources quicker (they are all done at one time), but they will be held for longer than needed. As with other aspects of program and system design, my preference is to keep things short and small. Smaller, shorter chunks provide better overall system usage. Therefore, I prefer the default values for most plans. There are a few cases where ALLOCATE and DEALLOCATE are good choices. If you are planning to use thread reuse for a CICS transaction (see Section 9.2), USE and COMMIT will not provide the full benefits of thread reuse. If a program issues frequent commits, the repeated acquiring and releasing of resources may be excessive. This can especially be a problem if the table spaces or index spaces have CLOSE YES. In this case, the datasets will be closed at each commit.

3.3.3.2 EXPLAIN

The EXPLAIN feature of DB2 is described in detail in Section 5.1. EXPLAIN tells you what DB2's choice of access path will be for an SQL statement—whether it will use an index (and which one) or do a table space scan. It is a key means of understanding and tuning program performance. EXPLAIN can be used on a single statement through SPUFI or QMF, or it can be used for a plan by specifying EXPLAIN(YES) on the BIND. EXPLAIN does not actually produce a report of the access. Instead, it inserts rows into a plan table, which you can then query to find out DB2's strategy. Since the plan table will have rows inserted each time the plan is bound, EXPLAIN(YES) should only be used when needed.

EXPLAIN should be used on every program at least twice. It should be run in the test system to see that the access paths are what is expected or reasonable. Since the test tables may not have the same volume or clustering of indexes as the production tables, it should also be done when the plans are bound for production.

Speaking of binding for production, it should always be remembered that DB2's access is dependent on the amount and distribution of data. This information is obtained from the catalog tables and is put into them only when the RUNSTATS utility is run. The important rule then is that binds for production programs should be run after the production tables are filled with data and RUNSTATS has been run. If the tables will initially only have a small amount of data but will grow much larger, then you should plan on running RUNSTATS again after a volume of data has been entered. At this point, a reorg may be desirable (prior to the RUNSTATS). The BIND should then be run again (with EXPLAIN(YES)). Don't forget to actually look at the results of the EXPLAIN. There is no point in asking for the plan and then not checking it. It is always better to do this before running in production, where surprises are not pleasant.

3.4 ATTACHMENT FACILITIES

In order for a program to access DB2, it must connect to the DB2 subsystem and establish a thread for the communication. DB2 runs in a separate region from the application programs. DB2 actually runs in three separate regions (and starting with Version 2.2, there is a fourth region). This is illustrated in Figure 3.26. A thread is a general term used to indicate an access path to a file or file system. The file system (whether DB2, IMS, or VSAM) must maintain control blocks to keep track of where it is within a file, the current status of the program's interactions with the file, and to return the results of a file access. Each task accessing these systems requires a thread.

These functions (and other housekeeping) are needed for each program, although, in general, the applications programs do not have to worry about any of this. The system software will do most of it for you (there are some tables that the system administrator or systems programmer must set up for the CICS or IMS/DC environment).

For DB2, this connection and thread creation processing are done through the attachment facilities. There are four attachment facilities provided by DB2, for the different operating environments. They are for CICS programs, IMS/DC, TSO/batch, and the call attachment facility (CAF). The call attachment facility is really one in which you do much of the work yourself. It is used where special functions are needed that cannot be handled by the TSO attachment. It is described in Section 9.1, where we will look in more detail at what the attachment facilities do.

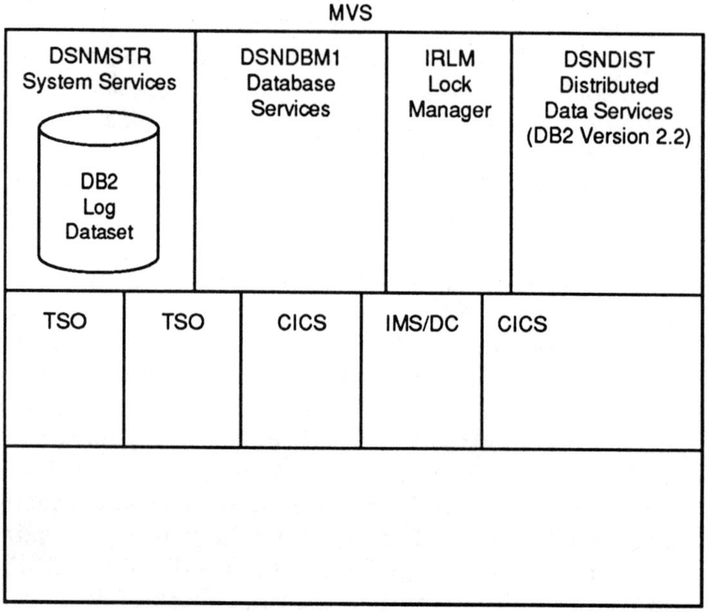

Figure 3.26. DB2 and Application Regions.

For the other three attachments, the applications programmer needs to know two basic things—how to link-edit a program, and how to invoke the program.

Preparing a DB2 program (compiling and link-editing) is very similar for CICS, IMS/DC, batch, and TSO programs. In each case, the source must go through the SQL preprocessor to create a DBRM and translate the SQL statements, through the compiler, and the linkage editor. A CICS program must also go through the CICS translator to translate CICS commands within the program. The difference comes in the link-editing. This is where you specify which attachment facility to use. You must specify the right one for the environment in which the program will be executed. Figure 3.27 has the basic link-edit statements for a TSO/batch program. The SYSLIB dd statement must have the DB2 load module library. This is where the attachment programs are located. DSNELI is the TSO/batch attachment program. For a CICS program, you use DSNCLI. For IMS/DC, you use the IMS interface module—DFSLI000. You must use the right one. If you don't, the program will probably abend at the first SQL call. To summarize:

TSO/Batch—DSNELI
    CICS—DSNCLI
        IMS—DFSLI000
        CAF—DSNALI

Notice that I refer to one attachment for TSO/batch. DB2 programs cannot run as normal batch jobs unless they use the call attachment facility. The simpler way to run them is under the TSO terminal monitor program. This has special requirements for the JCL. In fact, in both batch and TSO, the DB2 programs are not invoked directly, they run under control of the DSN command processor. DSN handles the TSO attachment facility. It does the connection to DB2 and creates the thread. In addition to running application programs, DSN also enables you to issue DB2 commands, such as BIND and DCLGEN, and to run SPUFI. Figure 3.28 has the command sequence to use DSN under TSO. DSN establishes the connection. The SYSTEM parameter identifies the DB2 subsystem with which to connect. The default is DSN, but a shop may use other names for the subsystems. A given installation may run only one DB2 subsystem for test and production, or it may run several. We will digress here briefly to mention that when you use the DB2 Interactive TSO panels (DB2I) for DCLGENs, SPUFI, program prep, etc., the DSN command is issued automatically for you. The subsystem is identified on the Defaults panel. You usually only access this panel once and then forget about it. Don't forget to set the subsystem value to your installation's requirements.

After DSN is issued, you can issue any number of other subcommands. The most common for a programmer will be the RUN subcommand. This executes a program. In this example, the program HSPAT07, which is in load module library HOSP.TEST.LOADBAT, will be executed using plan HSPAT07. The DSN command connected your TSO session to DB2. At the RUN command, the TSO

```
//* LKED THE PROGRAM
//LKED EXEC PGM=IEWL...
//   DD CARDS FOR THE LINKAGE EDITTOR
//SYSLIN DD DSN=&&LOADSET,DISP=(OLD,DELETE)   object module
//       DD DSNAME=SYSIN   for control cards
//SYSLIB DD DSN=DSN220.DSNLOAD,DISP=SHR
//       DD .... subroutine libraries
//SYSLMOD DD DSN=DB2T.DEV.LOADBAT(&MEM),DISP=SHR   load module
//* the control cards list modules to be included into the load
//* module.
//*  DSNELI is the DB2 TSO interface module
//*  for CICS it is DSNCLI
//*  for call attach it is DSNALI
//*  for IMS you use the IMS interface module - DFSLI000
//SYSIN DD *
  INCLUDE DSNELI
/*
```

Figure 3.27. Link-Edit a Program.

```
DSN SYSTEM(DB2T)
RUN PROGRAM(HSPAT07) LIB('HOSP.TEST.LOADBAT') PLAN(HSPAT07)
DCLGEN TABLE(THSADM0) LIBRARY('HOSP.TEST.INCLUDE(THSADM)') -
       ACTION(REPLACE) LANGUAGE(PLI) STRUCTURE(THSADM)
BIND PLAN(HSADM03) MEMBER(HSADM03) ACT(REPLACE) -
     LIBRARY('HOSP.TEST.DBRM') -
     ISOLATION(CS) RETAIN EXPLAIN(NO) VALIDATE(BIND) -
     ACQUIRE(USE) RELEASE(COMMIT)
END
```

Figure 3.28. Using the DSN Command Processor Under TSO.

attachment will open the thread, identifying to DB2 the plan to be used by your program. At the end of the program execution, the thread will be closed.

Other DB2 commands can also be issued while the connection is still established. In this figure, a DCLGEN is issued to create a table declaration for the THSADM0 table, and the plan HSADM03 is bound. When the END subcommand is given, the connection to DB2 is terminated and the DSN command ends.

To run a batch program, the same attachment facility is used. The program JCL must, therefore, invoke the TSO terminal monitor program (IKJEFT01). This JCL is in Figure 3.29. This batch job is in effect a batch invocation of TSO (i.e., there is no terminal attached). You need DD statements for any files that your applications need (you can invoke more than one application program within the same job step). The SYSTSIN DD statement identifies a set of TSO commands to be executed. These can be any valid TSO commands that do not require a terminal. In our case, we are invoking the DSN command and several subcommands of it. We are executing two programs and a BIND subcommand. The END statement is optional. When end of file on SYSTSIN is reached, DSN will be terminated as well as the entire terminal monitor program step. If we

```
// EXEC PGM=IKJEFT01,REGION=1M
//STEPLIB DD DSN=DSN220.DSNLOAD   DB2 load library
//SYSPRINT DD SYSOUT=*
//SYSTSPRT DD SYSOUT=*
//SYSTSIN DD *
DSN SYSTEM(DB2T)
RUN PROGRAM(HSPAT01) LIB('DB2.DEV.LOADBAT') PLAN(HSPAT01)
RUN PROGRAM(DSNTIAD) LIB('DB2T.DSN.RUNLIB.LOAD') PLAN(DSNTIA22)
BIND PLAN(HSADM03) MEMBER(HSADM03) ACT(REPLACE) -
     LIBRARY('HOSP.TEST.DBRM') -
     ISOLATION(CS) RETAIN EXPLAIN(NO) VALIDATE(BIND) -
     ACQUIRE(USE) RELEASE(COMMIT)
/*
//* THE SYSIN DD STATEMENT CONTAINS THE INPUT FOR DSNTIAD
//SYSIN DD *
  CREATE SYNONYM HSADM FOR GELLER.THSADM0;
/*
```

Figure 3.29. JCL for Executing Batch DB2 Programs and Commands.

wanted other TSO commands after DSN, then we would need the END subcommand to terminate DSN.

I will digress again to mention that the second program executed in this example (DSNTIAD) is one of the sample programs supplied by DB2. These samples are extremely useful not just as samples but in their own right. DSNTIAD is a dynamic SQL program that allows you to issue SQL statements in batch without writing a program. It can be used for any statement other than a SELECT that returns a set of rows. In particular, it can be used to issue CREATE statements. Therefore, tables, views, synonyms, etc., can easily be created in batch and not just through SPUFI or QMF. This program and the other sample programs are described in the Administration Guide. If they are not currently available for your use, check with your system administrator.

Other than the requirement to run the batch programs under the TSO terminal monitor program, there is really no other difference from running a normal batch program.

CICS and IMS/DC programs are also run as normal programs. The attachment facilities in these environments are for the most part transparent to the programmer. The exception as described earlier is the requirement for structuring the application plan based on the transaction flow. For the system administrator, there are additional considerations. A table must be created to identify which plan is to be used by each transaction, and to specify thread requirements for these plans. The reason for this additional complexity is that CICS and IMS/DC are multi-user systems. A TSO region processes one TSO user and one program at a time. The TSO attachment, therefore, needs only one thread at a time. The same is true for batch. However, CICS handles many concurrent users and programs. In fact, the same program may be used concurrently by several users all within the one CICS region. Therefore, this attachment facility needs to be able to open several threads concurrently. The details of these requirements and the performance implications of this table (called the RCT) are described in Chapter 9, as are the IMS attachment and call attachment facilities.

3.5 DYNAMIC SQL

3.5.1 Dynamic and Static SQL

SQL statements that are embedded in a program can be static SQL or dynamic SQL. Static SQL statements have a fixed format. The list of columns selected, the table(s) being accessed, and the format of the WHERE and ORDER BY clauses do not change. There is still a good amount of flexibility in that host variables can be used for any values in the WHERE clause and for inserting or updating columns. Most programs are written using only static SQL.

With dynamic SQL you can code programs where even the *format* of the statements changes at execution time. This has benefit where you need a general-purpose program that can do more things than is practical to code for. The simplest example involves the user (executor of the program) being able to enter any SQL statement that accesses any table and having the program execute it. This example sounds like QMF or SPUFI. In fact, QMF and SPUFI are programs that use dynamic SQL. In reality, there is no such thing as SQL being executed "by itself." Access to DB2 is always through a program.

The reasons that most programs use static SQL are that it is simpler to code and is generally more efficient. Actually, some types of dynamic SQL are not difficult to code as we will see below. Any program can have both static and dynamic statements. There is no restriction on having one kind or the other.

3.5.2 Performance of Dynamic and Static SQL

There are several ways in which dynamic SQL is less efficient. The basic reason is that whatever work DB2 must do to determine how to execute the statements must be done at execution time rather than at compile time. DB2 must interpret the statement to see what it is doing (it only needs to be interpreted once even if executed many times). For static SQL, this is done by the preprocessor. DB2 must then decide on an access path and do authorization checking. These are normally done in the BIND process. Each of these take time. How much? Not that much that it presents a problem for low volumes. You can see when you execute a QMF query that the time it takes before the query starts (i.e., when you get the panel showing the estimated cost) is not too long on a lightly loaded system. However, for a high volume transaction, the overhead is high enough that you should not use dynamic SQL unless necessary.

There are actually some cases where dynamic SQL can provide improved performance. When a static SQL statement uses host variables in the predicates of the WHERE clause, DB2 cannot always use the best access path because it does not know at compile time what values will be used in the host variables. The main example is the LIKE predicate. DB2 can use an index with a LIKE provided that the value does not start with a wild card. For example, Figure 3.30 asks for patients whose last name starts with the letters JON and have any number (including none) of additional characters. We have an index on LASTNAME (XHSPAT01). If we issue this statement under QMF, DB2 will probably use this index. Figure 3.31 has a SELECT looking for names that have VIER

```
SELECT * FROM HSPAT
   WHERE LASTNAME LIKE 'JON%'
```
Figure 3.30. LIKE Predicate with Wildcard.

```
SELECT * FROM HSPAT
   WHERE LASTNAME LIKE '%VIER%'
```
Figure 3.31. LIKE Predicate with Wildcard at the Beginning.

```
EXEC SQL DECLARE PAT1 CURSOR FOR
    SELECT PATID,LASTNAME,FIRSTNAME,BIRTHDATE FROM HSPAT
      WHERE LASTNAME LIKE 'JON%';
(a) with constant value for comparison


EXEC SQL DECLARE PAT2 CURSOR FOR
    SELECT PATID,LASTNAME,FIRSTNAME,BIRTHDATE FROM HSPAT
      WHERE LASTNAME LIKE :MATCHNAME;
(b) with host variable for comparison
```
Figure 3.32. Embedded SQL with LIKE Predicates.

somewhere in them, starting and ending with any arbitrary string of characters. DB2 can *not* use a matching index scan to find them because the name can start with any leading character(s). Figure 3.32 has two embedded SELECT statements. The first one looks for names starting with JON. This prefix is coded as a constant. Therefore, DB2 can use the index. The second select uses a host variable. It is more flexible in that the comparison value can be changed at execution time. However, at compile time, DB2 does not know what form the value will take. Will it be 'JON%' or will it start with a wildcard? Since the access path is decided on at BIND time, DB2 cannot use the index.

With dynamic SQL, the comparison value is also set at execution time, but the statement that DB2 looks at to determine the access path already has the value of the variable filled into the statement (as when you execute it under QMF). Therefore, it has more information available and can make a better choice of access path. This can result in a significant savings in processing time.

Other cases where DB2 can make a better choice involve selecting on ranges (Figure 3.33). When calculating filter factors, DB2 considers the size of the range as compared to the total range of values (using HIGH2KEY and LOW2KEY from the catalog table SYSIBM.SYSCOLUMNS). With dynamic SQL, the range in the BETWEEN is known when the calculations are made. With host variables in static SQL, the range is not known.

3.5.3 Authorization

There is another fundamental difference between static and dynamic SQL. With static SQL, the binder of the plan must have authorization to access all of the tables referenced in the program. The person who runs the program must be granted EXECUTE authority on the plan. This person does *not* need authority to access the individual tables. With dynamic SQL, the person who runs the program needs the authority to access the tables. This is what happens with

```
EXEC SQL DECLARE PAT3 CURSOR FOR
    SELECT PATID,LASTNAME,FIRSTNAME,BIRTHDATE FROM HSPAT
        WHERE LASTNAME BETWEEN :LOWNAME AND :HIGHNAME;
```
Figure 3.33. Embedded SQL with a Range.

SPUFI and QMF. These are dynamic SQL programs and you need to be granted authority for each table you access.

You have to give some thought to the whole authorization scheme. With static batch and TSO jobs, the idea is that if a user is allowed to run the program, you implicitly intend for him to be able to access anything the program does. It is, therefore, simpler just to grant execute authority on the plan. This user does not need authority for the individual tables unless he is also going to be using QMF. With dynamic SQL in the programs, you must also grant the necessary table authorizations.

In CICS, the situation is more complicated. TSO authorization is based on the current SQLID, which is usually the TSO logon ID (unless secondary IDs are being used). In batch, it is the USER parameter on the JOB statement. This is often the same as the TSO logon ID. In CICS, the authorization ID is decided on by the system administrator. There are several different choices. These are coded in the RCT table and are described in Section 9.2.

It is very important to understand which authorization ID is being used when the program has dynamic SQL. As discussed in Section 3.2, programs are often written using a synonym rather than the full qualified table name. For static SQL, the synonym is the one created by the binder of the program. For dynamic SQL, it will be the one for the authorization ID of the executor of the plan.

In most cases, a programmer clearly knows whether or not he has coded static or dynamic statements, although there are some exceptions. CSP (Cross System Product) is a "4th generation" application development package from IBM. It can be used to write applications, which can then be generated to run under TSO or CICS (as well as under other IBM software systems). When you use SQL statements in a CSP application, you have the choice of generating static or dynamic SQL for the executable module. In fact, even if you generate static SQL, when you execute the application you can request that dynamic SQL be used. There is no change in the source program. CSP takes care of the dynamic statement processing for you. This gives great flexibility in program development and testing (and provides an easy way to code dynamic SQL). However, you had better understand and know which way you are executing the application. Performance is a consideration, but setting up the correct authorization is critical.

3.5.4 Coding Dynamic SQL

We are not going to go into all of the details of dynamic SQL. These are described fairly well in the DB2 "Application Programming and SQL Guide." There are also several sample programs supplied with DB2 that can be examined in order to see the details. These are DSNTEP2 (written in PL/I), DSNTIAD (assembler, no SELECT statements), and DSNTIAUL (assembler, a general-purpose unload program). We will go over the basics, examining why dynamic SQL (in particular, SELECT statements) can be more difficult to code than static SQL.

First, let's distinguish three classes of SQL statements:

- Non-SELECT statements.
- SELECT with a fixed list of columns.
- SELECT with a variable list of columns.

This list is in ascending order of difficulty. The reasons are fairly simple. Non-SELECT statements do not return any data to the program. While the format of the statement may change, you do not have to worry about host variables to receive data. SELECT statements with a fixed list of columns need host variables to receive the data, but the same set of host variables can be used every time the statement is executed. The table they are selected from may change, as might the selection criteria, but the selected columns do not. Dynamic SELECTs usually also need a cursor just like static SELECTs. SELECT statements, in which the number of columns changes, are more difficult. You cannot simply code a list of host variables. Each time the SELECT is executed, a different set of variables may be needed. Therefore, you need code that can handle this. We'll describe this below.

3.5.4.1 Non-SELECT Statements

Let's start with non-SELECT statements. There is a two-step process. First, you prepare the statement (Figure 3.34). This tells DB2 what you plan to do—the statement is built. You follow this with the execution of the statement (Figure 3.35). In this simple example, the program reads a character string which contains an arbitrary SQL statement. If the program does not do any checking to ensure the validity of the statement, then DB2 might return an error SQLCODE after the PREPARE statement. The string representing the SQL statement to be prepared can be a varying length character string in COBOL (i.e., a structure containing a halfword binary length, followed by a string variable). In PL/I, it

```
DCL SQLSTRING CHAR(100) VARYING;

/* read in a value for SQLSTRING */

EXEC SQL PREPARE STMT1 FROM :SQLSTRING;
```
Figure 3.34. Preparing a Dynamic SQL Statement.

```
EXEC SQL EXECUTE STMT1;
```
Figure 3.35. Executing the Prepared Statement.

can be any expression that evaluates to a string. Figure 3.36 has a COBOL structure that can be used as the basis for an update of table THSADM0, in which the column being updated and the value it is being updated with are set at execution time.

Figure 3.37 has an alternative. EXECUTE IMMEDIATE combines the prepare and the execute into one statement. If the dynamic SQL statement is going to be executed once, then this is simpler to use and just as efficient. If the statement may be executed many times, then it is more efficient to prepare it once and then execute the prepared statement. You might ask at this point why you would execute the exact same statement several times. The answer is that the statement that you prepare can have parameter markers (Figure 3.38). These work similarly to host variables. In fact, the EXECUTE has the USING parameter, which substitutes the values of host variables for the parameter markers. In this example the DISDATE column of HSADM will be updated with a value for a particular patient ID. The values are changed for each execution.

```
01 ADM-UPDATE.
   02 FIXED-PART PIC X(30) VALUE
      'EXEC SQL UPDATE THSADM0 SET '.
   02 UPDATE-COL PIC X(18).
   02 EQUAL PIC X(1) VALUE '='.
   02 UPDATE-VALUE PIC X(50).


MOVE 'DISDATE' TO UPDATE-COL.
MOVE '1989-03-23' TO UPDATE-VALUE.
```

Figure 3.36. A COBOL Structure to Be Used as a Flexible UPDATE Statement.

```
EXEC SQL EXECUTE IMMEDIATE :SQLSTRING;
```

Figure 3.37. EXECUTE IMMEDIATE Can Be Used Instead of PREPARE.

```
DCL SQLSTRING CHAR(100) VARYING;
SQLSTRING = 'UPDATE HSADM SET DISDATE = ? WHERE PATID = ?;
EXEC SQL PREPARE STMT1 FROM :SQLSTRING;
EXEC SQL EXECUTE STMT1 USING :UPDATE_VALUE, :PATID;
```

Figure 3.38. Parameter Markers Can Be Used Like Host Variables.

3.5.4.2 SELECT with a Fixed List of Columns

The coding for a SELECT with a fixed number of columns is a combination of non-SELECT dynamic statements and static SELECT statements. Even if only one row will be returned, the use of a cursor is required. The process involves declaring a cursor, preparing the statement, opening the cursor, fetching in the rows, and closing the cursor. Figure 3.39 has an example. The FETCH lists the host variables to receive the data. This list is fixed. It is not part of the statement that is prepared. If this meets your requirements, then the coding is not too difficult. The table name, selection criteria, ordering, etc., can all be changed before the cursor is opened, but the list of columns selected cannot.

3.5.4.3 SELECT with a Variable List of Columns

If you need a variable list of columns, then the coding becomes more difficult. In QMF, for example, the user can enter any SELECT statement he wants. The QMF program must be able to build this statement and read in and display any combination of columns. Before we look at an example, I'll mention the first difficulty. The program must decide on where each returned column is to be stored in the program storage. It must then tell DB2 where this is. It does this using pointer (address) variables. COBOL does not have pointer variables and, therefore, cannot be used for variable list SELECT statements. COBOL2 can be used, as can PL/I, C, and assembler.

In order to handle this situation, the program communicates with DB2 with a control block called an SQLDA (Figure 3.40 has the PL/I declaration for the SQLDA that can be included into the program with %INCLUDE SQLDA;). Figure 3.41 has program code for the whole process. First, the program prepares the statement. After the PREPARE, the program issues a DESCRIBE statement. During the DESCRIBE (you can also combine the PREPARE and DESCRIBE into one statement), DB2 will fill in the SQLDA with information about each column that the statement requested. There is one occurrence of the substructure SQLVAR for each column. This information includes the column type (e.g., char, decimal), length, and name. It also fills in the number of columns (variable SQLD). The program can do whatever it wants with this information. It can prepare headings for a report and it can obtain or set aside storage to receive the data (the length and type of each column is useful for this). The program must then fill in some information into the SQLDA. The SQLDATA field of each occurrence of SQLVAR must contain the address of the place in storage where DB2 is to return this column when a row is fetched. It can point to a host variable. Or it can point to part of a general large storage area that the program has obtained. It is up to the program to set this field. The program can then open the cursor and fetch the rows.

There is one other situation where an SQLDA is used. A dynamic statement may also have a variable number of parameter markers. This, too, must be handled with trickier coding.

```
       DCL 1 SELECTSTMT,
            2 COLUMN_LIST CHAR(50)
              INIT('SELECT PATID,LASTNAME,FIRSTNAME FROM '),
            2 TABLE_NAME CHAR(18),
            2 WHERE_CLAUSE CHAR(100),
            2 ORDER_CLAUSE CHAR(50);
       DCL SQLSTRING CHAR(218) BASED(S_PTR);
        S_PTR = ADDR(SELECTSTMT); /* OVERLAY SQLSTRING ON SELECTSTMT*/
        TABLE_NAME = 'THSPAT0';
        WHERE_CLAUSE = ' WHERE BIRTHDATE >= '1980-01-01';
        ORDER_CLAUSE = ' ORDER BY LASTNAME,FIRSTNAME';

       EXEC SQL DECLARE SEL1 CURSOR FOR STMT1;
       EXEC SQL PREPARE STMT1 FROM :SQLSTRING;
       IF SQLCODE ¬= 0 then error
       EXEC SQL OPEN STMT1;
       IF SQLCODE ¬= 0 then error
       EXEC SQL FETCH STMT1
             INTO :PATID, :LASTNAME, :FIRSTNAME;
       IF SQLCODE = 100 /* THEN NONE */
          ELSE IF SQLCODE ¬= 0 then error
       /* if there are more than 1,           */
       /* then loop through until sqlcode=100*/
       EXEC SQL CLOSE STMT1;
       IF SQLCODE ¬= 0 then error
```

Figure 3.39. Dynamic SELECT with a Fixed List of Columns.

3.5.5 Controlling Resource Utilization

When a program is written with static SQL, the programmer can test the program and use the EXPLAIN function to see that it performs efficiently enough for its purpose. When dynamic SQL is used, you cannot control in advance whether it will perform well. There are two facilities available to prevent exces-

```
DCL 1 SQLDA BASED(SQLDAPTR),
      2 SQLDAID    CHAR(8),
      2 SQLDABC    BIN FIXED(31),
      2 SQLN       BIN FIXED,
      2 SQLD       BIN FIXED,
      2 SQLVAR     (SQLSIZE REF(SQLN)),
        3 SQLTYPE  BIN FIXED,
        3 SQLLEN   BIN FIXED,
        3 SQLDATA  PTR,
        3 SQLIND   PTR,
        3 SQLNAME  CHAR(30) VAR;
DCL SQLSIZE BIN FIXED;
DCL SQLDAPTR PTR;
```

Figure 3.40. SQLDA Declaration.

sive resource consumption. QMF has a governor facility that can set limits on the CPU time or number of fetched rows before pausing or stopping execution. DB2 Version 2 introduced a Resource Limit Facility (RLF) that can do a similar function for any dynamic SQL statement (whether executed through QMF or any other program). This is described in Section 8.6.

3.6 DB2I—SPUFI

3.6.1 DB2 Development Tasks

DB2I is a set of TSO panels and CLISTS to guide a programmer or DBA through many of the functions of DB2. Figure 3.42 has the menu panel for DB2I. There are several classes of functions available. Some of these are just as easy (or easier) to do in batch. Others are well-suited for interactive use.

The first class is program preparation (option 3)—putting a source program through the SQL preprocessor, a compiler, the linkage editor, binding the plan, and executing the program. I find that it is useful to go through these when first learning DB2, but that afterward it is easier and quicker to use batch jobs for compiling and binding. This assumes your data center provides quick turnaround for batch. Otherwise, it will be quicker to use DB2I. The usefullness of the interactive mode is that there is online help available for each step of the process. These help screens can explain the parameters that you can use. The same information can be obtained from the manuals, but the first time through it is nice to be guided through the process.

/* IN THIS SIMPLE EXAMPLE, THE DYNAMIC SELECT IS BEING ISSUED
   WITH A KNOWN SET OF COLUMNS. I AM THEREFORE USING HOST
   VARIABLES TO RECEIVE THE DATA. IF THE NUMBER OF COLUMNS
   WERE SET AT EXECUTION TIME, THEN I WOULD HAVE A LARGE BUFFER
   AREA AND WOULD USE THE LENGTH OF EACH RETURNED FIELD TO FIND
   THE PROPER OFFSET TO STORE EACH COLUMN */

%INCLUDE SQLDA;   /* THE DESCRIPTOR AREA */
/* SQLDA IS OVERLAYED ON A BUFFER AREA */
DCL BUFFER(20000) CHAR(1) BASED(B_PTR);
ALLOCATE BUFFER;
SQLDAPTR = B_PTR;

/* THIS SELECT STATEMENT ASKS FOR 3 COLUMNS */
DCL 1 SELECTSTMT,
      2 COLUMN_LIST CHAR(50)
         INIT('SELECT PATID,LASTNAME,FIRSTNAME FROM '),
      2 TABLE_NAME CHAR(18),
      2 WHERE_CLAUSE CHAR(100),
      2 ORDER_CLAUSE CHAR(50);
DCL SQLSTRING CHAR(218) BASED(S_PTR);
 S_PTR = ADDR(SELECTSTMT); /* OVERLAY SQLSTRING ON SELECTSTMT*/
 TABLE_NAME = 'THSPAT0';
 WHERE_CLAUSE = ' WHERE BIRTHDATE >= '1980-01-01';
 ORDER_CLAUSE = ' ORDERBY LASTNAME,FIRSTNAME';

EXEC SQL DECLARE SEL1 CURSOR FOR STMT1;
/* WE FIRST TELL DB2 THE MAXIMUM NUMBER OF COLUMNS WE MIGHT ASK
   FOR BY SETTING SQLN. THE PREPARE STMT WILL SET SQLD WITH THE
   ACTUAL NUMBER OF COLUMNS IN THE STMT */

Figure 3.41. Dynamic SELECT with a Varying List of Columns.

```
           SQLN = 300;
           EXEC SQL PREPARE STMT1 FROM :SQLSTRING;
           IF SQLCODE ¬= 0 then error
           EXEC SQL DESCRIBE STMT1 INTO SQLDA;
           IF SQLCODE ¬= 0 then error
           /* SINCE WE KNOW WHICH THREE COLUMNS ARE IN THE SELECT WE CAN USE
              PROGRAM VARIABLES */
           /* SQLDATA IS A POINTER TO A STORAGE AREA WHERE DB2 SHOULD RETURN
              EACH COLUMN OF THE SELECT LIST */
           SQLDATA(1) = ADDR(THSPAT.PATID);
           SQLDATA(2) = ADDR(THSPAT.LASTNAME);
           SQLDATA(3) = ADDR(THSPAT.FIRSTNAME);
           EXEC SQL OPEN STMT1:
           IF SQLCODE ¬= 0 then error
           /* THE FETCH DOES NOT MENTION VARIABLES (INTO CLAUSE).  INSTEAD
           IT TELLS DB2 WHICH DESCRIPTOR (SQLDA) TO USE TO FIND WHERE TO
              PLACE THE DATA */
           EXEC SQL FETCH STMT1
                USING DESCRIPTOR SQLDA;
           IF SQLCODE = 100 /* THEN NONE */
              ELSE IF SQLCODE ¬= 0 then error
           /* if there are more than 1,             */
           /* then loop through until sqlcode=100 */
           EXEC SQL CLOSE STMT1;
           IF SQLCODE ¬= 0 then error
```
Figure 3.41. (*Continued*)

There are two advantages to doing these functions in batch. Each program that you are compiling can have its own JCL jobstream saved in a program library. All the parameters that you want to use for binding and compiling can be saved. Therefore, you do not have to remember them all each time you recompile, and you do not have to retype them in. DB2I will remember the last set of parameters

```
                      DB2I PRIMARY OPTION MENU
                                                          USER - SYSADM
 ===>                                                     TIME - 09:58
 Select one of the following DB2 functions and press ENTER.
                                                          DATE - 89/02/08

  1  SPUFI              (Process SQL statements)
  2  DCLGEN             (Generate SQL and source language declarations)
  3  PROGRAM PREPARATION (Prepare a DB2 application program to run)
  4  PRECOMPILE         (Invoke DB2 precompiler)
  5  BIND/REBIND/FREE   (BIND, REBIND, or FREE application plans)
  6  RUN                (RUN an SQL program)
  7  DB2 COMMANDS       (Issue DB2 commands)
  8  UTILITIES          (Invoke DB2 utilities)
  D  DB2I DEFAULTS      (Set global parameters)
     DEMO               (DB2 Sample Phone Application)
  Q  QMF                (Query Management Facility)
  QT QMF MESSAGE TOOL   (Message Tool for QMF)
  X  EXIT               (Leave DB2I)

 PRESS: END to exit      HELP for more information
```

Figure 3.42. DB2I Menu (Courtesy International Business Machines Corporation).

you used, but if different parameters are used for different programs, it is nice to save them all. The other advantage is speed of execution. In most data centers, the compilers and the bind process will execute more quickly in batch. It all depends on the execution priorities set up for the system.

Any of the functions you execute under DB2I must be for a particular DB2 subsystem, just as in any other environment. In fact, all these functions are run under the DSN command processor (DB2I invokes it for you). The defaults panel contains several default values that you usually set once. The two most important are the subsystem, and the language to be used for DCLGENs and program preparation (see Figure 3.43).

The DCLGEN option (2) generates the DCLGENs (table and structure declarations) for a table. This can be executed in batch by using the DSNTIAD sample program which allows any non-SELECT SQL statement to be executed. You can save your DCLGEN parameters in a library and have them ready for reexecution in batch. However, I find that it is simpler for me to use this option and do it interactively. I use naming standards for my tables, the structures generated, and the library member name for the created declaration. Therefore, it is easy to know what to fill in for each table I want to do a DCLGEN for.

DB2 COMMANDS (option 7) allows you to enter DB2 commands, such as stopping and starting databases or table spaces. You may need this occasionally.

The UTILITIES panel allows you to create JCL for executing the various DB2 utilities. Again, for most of these I find it useful initially for learning purposes. Afterward, it is easier to set up jobstreams for each utility. You can get the necessary JCL from reading the "Command and Utility Reference" manual (SC26-4378) or from generating them once with DB2I. The manual "DB2 Version 2, Release 2 Utilities Guide" (#GG24-3390) also has useful information on running all of the utilities. Once created, it is easy to just edit each job to create new jobs for different tables. The one function that I run under this option is the Terminate Utility command. DB2 tries hard to not let you make mistakes that could compromise the integrity of the data. When a utility job is executed, DB2 records in its catalog the fact that this job is running. You must associate a utility ID (of your own choice) with each run. If the run has an error (other than a syntax error that is caught right away), it will terminate but not remove the catalog entry. Even if the error was not significant (e.g., a LOAD with REPLACE, which will replace all data anyway, is easily rerunnable), you will not be able to rerun the job without first telling DB2 to terminate the previous run. This is done with the Terminate Utility command. You must identify the type of utility that was running (e.g., RECOVER, LOAD, REORG) and the utility ID that you had used.

3.6.2 SPUFI

Finally, we come to SPUFI (option 1). SPUFI stands for Sequential Processing Using File Input (IBM's attempt at being cute). Basically, it is a program that allows you to enter any SQL statement (in an input file that you create), and execute it interactively. QMF is another tool for doing this. QMF is a full-fledged

```
                              DB2I DEFAULTS

===>

Change defaults as desired:

 1  DB2 NAME  ............    ===>  DB2T      (Subsystem identifier)
 2  DB2 CONNECTION RETRIES    ===>  0         (How many retries for DB2 connection)
 3  APPLICATION LANGUAGE      ===>  COB2      (ASM, ASMH, C, COBOL, COB2, FORTRAN, PLI)
 4  LINES/PAGE OF LISTING     ===>  60        (A number from 5 to 999)
 5  MESSAGE LEVEL  ........   ===>  I         (Information, Warning, Error, Severe)
 6  COBOL STRING DELIMITER    ===>  DEFAULT   (DEFAULT, ' or ")
 7  SQL STRING DELIMITER      ===>  DEFAULT   (DEFAULT, ' or ")
 8  DECIMAL POINT  ........   ===>  .         (. or ,)
 9  DB2I JOB STATEMENT:                       (Optional if your site has a SUBMIT exit)
    ===>
    ===>
    ===>
    ===>

PRESS: ENTER to save and exit      END to exit      HELP for more information
```

Figure 3.43. DB2I Defaults (Courtesy International Business Machines Corporation).

report writer and query package aimed at end-users. SPUFI is aimed at programmers and DBAs. It does not have QMF's formatting capabilities, but has several advantages for application developers:

- The input file is a sequential file (or member of a library) that is created with the TSO editor. It can be created either ahead of time, or after you have gone into SPUFI.
- It is, therefore, quicker to create and save queries with SPUFI than with QMF (you can save them under QMF, but it is simpler with the editor).
- It is also usually quicker to get into SPUFI to start the execution.
- Many SQL statements can be executed in one run. Each statement will need a semicolon (;) to indicate the end of the statement. This can be very useful for a number of functions—looking at several queries of the same table, looking at related data in several tables, doing an EXPLAIN and looking at the results, creating a table space, table, and indexes at one time.

Why is SPUFI useful? I just mentioned some of the things it can be used for. Even more basically, any SQL statement that you want to use in a program can first be tested under SPUFI to see if it works, without worrying about host variables and displaying the results. SPUFI will display the results for you. You can also try several variations easily without having to recompile a program each time.

Most important of all, SPUFI provides a simple accurate means of seeing what data is in the tables. Whenever you are writing a program that accesses a file of any kind, you cannot tell for sure that the program is coded correctly unless you know what is in the file. Since any SELECT statement can be issued, you can see precisely what is in every column of every row of the table. Or, you can selectively look at the data with certain conditions. You can easily update or insert test data for any conditions you want to test out. You can find out how many occurrences there are of all rows, or of specific values. SPUFI is the best testing tool that a programmer has. It is also the best debugging tool that a DBA has to verify the data in a table.

The DBA can also use SPUFI to execute the CREATE statements for the tables and other objects. A library can contain these statements for permanent access and reexecution. An alternative is to use the DSNTIAD sample program to execute them in batch. SELECT statements can be executed in batch with the DSNTEP2 sample program.

SPUFI is also a good vehicle for running the EXPLAIN function on individual statements. Chapter 5 describes EXPLAIN in detail. The results of an EXPLAIN are put into a plan table (called userID.PLAN_TABLE) which has to then be queried to read the results. This can be easily handled by having a member of a library with a sample EXPLAIN and a SELECT from PLAN_TABLE.

Figure 3.44 shows the SPUFI panel. Line 1 is where you identify the input dataset (using standard TSO naming conventions). Line 4 is the name of an output dataset, where SPUFI will put its output—your SQL statements and the results. At the end of the execution, you will be brought into Browse mode on this dataset, where you can use all the features of the ISPF Browse function. Lines 5 through 9 indicate (Y/N) which steps are to be executed. Defaults are usually only done once, the others each time. If you know that you need no changes, you do not have to edit the input. You certainly want to execute it. Autocommit will issue a commit for you to commit any updates that you have done. Otherwise, you will be prompted for whether you want the updates committed or rolled back. Finally, you certainly want to browse the output file to check on the results.

The SPUFI defaults (Figure 3.45) that you will want to change are the isolation level and the maximum number of lines to be returned on a SELECT. The default isolation level is RR (repeatable read). The advantages of CS (cursor stability) were discussed in Section 3.1. Since SPUFI is being used for testing purposes, programmers working on the same tables can get better concurrency if CS is used by all of them. MAX SELECT LINES sets a maximum number of rows that will be returned to you. The default is 250. This is often not enough. I find that 1000 is a more reasonable number, which will not result in excessive system resource consumption. If you do not have a high enough number, not only may you not see the data you want to see, but you may also be fooled into thinking that those rows are not there. The way to tell the difference is that after each SQL statement is executed, SPUFI displays the last SQLCODE. For a SELECT, this will be the code returned after the last FETCH. If all rows are returned, this will be 100 (no more rows). If the maximum was reached while there were still more rows to be fetched, then the SQLCODE will be 0 (the last FETCH found a row).

All in all, SPUFI is a tremendous aid to the DBA and the programmer.

3.7 QMF—QUERY MANAGEMENT FACILITY

QMF is an IBM product that uses DB2 (there is also a version for SQL/DS under VM or DOS/VSE). It is a query and report writer package. The DB2 version runs under TSO or can be run in batch. Starting with QMF Version 3.1, it can now also run under CICS.

You may be wondering why we need to discuss a report writer in a book on DB2 performance and development. The reason is that QMF is used by many DB2 shops and is a very important part of the application development effort. Being a heavily used product, it also has performance implications of its own, in addition to the DB2 access.

Good report writers are of tremendous benefit. Every DP shop should have one. Most reports can be written with QMF rather than having to use a programming language. They can be written more quickly and they can be written by nonprogrammers, including sophisticated end-users. This not only means that new reports can be created on a more timely basis, but also that a large burden can be lifted from the programming staff. It becomes practical to develop ad hoc queries

DESIGN AND DEVELOPMENT

```
                         SPUFI
===>

Enter the input data set name:       (Can be sequential or partitioned)
  1  DATA SET NAME      ===>  'DB2.DEV.TABLES(GTTELX)'
  2  VOLUME SERIAL      ===>         (Enter if not cataloged)
  3  DATA SET PASSWORD  ===>         (Enter if password protected)

Enter the output data set name:      (Must be a sequential data set)
  4  DATA SET NAME      ===>  OUTPUT

Specify processing options:
  5  CHANGE DEFAULTS    ===>  NO     (Y/N - Display SPUFI defaults panel?)
  6  EDIT INPUT         ===>  YES    (Y/N - Enter SQL statements?)
  7  EXECUTE            ===>  YES    (Y/N - Execute SQL statements?)
  8  AUTOCOMMIT         ===>  YES    (Y/N - Commit after successful run?)
  9  BROWSE OUTPUT      ===>  YES    (Y/N - Browse output data set?)

PRESS:  ENTER to process    END to exit    HELP for more information
```

Figure 3.44. SPUFI Panel (Courtesy International Business Machines Corporation).

PROGRAM DEVELOPMENT   149

```
                     CURRENT SPUFI DEFAULTS

===>

Enter the following to control your SPUFI session:

   1  ISOLATION LEVEL    ===>  CS      (RR=Repeatable Road, CS=Cursor Stability)

   2  MAX SELECT LINES   ===>  1000    (Maximum number of lines to be returned from a SELECT)

Output data set characteristics:

   3  RECORD LENGTH ...  ===>  4092    (LRECL=Logical record length)

   4  BLOCK SIZE .......  ===>  4096    (Size of one block)

   5  RECORD FORMAT ...  ===>  VB      (RECFM=F, FB, FBA, V, VB, or VBA)

   6  DEVICE TYPE .....  ===>  SYSDA   (Must be DASD unit name)

Output format characteristics:

   7  MAX NUMERIC FIELD  ===>  20      (Maximum width for numeric fields)

   8  MAX CHAR FIELD ..  ===>  80      (Maximum width for character fields)

   9  COLUMN HEADING ..  ===>  NAMES   (NAMES, LABELS, ANY or BOTH)


PRESS:  ENTER to proceed      END to exit      HELP for more information
```

Figure 3.45. SPUFI Defaults (Courtesy International Business Machines Corporation).

and reports that will only be used once. With the increased ease of development, the data becomes more useful and the system can generate more information. Many shops have been reluctant to use QMF because they do not allow the end-users access to TSO. With the new ability to run QMF under CICS, there will be an increased use of the product.

QMF can be used by itself for online report generation and it can be used in batch. You can also interface TSO applications (programs, CLISTS, and ISPF panels) with QMF. If you are developing applications for the TSO environment, this gives you an added option. You do not need programs for all of the functions, QMF can be used for much of it.

Performance becomes an issue because QMF is so easy to use. With a means of getting their own data, end-users will make heavy use of the system. QMF reports will often be more resource intensive than other online work. Most online transactions are direct inquiry or update that are designed for quick response time. Reports that require larger amounts of data are usually done in batch, often at night. QMF enables the user to run this type of report whenever he wants. Since it is easy to create new reports, many more will be run throughout the day. The user may not be as aware of DB2 performance issues and may not know the best ways to code SQL statements. All in all, the introduction of QMF may result in a tremendous increase in computer utilization. This is not all bad in that it is for a purpose—providing the user with information. However, this increased use must be planned for and controlled.

There are four basic components to a QMF report—the query, the form, the report, and (optionally) a proc (procedure). The query is the SQL statement to be executed. Query is a misnomer. You can execute any SQL statement (DML, DDL, DCL) under QMF. Tables can be created, privileges granted, data updated or deleted as well as selected. SELECT statements are the most common. Updating of data is a function for which you usually need application constraints and validity checking. Therefore, they are usually done through a program.

3.7.1 The QMF Languages

3.7.1.1 SQL

QMF provides four languages for the composition of a query: SQL, QBE (Query By Example), the Prompted query (introduced in QMF Version 2.3), and the new SAA Language Access—a natural language query interface (i.e., English). SQL is the standard SQL as used in programs or through SPUFI. Most programmers are familiar with SQL and prefer using it for their queries. The other languages are internally translated by QMF into SQL before execution. There are some SQL capabilities that the others do not have.

3.7.1.2 QBE

QBE is a language that I find to be extremely easy to use for simple queries and for inserting or updating test data. Figures 3.46–3.51 present some sample QBE queries. You start by asking for a skeleton of a table by typing in the table name and hitting a PF key to tell QMF to draw the skeleton (Figure 3.46). To indicate which columns should appear on the report, you enter a P. under each column name (Figure 3.47). If the P. is placed under the table name, then all fields are listed. This would be done in SQL as:

SELECT * FROM THSPAT0

Selection criteria (the WHERE clause of SQL) are done by placing the data values under the columns (Figure 3.48). In this example, active, male patients are selected. Ordering is done with functions AO(1)., AO(2)., DO(3)., etc. The A is for ascending, D for descending. The number in parentheses indicates the sort order. The column with O(1) is the high-order field of the sort. To sort by patient ID and birth date you would mark the screen as in Figure 3.49. To compare fields to each other or perform arithmetic on a column requires extra work. You create a blank column, make field references, and relate them in the blank column (Figure 3.50). We've created a column that has total hours as being regular hours plus overtime hours.

Joins are also handled with references. You draw the two tables, mark the join criteria columns where the match is to be made, and indicate the fields that are to be printed. P. can only appear in one of the table lines. Figure 3.51 is a join

```
THSPAT0|PATID     |LASTNAME    |FIRSTNAME|SEX|BIRTHDATE  |ACTIVEFLAG
_____
       |          |            |         |   |           |
```
Figure 3.46. QBE Table.

```
THSPAT0|PATID     |LASTNAME    |FIRSTNAME|SEX|BIRTHDATE  |ACTIVEFLAG
_____
       |P.        |P.          |P.       |   |P.         |
```
Figure 3.47. List Several Columns.

```
THSPAT0|PATID     |LASTNAME    |FIRSTNAME|SEX|BIRTHDATE  |ACTIVEFLAG
_____
       |P.        |P.          |P.       |M  |P.         |Y
```
Figure 3.48. QBE Selection Criteria.

```
THSPAT0|PATID     |LASTNAME    |FIRSTNAME|SEX|BIRTHDATE  |ACTIVEFLAG
_____
       |P.AO(1).  |P.          |P.       |M  |P.AO(2).   |Y
```
Figure 3.49. Sorting a QBE Report.

EMPLOYE	EMPID	LASTNAME	REGHOURS	OVERHOURS
P.			_R	_S	_R+_S

Figure 3.50. QBE Operations on Fields.

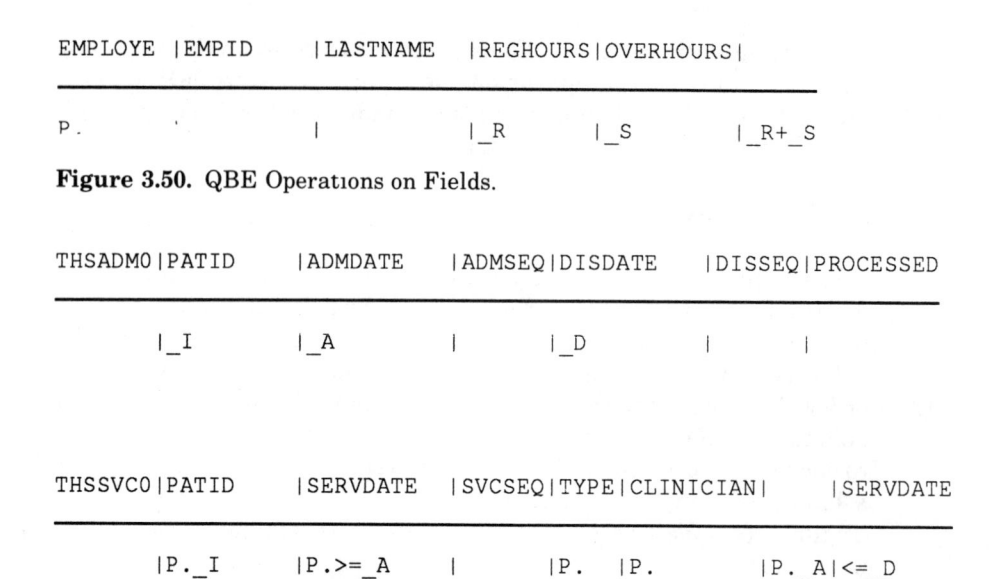

THSADMO	PATID	ADMDATE	ADMSEQ	DISDATE	DISSEQ	PROCESSED
	_I	_A		_D		

THSSVCO	PATID	SERVDATE	SVCSEQ	TYPE	CLINICIAN	SERVDATE
	P._I	P.>=_A		P.	P.	P._A<=_D

Figure 3.51. QBE Join of Two Tables.

of admit and service data (service date between the admit date and the discharge date). Simple queries are very easy with QBE but things can get more difficult as you try to do more complex queries.

QBE requires many fewer keystrokes than SQL. If you have forgotten the column names but know the table name, you can easily have QMF supply them for you. You can draw a skeleton SELECT in SQL also, but it lists all fields in the select list. If you don't want them all, you then have to delete or comment out the ones you don't want. This is a lot more work. Inserting several rows of test data is also very easy with QBE. After each INSERT, you just change the columns for which you want different values. It's all lined up neatly and easy to read. I use QBE as my default language in QMF.

There are several drawbacks to QBE. It can become more cumbersome than SQL for complex queries—those with joins and selection criteria that have expressions involving several columns. A more serious drawback is that it appears that QBE is a stepchild in IBM's eyes and they are not treating it as a strategic product. There have been new functions added to SQL that have not been added to QBE. These include the date and time built in functions. This severely limits its usefullness. I would be afraid to invest user education or production user reports in QBE as future support may not be the same as for SQL.

3.7.1.3 Prompted Query

The prompted query is a newer feature aimed at end-users (and programmers who are new to DB2). It leads you through the building of a query, step by step. It first prompts you for a table name (or several for a join). If you do not know the table name, you can request a list of tables and choose one from the list. You are then presented with a list of columns from the table(s). You can choose all or some of them to be in the select list. The WHERE clause is built by prompting the user for a column, a relational operator, and a comparison value. Additional criteria can then be entered with an AND or OR connector. Sort criteria are then prompted for.

All of this is rather straightforward and a user can easily build a report without any knowledge of SQL. The user can then ask to see the equivalent SQL statement (this is a good means of learning the basics of SQL). The query can optionally be converted to an SQL query. However, once converted to SQL, you cannot convert it back to a prompted query. If you want it both ways, save the prompted query first, before converting.

3.7.1.4 Language Access

This is a new IBM product. It allows users to formulate their query in their natural language (e.g., English). QMF will have an interface to this product, and allow the QMF queries to be written in this format.

3.7.2 Form, Report, and Proc

Every query has a form associated with it. The default form simply lists each selected row, with column headings that are the names of the columns. You can customize the form in many ways. You can put in page headings, new column headings, and have variables (i.e., column values) in the headings and footings. Control breaks can be specified (to group data by a set of columns) and arithmetic functions can be applied at control breaks. You can get counts and sums of columns through the form. This enables you to get row details as well as summation in one report (SQL provides summation by groups, but then you cannot see each row).Each new release of QMF has introduced new features for formatting and you can now create quite an attractive report with just the forms. You can save several different forms to be used with the same query with different formatting, control breaks, and the order (or appearance) of columns.

The report is the result of the query after formatting with the form. You can switch between the report and the form screens to try out different variations without having to rerun the query. This can be a tremendous savings in time (yours and the computer's) as the rows do not have to be fetched again. The selected rows are simply reformatted each time.

A Proc (procedure) is a set of QMF commands to be executed in sequence. This simplifies execution of a query with a specific form, and enables the consecutive execution of several queries (this is especially useful in batch). One query can also act on the results of a preceeding query. The data selected by a query can be saved (with the SAVE DATA command) into a table that QMF will build on the fly for you. A subsequent query can then select data from this table. This can be useful where you have a complex request that cannot be satisfied with a single SQL statement.

Starting with QMF 3.1, the proc can include REXX commands. REXX is a powerful procedure langauge used with VM and with TSO. By incorporating it into QMF, the QMF proc can do many more things. For example, it can now have conditional logic (i.e., the same procedure can execute different queries based on the setting of variables).

3.7.3 Controlling Performance

Since QMF will be so heavily used, it is important to control this usage to prevent it from getting out of hand. There are several ways to do this. With large tables, it is easy to create queries that will take a very long time to run. Even medium-sized tables, which are joined or have subselects, can result in hour-long queries. If you simply want to prevent some or all users from running excessively long queries, you can use the QMF governor or the DB2 Resource Limit Facility (RLF), which was introduced in DB2 Version 2. Both of these can stop a query after it has reached a set limit. They are described in Section 8.6. The DBA should read that section to learn how to control QMF usage. QMF users should read it to understand what limits are placed on their usage of DB2.

Preventing very long queries is only a partial answer. Many shorter queries can add up to heavy system usage. Also, these very long queries may not need to run so long. They may just be coded poorly or incorrectly. The first step in effective QMF use is training of the users and ongoing monitoring of usage. There must be a QMF expert in the organization whose primary function is training users in correct and efficient SQL coding. This includes understanding their data, the volumes, and indexes available. The second part of his job is to monitor the use of QMF—see how much of the system resources it is using, plan for growth, and monitor individual users' queries and CPU utilization. When necessary, he or she should advise users on better ways to do their job, or should use the governor to limit their online use.

Without effective monitoring and training, usage can get out of hand. There are likely to be many valid queries that are not coded as efficiently as possible. There are also likely to be many incorrect queries. An SQL statement that is not coded correctly will certainly not return the desired results (although it may not be obvious if the user does not know exactly what results to expect). An incorrect statement may also perform very poorly. If you meant to use a selection criteria on a column which is indexed, but instead used a different (perhaps similarly named) column, the query may run for hours.

Any user, including experienced programmers, will make some mistakes as they develop their queries. Even without mistakes, they may make changes as they see the results from the first run. If query development is done on large production tables, a great amount of time (user and CPU) will be wasted during the development process. Programmers are used to having small test databases for development. End-users should have them also. The DBA or QMF administrator should set up test tables for end-users to use in order to develop their queries. They will not only run faster, but the amount of data will be manageable, enabling the user to more easily verify if the query is correct. Then the user can run against the production tables.

For tables that have heavy production transaction activity, there is also a potential contention problem. The nature of DB2 contention is described in Section 6.3. If contention with QMF users is a problem, it might be necessary not to provide access directly against the production tables. Instead, copies of the tables could be made nightly (or less frequently). Most of the QMF users would then run their reports against these tables. The data would not be up to the minute, but this might suffice.

Other ways to limit resource consumption on a heavily loaded system might include restricting much of the QMF access to batch, or overnight runs. If the installation has several processors, QMF access to copies of the production data could be done on a separate processor.

QMF is a very useful product, but you must be careful with its use. The governor or the RLF can help in this task, but effective monitoring and training are essential, too.

3.8 SUMMARY AND KEY GUIDELINES

- There are two forms of SQL statements:
  - Static: The format of the statement is fixed, but values can be supplied by program variables. Static SQL is used in most programs.
  - Dynamic: The program builds the statement at execution time. SPUFI and QMF are programs that use dynamic SQL.
- DCLGEN creates host language structures for tables. Using DCLGEN (and keeping the structures up to date) is a good means of ensuring the accuracy of record declarations).
- SELECT statements that may return more than one row must use cursors.
- If DB2 uses an index for a cursor-controlled select, and does not need to sort the rows, then it does not build an internal results table. One row is accessed for each FETCH statement. This enables you to fetch one screen's worth of data without having DB2 access all qualifying rows.
- CS vs. RR—With Cursor Stability, rows are protected (pages locked) while the cursor is positioned on the row. The lock is released when the program moves to a row on another page. With Repeatable Read, the locks are kept until a commit point. This reduces concurrency because the locks are held longer. You should use CS most of the time.
- Do not use SELECT * in programs. It is much better to list the columns you need (the same is true for INSERT). The program will have more data independence (not as affected by changes to the table) and will be more efficient.
- Decimal columns must be given valid decimal data. Invalid data used to result in an abend, but now (Version 2.2) returns a negative SQLCODE. This happens most frequently with INSERT statements

that do not have a column list (e.g., all columns) for which not all of the variables have been initialized.
- Programs should use synonyms rather than hardcoding a specific creator ID for the tables. In this way the same program can be used for production and test tables (as well as several different sets of test).
- Each of the different execution environments (e.g., CICS, IMS/DC, TSO/Batch) uses a different interface module. When you link-edit the program, you must include the correct one.
- Everytime you recompile a program, you must also BIND the plan—even if you have not changed any of the SQL statements. This is because of the timestamp put in by the SQL preprocessor.
- The person who binds a plan is the owner of the plan. By default he is the only one who can execute the plan or BIND it again. To allow others to do so, he must GRANT EXECUTE or BIND authority.
- Dynamic SQL is generally less efficient than static because DB2 must determine an access path and check authorizations at execution time. It can, however, sometimes be more efficient because DB2 will know the values in the WHERE clause. The static SQL may use host variables and DB2 will not have as much information.
- SPUFI can be a very useful tool for the programmer. It is generally quicker and easier to edit and save a request than can be done through QMF. You can also execute several SQL statements at one time. Everyone should change the SPUFI defaults. The Isolation Level should be changed to CS. The number of rows returned should be increased above the default of 250.
- QMF is very good for end-user computing. However, it is essential that its use be monitored and controlled (the governor) and that the users be educated on efficient SQL.

part 2

Access Path Selection

4

Access Paths—The Basics of Performance

To design and develop efficient systems, it is necessary to understand all the components of DB2 performance and how they interact. They *do* interact. The table and index design affects how the programs should be coded. The application requirements affect how the tables should be designed.

The components that affect DB2 performance include:

- Database design
  - Table design
  - Choice of indexes
  - Table space and index parameters
- Programming (SQL statements in programs and in QMF queries)
- DB2 Optimizer—understanding the possible DB2 access paths and how DB2 determines which access path to use
- System parameters
- Data volumes and distribution of data values
- Data layout—how the data was loaded and/or reorganized
- Running RUNSTATS to place statistics into the catalog and updating those statistics manually to influence DB2's access path choices

The best way to achieve good performance is to understand how DB2 accesses data and then to design and code to take best advantage of that knowledge, followed by using EXPLAIN to see the results. It is most important to learn how to reduce the number of IOs needed. To learn about DB2's methods, you can read this chapter and the next and the following DB2 manuals (Version 2.2):

Administration Guide, Volume III
Application Programming and SQL Guide

The Application Design and Tuning Guide is an older manual from the IBM System Support Centers (a red book), which contained much of the performance information and was widely read. This manual is now out of date as it is based on DB2 Version 1.2.

Reading about the DB2 optimizer gives you the basics of how and when indexes are used, but it also helps to get a feel for it in action. EXPLAIN is not just an after-the-fact tool for verifying SQL statements. You should use it extensively on a variety of queries and tables. In this way you can increase your knowledge and intuitive feel for what makes an efficient design and learn how to code to take advantage of DB2's capabilities.

This chapter and the next one will examine in detail the processing of SQL statements. In this chapter, we examine the possible access paths for different SQL statements. Chapter 5 describes the EXPLAIN feature, how to read its output, and how it fits in with the access paths. In effect, this is a picture of DB2's actions. Other chapters cover other aspects of performance—system parameters, table space and index parameters and table design. However, the most important aspect is the choice of access path. All DBAs and programmers should have a good understanding of this area. The performance of even the simplest SQL requests can vary greatly, based on the factors that determine the access path.

4.1 ACCESS PATHS TO ONE TABLE

There are two components to the processing of a request—CPU time and IO time. Each SQL statement can take a fair amount of CPU time. The more you ask for and how you ask for it can make a substantial difference. We will look at some of the important aspects of this later. However, the single most important component of performance is the number of IOs that are needed. SQL is a powerful data manipulation language. What makes it so useful is that any data can be requested from the database regardless of whether or not there are any indexes on any of the columns. In addition, each DML statement can process a set of rows, not just one row at a time. When a request processes a single row and an index is used, there will be very few IOs. If a large set of data is processed or if no indexes are used, there may be many IOs.

Any transaction that only needs a few IOs will perform well. A 3380 disk drive can process about 40 random IOs per second. The key goal is, therefore, to keep the number of IOs small. The programmer cannot tell DB2 how to access the data. DB2 will decide for itself what it thinks is the best way. It bases this on which columns are being accessed, what the selection criteria are, which indexes exist, any sort criteria, and statistics of how many values there are for each index. Since IOs are so important, it is good to know that DB2 handles IOs fairly efficiently.

There are several basic ways in which DB2 can find a row of data that meets a search criteria. It can use an index for a direct lookup, or it can read through the entire table space checking each row. There is also an index scan in which DB2 will read through an entire index looking at each index record. Figures 4.2, 4.4, and 4.5 have three SELECT statements to retrieve data from the patient table THSPAT0. Each illustrates one of the types of access paths.

4.1.1 Direct Index Lookup

There is an index on PATID as shown in Figure 4.1 (the other indexes and the table layout are in Appendix A). The first statement (Figure 4.2) asks for rows with patient ID equal to '223344556'. Since this happens to be a unique index, there can be at most one such row. Even if it weren't a unique index, the nature of the data is such that there would probably only be a few rows with that value. Assuming that RUNSTATS has been run, DB2 will probably determine that the quickest way to access the data will be to use index XHSPAT02. This will involve:

- reading the index to find the row(s) with ID = '22334445556';
- reading the data rows (from the table) to retrieve the actual row;
- pulling out the requested columns.

The number of IOs needed for this direct lookup will depend on how many index levels there are (which, in turn, depends partly on how many rows there are in the table) and on whether or not any of the index pages are in a buffer. The number of levels is usually not too high. A small- to medium-sized table of 100,000 rows or less may only have two levels. A million-row table may have three levels. The highest index level will usually be in a buffer for a heavily used table. Therefore, a typical access for a unique value will require two or three IOs. If there were, say, 10 rows that meet the search criteria, it is likely that the index entries will all be on one page (or two at most). The data rows might all be on the same page if the index is clustered or they might all be on separate pages if the index is not clustered. We'll talk about clustering in more

```
CREATE UNIQUE INDEX GELLER.XHSPAT02 ON GELLER.THSPAT0

(PATID)

USING STOGROUP STG1 PRIQTY 10000 SECQTY 200

SUBPAGES 4 CLOSE NO
```
Figure 4.1. Create Index on PATID.

```
SELECT PATID,LASTNAME,FIRSTNAME,SEX,BIRTHDATE
   FROM THSPAT0
   WHERE PATID='223344556'
```
Figure 4.2. SELECT with a Matching Index Scan.

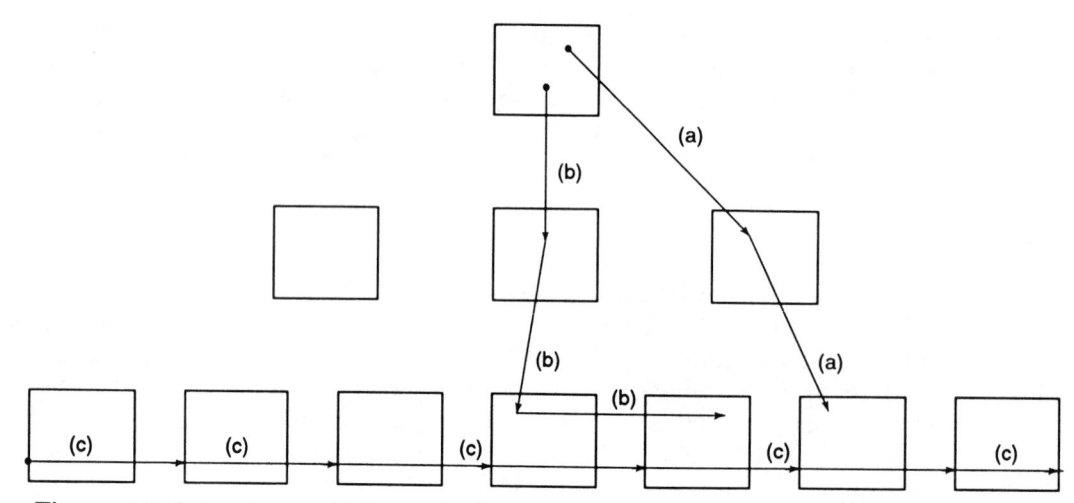

Figure 4.3. Index Access: (a) Direct Lookup; (b) Matching Index Scan; (c) Nonmatching Index Scan.

detail below, but as you can see, clustering can make a big difference when a set of rows is to be returned. This example would take approxiamately 3 vs. 12 IOs, depending on whether the selected rows were all on the same page or spread throughout the table space.

Figure 4.3 shows various types of index access. The direct lookup is shown by the lines labeled (a). One page from each index level must be read.

4.1.2 Table Space Scan

The SELECT statement in Figure 4.4 has search criteria for columns BIRTH-DATE and SEX. There is no index on these fields. Regardless of the statistics on the table, DB2 has no choice but to scan through every row in the table space, checking the values of each one. This is called a table space scan. Table space scans are not necessarily a problem, depending on the size of the table space and the transaction environment (i.e., 5 second response time is not great for a high volume CICS transaction but is fine for batch or an occasional query). When doing a table space scan, DB2 does not always require one IO for each page. It can read ahead many pages per IO. This is called sequential prefetch. For reading, DB2 does 8 pages per IO for small buffer pools (under 224 buffers), and 16 pages per IO when the buffer pool is between 224 and 999 buffers. For larger

```
SELECT PATID,LASTNAME,FIRSTNAME,BIRTHDATE
  FROM THSPAT0
    WHERE BIRTHDATE = '1962-03-17' AND SEX='M'
```
Figure 4.4. SELECT with Table Space Scan.

buffer pools, it will do 32 pages at a time. Utilities may read up to 64 pages per IO. When writing an entire table (such as with the LOAD or RECOVER utilities), it will do 32 pages per IO. This is very good.

Not only does prefetch read many pages per IO, but it also does this asynchronously. This means that DB2 will issue the prefetch request while the program (and DB2) continue to do other processing. The request is done for an upcoming set of pages. Therefore, the program does not have to wait for the IO to complete.

Let's look at an example. The THSCHR0 table has rows that are just under 100 bytes long (95 including overhead). That means that approxiamately

- 40 rows will fit in each page.
- 32 pages can hold 1280 rows.

A 3380 can process 40 IOs or more per second (assuming no other program is accessing the disk concurrently). Therefore, 51,200 rows can be read in 1 second. That is quite a bit (of course, I have ignored other things like the processing of the rows). One second is a pretty quick response time. A much larger table will, of course, take longer. If there were four million rows, the table space scan would require 100 seconds—no longer that amenable to ad hoc query, but still acceptable for batch.

I use 40 IOs per second as a lower bound. Random disk reads take about 25 milliseconds (40 per second). When blocks are read sequentially, the disk drive is already positioned at the correct disk cylinder most of the time. Thus, the disk seek is eliminated. When there isn't contention for the drive, these IOs may only take 10 ms. You can then get up to 3200 pages read in a second (100 IOs times 32 pages per IO).

This example used a 100-byte row. If the rows were 200 bytes, then only 20 would fit in a page. It would take twice as many IOs and twice the IO time to do a table space scan. For queries that are on the borderline of acceptable online performance, the row size can make a big difference. DASD is relatively cheap compared to 10 years ago. The amount of storage data requires is no longer as great a concern as it was then, strictly in terms of storage space. However, storage space does directly affect the performance of any function that requires reading the entire file. This includes the utility programs, such as backups and recoveries. However, for DB2 it also includes any access that does not use indexes. Performance is not the only criteria in table design, and you should not compromise your design just to reduce storage. However, you should be careful not to waste space. Space can be wasted by making fields much larger than needed or by unnecessarily denormalizing tables. This is discussed in Section 2.1. Denormalizing may be of benefit in some cases, but it will increase the size of table spaces and, therefore, increase the time to do a table space scan. You must analyze the types of access that will be done for each table individually.

The scanning of every row is called a table space scan because for simple and partitioned table spaces, DB2 must look at every row in the table space, including the rows of any other tables. This is because the rows are intermixed. Segmented table spaces (see Section 2.4), however, keep the rows of different tables on different pages. When a table space scan is used, only the pages of the one table need to be read. This is a great improvement for table spaces with more than one table.

DB2 does not automatically start off a table space scan by using sequential prefetch. It will only consider using prefetch if it thinks that there are enough pages to make it worthwhile. This determination is normally made at bind time. Up through Version 2.1, the threshold was 40 pages. Starting with Version 2.2, the threshold has been reduced to 8. With Version 2.3, even if at bind time DB2 did not choose prefetch, it may detect at run time that prefetch will be beneficial. The number of pages in the table space is obtained from the catalog statistics (see Section 4.4). As described there, the statistics are only updated when the RUNSTATS utility is run and may not accurately reflect the true size of the table space. If prefetch is considered, then DB2 starts by reading pages one at a time. Prior to Version 2.2, it did not initiate sequential prefetch until it reached its threshold (8, 16, or 32). It is not the next set of 8, 16, or 32 pages which are fetched, but rather the third set. For example, if 16 pages are to be read at a time, when the 16th page is read, DB2 will request the fetching of pages 33–48. While these are being read in, DB2 will continue reading pages 17–32 one at a time. When page 32 is read, a prefetch of pages 49–64 will be initiated. This process allows DB2 to continue while the large set of pages are being obtained. The set of pages will be ready in the buffer pool for DB2 when it is ready to use them. Because of this single page reading, when calculating the number of IOs that will be done, you had to add in that first 32 or 64.

Waiting until the 16th or 32nd page before initiating prefetch seems a little wasteful. At bind time, DB2 decided that it was worth doing the prefetch, so why not initiate it right away. In fact, that is what is now done (starting with 2.2). After the first IO, DB2 will initiate two prefetches. One will be for the second set of pages (e.g., pp. 33–64). However, at the same time, it will also do a prefetch of the remaining pages of the first set (e.g., pp. 2–32). It will continue reading them one at a time while waiting for the prefetch to be completed. With this new scheme almost all of the pages are prefetched and there are fewer synchronous IOs.

With prior releases, a medium-sized table may actually perform better with a pool of 999 buffers than with a pool of 1000, since the number of single page IOs prior to the start of prefetch is based on the size of the buffer pool. With a 1000 buffers, there will be 64 synchronous IOs. With 999, there will be 32. Let's look at two examples:

Table space A—600 pages

Buffer pool < 1000 pages

32 IOs for the first 32 pages. That leaves 568 more pages. At 16 pages per IO, it will take 35 more IOs. Total = 67 IOs.

Buffer pool >= 1000 pages

64 IOs for the first 64 pages. That leaves 536 more pages. At 32 pages per IO, it will take 17 more IOs. Total = 81 IOs.

However, with larger tables, the larger prefetch size will greatly reduce the number of IOs.

Table space B—10,000 pages

Buffer pool < 1000 pages

32 IOs for the first 32 pages. That leaves 9968 more pages. At 16 pages per IO it will take 623 more IOs. Total = 655 IOs.

Buffer pool >= 1000 pages

64 IOs for the first 64 pages. That leaves 9936 more pages. At 32 pages per IO, it will take 311 more IOs. Total = 375 IOs.

Now that prefetch is started after the first IO, there is no longer a penalty of more synchronous IOs with larger buffer pools. Those shops which have kept their buffer pools under 1000 for this reason should now change the pool size.

4.1.3 Nonmatching Index Scan

The SELECT in Figure 4.5 asks for records with discharge date between 5/20/89 and 5/24/89. There is no index that has DISDATE as the first column of the index, but index XHSDIS01 (Figure 4.6) is on PATID and DISDATE. DB2 might choose to read through this index, looking at every index entry for rows with DISDATE in the requested range. Then, for each one found, it will go read the data row. This is called an index scan. DB2 might choose this route because there are many fewer index pages than data pages. Each index page is also 4K bytes and each index entry is smaller than the data row (for this example). The

```
SELECT PATID,DISDATE,CONDITION
  FROM THSDIS0
  WHERE DISDATE BETWEEN '1989-05-20' AND '1989-05-24'
```
Figure 4.5. SELECT with Nonmatching Index Scan.

```
CREATE UNIQUE INDEX GELLER.XHSDIS01 ON GELLER.THSDIS0
(PATID,
 DISDATE,
 DISSEQ)
CLUSTER
USING STOGROUP STG1 PRIQTY 10000 SECQTY 200
SUBPAGES 2 CLOSE NO
```
Figure 4.6. Index for Discharge Table.

index scan may also use prefetch in reading the index pages. This would mean 16 or 32 pages per IO so it will take fewer IOs to read through the entire index space than through the entire table space. Figure 4.3 shows a nonmatching index scan [the lines labeled (c)]. Each index page at the lowest level is read.

I said that DB2 might choose this route. It might not. The factors that DB2 must weigh are how many rows it thinks will be selected, whether the index is clustered, and the fact that DB2 uses more CPU time to check index entries to evaluate a predicate than to do the evaluation with the data rows. The selected rows are likely to be scattered throughout the table space. If they are scattered, then each one may require an IO and the total number of IOs to read each data row plus the IOs for the index scan may be more than the number of IOs to do a table space scan. If the index is clustered, then at least the selected rows will be in the same order as the index. Let's look at a few sample cases. We will assume a buffer pool of at least 1000 (32 pages per prefetch IO) and Version 2.2 (prefetch started immediately).

100,000 rows in the table—200 bytes each
5000 pages in the table space
500 pages in the index space
Column YYY is in the search criteria and is a low-order column of an index
Selected range: 30–32

Case 1.

Number of values for YYY: 1000
Expected % of rows: 3 out of 1000 = 0.3%
On average 300 rows will be selected; DB2 assumes a uniform distribution of data values; it does not know if the data is skewed (i.e., 99% have value 31)

The index scan would take about (500/32 + 1) = 17 IOs
The table space scan would take about 5000/32 + 1 = 168 IOs

Since the column YYY is not the high-order column of the index, it is likely that the selected rows will be spread through the table space. With earlier releases of DB2, the 300 rows may require 300 IOs to retrieve. The index scan plus the data row access may, therefore, total 317 IOs, which is twice as many as the table space scan would require.

With Version 2.2, DB2 might use a new feature called list prefetch. It would sort the selected index entries by the row ID (RID) of the data row and then use prefetch to read the needed data pages. With this approach, the selected data rows would require at most 168 IOs (the same as for a table space scan). It would need this many if the pages were spread throughout the table space. If they were grouped closer together, then fewer prefetches would be needed. However, the 168 IOs for the list prefetch would be in addition to the 17 IOs for the index scan. It would still be cheaper to just do the table space scan.

Case 2.

Number of values for YYY: 10,000
Now, 30 rows are expected to be selected

The 30 rows will take up to 30 IOs. An index scan plus data access would then take only 47 IOs—much less than the table space scan. In this case, the index scan would be chosen.

Case 3.

Number of values for YYY: 10,000
Row size = 100
2500 pages in the table space

Now the table space is smaller. It would take 79 IOs for a table space scan. This is still more IOs than the index access would take. However, DB2 might choose to do the table space scan because of the extra CPU cost of processing the index. The total elapsed time might be greater for the index scan even though there are fewer IOs.

This example covers the basics of DB2's choice of access path. The optimizer analyzes the expected number of selected rows and the expected number of IOs necessary through each possible path. It is really the total time required that the optimizer calculates. This includes other factors such as whether a sort is necessary and total CPU processing; but this is a good basis for understanding the main criteria.

4.1.4 Matching Index Scan

Let's look at another variation of index scans. In the above example, column DISDATE was the second column of an index. DB2 had to read *all* index entries to find matching records. In Figure 4.7, the request is for names that have a last name of JONES. Index XHSPAT01 is on last name, first name. DB2 can use the index structure to quickly find the first entry with last name JONES. It can then scan the index entries until the last name is greater than JONES. This is called a matching index scan. The entire index does not have to be searched, only those with JONES as the last name. Obviously, the more columns that produce exact matches, the fewer records (and pages) have to be read and the request will take less time to process. This index access is shown in Figure 4.3 [the lines labeled

```
SELECT PATID,SEX,LASTNAME,FIRSTNAME
  FROM THSPAT0
    WHERE LASTNAME='JONES'
```
Figure 4.7. SELECT of a Set of Names.

(b)]. One page at each level is read to find the starting point of the index scan. Only some of the index pages need to be read at the lowest level.

For this type of access, it makes a big difference whether or not the index is clustered. If it is clustered, then the selected rows will be grouped on the same data pages and fewer IOs will be needed to retrieve them. I have made XHSPAT01 the clustering index for the patient table for this reason. It is much more common for transactions to need a set of patient rows with similar names (and in alphabetical order). It is less often that we would need the same function by patient ID.

4.1.5 Index Only Access

All of the above examples involved accessing the data rows, perhaps after first accessing the index. Many queries can be satisfied with only accessing the index. If all the columns mentioned (in the selection list, WHERE clause, ORDER BY clause, etc.) are in an index and DB2 uses that index, then there is no need for DB2 to access the data rows at all. This type of query will certainly be processed more quickly. Figure 4.8 contains such a query. The index XHSDIS01 is on PATID,DISDATE. A nonmatching index scan will find all of the entries within the discharge date range. The only column selected is PATID, which can be obtained directly from the index entries.

4.1.6 Indexes for Sorting

There are a number of SQL operations that require the data to be put into some order. ORDER BY and GROUP BY clauses do so. So does the DISTINCT function (to select distinct values), and UNION without the ALL parameter. Joins may require data to be sorted, depending on the method DB2 uses to do the join. DB2 may not have to actually perform a sort operation on the data to meet each of these needs. If there is an index in the required order and if DB2 uses this index to process the request, then a sort might not be necessary. The word "might" is important. DB2 may still find it necessary to do a sort and whether or not it does may change from one release of DB2 to the next. For example, SELECT DISTINCT (as in Figure 4.9) always resulted in a sort in DB2 Version 1, even if an index on that column was used to read the records. In DB2 Version 2, the optimizer was improved to recognize that in these cases, if the index is used (such as the patient ID index in this figure), there is no need to sort the rows to find distinct values. However, this is only true if it is a unique index and

```
SELECT PATID
   FROM THSPAT0
   WHERE DISDATE BETWEEN '1989-05-20' AND '1985-05-24'
```
Figure 4.8. SELECT with Index Only Access.

```
SELECT DISTINCT PATID

FROM THSPATO

WHERE PATID BETWEEN '200000000' AND '200000100'
```
Figure 4.9. DISTINCT May Not Require a Sort If an Index Is Used to Find the Rows.

the select list contains all of the columns of the index. If you ask for SELECT DISTINCT LASTNAME, a sort will still be used by DB2.

Whether or not an index in the sort order will be used will depend on the rest of the query and the catalog statistics. In a query such as in Figure 4.10, the WHERE clause uses the same columns as the ORDER BY and uses the equal predicate. In this example, DB2 is very likely to use the name index to satisfy the query. In Figure 4.11, the WHERE clause selects rows within a particular range of PATIDs. If DB2 determines that this will probably only return a few rows, it may choose to use the index on the PATID column and then sort the selected rows in name order. This will be much cheaper than going through the entire name index, reading the data row for each patient, and then checking the PATID field. Similarly, for the query in Figure 4.10, if the name index were not clustered, DB2 might choose to do a table space scan to find the names that start with J and then sort by LASTNAME.

Let's review what we have so far.

- DB2 analyzes the request to determine what it thinks is the cheapest path based on IO and CPU cost models.
- It uses the catalog statistics on the number of values (called cardinality) in the table and indexes, the number of pages in each table space and index space, the clustering of the indexes and sort criteria.

```
SELECT PATID,LASTNAME,FIRSTNAME

FROM THSPATO

WHERE LASTNAME LIKE 'JOHN%'

ORDER BY LASTNAME
```
Figure 4.10. Sort May Not Be Needed If Index Is Used.

```
SELECT PATID,LASTNAME,FIRSTNAME

FROM THSPATO

WHERE PATID BETWEEN '200000000' AND '200000009'

ORDER BY LASTNAME
```
Figure 4.11. Sort Will Be Needed If Index Is Not Used.

- The most important goal is the minimizing of IOs.
- For a request that processes at most a few rows, the quickest path would be through an index on the columns of the WHERE clause, provided that the search criteria match the structure of the index.
- If many rows are returned or must be looked at to fully satisfy the search criteria, then an unclustered index is not as useful as a clustered one. However, starting with Version 2.2, unclustered indexes are much more useful than previously.

Our goals as database designers and programmers is to have indexes on those columns that are frequently used as search or sort criteria, and to code the SQL statements to take advantage of those indexes. That last point is important. We cannot tell DB2 to use or not use an index, but the way the SQL statement is coded can make a difference in what DB2 chooses to do. We will look at some examples later.

Another important point is that it is not necessarily beneficial to create indexes on every possible combination of fields. Indexes are not free. They take up space and there is overhead when the table is updated, as each index also has to be maintained. Unclustered indexes were less likely to be used by DB2 unless the request was expected to return only a few rows. There is, therefore, a balancing act that the DBA must do. He must understand the application requirements to determine the best set of indexes to create. The DBA can then review his decisions by using EXPLAIN on the programs and queries that access the tables. If necessary, additional indexes can be created, and others changed or dropped. One of the very nice features of DB2 is that it is fairly easy to add or modify indexes at a later time.

4.1.7 One Index at a Time vs. Multiple Indexes

There is one possible access path that, prior to Version 2.2, DB2 did not do. That is to use more than one index at a time to access a table. It can do so now. For example, the query in Figure 4.12 is requesting patients who entered ward 0003 on January 12, 1987 and are still there. There is an index on PATID,LOCDATE and another on CURRENTFLAG,WARD. Assuming that there are only a handful of patients meeting both criteria, the quickest way to find them might be to use the second index to find those people currently in ward 0003 and use the first index to find people who entered a location on 1/12/87. These two lists could

```
SELECT PATID
  FROM THSLOC0
  WHERE WARD = '0003' AND LOCDATE = '1987-01-12' AND
        CURRENTFLAG = 'Y'
```

Figure 4.12. DB2 Can Now Use More Than One Index to Access a Table.

then be merged (the intersection of the two lists) to find the requested subset. DB2 will not do this with earlier versions. It will either do a table space scan or choose *one* of the indexes to resolve one of the predicates. It will then take the ones satisfying that predicate and read the data rows to resolve the other. For example, it may choose first to find patients in ward 0003, then read their data rows to see if the LOCDATE is 1/12/87. With Version 2.2, DB2 can make use of the two indexes, using the intersection of the row IDs to find the rows that meet both criteria.

The preceding example involved the ANDing of two predicates. The ORing of two predicates also prevented DB2 from using *any* index unless the predicates used the same column of the same index. For example, in Figure 4.13, we are asking for patients who have received service type 'A243' or received any service by clinician '642356'. There is an index on TYPE and a different index on CLINICIAN, but neither one could be used. If the first index alone is used, it will only find rows with TYPE='A243'. It will miss those rows that had CLINICIAN='642356' but not TYPE='A243'. This does not satisfy the query. Therefore, a table space scan was required.

It is important to remember that this does not hold true when the same column of the same index is used. In Figure 4.14, there is an OR of two predicates. Both of them use the first column of the index XHSSVC03. DB2 *can* use this index to satisfy the criteria.

With Version 2.2, the ORing of predicates can now be satisfied with indexes. DB2 can use the first index to find all rows with TYPE='A243' and the second index to find all rows with CLINICIAN='642356'. It will then merge the two lists, eliminating duplicates (i.e., index entries that point to the same data row).

The predicates:

(TYPE='A123' AND PATID='111222333') OR
(TYPE='B333' AND PATID='999888777')

would not have been handled with the use of a single index. DB2 did not rec-

```
SELECT PATID,CLINICIAN,TYPE
   FROM THSSVC0
   WHERE TYPE = 'A243' OR CLINCIAN = '642356'
```
Figure 4.13. DB2 Can Use Multiple Indexes When OR Is Used.

```
SELECT PATID,CLINICIAN,TYPE
   FROM THSSVC0
   WHERE TYPE = 'A243' OR TYPE = 'A350'
```
Figure 4.14. DB2 Could Always Use an Index for OR with the Same Column.

ognize that this situation can be done easily with one index. Now it will treat it as a multiple index access, using the same index twice.

DB2 will not always use multiple indexes to satisfy queries of these types. If too many rows match an OR criteria, then it might still be more efficient to do a table space scan. If too few satisfy one criteria of an AND, then it may be cheaper to read all of those data rows to check the other criteria than it would be to search the second index. With Version 2.2, the thresholds are (approximately):

> AND—if fewer than 32 rows from one of the indexes are expected to satisfy the criteria, then multiple index access will not be used.
> OR—if more than 25% of the rows of any of the indexes will qualify, then multiple indexes will not be used.

There is a very good chance that these specific criteria will change with future releases. But these numbers give you a guideline to the basic concept.

4.1.8 Summary of One Table Access Paths for a SELECT

- Matching Index Access—this is the fastest way to get specific rows. The DBA and application designer must work together to identify the columns most often used for selection and ordering. Indexes should be created on these columns.
- Table space scan—when accessing a single table in batch or an ad hoc query, table space scans are *not* too costly. Sequential prefetch can provide very efficient processing of the entire table. However, while a 3-second scan is adequate for an occasional query, it is not acceptable for high volume transactions.
- Multiple indexes—starting with Version 2.2, a single query may use more than one index to resolve the predicates. This can provide a tremendous improvement for certain queries.
- Index only access—as a general rule, a SELECT should only list the columns that are needed. This reduces the CPU costs for the query. If the columns in the select list are all in an index which is used for the access, then DB2 does not need to read the data rows at all. This reduces costs even further.

4.1.9 Insert Processing

So far, we have looked at how DB2 goes about selecting rows. Now we will look at how it processes the other DML statements. An INSERT statement puts data into a table. The simple INSERT (i.e., one that does not have a subselect) stores one row at a time. A data row is stored in a table space page, and index entries are added to each index defined on the table.

When inserting a row, DB2 will first try to place it in clustering index order. That is, it will put the row on the same page as rows with similar key values. If there is no room on that page, the search algorithm depends on whether the table is in a segmented table space or not.

For a nonsegmented table space, DB2 will next try to insert the row on a nearby page. Nearby means within 16 pages. First, it will search forward 16 pages and then it will search the preceeding 16 pages. DB2 does not have to actually read all of these pages to see if there is room. DB2 maintains a space map for each table space. This space map will tell DB2 whether or not there is room on each page for a new row. If a page with room is found, the data row will go on that page.

If no room is found on a nearby page, then the space map is searched for any page with space, starting from the beginning of the table space. If there is no room in any page in the table space, then the row will get inserted at the end. If there are no unused pages at the end of the current extent, then a new secondary extent will be obtained. Actually, the secondary extents are obtained prior to when they are first needed so that DB2 and the application do not have to wait for the space to be allocated.

For segmented table spaces, DB2 does less searching. When there is no room on the page with similar clustering index keys, the other pages of the same segment are searched for room (a segment is a set of pages). If there isn't any, then the last segment of the table space is checked. If this, too, is full, then a new segment is created for the table.

Are these search algorithms of concern? The programmer does not have to worry too much about it. Other than checking the space map pages, the only IO is for the page that the row will end up on. Therefore, inserting the data row is fairly efficient. The DBA, though, does have to be aware of the frequency of inserts that will occur. As the amount of available space declines, the data rows will often not be inserted in clustering order. The DBA must specify a free space amount based on this frequency. For an active table, he should also plan to reorg the table space on a frequent basis so as to reestablish free space.

The clustering index is also updated. An entry for the new row is put in. Index entries are also stored in pages. If there is room on the index page for another entry, it will go there. If not, room has to be made. After all, the index entries must be kept in order, DB2 cannot just stick the entry at the end of the index. To make room, DB2 will take an empty page and move some of the index entries from the full page to the empty one. Where does this empty page come from? There are two possibilities. If the FREEPAGE parameter on the CREATE INDEX statement was greater than zero, then after every few pages, an empty page was left when the index was created. If there is no empty page available nearby, then a page will be taken from the end of the index.

The process of splitting a page takes time. For tables that will have a lot of insert activity, it is therefore a good idea to have free space available. When index pages have to be acquired from the end of the index, the index becomes disorganized. Processing of indexes is much quicker if all of the entries are in physical order. Therefore, it is useful to have free pages for indexes with a lot of insertions.

Indexes are actually tree structures. There are several index levels. The bottom level is the one with the actual index entries. The pages at this level are called leaf pages. The higher index levels contain entries that tell DB2 which set of index values can be found on each leaf page (i.e., they contain the highest value found on each leaf page). This enables efficient searching of the index. At the top of the tree is the highest level. This contains one page called the root page. The index structure is illustrated in Figure 4.15. When new index entries are added, the higher level pages may also need updating. This will occur if the leaf page contains a new highest key value. Whenever a new leaf page is needed (i.e., when a split is necessary), then a new entry must be put into the higher level index page. Eventually, these pages may also need splitting. When the root page is full and requires splitting to add a new entry, an additional index level is created.

Not only does it take time to split a page, but it also reduces concurrency. Whenever an index page is updated, the subpage receives an 'X' (exclusive) lock—no other task can access any of the entries on the subpage until a commit point is reached. If a page is split, then the whole page is locked and the higher level index page is updated to record the information about the new page. This higher level page, therefore, receives an 'X' lock. Now, all of the index entries on any of the pages controlled by this one are unavailable to other tasks until the commit.

Tables can have many indexes. Whenever a row is inserted, every index requires a new entry to point to the new row. The process of updating the clustering index is then repeated for every other index on the table. How does DB2 find the right spot in each index? Essentially, it uses a matching index lookup to get to the right position. When a row is inserted, there are values for every column. Some columns may be given the default value or NULLs, but as far as indexes are concerned, these are values, too. Therefore, the process of finding the right spot is fairly efficient.

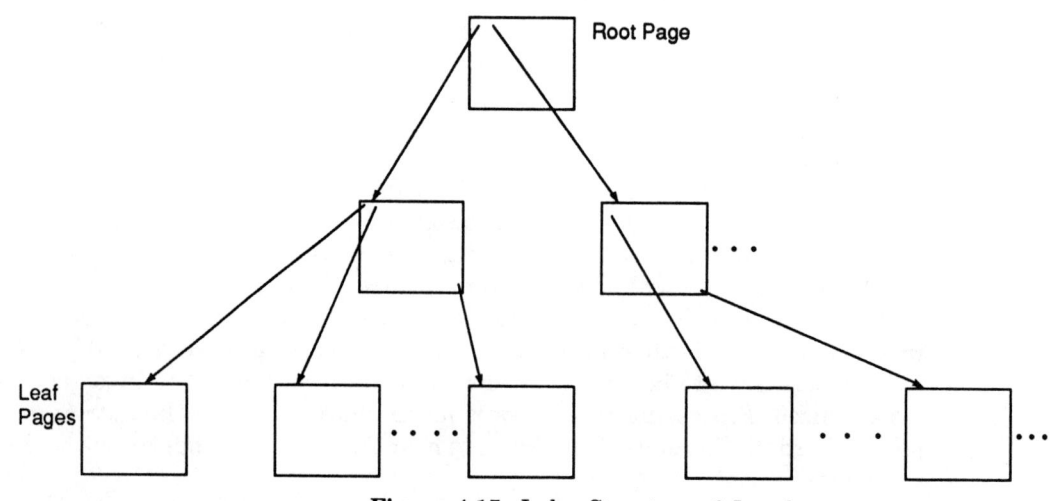

Figure 4.15. Index Structure—3 Levels.

ACCESS PATHS—THE BASICS OF PERFORMANCE

While DB2 is going about inserting index entries, there is one problem it could run into. If any of the indexes are defined as being UNIQUE, duplicate values are not allowed. If *any* unique index already has an entry matching the columns of the new row, then the INSERT statement is rejected. None of the index entries or the data row are kept and an SQLCODE of −803 is returned.

To summarize the insert processing, we can give the following guidelines:

- The insertion of a row with one or two indexes is fairly efficient.
- Each index must be updated. The more indexes a table has, the longer it takes to insert a row. There is a greater chance of contention problems for tables with high insert volumes.
- It takes more time to add an entry when a page split is required than when there is enough room on the index page. If new pages are needed from the end of the index dataset, then the index becomes disorganized. Therefore, if much insert activity is anticipated, free space and free pages should be defined, and reorganization of the index may be needed on a regular basis (see Section 7.3). Free space in the table space is also desirable when there is much insert activity.

4.1.10 Update Processing

In some ways, an UPDATE can be thought of as a combination of SELECT and INSERT. You must identify which rows you want to update (with a WHERE clause) and which columns to give new values. The UPDATE in Figure 4.16 will change any row that has PATID = '123456789' and SERVDATE = 5/23/90. Just as in a SELECT, there may be no rows meeting the criteria, one row, or a set of rows. The first step is for DB2 to find the rows. It will do this the same way it processes a SELECT (with one exception described below). Therefore, there is nothing new to describe here. Any of the access paths we have discussed might be used—table space scans, matching index scans, or nonmatching index scans.

Once the row(s) have been found, the columns are changed. In Figure 4.16, the TYPE column is set to A300 and the CLINCIAN column is set to 8887776 for each row. In most cases, the data is changed in place. There is no need to move the row to a different location. One exception is the handling of varying length fields. If the updated value is longer than the original value, the row itself will require more space. If there is room on the page, the other rows on the page will be moved over to make room. If there is not enough room, then the row is stored on a different page that does have room. In the spot where the row had been,

```
UPDATE THSSVC0
   SET TYPE = 'A300',
       CLINICIAN = '8887776'
   WHERE PATID = '123456789' AND SERVDATE = '1990-05-23'
```
Figure 4.16. An UPDATE Statement.

DB2 will leave a header with a pointer to the new location of the row. Any subsequent access to the row will require two IOs, one to the original page and then another to the actual row. The other exception happens after a new column has been added to the table with the ALTER TABLE statement. The ALTER does not change any existing rows. When a row is updated and data is filled in to the new column, the row is again lengthened and room must be found for it.

Updating a row may also require some indexes to be updated. For each column that is changed, any index that has that column will be affected. The old entry must be deleted and a new entry put into the index. The index may have other columns besides those being updated. Once DB2 has retrieved the data row, it has all the other columns available and so it can find the index entries with a matching lookup. The updating of the indexes has the same performance implications as for inserting of new rows. Uniqueness must be checked where appropriate. However, instead of all indexes being updated, only those with the changed columns are affected.

We mentioned that there were some differences in finding the qualifying rows in an UPDATE vs. a SELECT. For a SELECT, any index might be used to find the rows. Prior to Version 2.2, for an UPDATE, some indexes would not be used if the indexed columns are being updated. It will depend on the type of update and the types of predicates. For example, in Figure 4.17, we are setting EDUCATION to EDUCATION + 2 for any row with EDUCATION > 15. If there is an index on EDUCATION, DB2 would not have used it to find the rows even though this would be the fastest way. Since we are adding 2 to each occurrence of EDUCATION, then if DB2 used the index on this column, it would encounter the same row over and over. Each time it is updated, the old entry is deleted and a new entry is stored. The new entry will be further down the index as it has a higher value. To avoid this problem, DB2 would only use an index that has the updated columns, if there is no chance of the row being encountered again. For example, if we:

SET ADMDATE = ADMDATE + 1 DAY
WHERE ADMDATE = '1990-09-15'

then once an index entry has been changed to '1990-09-16' it would no longer satisfy the search criteria. However, if we had:

SET ADMSEQ = ADMSEQ + 1
WHERE ADMDATE = '1990-09-15'

```
UPDATE THSCHRO
  SET EDUCATION = EDUCATION + 2
  WHERE EDUCATION > 15
```

Figure 4.17. This UPDATE Could Not Use an Index on EDUCATION Prior to Version 2.2

then if an entry with ADMSEQ = 1 were changed to 2, the new entry would again satisfy the criteria and be incremented again.

This type of processing has been improved with Version 2.2. As described below in Section 4.3, when processing an index, DB2 can now gather a list of row IDs (RIDs) selected from the index before processing the data rows. When used with an UPDATE of an indexed column, DB2 can build this list of rows to be updated. Now, each row will only get updated once, as all qualifying rows will be selected from the index before any of the updating takes place.

4.1.11 Delete Processing

DELETE statements also can process sets of rows at a time. DB2 will use the same types of access paths to find the rows as it does with SELECTs and UPDATEs. Once each row is found, it is deleted from the table space. This simply involves marking the space as being unused and available. Then, each index must also be updated. With an UPDATE statement, only some of the indexes may be affected, but with a DELETE, they all are. The entries for each deleted row must also be deleted. Finding the index entries is generally quick enough. Once again, all the fields are available to DB2 to do a matching lookup. Finding the entry is fast for unique indexes and for nonunique indexes if there are only a few duplicates of the value being searched. If there are many duplicates (e.g., an index with many blank or NULL entries), then these entries must be searched sequentially to find the one with the matching RID. This could potentially take a long time. Removing an index entry is generally quicker than adding an entry as there are no index page splits necessary. However, it does take longer to delete a row from a table with 10 indexes than from a table with only two indexes.

4.1.12 GROUP BY

Column functions such as SUM, COUNT, MAX, MIN, and AVG can be applied to a table to produce a single result. Alternatively, you can apply these functions to several subsets of a table by using the GROUP BY clause. In Figure 4.18, we are asking for the number of people who are currently in each ward. To produce the result, DB2 must group the location rows by ward and then apply the function. To do the grouping, the rows must be in order of the GROUP BY columns. If there is an index on these columns, then DB2 can use the index to access the rows in order, and do the grouping as it goes along. If there is no index, then the rows must be sorted first.

Prior to Version 2.2, even if a sort was not needed, any qualifying rows were

```
SELECT COUNT(*) FROM THSLOCO
    WHERE CURRENTFLAG = 'Y'
    GROUP BY WARD
```

Figure 4.18 GROUP BY Clause.

```
SELECT COUNT(*) FROM THSLOC0
  WHERE CURRENTFLAG = 'Y'
  GROUP BY WARD HAVING MAX(LOCDATE) <= '1988-12-31'
```
Figure 4.19. HAVING Clause.

first extracted and placed into a work table. Then a pass was made over the work table to apply the function. With Version 2.2, the function can be applied as the rows are extracted. Even with a sort, the function can be applied on the sorted rows. They do not necessarily have to be written to the work file.

Selection criteria can also be placed on the groups. This is done with a HAVING clause. HAVING clauses are like WHERE clauses except that they apply to the group, not to individual rows. In Figure 4.19, we only want wards where everyone has been there since at least 1988. The selection criteria in this case does not require additional access.

4.2 ACCESS PATHS TO MULTIPLE TABLES—JOINS AND SUBQUERIES

So far, we have looked at basic SQL statements that access a single table. Joins and subqueries involve access to two or more tables. Actually, they may involve only one table that is accessed two or more times. There are several methods by which DB2 will join two tables, but the basic access paths to each one are the same as for the access in a simple SELECT from one table. The choices are table space scans, index access, or nonmatching index scans. Sorts may or may not be needed to do the join (in addition to sorting needed for an ORDER BY).

Joins and subqueries can often be used interchangably to access the same set of data. Usually, however, joins are more efficient. Figure 4.20 has a join of data from the patient and admission tables. Figure 4.21 has the results for a small set of data in each. Let's first review what join criteria are and then we will look more closely at these examples.

4.2.1 Join Criteria

When you join two tables, you must tell DB2 how to match up the rows. This is done in the WHERE clause with predicates that involve columns from both tables. In addition to join criteria, the WHERE clause can, of course, have other

```
SELECT PAT.PATID,LASTNAME,ADMDATE
  FROM THSPAT0 PAT, THSADM0 ADM
  WHERE PAT.PATID = ADM.PATID
```
Figure 4.20. A Join Between Patient and Admission Data.

predicates that restrict the number of rows selected. In Figure 4.20, we are asking DB2 to match rows with identical patient ID numbers. One patient row may match up with several admission rows. This is a simple example. The predicate can have other operators, too. A join where the join criteria requires that a column from one table be equal to a column of the other table is sometimes referred to as an equijoin.

In Figure 4.22, we are matching locations with the admissions they occurred during. The patient IDs must be equal and the location date must be greater than or equal to the admission date and less than or equal to the discharge date. In this case, one admission row may match up with several location rows. Since

```
Patient table         Admit table

ID    Name            ID    Admit date

 2    JONES            2    1983-02-23

 3    SMITH            2    1985-11-12

 7    ABLE             3    1981-05-19

10    BAKER            7    1979-02-06

                       7    1982-10-30

                      10    1989-08-04


Results

 2    JONES           1983-02-23

 2    JONES           1985-11-12

 3    SMITH           1981-05-19

 7    ABLE            1979-02-06

 7    ABLE            1982-10-30

10    BAKER           1989-08-04
```

Figure 4.21. The results of a Join.


```
SELECT ADM.PATID,ADMDATE,LOCDATE,WARD
  FROM THSADM0 ADM, THSLOC0 LOC
  WHERE ADM.PATID = LOC.PATID AND
        LOCDATE >= ADMDATE AND LOCDATE <= DISDATE
```
Figure 4.22. Joins Can Match Several Rows of Each Table.

the join criteria allow rows from the location table to fall within a range of admission values, this type of join is called a non-equijoin.

It is also possible for several rows of each table to match several rows of the other. This would happen if the columns used as the join criteria were not unique in either table. In Figure 4.22, if we only had the predicate:

HSADM.PATID = HSLOC.PATID

then for each patient, we would join all of his locations to each of his admissions, not just the one for the correct time period.

On the other hand, if in Figure 4.22 we *left out* the predicate

HSADM.PATID = HSLOC.PATID

then every location record would match every admission whose time period it fell within, regardless of patient. I give this example, not as a practical request, but as an example of a common coding error and the results that entail.

If no join criteria are given, then every row of the first table will match every row of the second table! This is called a cartesian product.

As I said, this is a common error, especially when you are joining three or more tables. For example, in Figure 4.23, we are joining patients with their admissions, but also want data from the characteristics and address tables. Other criteria limit the request to admissions in 1989 (there are 3000) and people who live in New York (80% of the patients). I remembered to ask for PAT.PATID = ADM.PATID and for PAT.PATID = CHR.PATID, but I forgot to give any criteria to combine the address rows. Therefore, for each selected patient admission, DB2 will join the data with every single New York address row in the table, regardless of patient. If there are 100,000 patients and 150,000 admissions, we really wanted a result with at most 3000 rows—one per 1989 admission. Instead, we will get 3000 admissions matched with 80,000 addresses each. This gives us a total of 240,000,000 (240 million) rows! Not only is this not what we wanted, but the query may run for a while!

```
SELECT PAT.PATID,LASTNAME,ADMDATE,CITY,STATE,EDUCATION
  FROM THSPATO PAT, THSADMO ADM, THSCHRO CHR, THSADDO ADD
  WHERE ADMDATE BETWEEN '1989-01-01' AND '1989-12-31' AND
        CITY = 'NEW YORK CITY' AND
        PAT.PATID = ADM.PATID AND
        PAT.PATID = CHR.PATID
```
Figure 4.23. Forgetting Some of the Join Criteria Can Be Disastrous.

4.2.2 Join Methods

There are two basic join methods that DB2 has used:

- Nested loop
- Merge scan

With Version 2.3, there is a new join method. This is a hybrid join which combines some of the characteristics of the other two methods.

DB2 will decide on which one to use based on the availability of suitable indexes, the catalog statistics, and the selection and join criteria. If you are joining three or more tables, DB2 will first join two of them, then join the intermediate results with a third table, and so on.

4.2.2.1 Nested Loop Join

The nested loop join involves one table being chosen (by DB2) as the outer table and the other as the inner table. The outer table is accessed to find all rows that meet the nonjoin criteria. This access may be a table space scan or may use an index. For each row selected, the inner table will be accessed using the join criteria to find matches. This access may also be via an index or a scan of the whole table space. In the join of Figure 4.20, the patient table may be chosen as the outer table and will be accessed with a table space scan as we have not limited which patients are to be selected. The admissions will be the inner table. For each patient row, the XHSADM01 index will be used to find the admissions for that patient.

As with all access path decisions, DB2 will calculate an estimated cost of each possible path. It must choose what it calculates to be the cheapest alternative between nested loop and merge scan, and now a third method, with each of the two tables as the outer table. If nested loop is chosen, the choice of outer and inner tables will be guided by two main factors. It is preferable that there be selection criteria on the outer table to reduce the number of selected rows from this table since for each one selected, the inner table must be scanned. If the selected outer rows can be found with an index, even better. It is also desirable for the inner table to be accessed via an index to satisfy the join criteria, assuming that only a few will match up with each outer row. In Figure 4.24, we want the admission and discharge data for patient '123456789'. This is a good candi-

```
SELECT *
  FROM THSADMO ADM, THSDISO DIS
  WHERE ADM.PATID = '123456789' AND
        ADM.PATID = DIS.PATID AND
        ADM.DISDATE = DIS.DISDATE
```

Figure 4.24. When Indexes Are Available, Nested Loop Join May Be Used.

date for a nested loop join with the HSADM table as the outer table. The XHSADM01 index can quickly find rows for patient '123456789'. Only for these will DB2 have to access the discharge table. It can use the discharge date from the HSADM row along with the PATID value of '123456789' to quickly access the HSDIS table through the XHSDIS01 index.

Contrast this with the join of Figure 4.20. Since all patients are requested, the entire HSPAT table will have to be scanned regardless of which table is the outer table. This will be more costly.

4.2.2.2 Merge Scan Join

The merge scan join takes both tables, sorts them into the order of the join columns (unless an index in that order is available), and then merges them. Actually, until Version 2.3, only one of the join columns was used to order the two tables. With the new version, all of the join columns will be used.

Nonjoin criteria are applied before the sort and it is intermediate result tables that are merged. Prior to Version 2.3, only one index could be used to satisfy the predicates of the inner table. With 2.3, multiple index access can be used. Again, an outer and an inner table are chosen. A row from the outer table is read, then rows from the inner table are read. If the join columns match, a row is selected and the next row from the inner table is read. This continues until an inner row with a higher value on the join columns is encountered. The next row of the outer table is then read. If it has the same value in the join columns as the previous row from the outer table, DB2 will back up in the inner table to the beginning of the rows with this value. This is a case of several rows of each table matching. If the outer row has a higher value, then the next row is read from the inner table. The merge scan join is illustrated in Figures 4.25, 4.26, and 4.27.

If there are no efficient access paths to the inner table, then a merge scan join may be better than a nested loop join. Figure 4.26 is an example of this situation. The two tables are being joined on the phone (calling number) column. Let's say there are 10,000 calls and 1000 employees, and 100 rows of each meet the nonjoin search criteria. There are no indexes on any of the columns in the WHERE clause. Access to either table will have to be with a table space scan. If nested loop were used, then for each row selected from the outer table the entire inner table would have to be scanned. This is costly (100 table space scans). With merge scan, each table is scanned only once. The 100 rows from each will be put into a work table and sorted. They will then be merged. This is much faster.

The new hybrid join will be useful where the join columns of the inner table are in an unclustered index. The outer table will be scanned once in join column order (either through an index or after sorting). The inner table's index will be scanned. Only the row IDs (RIDs) will be joined with the outer table rows. These partial rows will then be sorted into RID order. List prefetch will then be used to access the data rows of the inner table, to pick up the rest of the data that is needed. This method provides an efficient access path through an unclustered index of the inner table. With this method, the inner table rows are only accessed once, even if the outer table has duplicate rows.

ACCESS PATHS—THE BASICS OF PERFORMANCE   **183**

```
CREATE TABLE TELEPHONE
 (CALLEDNUM  CHAR(10),
  CALLDATE   DATE,
  CALLINGNUM CHAR(10),
  COST       FIXED DEC(7,2),
  DURATION   FIXED DECIMAL(3));

CREATE TABLE EMP
 (EMPID   CHAR(7),
  NAME    CHAR(25),
  PHONE   CHAR(10),
  DEPT    CHAR(2))
```

Figure 4.25. Telephone and Employee Tables to Be Joined.

```
SELECT EMPNAME, CALLDATE, CALLEDNUM
  FROM EMP, TELEPHONE
  WHERE DURATION > 60 AND DEPT = '23' AND
        PHONE = CALLINGNUM
```
Figure 4.26. Joining on Nonindexed Columns.

Intermediate tables created with 1 tablespace scan of each table

```
Telephone rows
with DURATION>60      EMP rows with DEPT='23'
CALLINGNUM                   PHONE
   1234  ←──────────────────→ 1234
   1359  ←──────────────────→ 1359
   1359  ←──────────────────→ 1359
   6587                       1499
```

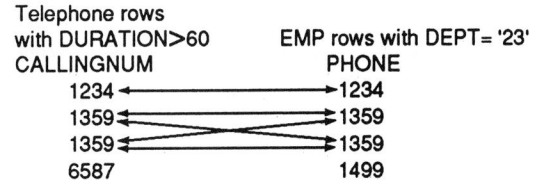

Figure 4.27. A Merge Scan Join Is Used.

4.2.2.3 Joining Three or More Tables

When three or more tables are joined, DB2 may have to create an intermediate results table after joining the first two. This results table will then be joined with the third table. However, it is not always necessary to create an intermediate table first. If a nested loop join is used with indexes on the join columns, DB2 will do the three-way join, one row at a time. For example, in Figure 4.28,

```
SELECT *
FROM THSPAT0 PAT, THSCHR0 CHR, THSADM0 ADM
WHERE PAT.PATID = CHR.PATID AND
      PAT.PATID = ADM.PATID
```

Figure 4.28. Joining Three Tables Does Not Require an Intermediate Table to Be Created.

we are joining patients with their characteristics and admissions. DB2 will do a nested loop join perhaps with the patient table as the outer table. Either of the other two may be the second table.

DB2 will do a table space scan through the patient table. As it reads each patient row, it will get the corresponding characteristics row by doing a direct index lookup using index XHSCHR01 (which has PATID as the high-order column). Then it will read the corresponding admission rows using the XHSADM01 index (which also starts with PATID). For each one, it will return a resulting joined row. DB2 will then continue with the next patient.

4.2.2.4 Summary of Join Methods

- Regardless of join method, it is critical that the programmer specify the correct join criteria. Otherwise, the tables will not be matched up correctly.
- You get the most efficient join access if there are indexes on the join criteria columns.
- If there are such indexes, and especially if an equijoin is requested, DB2 will probably use a nested loop join.
- If there are no such indexes, a merge scan join will probably be a better choice for an equijoin.

4.2.3 Subqueries

The selection criteria for a column may depend on the data in another table or in other rows of the same table. This can be done with a subquery. A subquery can appear in either a WHERE clause or a HAVING clause. To find the youngest patients, we ask for the patients whose birthdate is equal to the highest birthdate in the table (Figure 4.29). Note that you cannot just say:

WHERE BIRTHDATE = MAX(BIRTHDATE)

The columns in the WHERE clause refer to the value of that column in each row, one row at a time. MAX is a column function. MAX(BIRTHDATE), therefore, refers to the full set of values of the BIRTHDATE column and it cannot appear in that form in the WHERE clause.

```
SELECT PATID,LASTNAME,FIRSTNAME
  FROM THSPAT0
  WHERE BIRTHDATE =
    (SELECT MAX(BIRTHDATE) FROM THSPAT0)
```
Figure 4.29. Subquery to Find the Youngest Patient.

4.2.3.1 Types of Subqueries

There are four different forms of subqueries, and each of these can be either correlated or noncorrelated. The four kinds differ in the number of values returned by the subquery, and the type of comparison used. The first three types all involve comparing a single column of the outer table to the results of the subquery. The result must be a single column or expression.

You can get the names of patients who have been in WARD 0100 (Figures 4.30 and 4.31). The first of these is called a noncorrelated subquery; the second is a correlated subquery. The difference is that in the second one we are tying together (correlating) a row of the inner query with a specific row of the outer query. Both of these queries could also be done with a join of the two tables (Figure 4.32). The subquery types are:

1. Any of the relational operators are used (=, <, >, etc.). A single value is returned by the subquery. Figure 4.29 is an example of this type. The subquery finds the maximum birthdate in the patient ta-

```
SELECT PATID,LASTNAME,FIRSTNAME
  FROM THSPAT0
  WHERE PATID IN
    (SELECT PATID FROM THSLOC0
       WHERE WARD = '0100')
```
Figure 4.30. Noncorrelated Subquery.

```
SELECT PATID,LASTNAME,FIRSTNAME
  FROM THSPAT0 PAT
  WHERE PATID IN
    (SELECT PATID FROM THSLOC0 LOC
       WHERE WARD = '0100' AND
          PAT.PATID = LOC.PATID)
```
Figure 4.31. Correlated Subquery.

```
SELECT PATID,LASTNAME,FIRSTNAME
  FROM THSPAT0 PAT, THSLOC0 LOC
  WHERE PAT.PATID = LOC.PATID AND
      WARD = '0100'
```

Figure 4.32. A Join Can Often Be Used Instead of a Subquery.

ble. Then, each patient row (which meets any other search criteria) is looked at to see if BIRTHDATE is equal to this value.

2. The keywords ALL, ANY, or SOME are used with any of the relational operators. Any number of rows may be returned by the subquery, but only one column. If ALL is used, then for each row of the outer table, the comparison column is checked to see how it compares to all of the subquery rows. ANY or SOME require a match on at least one row. In Figure 4.33, we have a correlated subquery to find any active patients who were admitted when they were less than 20 years old (BIRTHDATE + 20 YEARS > ADMDATE). If any of the admissions for each patient satisfy the comparision, then the patient is selected.
3. The keyword IN is used (Figure 4.30). The subquery returns a set of values. For each row of the outer table, if the column's value is in the returned set, the row is selected. You can also use NOT IN to find rows that do not have a match with the subquery.
4. EXISTS (or NOT EXISTS) (Figure 4.34). Each of the other types of subquery involved comparison with a single column. With the EXISTS keyword, no specific data is returned by the subquery. Instead, a row from the outer table is selected if there is a row in the table of the subselect with a given set of criteria. EXISTS is generally more meaningful with a correlated subquery. This figure is equivalent to the one in 4.31. We want patients who have been in WARD 0100. The advantage of EXISTS is that the comparison is not dependent on a single column. IN could be used in this example because PATID

```
SELECT PATID,LASTNAME,FIRSTNAME,BIRTHDATE
  FROM THSPAT0 PAT
  WHERE ACTIVEFLAG = 'Y' AND
      BIRTHDATE + 20 YEARS > ANY
    (SELECT ADMDATE FROM THSADM0 ADM
        WHERE PAT.PATID = ADM.PATID)
```

Figure 4.33. Subquery with ANY.

```
SELECT PATID,LASTNAME,FIRSTNAME
  FROM THSPAT0 PAT
  WHERE EXISTS
      (SELECT PATID FROM THSLOC0 LOC
              WHERE WARD = '0100' AND
                    PAT.PATID = LOC.PATID)
```
Figure 4.34. Subquery with EXISTS.

is a unique single column field. If the primary keys of these tables consisted of several columns, EXISTS would be the only alternative. Since no data is actually returned, you can use anything for the column list—*, a set of columns, or a single constant.

4.2.3.2 Subquery Access Paths

The access path for a subquery depends on several things:

- Correlated or noncorrelated
- The type of subquery
- The presence of indexes on the comparison column
- Any other search criteria

In a join, DB2 can choose any of the join methods, with either table as the outer table. With subqueries, there is less flexibility. The performance of a particular query may be greatly affected by the way you code it. Subqueries are less often used to find specific rows based on a key value. They usually involve searching one or more tables to find rows with related values. With additional search criteria to limit the number of rows looked at, performance can be good. However, if you are searching all rows of both tables, without use of indexes, performance can be very bad.

The method for evaluating the query is dependent on whether it is correlated or not. For a noncorrelated query, the subselect is always evaluated first. For the qualifying rows, the values returned are sorted, duplicates eliminated, and the values are placed in an intermediate results table. Then, the outer SELECT is evaluated. Any row that meets the other search criteria is compared against this intermediate table to find a match. The method of comparison (and the performance) depend on the type of subquery.

For a correlated subquery, the outer table is evaluated first. For each qualifying row, the subquery is evaluated. The row from the outer table is then compared to the subquery result to determine if it will be selected. Generally, this means that the subquery will be evaluated many times. Now let's look at the specific operation of the different types of subquery.

4.2.3.3 Noncorrelated Subqueries

The first type of subquery returns a single value. The subquery is evaluated by whatever access path is appropriate. In Figure 4.29, MAX(BIRTHDATE) is found by a table space scan of the patient table. The evaluation of the outer SELECT will depend on whether or not there is an index on the comparison column. BIRTHDATE does not have an index, so a table space scan will be used. If there was an index on BIRTHDATE, it could be used, because we are comparing it to a specific value.

When ALL or ANY are used, a set of values are returned by the subquery. For each outer table row, this set must be scanned. With ALL, the comparison must hold true for all values in the set. For ANY or SOME, as soon as one match is found, the outer row is selected. This process was always used prior to Version 2.2. Now, in some cases, the process can be speeded up. If a > or < operator is used, then the comparison is equivalent to MAX or MIN. For example, > ALL is equal to > MAX; > ANY is equal to > MIN. DB2 will recognize this and will throw away all values except for the highest or lowest. The comparison will, therefore, be much quicker.

The IN operator provides a flexible means of finding matching rows. = can only be used if a single value is going to be returned. In Figure 4.30, we asked for patients in a particular ward. Since there may be more than one, IN allows the set of PATIDs to be returned. The outer table can now be searched to find patients with IDs in this set. However, for the IN operator, DB2 will *not use an index* on PATID in the patient table to find the matching patients. It will always do a table space scan of the patient table. For each one, it will scan the intermediate result table. If the subquery returns thousands of rows, then there will be an awful lot of scanning. Performance of this type of subquery can be very, very bad when the subquery returns many rows. If there is an equivalent correlated subquery or join, they should be used instead.

4.2.3.4 Correlated Subqueries

For a correlated subquery, the subquery is evaluated for each outer row. If there is an index on the correlation columns of the inner table, then performance can be fairly good. If both tables are clustered on these columns, then performance will be fine. However, if there are no indexes on the columns and the inner table is large, then performance can be very bad. It could involve a table space scan of the inner table for every row of the outer table (which meets the other search criteria).

Some improvement has been made in Version 2.2 for the processing of correlated queries. If the subquery returns one value, it is saved in a work area. For the next outer row, if the correlation columns have the same values as the previous row, DB2 does not have to reevaluate the subquery. It already has the value. In Figure 4.35, we are selecting services that patients have received during their most recent admission (SERVDATE > = MAX(ADMDATE)). The outer table requires either a table space scan or a nonmatching index scan since we

```
SELECT PATID,SERVDATE,TYPE,CLINICIAN
  FROM THSSVC0 SVC
  WHERE SERVDATE >=
    (SELECT MAX(ADMDATE) FROM THSADM0 ADM
          WHERE SVC.PATID = ADM.PATID)
```

Figure 4.35. Correlated Subquery May Not Need Reevaluation for Every Row.

want to examine all services. Finding the maximum admission date for each patient can be done with a matching index lookup of THSADM0. However, each patient may have a large number of services. Prior to Version 2.2, the admission lookup would be repeated for each service. Now, the lookup will only be done once per patient.

4.2.3.5 Joins vs. Subqueries

Subqueries with IN and with EXISTS are often equivalent to a join. Generally, the join will perform better. With a join, DB2 will choose either table as the outer table and will choose either of the join methods based on the cost estimates of the possible access paths. When there are no indexes on the join columns, the merge scan join can provide reasonably good performance. With a subquery, there is less flexibility in the ways DB2 will access the data, and the most efficient path may not be an available choice. Therefore, when possible, use a join.

Joins and subqueries do not necessarily produce the same results. If a nonunique column is used as the join criteria, then several rows of each table may match several rows of the other. With a subquery, each row from the outer table will be selected only once. You could use the DISTINCT option on the join to eliminate duplicates. Figure 4.36 has an equivalent join and subquery.

There are also many situations where a subquery can be used for something that cannot be done with a join. Figure 4.29 is an example of such a query. A major class of query that requires a subquery is finding rows in one table that do *not* match any row in a second table. This is sometimes called an outer join. However, it cannot be done with a join of two tables. In Figure 4.37, we want to find active patients who have not had services in 1990. Joins can only find patients with rows in both tables. The NOT EXISTS predicate is used to find the nonmatches. Again, if there are indexes, use a correlated subquery.

4.2.3.6 Summary for Subqueries

- Subqueries can be correlated or noncorrelated.
- Subqueries return either a single value or a set of values for comparison with one column. The EXISTS keyword is used when the comparison is dependent on the existence of matching rows, rather than on a single column.

```
SELECT LOCDATE,PATID
  FROM THSLOC0
  WHERE PATID IN
    (SELECT PATID FROM THSADM0
       WHERE ADMDATE BETWEEN '1986-01-01' AND '1986-01-31')
```
(a) the subquery

```
SELECT DISTINCT LOCDATE,PATID
  FROM THSADM0 ADM, THSLOC0 LOC
  WHERE ADM.PATID = LOC.PATID AND
       ADMDATE BETWEEN '1986-01-01' AND '1986-01-31'
```
(b) the join

Figure 4.36. A Subquery and Equivalent Join.

```
SELECT PATID,LASTNAME,FIRSTNAME
  FROM THSPAT0 PAT
  WHERE ACTIVEFLAG = 'Y' AND NOT EXISTS
    (SELECT PATID FROM THSSVC0 SVC
       WHERE SERVDATE BETWEEN '1990-01-01' AND '1990-12-31'
       AND PAT.PATID = SVC.PATID)
```
Figure 4.37. Subquery with NOT EXISTS to Find Rows *Not* in a Table.

- The performance of a subselect depends on the number of rows that satisfy the other search criteria as well as whether or not there are indexes on the subquery table.
- The performance choice between correlated and noncorrelated can be summarized as follows:
    - No index on the correlation columns of the subquery
        For a correlated subquery, the inner table is scanned for each outer row. If there is no index on the column being used, then this is a table space scan of the inner table for *each* row of the outer table selected. This is *very* costly. For the noncorrelated query, the inner table is scanned once with only some of its rows put into an intermediate table for scanning with each outer row.

```
SELECT PATID
  FROM THSPAT0 PAT
  WHERE BIRTHDATE = '1950-01-09'
    AND EXISTS
      (SELECT PATID FROM THSLOC0 LOC
          WHERE WARD = '0100' AND LOC.PATID = PAT.PATID)
```

Figure 4.38. A Correlated Subquery Is Good When There Are Only a Few Rows Selected from the Outer Table.

Therefore, if few subquery rows are returned and there is *no* index, then the noncorrelated query will be better.

— Index on inner table

If, on the other hand, only a few outer rows are used (Figure 4.38) and there is an index on the subquery column, then the correlated query is better. In this example, only a few patients are selected with the birthdate criteria. The XHSLOC01 index on the HSLOC table will be used to find the location rows for those patients. Therefore, there will be no full scan needed on the location table.

In general, however, joins are faster as DB2 can choose either table as the inner or outer and use any available indexes. In the example in Figure 4.32, DB2 will probably use the XHSLOC02 index to find entries with WARD 0100, and then use the XHSPAT02 index to find the patient records.

4.3 CLUSTERED INDEXES

4.3.1 Access Through an Index

For a row to be selected, it must satisfy the entire WHERE clause. There may be several columns referenced, not all of which are in the same indexes. If DB2 uses an index, it will first evaluate those parts of the expression that only have columns in that index. Any row which meets that part of the expression will then have to be read from the table. The rest of the expression will be evaluated to determine if the row satisfies the criteria and should be processed. The more rows that are eliminated by looking at the index columns, the fewer data rows that have to be read from the table space.

To read a row from the table space, DB2 will read the data page into a buffer. If another row is needed from the same page, and the page is still in the buffer pool, there will be no IO. Therefore, it is beneficial for the data rows to be in the same general order as the index entries that are being searched. If they are, then as DB2 goes from one index entry to the next, it is likely that the row will be on the same page or the next one. Only one IO will be necessary for each page. When a clustered index is used to access the data, DB2 might also use sequential prefetch of the data rows, further reducing the number of IOs to read the data pages.

If the data rows are in a very different order from the index, then each row that is read is likely to be on a different page. A separate IO may be necessary for each row. Even if the full set of rows returned has many rows on the same page, if the order is different from the index order, by the time the same page is needed again, it may very well no longer be in the buffer pool and will have to be read again.

If a table has an index, the data may, or may not, be physically stored in the same order as the columns of the index. Indexes which are in the same order as the data rows are clustered. Indexes which are not are unclustered. Clustered indexes are much better than unclustered ones! Access through each type is illustrated in Figures 4.39 and 4.40.

We have to distinguish between these terms, and the term, clustering index. When you create indexes for a table, you can specify one of them as being the clustering index (with the CLUSTER keyword). DB2 will use this index on INSERT statements to try to keep the rows in order by this index. On a reorg of the table space, the rows will be reloaded into the table in exact order by the clustering index. Therefore, after a reorg, the clustering index will be clustered. Before the reorg it may or may not be. If there is heavy insert activity and there is not enough free space in each page, then inserted rows cannot be placed on the same page as other rows with similar keys.

Rows are added to a table either with INSERT SQL statements or through the LOAD utility. Many tables are refreshed (i.e., all existing rows are replaced with new ones), with the LOAD utility and the REPLACE option. This is often done for tables whose data come from another system. LOAD with REPLACE does *not* use the clustering index to place the data rows. The rows are loaded in the same order as the input file. Therefore, it is very important to first sort the rows into the order you want them to be in physically, before inputting them through the LOAD utility.

The other indexes that are created (i.e., those that are not the clustering index) may or may not be clustered. If the index columns are similar to those of the clustering index, this index may also be clustered. For example, the drug table has a clustering index on PATID and DRUGDATE and another index on PATID, DRUGCODE, and DRUGDATE. Figure 4.41 has the create statements for these indexes. If the table is in clustering order by the first index, it may also be in order by the second index as they both have PATID as the high-order column. Another index may also be clustered if the data was loaded with the LOAD utility and the input file was in the order of this other index.

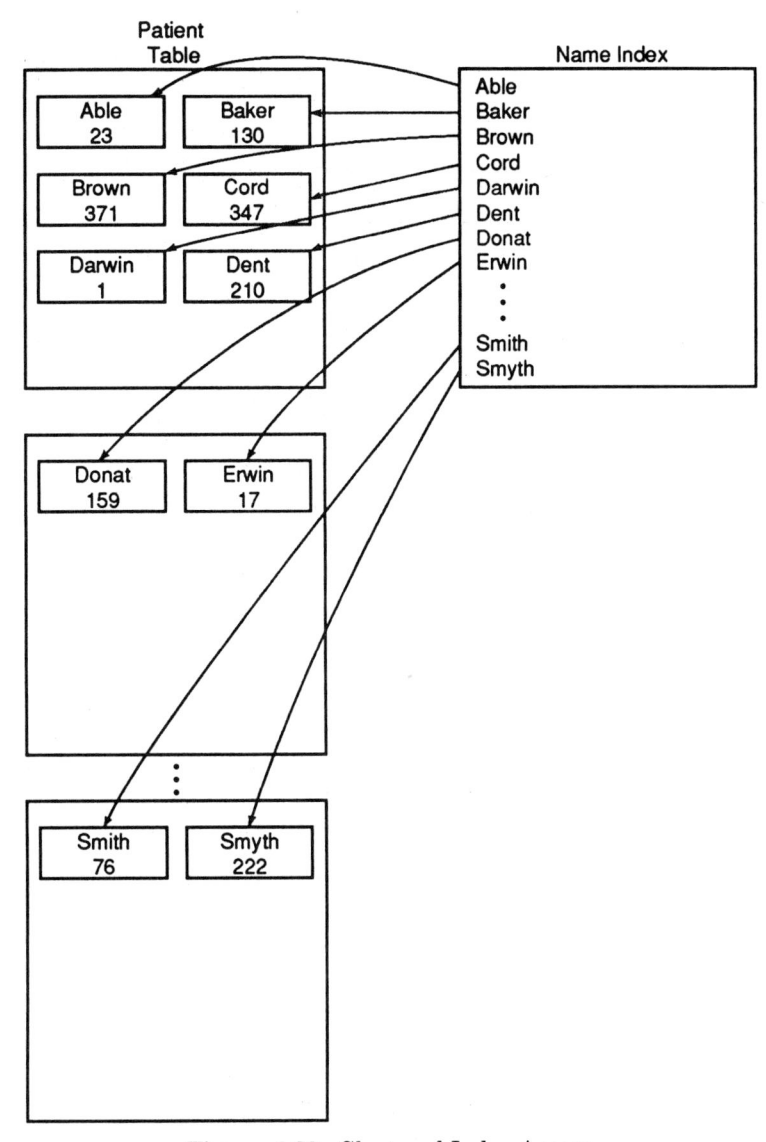

Figure 4.39. Clustered Index Access.

4.3.2 Sorting the Index Entries

Version 2.2 introduced a new way of processing unclustered indexes, which has greatly increased their usefullness. As we have seen, when rows are selected through an unclustered index each one is likely to be on a different page than the preceding row. When many rows are selected, several may actually be on the same data pages, but by the time DB2 is ready to read a second data row from a page, that page may no longer be in the buffer pool. In the worst case,

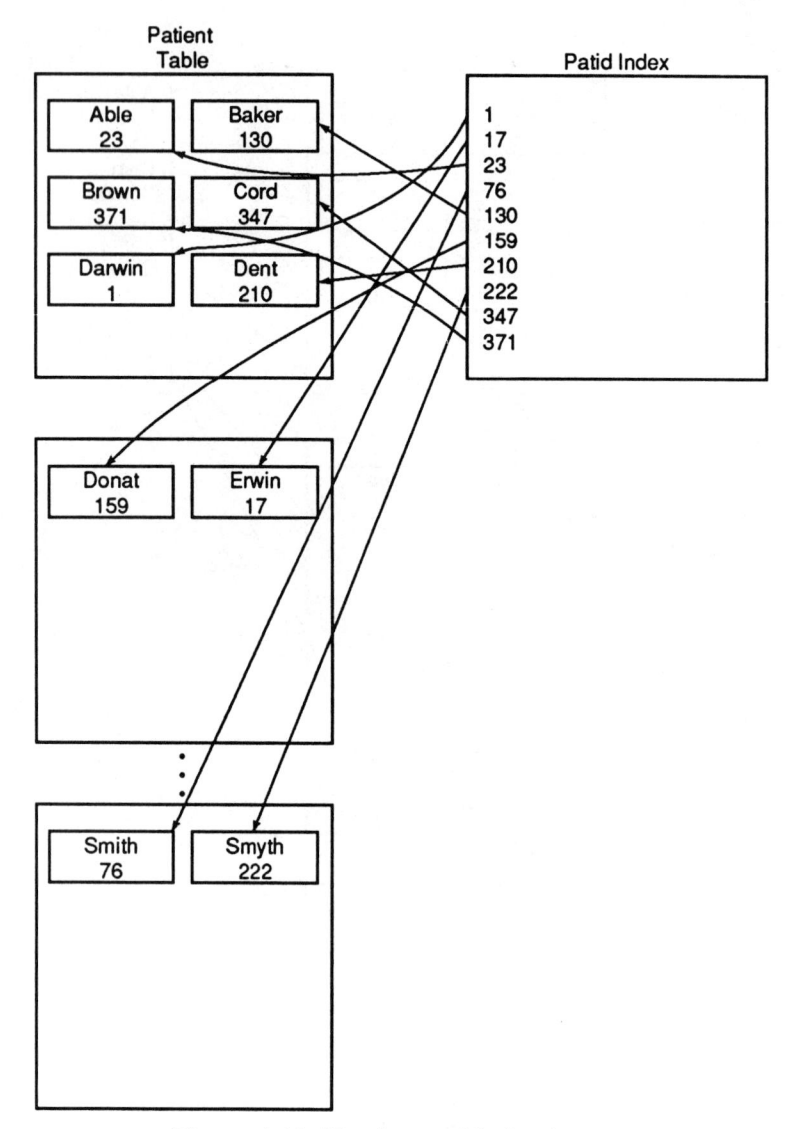

Figure 4.40. Nonclustered Index Access.

every row may require an IO. With clustered index access, there will only be one IO for each needed data page regardless of how many rows are needed from that page. Again, the existence of a clustering index does not guarantee that the data rows are clustered.

Now, DB2 may choose to process the index in a different manner. Normally, it will read each data row right after reading the index entry. Instead, it may find all index entries that match the search criteria and then sort the entries by

```
CREATE INDEX GELLER.XHSDRG01 ON GELLER.THSDRG0

(PATID,

 DRUGDATE DESC)

CLUSTER

USING STOGROUP STG1 PRIQTY 1000 SECQTY 1000

SUBPAGES 2 CLOSE NO;


CREATE INDEX GELLER.XHSDRG02 ON GELLER.THSDRG0

(PATID,

 DRUGCODE,

 DRUGDATE DESC)

USING STOGROUP STG1 PRIQTY 1000 SECQTY 1000

SUBPAGES 2 CLOSE NO;
```

Figure 4.41. Both Indexes May Be Clustered Even Though Only One Is the Clustering Index.

row ID (RID). Then it will read the data pages in RID order. This way, each data page will only be read once as with clustered index access. The cost is the time and storage needed to do the sort. On the whole, this cost is small compared to the savings in IO. Figure 4.42 illustrates this process. First, the index entries are found, then sorted, and finally the table space is accessed in RID order.

Unclustered indexes will not always be processed in this manner. If DB2 expects to select only a few rows, then these rows are likely to be all on different pages anyway. The same number of pages will need to be read whether or not they are read in order. Therefore, it does not pay to bother sorting the entries. There is no exact number of rows that represent a cutoff. When more rows are to be read for a given sized table space, there is a greater chance that more than one will be on the same page. The bigger the table space, the less likely several rows will be together. As with all other possible access paths, the DB2 optimizer will estimate the cost of these alternatives.

If a very high percentage of rows are going to be selected, then it is likely that DB2 will choose to do a table space scan. This will be cheaper than finding the index entries, sorting them, and then reading most of the table space pages anyway. With prior releases of DB2, unclustered indexes were only used when a fairly small number of rows were needed. Now, these indexes are much more useful and can be processed efficiently even when a larger number of rows are needed.

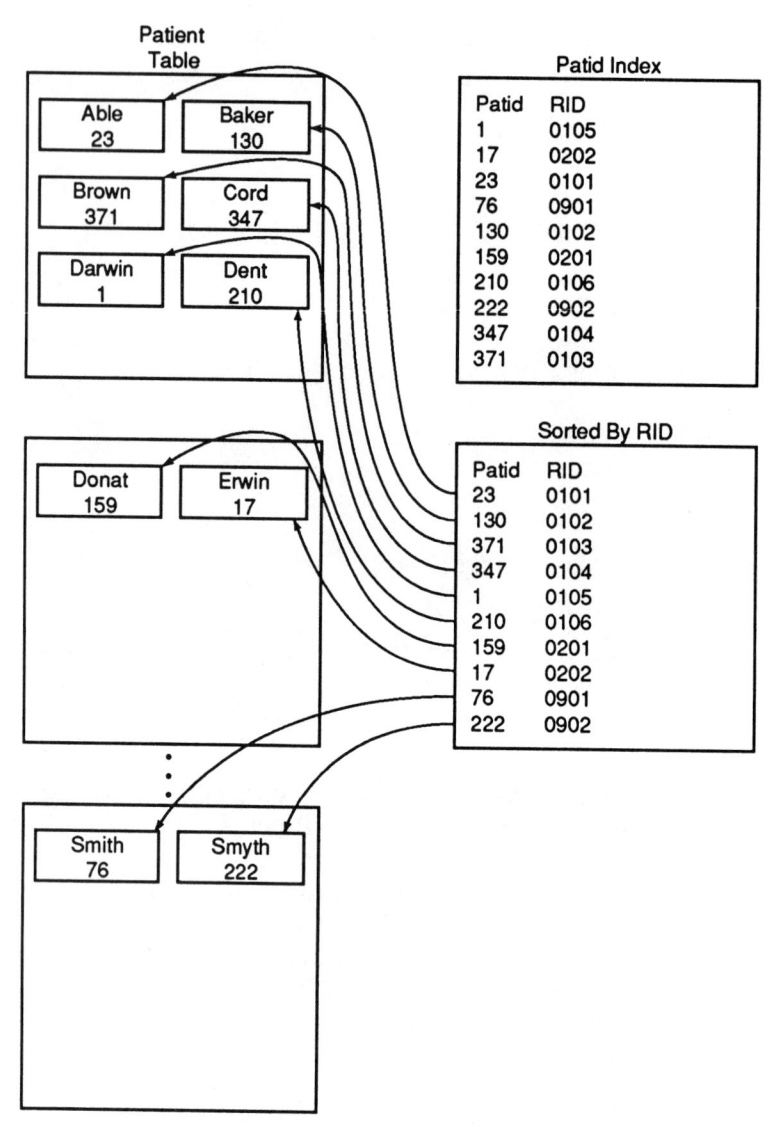

Figure 4.42. Sorting the Index Entries by RID.

4.3.3 Multiple Index Access and RID Sorting

Whenever DB2 chooses to use multiple indexes to access the data, it must also sort the index entries into RID order. It must do so for each index used in order to merge the index entries. When an AND predicate is used, the intersection of the index lists must be produced—only those entries that appear in both lists are selected. With an OR predicate, the union of the lists is produced—those that appear in either list. However, the same data row should not be selected twice, so duplicate RIDs must be eliminated. Therefore, multiple index access also gains the benefit of accessing the data rows in physical order.

4.3.4 List Prefetch

When rows are processed in RID order, you get the benefit of having only one IO per page. As discussed above, when many pages in a row are going to be read, DB2 might use sequential prefetch to read in multiple pages ahead of time. This means it might only take one IO per 16 or 32 pages. Sequential prefetch is used for table space scans and can also be used for index scans. The index pages themselves might be read with prefetch and with a clustered index, the data pages might also be read with prefetch. However, this prefetch is only done and only useful if all or most of the data pages have to be read. However, there are cases when large disjoint sections of the table space are needed. Being able to read these sections in chunks of pages would be beneficial. For example, in Figure 4.43, we are selecting employees with one of two job codes. If there is an index on job code, DB2 will probably use that index to select the records. There may be many rows that satisfy each of the two job codes. If the index is clustered, the data rows for one job code will be on the same set of pages, but the two sets might be well-separated. Furthermore, of course, there may be many pages that only contain rows with different job codes. For an unclustered index, sorting the entries into RID order may also produce disjoint groups of pages that are needed.

Version 2.2 has introduced a new way of processing this type of situation. It is called list prefetch. When processing the index, DB2 will keep a list of data pages that will be needed. Blocks of pages that are consecutive may be prefetched. Those blocks of pages that are not needed can be skipped. Prefetch will continue with the next set of pages that can benefit. This type of processing can greatly speed up some queries.

4.3.5 Disorganized Indexes

We also have to distinguish between a clustered index and a well-organized index. As records are added to the table, or the indexed columns are updated, the index entries are also maintained. The index is similar in nature to any other index file, such as a VSAM KSDS index. Ideally, the index entries should be physically in exact key order. However, as index entries are added and deleted, there may not be room in the index page where the entry should go. If an index subpage is full, it is first split and some entries are moved to another subpage in the same page. If there is no room at all in the index page, then it is split

```
SELECT *
  FROM THSEMP0
  WHERE JOBCODE = '23' OR JOBCODE = '25'
```
Figure 4.43. Selecting Two Distinct Ranges.

with a new page obtained elsewhere in the index dataset. If the FREEPAGE parameter is not 0, then a new page may be found nearby. Either way, the index itself becomes disorganized. If the index entries are out of physical order, it will take longer to read the index regardless of where the data rows are placed. Indexes can be put back in physical order by reorging either the individual index or the entire table space.

4.4 CATALOG STATISTICS

How do you tell if an index is well-organized and/or clustered? The DB2 catalog provides these answers (as well as many other answers).

DB2 maintains statistics in its catalog for tables, indexes, table spaces, and columns. These statistics serve two purposes:

- DB2 uses some of them at bind time to help it decide on which access path to use.
- The DBA can use them to find out how much data is in the database, and to determine when to reorganize the table spaces and indexes.

4.4.1 RUNSTATS

The statistics are *not* kept on the fly by DB2 as the tables get updated. They are only updated by the DBA in one of two ways. The basic way to update the statistics is to run RUNSTATS on the table space (see Figure 4.44 for the JCL and control statements). RUNSTATS should be run whenever there is a substantial change in the file—either many rows have been added, much update activity, or after a reorg. RUNSTATS gathers statistics on the table and indexes and places them in the DB2 catalog. The other way some statistics can be updated is through the SQL UPDATE statement (see Section 7.2).

Since DB2 uses these statistics during the BIND process (or at execution time for dynamic SQL, such as through QMF) to determine its access path, it is very important to bind production plans after there is a full volume of data and RUNSTATS has been run. If RUNSTATS has never been run for a table space, DB2 will use some default values instead. These default values are fairly reasonable

```
//RUN EXEC DSNUPROC,SYSTEM=DB2T,UID='RUNSTATS'    utility proc
//DSNUPROC.SYSIN DD *
 RUNSTATS TABLESPACE GELLER.SHSPAT0 INDEX(ALL) all indexes
 RUNSTATS INDEX GELLER.XHSADM01    for one index
 RUNSTATS TABLESPACE GELLER.SHSDIS0 TABLE(GELLER.THSDIS0)
    INDEX(ALL)    for all columns of table THSDIS0
```

Figure 4.44. JCL and Control Statements for RUNSTATS.

and, in general, provide good results. If RUNSTATS is run when only a small set of test data is present, and then not run again with normal volumes, you will probably get poor results. Therefore, when putting new tables into production, you should use the following sequence:

- load the table with data
- if the data is loaded with INSERT statements, you might want to run a REORG (see Section 7.3) at this point
- run the COPY utility to have a backup of the table space
- run RUNSTATS
- bind the plans

If the table will initially be very small, with most of the data inserted later on, then:

- do *not* run RUNSTATS at all
- bind the plans
- plan on running RUNSTATS a month or so later when a larger volume of data is present

You might think that you could just run RUNSTATS weekly and always be fairly up to date. This would be good for ad hoc query (e.g., dynamic SQL), but not good for the static SQL programs. It is likely that some programs will be moved into production during the first couple of weeks and then never have their plans bound again. These plans would be based on small table sizes and may not perform well when the table grows.

Figure 4.44 shows several different forms of the RUNSTATS control statement. The basic format is to update the statistics for a table space, although there are several options. If you want statistics for the indexes, you must ask for them. In the first control statement we ask for statistics for all of the indexes for the table space SHSPAT0. This is regardless of whether there is only one table in the table space or many. You can also request that only the index statistics be updated, and not the statistics for the tables or the table space. In the second control statement we are only updating those for index XHSADM01.

Finally, by default, RUNSTATS does not gather statistics on every individual column, only those that are the high-order column of some index. If you want statistics for other columns, you must ask for them. You can ask for specific columns or all columns for a table. If you want all columns for a table, you can leave out the COLUMN parameter (as in the third control statement), but you must include the TABLE parameter to identify a specific table (THSDIS0), or all tables (TABLE by itself). The option for column statistics was introduced in Version 2.1. For that version, the RUNSTATS execution time was much longer with this option. With Version 2.2, the execution time has been substantially reduced.

With Version 2.3, there is a new option that allows you to choose which catalog tables to update with an execution of RUNSTATS. You might choose to only update those used by the optimizer for access path selection. Or you might choose to update the ones that provide the DBA with tuning information.

Prior to Version 2.3, the only way to see the statistics in the catalog is through normal SQL SELECT statements. With 2.3, there are two other methods. RUN-STATS will now also be able to produce a report of the statistics (previously it just listed which catalog tables it updated). There will also be new interactive panels to guide you through the DB2 catalog, showing the information it contains (and not just the statistics data). This will provide easier access to the catalog data for novice DB2 users.

4.4.2 Index Statistics

There are a number of columns of several tables that are updated by RUNSTATS. First, we will look at those that tell us how well-organized the indexes are and whether or not they are clustered. The two catalog tables we will look at are SYSIBM.SYSINDEXES and SYSIBM.SYSINDEXPART. We find out what is in them by issuing SQL SELECT statements (e.g., through SPUFI). There are many columns in each of these tables, but we only need to look at a few of them. Figure 4.45 has the SELECT statements to retrieve the relevant fields for the indexes for the THSPAT0 table. Figure 4.46 has the sample output from these queries. They tell us similar information in different ways.

```
SELECT NAME,CLUSTERED,FIRSTKEYCARD,FULLKEYCARD,NLEAF,NLEVEL,
       CLUSTERRATIO
    FROM SYSIBM.SYSINDEXES
    WHERE TBNAME='THSPAT0';
SELECT IXNAME,CARD,NEAROFFPOS,FAROFFPOS,LISTDIST
    FROM SYSIBM.SYSINDEXPART
    WHERE IXNAME LIKE 'XHSPAT0%';
```

Figure 4.45. Querying the Catalog for Index Statistics.

NAME	CLUSTERED	FIRSTKEYCARD	FULLKEYCARD	NLEAF	NLEVELS	CLUSTER RATIO
XHSPAT01	Y	91520	97863	800	2	100
XHSPAT02	N	100000	100000	500	2	20

IXNAME	CARD	NEAROFFPOS	FAROFFPOS	LEAFDIST
XHSPAT01	100000	1	0	0
XHSPAT02	100000	20000	30000	0

Figure 4.46. Output from Index Statistics.

4.4.2.1 SYSINDEXES

SYSINDEXES directly tells us whether or not DB2 considers the index to be clustered.

- CLUSTERED—Y if the index is, and N if it is not. The CLUSTERING column identifies which index was defined as the clustering index.
- CLUSTERRATIO—gives a more exact breakdown. If the value in this column is 95 or greater, then the index is considered clustered.
- NLEVELS can give us a clue as to how well-organized the index is. Indexes contain several levels. The lowest level has the actual index entries for each row. If this were the only level, then any index access would have to scan from the beginning of the index to find an entry. Therefore, there are higher levels of index which point the way into parts of the index so as to speed up the search. The index levels make up a hierarchy of values. The bigger the table, the more index levels are needed. In this medium-sized table, only two levels are needed. A million row table will need three. If a table becomes disorganized, the number of index levels may go up. Therefore, by comparing NLEVELS with the value from a prior run, you can check for an increase. This may just reflect an increase in volume, but it may also indicate a need to reorganize the index.
- NLEAF gives the number of leaf pages in the index. These are the pages of the lowest level of the index. DB2 uses this to determine the number of IOs for an index scan. You can use it when trying to understand DB2's choices.
- FIRSTKEYCARD and FULLKEYCARD provide useful information for tuning, coding, and just understanding what you have in your table. Card means cardinality—how many values there are. FULLKEYCARD is the number of distinct values for the index. In this example, there are 97,863 different values for XHSPAT01—the name index. If this number is the same as the number of rows in the table (CARD column in SYSIBM.SYSTABLES), then there are unique values for this index (the index may or may not be constrained to unique values). FIRSTKEYCARD tells you how many unique values there are for the first column of the index. For index XHSPAT01, this is 91,520. That means that there are 91,520 different last names.

DB2 does not maintain the number of distinct values for each partial key, only the first column of the index and the full index. These are important numbers that DB2 uses to help guess how many rows will satisfy predicates involving columns of the index. These rows may then have to be read from the table to finish checking the search criteria. The higher the cardinality the better. Fewer rows would satisfy predicates with an equal operator. For each column of the index in turn, if there is an equal operator, then a direct index match can be made. For example, the SELECT in Figure 4.47a will result in an index lookup

```
SELECT * FROM THSDIS0
   WHERE PATID='987654321'
(a) 1 matching column


SELECT * FROM THSDIS0
   WHERE PATID='987654321' AND DISDATE > '1987-01-01'
(b) 2 matching columns


SELECT * FROM THSDIS0
WHERE PATID='987654321' AND DISDATE = '1987-05-17' AND DISSEQ = 1
(c) 3 matching columns


SELECT * FROM THSDIS0
   WHERE DISDATE = '1987-09-13'
(d) no matching columns
```

Figure 4.47. SELECTs with index access.

with one matching column. That in Figure 4.47b will have two matching columns; the one in 4.47c will match all three columns of the index. Finally, the SELECT in Figure 4.47d will result in an index scan. There are no matching columns, since the first column of the index is not part of the search criteria. The entire index will have to be scanned. In a and b, the entire set of columns is not used. FIRSTKEYCARD is, therefore, the statistic that DB2 will look at to see if the index should be used. For the XHSDIS01 index of the discharge table, FIRSTKEYCARD would be over 90,000 (most patients are no longer active). This is a high percentage of the total number of rows, so it is likely that DB2 will use the index for these queries. There will probably be only a few rows with a specific PATID. In Figure 4.47c, we are matching on all three columns of the index with equal operators and DB2 will use FULLKEYCARD to determine its choice of access path.

Similarly, for the index on name (XHSPAT01), FIRSTKEYCARD is 91,250, which is almost as high as the FULLKEYCARD. Queries that use LASTNAME but not first name are just as likely to use the index.

On the other hand, let's say we had an index with a FIRSTKEYCARD of 8 and a FULLKEYCARD of 100,000. A query that only used the first column of the index would probably not use the index for access because an average of 12,500 rows would be selected.

4.4.2.2 The Distribution of Column Values

In talking about the actual distribution of values in a column, we must distinguish between Version 2.2 and all prior versions. Prior to 2.2, DB2 did not know the actual distribution of values of LASTNAME. If FIRSTKEYCARD were 8, but there were only 3 rows with a requested value, DB2 did not know this when building the plan. It would assume 12,500 and would probably not use this index. Conversely, if LASTNAME had 2000 values, then the average would be 50 apiece. In this case, DB2 might very well have used this index when you asked for LASTNAME = value. If it turned out that this particular value had 98,000 occurrences, and there was one occurrence for each of the other values, you might get very poor performance if the index were not clustered. However, DB2 would not know the distribution when making its plan. It would assume that 50 rows would be returned. Nonuniform distributions can create problems that are tricky to solve.

With Version 2.2, DB2 can keep statistics on the distribution of values for some columns. It will only do so for the first column of indexes. It does not do so for other columns. There is also no need to do so for a unique single column index as the distribution has to be 1 row per value due to the uniqueness of the index. The distribution will, of course, only be kept if RUNSTATS is run for the table space.

DB2 does not keep a record of the complete distribution of values, but rather just the 10 most frequently occurring values of the column. It stores this as a percentage of the total number of rows. For example, on the name index (XHSPAT01), it might record the following distribution:

SMITH—5%
JONES—4%
JOHNSON—1%
CARTER—0.4%
6 others—each with some small percent

With these statistics, DB2 will know that a query requesting LASTNAME='SMITH' will return 5000 rows, whereas LASTNAME='CARTER' will return 400 rows. Any name which does not appear as one of the 10 most frequent names will have fewer occurrences than the tenth one on the list. Now DB2 has much more information to make an intelligent estimate of returned rows for queries involving the high-order columns of indexes. Of course, it can only do so when constant values are used in SQL statements. If host variables are used (e.g., ADMDATE > :HOSTDATE), then DB2 has no idea what value will be in HOSTDATE when it is choosing its access path. Therefore, it still assumes a uniform distribution for ADMDATE and an average value for HOSTDATE.

4.4.2.3 SYSFIELDS

The column distribution statistics are stored in the table SYSIBM.SYSFIELDS. This is *not* a new table with Version 2.2. It is also used to store information about field procedures that have been defined for columns. Now it is used for both purposes. There are rows in here for each column that has a field procedure. These rows will have column FLDPROC filled in. It will be blank for a statistical row. For each column whose distribution is recorded, there will be up to 10 rows, each with one of the 10 most frequent values. If there are fewer than 10 different values, then there will be fewer than 10 rows. The two fields used to record the distribution are EXITPARM and EXITPARML.

- EXITPARM contains the data value and EXITPARML contains the percentage of rows (times 100).
- EXITPARML is a small integer. If a value appears in 5% of the rows, it will be stored as 500 in EXITPARML.

Looking at and understanding the values in SYSINDEXES and SYSFIELDS is something that the DBA must do to plan for reorgs of the tables and to decide on new indexes. It is also something that the programmer must use to plan his use of SQL. We'll see below how the code you use can affect DB2's choice of access.

4.4.2.4 SYSINDEXPART

SYSINDEXPART has one row for each index partition. For a partitioned table space, the clustering (partitioning) index has one index partition for each table partition. For nonpartitioning indexes, there is one index partition per index.

- CARD is the number of index entries (counting duplicate values). For a nonpartitioning index, this should equal the number of rows in the table. For a partitioning index, it is the number of rows in each partition. Note that in DB2 Version 1 it was possible for CARD to be less than the number of rows. The LOAD utility upon finding a duplicate index value for a unique index, discarded the duplicate index entry but retained the duplicate data row. You had to manually fix this up yourself. Fortunately, in Version 2, the LOAD utility has been improved to also remove the duplicate data row, while still giving you an error message.
- NEAROFFPOS and FAROFFPOS help you figure out how well-clustered the indexes are. When doing an index scan, if many rows have to be read from the table, DB2 may do sequential prefetch of the table space pages. If consecutive pages are needed, the same algorithm is used for initiating prefetch as for a table space scan. Therefore, for a clustered index, the number of IOs of the table space may be substantially less than one per page. The more clustered the index, the better the performance of the table access. NEAROFFPOS tells how many rows are within a nearby page of the preceeding row (in index

order). Nearby means within 16 pages (under Version 2). FAROFFPOS tells how many rows are further away. By subtracting these numbers from CARD you get how many rows are in the same page (or the next one) as the preceeding row. With DB2 Version 1, a fully clustered index had NEAROFFPOS equal to the number of data pages, as the first row on each page was counted in NEAROFFPOS. Under Version 2, the first row of each page is no longer counted in NEAROFFPOS. Therefore, a fully clustered index should have NEAROFFPOS equal to 1. It is not 0 as you might think, because the very first row is counted in NEAROFFPOS. To make things confusing, IBM did not update the Version 2.1 manuals to reflect the change in algorithm. The manuals still described NEAROFFPOS as for Version 1. The Version 2.2 manuals have been updated.

When processing rows in order of an index that is fairly well-clustered, each data row has a good chance of being on the same page as the preceding row. The first one on a page may require an IO, but then the page will be in a buffer so subsequent IOs may not be necessary. When sequential prefetch is used, many consecutive pages are read at once, so no additional IO is necessary for the nearby pages. Therefore, rows that are in nearby pages (and counted in NEAROFFPOS) do not cause much of a performance problem when sequential prefetch is used. On the other hand, a high value for FAROFFPOS is a sign that the index is not clustered. Performance will suffer in this case. The next row needed might not have been fetched with the preceeding row. DB2 will have to jump back and forth through the table space. If FAROFFPOS and NEAROFFPOS are fairly high even if the index is marked as clustered, performance will not be as good as for an index where FAROFFPOS and NEAROFFPOS are low. There will be more IOs needed to process the table.

- LEAFDIST gives you an indication of when an index needs to be reorged. The method of calculating LEAFDIST also changed with DB2 Version 2. A well-organized index now will have a value of 0 for this column. In Version 1, a well-organized index had a value of 100. When doing an index scan, each leaf page is read in succession. When entries are inserted into an index, the entries go into the page where they belong in sequence. If that index page is full, then a new leaf page must be used. This new leaf page will not be in consecutive physical order unless the FREEPAGE parameter of the create index was used to leave free pages in the index after initial loads and reorgs. When the next leaf page is not physically next to the preceding one, the index scan will take longer. LEAFDIST is the average distance between successive leaf pages times 100. In Version 1, the next physical page was considered to have a distance of 1, two pages over had a distance of 2, etc. Therefore, if the index were perfectly organized, the average distance would be 1 and the value of LEAFDIST would be 1 * 100 = 100. In Version 2, the next physical page is now considered to have a distance of 0, two pages over has a distance of 1, etc. A perfectly organized index with no free pages will have an average distance of 0 and LEAFDIST will equal 0. Note that if FREEPAGE is not 0, then the average distance will be greater than 0 after a reorg because the free pages do not have any data and the next successive page will not always be the next physical page.

4.4.3 Other Catalog Statistics

While we're on the subject of catalog statistics, let's look at the other ones put in by RUNSTATS. The other tables updated by this utility are SYSIBM.SYSTABLES, SYSIBM.SYSTABLEPART, SYSIBM.SYSTABLESPACE, and SYSIBM.SYSCOLUMNS. These statistics are used by the DB2 optimizer to help decide on the access path selection. They can be used by you to monitor growth patterns, the need for reorg and to understand the choice of access path for different SQL statements.

4.4.3.1 SYSTABLES

In SYSTABLES, the columns that are updated are CARD, NPAGES, and PCTPAGES. Figure 4.48 has the SELECT statement to display these values for table THSPAT0.

- CARD is the cardinality of the table—the number of rows. Right after the RUNSTATS this will be equal to SELECT COUNT(*) FROM THSPAT0, but, of course, CARD will not get updated as rows are inserted and deleted from the table until the next time that RUNSTATS is run.
- NPAGES is the number of pages that have rows from this table. For a nonsegmented table space, if there is only one table (and the table has not previously been dropped without a reorg), then this is fairly

```
SELECT NAME,CARD,NPAGES,PCTPAGES
  FROM SYSIBM.SYSTABLES
  WHERE NAME='THSPAT0'
```

(a) SELECT statement

```
NAME         CARD       NPAGES     PCTPAGES
THSPAT0      100000     1200             99
```

(b) Results

Figure 4.48. Querying SYSTABLES for Statistics.

close to the number of pages that will have to be read in a table space scan. NACTIVE in SYSIBM.SYSTABLESPACE (Figure 4.49) will give the actual number of pages in the table space. For the BIND process, DB2 will use NACTIVE to estimate pages for nonsegmented table spaces, and NPAGES for segmented table spaces. In general, NPAGES is most reflective of how much space this table takes up, regardless of the type of table space or other tables in the same table space.

- PCTPAGES is the percent of pages that actually have data. For a nonsegmented, nonpartitioned table space this will normally be 99—every page has data except for the header and space map pages. If there have been many deletes or if the FREEPAGE parameter is greater than 0, whole pages may be empty and the number will be less. For a partitioned table space, some of the partitions may not have data and the percent will be lower. For a segmented table space, this number reflects the percent of the pages which are in segments for this table only.

4.4.3.2 SYSTABLESPACE

- NACTIVE as described above.

4.4.3.3 SYSTABLEPART

SYSIBM.SYSTABLEPART (Figure 4.50) has one row for each nonpartitioned table space and one row for each partition of a partitioned one.

- CARD is the number of rows in each partition.
- PERCACTIVE is the percent of the pages that actually contain data rows. It reflects how much space is actually being used within the pages.

```
SELECT NAME,NTABLES,NACTIVE,SPACE
  FROM SYSIBM.SYSTABLESPACE
  WHERE NAME='SHSPAT0'
```

(a) SELECT statement

```
NAME        NTABLES     NACTIVE     SPACE
SHSPAT0           1        1200      4800
```

(b) Results

Figure 4.49. Querying SYSTABLESPACE for Statistics.

```
SELECT TSNAME,CARD,NEARINDREF,FARINDREF,PERCACTIVE,PERCDROP
  FROM SYSIBM.SYSTABLEPART
  WHERE TSNAME='SHSPAT0'
```
(a) SELECT statement

TSNAME	CARD	NEARINDREF	FARINDREF	PERCACTIVE	PERCDROP
SHSPAT0	100000	0	0	90	0

(b) Results

Figure 4.50. Querying SYSTABLEPART for Statistics.

- PERCDROP tells how much of the space is take up by tables that have been dropped (a reorg reclaims the space). For production table spaces you always want this to be 0, there is no reason to leave the wasted space.
- NEARINDREF and FARINDREF are only greater than zero when there are variable length columns or a column has been added with ALTER TABLE. When a variable length column is updated, the new data may be longer or shorter. If it is longer and there is no room in the page for it to be replaced, DB2 will have to move it to another page with a reference from the old page to the new page. If this new page is nearby, then it will be counted in NEARINDREF. If it is further, then it will be counted in FARINDREF.

The columns in SYSTABLEPART are not used by the optimizer, but can be used by the DBA to monitor the table organization.

4.4.3.4 SYSCOLUMNS

SYSIBM.SYSCOLUMNS (Figure 4.51) has a row for every column of every table. The three columns that are updated are COLCARD, HIGH2KEY, and LOW2KEY. In Version 1, the only rows that are updated are for columns that are the high-order column in an index. None of the other columns got statistics. In Version 2, you have an option when you run RUNSTATS to ask for statistics on all columns of a table. Figure 4.52 shows the control statements for this option. The default in running RUNSTATS is for all tables in a table space. In order to get statistics on nonindex columns, you must explicitly ask for the tables (even if there is only one) by using the TABLE parameter. You do not have to actually list the table name. TABLE by itself defaults to TABLE(ALL)—all tables. You can ask for all columns of the table (b), or just some of them (c).

```
SELECT TBNAME,NAME,HIGH2KEY,LOW2KEY,COLCARD
  FROM SYSIBM.SYSCOLUMNS
  WHERE TBNAME='THSPAT0'
```
(a) SELECT statement

TBNAME	NAME	HIGH2KEY	LOW2KEY	COLCARD
THSPAT0	PATID	876123445	000000112	100000
THSPAT0	LASTNAME	ZACHARY	ABLE	91520
THSPAT0	FIRSTNAME			-1
THSPAT0	SEX			-1
THSPAT0	BIRTHDATE			-1
THSPAT0	ACTIVEFLAG			-1

(b) Results

Figure 4.51. Querying SYSCOLUMNS for Statistics.

```
RUNSTATS TABLESPACE DHSPAT0.SHSPAT0 INDEX(ALL)
```
(a) Indexes, but no columns

```
RUNSTATS TABLESPACE DHSPAT0.SHSPAT0 TABLE(GELLER.THSPAT0) INDEX(ALL)
```
(b) Indexes and all columns for table THSPAT0

```
RUNSTATS TABLESPACE DHSPAT0.SHSPAT0 TABLE(GELLER.THSPAT0) INDEX(ALL)
   COLUMNS(PATID,LASTNAME,FIRSTNAME,BIRTHDATE)
```
(c) Indexes and some columns for table THSPAT0

Figure 4.52. RUNSTATS Control Cards.

- COLCARD is the cardinality (number of values) of this column. For columns that are the high-order part of an index, this value should match the FIRSTKEYCARD value of the SYSIBM.SYSINDEXES row for that index. In general, the higher the cardinality for a column, the fewer the number of rows that will be returned for most search criteria. For example, if COLCARD for LASTNAME is 90,000 and the number of rows is 100,000; then LASTNAME='JONES' will on av-

erage return 1 or 2 rows. Of course, as we mentioned, DB2 (prior to Version 2.2) didn't know that there may really be 2000 people named JONES.
- HIGH2KEY is the second highest key value for the column. LOW-2KEY is the second lowest key value. These are used by DB2 for queries that involve greater and less than operators (and BETWEEN). DB2 assumes a uniform distribution between LOW2KEY and HIGH-2KEY.

4.4.4 Summary of Statistics Produced by RUNSTATS

Columns used by BIND:

- SYSINDEXES
  CLUSTERED
  CLUSTERRATIO
  FIRSTKEYCARD
  FULLKEYCARD
  NLEAF
  NLEVELS
- SYSTABLES
  CARD
  NPAGES
  PCTPAGES
- SYSTABLESPACE
  NACTIVE
- SYSCOLUMNS
  COLCARD
  LOW2KEY
  HIGH2KEY
- SYSFIELDS
  EXITPARM
  EXITPARML

Columns used by DBA for tuning:

- SYSINDEXPART
  CARD
  NEAROFFPOS
  FAROFFPOS
  LEAFDIST
- SYSTABLEPART
  CARD
  PERCACTIVE
  PERCDROP
  NEARINDREF
  FARINDREF

4.4.5 An Example of Uneven Data Distribution and Its Effect

Figure 4.53 has an example of the interplay of the catalog statistics and SQL code. The queries were run initially under Version 2.1. The first query does a join of two tables. COLJ of each table are the join columns. This query ran in 10 seconds. The user then added one more selection criteria (COLC = Z). Fewer rows will now be selected and the user expected a similar run time. Instead, it took over 20 minutes. Several pieces of investigation were needed to solve the problem.

The first step was to run EXPLAIN to find out what access path DB2 was using. The first query used a merge scan join, whereas the second one used a nested loop join. The outer table (TABA) was accessed with an index, but the inner table used a table space scan. Well, a table space scan of the inner table of a nested loop will often perform terribly. Why did DB2 choose this method?

The next step was to check on what indexes existed on these tables. The join columns (COLJ) were not in any index. Therefore, a merge scan join was probably the best method. Indeed, the merge scan join took only 10 seconds. So again, why the nested loop?

The index which was used on TABA was on COLC and COLB. COLC was the new predicate introduced. To try to understand DB2's choice, I checked the statistics on the tables. These included:

```
SELECT * FROM TABA A, TABB B
    WHERE
        A.COLA = X AND
        A.COLB = Y AND
        A.COLJ = B.COLJ
(a) a Merge scan join is used


SELECT * FROM TABA A, TABB B
    WHERE
        A.COLA = X AND
        A.COLB = Y AND
        A.COLJ = B.COLJ AND
        A.COLC = Z
(b) a Nested loop join is used with a table space scan of inner table
```

Figure 4.53. The Performance of the Second Query Is Suprisingly Much Worse Than the First, Due to Uneven Data Distribution.

- 8000 rows in TABA.
- 50,000 rows in TABB.
- 80 different values for COLC (determined from FIRSTKEYCARD).
- COLB had -1 for its cardinality. This means that RUNSTATS was not run with the option for column statistics. Therefore, DB2 assumed 25 different values.

With 8000 rows in TABA and 80 different values for COLC, DB2 estimates that 100 rows (8000/80) will satisfy the COLC=Z predicate. With 25 different values for COLB, DB2 estimates that 4 rows (100/25) will satisfy (COLC=Z AND COLB=Y). Therefore, the nested loop join would involve 4 rows selected from TABA and, therefore, 4 table space scans of TABB. This apparently came out cheaper than the merge scan, which would include table space scans of TABA and TABB, a sort of each of them, and then the merge.

Okay, now we think we know why DB2 chose this method. So, why did the query take so long? DB2 assumed an even distribution of values. To find out the actual distribution, I entered some queries selecting the count of rows for the particular value COLC=Z. I also checked on how many values COLB really had. It turned out that 5000 rows had COLC equal to Z. COLB had only *five* different values, not 25. Therefore, in reality, there were 5000/5 = 1000 rows selected from TABA, and 1000 table space scans of TABB!

Now we need some solutions. There are three of them.

1. Run RUNSTATS with the option for all column statistics. This was the simplest and best solution. Now DB2 will assume 100/5 = 20 table space scans rather than only four. This is more costly and the merge scan join was chosen.
2. Change the query to have the predicate COLC IN(Z,Z,Z,Z). This looks strange, but works well. The other three Zs are redundant. The same rows will satisfy this predicate. However, when DB2 estimates the cost, it thinks that there will be four times as many rows selected; therefore, there will be 4 * 4 = 16 table space scans. Again, the merge scan was chosen. Of course, this form of the query works well with the particular distribution of data and statistics that exist at the moment. It might not work as well when the data distribution changes.
3. Move to Version 2.2. With the new distribution statistics, the catalog will record the distribution of COLC because it begins an index. DB2 will know that 67.5% of the table has COLC=Z, not 1%.

This example illustrates the interplay of the SQL statement, the indexes on the tables, RUNSTATS, and the actual data distribution. It shows that there are a number of different things to check to solve a performance problem, and that the solutions may involve changes to the SQL code, or just to the catalog statistics.

4.5 PREDICATES

4.5.1 Will an Index Be Used?

We've looked at the basic choice between index access and table space scans. Things are not quite that simple. First, the WHERE clause may have predicates involving a number of columns with different relational operators, and there may be several indexes with different combinations of columns. DB2 must decide which ones (if any) to use. The access to any one table in a query might use one index. Or it might use multiple indexes to find subsets of rows matching parts of the search criteria. If a table is used multiple times in a SELECT statement (i.e., in a join with itself or in a subquery), then different access paths may be used to satisfy the different parts of the query.

Deciding to use an index is not simply a matter of the index columns being in the WHERE clause. The types of predicates (i.e., the operators involved) affect whether or not an index will be considered. Some predicates cannot be satisfied through index access. Others can, but the index access path may not be the most effective. Index IOs vs. table space scan IOs are only one part of the overall cost. Also included are sorting costs and CPU processing. In the current versions of DB2, the CPU costs are higher to evaluate index entries than to evaluate predicates using the data rows. For example, the COUNT function can be evaluated either by counting each row, or by counting the index entries of an index. The CPU utilization will be lower if the data rows are used. However, more IOs are needed to do the table space scan as the table space is usually larger than the index space. If they are close in size, then the overall cost of the table space scan may be cheaper.

Before we look at some examples of how the predicates affect the choice of access path, we will define some terms.

- Indexable predicate: A predicate that can be satisfied by matching an index. PATID = '123456' is indexable. Index XHSPAT02 is on PATID and can be used for a direct lookup. PATID ¬ ='123456' is not indexable. DB2 could do an index scan to resolve the predicate, but it cannot use the index structure to find it quickly. Figure 4.54 shows some other indexable and nonindexable predicates.
- Stage 1 and Stage 2 predicates: The processing of the search criteria goes through two stages. Rows that satisfy the stage 1 criteria are passed to the second stage. The fewer the rows that have to go through stage 2 the better. Therefore, it is preferable to have stage 1 predicates. Indexable predicates are also stage 1.
- Sargable and Nonsargable predicates: These are older terms for stage 1 and stage 2. Sargable is short for search-arguable.

Stage 1 processing is done by a component of DB2 called the Data Manager. This component handles the processing of the table space and indexes and the retrieving of the rows. Stage 2 processing is done by the Relational Data System (RDS) component.

Predicate	Indexable	Non-indexable	
col op value	X		(op is =,>,< etc.)
x.col1 op x.col2		X	
x.col op y.col	X		
col ¬= value		X	
col LIKE 'aaaa%'	X		
col LIKE '%aaaa'		X	
col IN (.....)	X		
col anyop (subquery)		X	
col = expression		X	

predicate AND predicate - indexable if both predicates refer to columns of the same index

predicate OR predicate - not indexable unless both predicates refer to the same column with = operator (e.g. sex='m' or sex='f')

Figure 4.54. Indexable and Nonindexable Predicates.

4.5.2 Filter Factors

DB2 estimates the processing (CPU) cost and IO cost of each possible access path. From the catalog, it gets the number of pages for each index and the table space. For each column that it has statistics on, it gets the cardinality. The type of predicate is used along with the column and index cardinality to estimate the number of rows that satisfy that predicate. For example, let's say there are 100,000 rows in a table. If there are 50 values for column YYY, then YYY = 23 will on average return 100,000/50 = 2000 rows. YYY IN(23,52,88) will return 6000 rows on average. The ratio of predicate cardinality to table cardinality is called the filter factor. For the first example, this is 2000/100000 = 0.02 (2%). For the second example, it is 0.06. The predicate

YYY BETWEEN 10 AND 50

will be evaluated as follows. Let's say HIGH2KEY is 90 (this is the second highest value for YYY) and LOW2KEY is 2. Then, DB2 assumes a uniform distribution between 2 and 90. The requested range represents (50−10)/(90−2) percent of the rows. This is equal to 40/88 = 43%. Therefore, the filter factor is 0.43. DB2 assumes that 43% of the rows (43,000) will satisfy this criteria.

If there were an index on YYY, it would probably not pay for DB2 to use it for this query, as close to half of the rows would be passed on for further processing. On the other hand, the predicate

```
SELECT * FROM THSPATO
  WHERE SEX='M' AND BIRTHDATE BETWEEN '1932-01-01' AND
      '1933-12-31';
```

Figure 4.55. Order of Predicates Can Affect Performance.

YYY BETWEEN 50 AND 51

will have a filter factor of 2/88 = 0.02. On average, 4000 rows will satisfy the predicate. If the index is clustered, index access may be beneficial—although for an unclustered index, it might not (and, certainly not, prior to Version 2.2).

The order of the predicates in a query will usually not affect whether or not DB2 uses an index, but they can affect the performance of the query. Figure 4.55 has a SELECT with two predicates in the WHERE clause. The first predicate will return (on average) 50,000 rows. The second predicate will return 1000. Assuming that there are no indexes, it is much cheaper to do the second test first. If you do, then only 1000 rows will need the second predicate applied to them. If the first one is done first, then 50,000 rows will need the second predicate applied to them. The same 500 rows will be selected by the whole set of criteria, but the testing will be cheaper.

4.5.3 Stage 1 and Stage 2 Predicates

All else being equal, DB2 will apply predicates in the order they appear in the WHERE clause. Therefore, you can speed up the processing of some queries by reordering the predicates. "All else being equal" means that indexable predicates are applied first, followed by stage 1 predicates, and then stage 2 predicates. For stage 1 and stage 2 predicates, within each of these stages, '=' predicates will be evaluated first, then range predicates (e.g., >, <), then other predicates. You can influence the order within these groups. For example

SEX='M' AND BIRTHDATE='1950-03-25'

will result in each row being first checked for SEX='M' and then birthdate being checked. Reversing the order of the predicates will significantly speed things up. However, in the following:

BIRTHDATE BETWEEN '1989-04-23' AND '1989-04-24' AND SEX='M'

the SEX predicate will be evaluated first because it has an = operator and BIRTHDATE has a range. You could influence DB2 by making the predicate more complicated:

SEX BETWEEN 'M' AND 'N'

This will still result in only males being selected, but will cause DB2 not to give priority to this predicate.

4.5.4 Indexable Predicates

In order to do a matching index lookup, there must be an indexable predicate on the high-order columns of the index. The columns of index XHSADM01 are PATID, ADMDATE, and ADMSEQ. The index XHSADM02 has ADMDATE. The predicate PATID = '223344556' will match the first column of index XHSADM01. ADMDATE > '1989-04-01' will match index XHSADM02 but not XHSADM01. However, the predicates PATID='223344556' AND ADMDATE > '1989-04-01' will match either index. It will match the first two columns of XHSADM01 and the first column of XHSADM02. Most likely, DB2 will choose the first index for this predicate. Fewer rows will be chosen by the exact match on PATID, followed by selecting a subset of admissions. If the second index were chosen, a great many rows may be selected for further checking. The data rows for each of these would have to be read to see if they are for that particular patient.

Surprises may occur even in this "obvious" example. If RUNSTATS was run only when a small amount of test data was loaded, the statistics may be so skewed as to get DB2 to use a different access path. If there were only two patients with 100 admissions each, the filter factor for PATID='223344556' would only be 1/2. Half the rows would pass this test. The filter factor for ADMDATE may be much less in this case, and so the second index may be chosen.

Using columns that appear in indexes is not enough. Prior to Version 2.2, a Boolean expression that used the OR operator would often make it impossible to use an index. PATID='223344556' OR LASTNAME = 'JAMESON' cannot use a single index. If either index were used, many rows that match one part of the expression will not even be looked at because they don't satisfy the other part. An exception is if the same column is used in both parts of the expression—PATID='223344556' OR PATID='665544332'. This expression could always be handled with a single index lookup.

The type of relational operator affects whether a predicate is indexable. This is a good place to remind you that IBM is continually improving the optimizer. Not only are the algorithms for determining the best path being improved, but also the processing of different predicates. Some operators that did not match indexes in previous releases do so now. Likewise, some that still do not may do so in the future. Figure 4.54 lists some of the predicates that are indexable. A more complete list can be found in the DB2 Administration Guide. From this list we can get an idea of the types of operators that can be used effectively. Essentially, if the high-order part of a column's value is given, then the index structure can be used.

- "COL operator value" is indexable. Operator is any of =, >, <, >=, <=. COL ¬= value is not indexable.
- LIKE is indexable if the operand starts with an explicit character string and then has a wildcard (% or _), and is not indexable if it starts with a wildcard.
- LIKE a host variable is not indexable because at bind time DB2 has no idea whether the host variable will start with a wildcard or an-

other character. This has been true up through Version 2.2. However, Version 2.3 does allow this type of predicate to be indexable.
- If the operand (value) involves an expression, then an index will not be used because expressions are not evaluated until stage 2. This is true even for a simple expression, such as PAYAMOUNT = 2000 + 100.
- If the operand uses a function, the predicate is stage 2. This is true even if the function extracts the high-order part of the column [e.g., YEAR(ADMDATE)=1990, SUBSTR(LASTNAME,1,4)='JOHN']. In these cases, it is better to use the entire column with a BETWEEN (e.g., ADMDATE BETWEEN '1990-01-01' and '1990-12-31').

Figure 4.56 has some predicates that, while not being indexable, are stage 1. Figure 4.57 shows stage 2 predicates. As of DB2 Version 2, the guidelines for determining whether or not a predicate is stage 1 or stage 2 are fairly simple. If a column is being compared to a specific value, it is stage 1. If it is not, then it is stage 2. Expressions are not calculated until stage 2. Subqueries mostly return values that are not preset, and so comparison to a subquery is usually stage 2. With Version 2.2, however, some subquery processing has been improved. Comparison with the ANY or ALL keywords can be stage 1.

Predicate	Stage 1
col op value	Y
x.col op y.col	Y
col ¬= value	Y
col LIKE 'aaaa%'	Y
col LIKE '%aaaa'	Y
col IN (.....)	Y
predicate AND predicate	Y
predicate OR predicate	Y
col op ANY subquery	Y

Figure 4.56. Stage 1 Predicates.

Predicate	Stage 2
x.col1 op x.col2	Y
col op (subquery)	Y
col = expression	Y

Figure 4.57. Stage 2 Predicates.

Comparing a column to another column in the same table (i.e., the same row) also is stage 2, as the second column will have a different value for each row. However, comparing a column to a column of a different table *is* stage 1. This has to do with the fact that this comparison is part of the join criteria.

Of course, any of the above may change with new releases of DB2. It is very important to read the new manuals to find out what has changed in the access path selection and in other performance areas. Existing queries and programs may be affected, both positively or negatively. You may also want to change your coding practices to take advantage of new capabilities.

4.6 SUMMARY AND KEY GUIDELINES

The most important aspect of performance is DB2's choice of access path. It is determined by the SQL statement, the indexes, the statistics in the catalog, the table design, and the way in which the data was loaded.

The primary goal in achieving good performance is to limit the number of IOs.

Table space scans of small- to medium-sized tables do not take too long for ad hoc queries but are not good for transaction processing. Repeated scans (e.g., for the inner table of a join) can cause incredibly long response times.

Clustered indexes are much better than unclustered indexes. Prior to Version 2.2, DB2 only used an unclustered index when it expected a few rows to be returned. Now, it can make better use of these indexes.

The different types of access paths are:

- Table space scans
- Index scans
- Matching index lookups
- Multiple index access
- Sorts
- Index Only access—for which there is no need to get the data row

In addition to being used for selection criteria, indexes can also be used to avoid the necessity to do a sort.

Joins and subqueries can often be used to satisfy the same type of query. Joins will usually be more efficient.

It is important to query the DB2 catalog to understand the choice of access path. It is especially important to verify whether or not the indexes are clustered. The tables to look at are:

- SYSIBM.SYSINDEXES
- SYSIBM.SYSINDEXPART
- SYSIBM.SYSTABLES
- SYSIBM.SYSTABLEPART
- SYSIBM.SYSCOLUMNS
- SYSIBM.SYSTABLESPACE

SQL statements that use indexable and stage 1 predicates are generally more efficient. The order of predicates in the WHERE clause can make a difference.

5

EXPLAIN

5.1 WHY EVERYONE SHOULD USE EXPLAIN

5.1.1 Why EXPLAIN Is Needed

For the DBA or programmer who cares about performance, EXPLAIN is the best tool he or she has. The most common cause of poor performance is an inadequate choice of access path for the SQL statements. Inadequate does not mean the wrong choice. If there are no indexes available for the columns in the search criteria, then DB2 *must* do a table space scan. By knowing what the access paths will be, the systems developers can determine whether the program code or the database design need improvement.

Many programmers do not bother trying to find out how DB2 will access the data; they do not care, and will take whatever is given them. You, however, do care. That is why you are reading this book. There are several ways to determine the access path. First, an educated guess can be made based on knowing what indexes exist, which is the clustering index, the amount of data in the table, and the DML statement being coded. This, in fact, is what you do when you write the SQL code. SQL supposedly does not require any navigation on your part, or detailed knowledge of the data layout. However, the way you code *can* affect the choice of access path. You must know the organization of the table and indexes to code effectively.

To get a closer guess as to what DB2 will do, a detailed calculation of the cost of each path can be done. An approximate number of IOs can be determined from the number of pages of each index and the table space, and from how clustered the indexes are. This calculation will not match DB2's exactly, however, as we do not know the exact formulas that the DB2 optimizer uses. This type of exercize is time-consuming and is not an effective way to look at all queries. However, it is useful in trying to learn and understand how DB2 makes its choice, especially when DB2's choice is not what was expected.

The easiest way to find out the access path is to ask DB2. The EXPLAIN function does just that. You ask DB2 to explain what access path it is going to use.

IBM and other vendors have products which take the EXPLAIN data and format it into a report that is somewhat more readable than that provided directly by the function. Some of them also automatically incorporate catalog data (such as the keys of the indexes) and data such as the filter factors involved. While these tools can help in reading the results, they do not remove the need to understand the data. Therefore, it is important to learn how to use EXPLAIN. Then you will be in a better position to evaluate any of these products.

5.1.2 When to Use It

When should you use EXPLAIN? It can be run on an exception basis or as a regular part of the development and implementation process. It should certainly be used any time that a program or QMF query is not performing as well as expected. It could also be run for every program or canned query as it is being developed and, again, when it is put into production. Rather than waiting for a problem, the programs can be checked in advance to see that they are going to use the best possible access path. This analysis can be part of the program walkthrough. The reason for running it again when the program goes into production is that the access path selected is highly dependent on the statistics in the catalog and on the volume of data. Production plans should be bound after a full volume of data is in the tables and after RUNSTATS has been run. The EXPLAIN for a program is done with the BIND of the plan. Many shops save the EXPLAIN output of all production plans for trouble and problem analysis.

5.1.3 Reasons for Unexpected Access Paths

As we look at the EXPLAIN results for some queries, we should bear in mind what some of the causes are for an unexpected access path. These may be due to the database or to the program. Certainly, if there is no index available on the columns being checked, then index access cannot be done.

The program code can also make a difference. The programmer may not fully understand the factors involved and may not have coded optimally. Even if you do understand the details, it can be tricky to take best advantage of what's there. DB2 does not have complete statistics on the data distribution. When host variables are used with static SQL, there is even less information available to help DB2 make the choice. Rewording an SQL statement may improve the access path. Sometimes additional redundant predicates will give DB2 more information to work with. They can influence DB2 to avoid a path that *you* do not think will be best. An example of a redundant predicate is shown in Figure 5.1. We

```
SELECT *
  FROM THSADM0
  WHERE PATID = '666555444'
  ORDER BY ADMDATE;
```

Figure 5.1. Ordering Admissions for a Patient.

are asking for admissions for one patient and we want them sorted by admit date. Since there is an index on PATID and ADMDATE, no sort is needed. However, in DB2 Version 1, unless you code the ORDER BY as PATID,ADMDATE, DB2 did a sort on admit date. It is now smart enough not to require the PATID column in the ORDER BY clause, but previously the programmer had to include it.

The SQL statement may also not be correct. If there are several columns with similar names and you use the wrong one, you will get both wrong results and possibly an access path that you did not expect. EXPLAIN is, therefore, also a good debugging tool.

The SQL statements may be coded as well as they can be, but the database may not be optimal:

- Perhaps there are no useful indexes for this statement. If so, the DBA must determine whether or not a new index should be created. This depends on how many transactions would take good advantage of such an index.
- If there are indexes, they might not be clustered even if they are the clustering index. Maybe a reorg is needed.
- If the catalog statistics are not present, then the problem may be as simple as RUNSTATS having not been run for the table space.
- Finally, even if everything looks good, the database design as a whole may not permit efficient processing of this statement. Each table can be clustered in one order. If there are many diverse online needs for the data, it may be difficult to design the tables to effectively accommodate all of them. Even if there is little that can be done short of a complete redesign, it is worth knowing which functions will not perform well.

5.1.4 How to Run EXPLAIN

EXPLAIN can be run either for a program (as part of the BIND operation) or for an individual SQL statement through SPUFI or QMF. Unfortunately, EXPLAIN does not directly tell you anything. It does not produce an output report pinpointing potential trouble spots. Instead, it writes the access path information to a table called the plan table. You then have to issue an SQL SELECT against that table, and try to figure out what it means. The appearance of this data is a bit cryptic. This has scared off many programmers from running EXPLAIN and trying to use it. However, it is not really difficult to understand once you know the important parts to look for. This chapter will try to show you how to look at the output and quickly pick up the important information. Once you have the basics, it is really an easy-to-use tool.

The plan table is a DB2 table called PLAN_TABLE. Each person who is going to run EXPLAIN must have a plan table of his own. So, the first step is to create one. Figure 5.2a has the CREATE statement for this table. There is no need for each person to type all this in herself, one person in the organization (the DBA) can do it and make the source code available to every one else. To create a table of any kind, you must have a table space in which you have authority to create tables. In this example, I am assuming that the programmer was given his own table space for creating small tables. The DBA should provide this for each programmer. If this has not been done, then there is a default table space that can be used, provided this has been made available for PUBLIC use. When in doubt, check with the DBA or system administrator. I am not going to describe all of the columns here. As we look at some EXPLAINs, I will describe the relevant columns. It is important to note, however, that the last three columns are new with Version 2.2. If you already have a plan table from a prior release of DB2, you can ALTER the table to add the three columns (Figure 5.2b).

EXPLAIN can be run with the BIND of a plan. This is done by setting the EXPLAIN parameter to YES (Figure 5.3). Entries will be made in the plan table for each SQL DML statement in the program. The owner of the plan is the person whose plan table is updated by the EXPLAIN. It can also be run for an individual SQL statement outside of a program, through SPUFI or QMF (with SPUFI, you can issue the EXPLAIN and the SELECT from the plan table in one execution). Figure 5.4 shows the format of running an EXPLAIN on a SELECT statement and then selecting the results. When you issue the EXPLAIN statement, the statement you are explaining is not executed. Only PLAN_TABLE is updated.

5.2 EXPLAIN RESULTS—INTERPRETING THE PLAN_TABLE

5.2.1 Identifying Each Explained Statement

QUERYNO is a column of PLAN_TABLE. It is the way you identify which row(s) of PLAN_TABLE corresponds to the statement you are explaining. You can set it to any integer value. Notice that I first delete any rows that have this query number. There is no unique index on this column, and EXPLAIN will just add new rows with the same QUERYNO. You may want to leave the old ones there for comparison, but it can get confusing as to which one is which. I find it better to delete any old ones first. If I want to keep them, then I will use new numbers for subsequent EXPLAINs.

When you explain through BIND, QUERYNO is set to the program statement number. Different programs will have similar program numbers. Therefore, to

```
CREATE TABLE PLAN_TABLE
    (QUERYNO        INTEGER       NOT NULL,
     QBLOCKNO       SMALLINT      NOT NULL,
     APPLNAME       CHAR(8)       NOT NULL,
     PROGNAME       CHAR(8)       NOT NULL,
     PLANNO         SMALLINT      NOT NULL,
     METHOD         SMALLINT      NOT NULL,
     CREATOR        CHAR(8)       NOT NULL,
     TNAME          CHAR(18)      NOT NULL,
     TABNO          SMALLINT      NOT NULL,
     ACCESSTYPE     CHAR(2)       NOT NULL,
     MATCHCOLS      SMALLINT      NOT NULL,
     ACCESSCREATOR  CHAR(8)       NOT NULL,
     ACCESSNAME     CHAR(18)      NOT NULL,
     INDEXONLY      CHAR(1)       NOT NULL,
     SORTN_UNIQ     CHAR(1)       NOT NULL,
     SORTN_JOIN     CHAR(1)       NOT NULL,
     SORTN_ORDERBY  CHAR(1)       NOT NULL,
     SORTN_GROUPBY  CHAR(1)       NOT NULL,
     SORTC_UNIQ     CHAR(1)       NOT NULL,
     SORTC_JOIN     CHAR(1)       NOT NULL,
     SORTC_ORDERBY  CHAR(1)       NOT NULL,
     SORTC_GROUPBY  CHAR(1)       NOT NULL,
     TSLOCKMODE     CHAR(3)       NOT NULL,
     TIMESTAMP      CHAR(16)      NOT NULL,
     REMARKS        VARCHAR(254)  NOT NULL,
     PREFETCH       CHAR(1)       NOT NULL WITH DEFAULT,
     COLUMN_FN_EVAL CHAR(1)       NOT NULL WITH DEFAULT,
     MIXOPSEQ       SMALLINT      NOT NULL WITH DEFAULT)
IN database.tablespace
(a) Creating the table
```

Figure 5.2. PLAN_TABLE.

```
ALTER TABLE PLAN_TABLE
   ADD PREFETCH CHAR(1) NOT NULL WITH DEFAULT;
ALTER TABLE PLAN_TABLE
   ADD COLUMN_FN_EVAL CHAR(1) NOT NULL WITH DEFAULT;
ALTER TABLE PLAN_TABLE
   ADD MIXOPSEQ SMALLINT NOT NULL WITH DEFAULT;
```
(b) Altering the table

Figure 5.2. (*Continued*)

```
BIND PLAN(HSPAT01) MEMBER(HSPAT01) ACTION(REPLACE) RETAIN
ISOLATION(CS) VALIDATE(BIND)
EXPLAIN(YES)
```
Figure 5.3. BIND Asking for an EXPLAIN.

```
DELETE FROM PLAN_TABLE WHERE QUERYNO=3;
EXPLAIN PLAN SET QUERYNO=3 FOR
SELECT * FROM THSPAT0
   WHERE PATID='666555444';
SELECT * FROM PLAN_TABLE WHERE QUERYNO=3;
```
Figure 5.4. Explaining a Single Statement.

identify the plan for a particular program, you can use the APPLNAME and PROGNAME columns. APPLNAME is the plan name, PROGNAME is the individual program (DBRM) name. Figure 5.5 selects the plan information for an application plan. Again, you may want to delete the previous rows before rebinding. Also, if you are finished asking for an explanation, don't forget to change BIND's EXPLAIN parameter back to NO so that you don't keep writing to PLAN__TABLE.

You can run EXPLAIN through SPUFI on a statement before embedding it in a program as a first checkout. But don't forget that dynamic SQL is not exactly the same as static. When host variables are used in the statement, DB2 has less information on what the query will be looking for, than when constants are used. You can simulate host variables by using a ? instead of a constant in the statements you are explaining.

Now let's look at our first EXPLAIN for the query in Figure 5.4. The results are shown in Figure 5.6a. Notice that the output is spread over four sets of lines. There are too many columns to fit across the page. Through SPUFI or QMF, you would page to the right to see all the information. In Figure 5.6b, I have short-

```
SELECT * FROM PLAN_TABLE WHERE APPLNAME='HSPAT01';
```

Figure 5.5. Getting the EXPLAIN Output for a Plan.

ened the output to three sets of lines by combining the sort fields into one field. This could be done by concatentating the columns in the select list (or using a view which does the concatenation). As I said, there are many columns in PLAN__TABLE and it can be a little daunting the first time you look at the output. However, there are really only a few columns that you need to look at most of the time. In fact, I have left out the REMARKS column from all of the examples since it is not filled in by EXPLAIN. It can be updated by the programmer to make whatever notes he wants. I also left out the TIMESTAMP column which tells you when the EXPLAIN was run.

There will be one row for each table being accessed. For example, if you are joining three tables, then there will be three rows in the plan table. There may be additional rows for any additional sorting that may be needed after several tables are joined (e.g., if DISTINCT is used). This sort is not part of the access for either individual table, so it has its own row. Also, starting with DB2 Version 2, the sort done by any ORDER BY, GROUP BY, or DISTINCT operation on a single table will also result in a separate row. Starting with Version 2.2, multiple indexes can be used to access a single table. In this case, there will be one row to indicate a multi-index operation, one row for each index used, and a row to indicate whether the intersection (AND) or union (OR) of the indexes is needed.

5.2.2 The Access Path

5.2.2.1 ACCESSTYPE

First, you check QUERYNO to make sure you are looking at the right line. The next column to look at is ACCESSTYPE. This tells you whether or not indexes are going to be used. For this query the value is 'I', meaning that an index will be used. The possible values are:

> 'I'—for a single index access.
> 'R'—for a table space scan.
> blank—a blank is used in several situations.
>
> - For an insert statement. DB2 will always use the clustering index to find a desirable place to store the data. It will then update all indexes.
> - For rows from sort operations.
> - For UPDATE and DELETE statements which have WHERE CURRENT OF CURSOR

There are several new values added with Version 2.2. They are described in more detail later:

ACCESS PATH SELECTION

QUERYNO	QBLOCKNO	APPLNAME	PROGNAME	PLANNO	METHOD	CREATOR
3	1		DSNESM68	1	0	GELLER

TNAME	TABNO	ACCESS TYPE	MATCHCOLS	ACCESS CREATOR	ACCESS NAME	INDEXONLY
THSPAT0	1	I	1	GELLER	XHSPAT02	N

SORTN UNIQ	SORTN JOIN	SORTN ORDERBY	SORTN GROUPBY	SORTC UNIQ	SORTC JOIN	SORTC ORDERBY	SORTC GROUPBY	TS LOCKMODE
N	N	N	N	N	N	N	N	IS

PREFETCH	COLUMN FN EVAL	MIXOPSEQ
		0

(a) With each sort column separate

QUERYNO	QBLOCKNO	APPLNAME	PROGNAME	PLANNO	METHOD	CREATOR
3	1		DSNESM68	1	0	GELLER

TNAME	TABNO	ACCESS TYPE	MATCHCOLS	ACCESS CREATOR	ACCESS NAME	INDEXONLY
THSPAT0	1	I	1	GELLER	XHSPAT02	N

NNNNCCCC UJOGUJOG	TS LOCKMODE	PREFETCH	COLUMN FN EVAL	MIXOPSEQ
NNNNNNNN	IS			0

(b) With the sort columns combined

Figure 5.6. The Contents of PLAN__TABLE.

'I1'—one fetch index scan
'N'—index scan for predicate with IN keyword
'M'—each of the values that start with 'M' are for multiple
'MX'—index access
'MI'
'MU'

5.2.2.2 ACCESSNAME

After seeing that an index is going to be used, the next thing to look for is which index. This is found in column ACCESSNAME. For our first query, we see that XHSPAT02 will be used. This is the index on PATID. This is what we would expect. We know that this is a unique index and our query asked for a specific patient. There will be (at most) one row to satisfy our query and this is clearly the fastest way to access the data.

This represents our first guideline. The first thing to look for is whether or not the access will be via an index or via a table space scan. We want to be wary of table space scans. This does not mean, however, that they should always be avoided. Not all table space scans are a problem. For a one-time report selecting on a nonindexed column, we can afford the extra time. If this column is not used for online selection, then it is not worth the maintenance overhead for an index. For small reference tables that occupy at most several pages (which could contain hundreds of rows), a table space scan is quick. It will involve at most a few IOs, which is what an index access will require.

5.2.2.3 Sequential Prefetch

Our next example (Figure 5.7a) looks at patient data by name. This SELECT asks for all patients whose last name is greater than or equal to J (this includes names that start with K, L, etc.). The EXPLAIN output is in Figure 5.7b. Note that DB2 is going to use a table space scan (R in column ACCESSTYPE), even though there is an index on LASTNAME,FIRSTNAME and this is the clustering index. The reason for this is that DB2 has determined that about half of the rows will satisfy this criteria, so, rather than scanning the index and a large percentage of the data pages, it will be quicker to just read through all the data pages. However, if we wanted names greater than or equal to 'Z', then the assumption is that a small percent of rows will be returned and the index would be used. In fact, for this table space scan, sequential prefetch is likely to be used. One IO will read in up to 32 pages at a time (based on the buffer pool size). The new column PREFETCH indicates whether DB2 is planning on doing prefetch. The value 'S' shows this.

5.2.3 Sorting

5.2.3.1 ORDER BY—Will a Sort be Needed?

Now let's look at some variations. Figure 5.8a has the same query but with an ORDER BY on LASTNAME,FIRSTNAME. We are requesting that the selected data be sorted into the same order as the name index. Now DB2 determines that

```
DELETE FROM PLAN_TABLE WHERE QUERYNO=4;
EXPLAIN PLAN SET QUERYNO=4 FOR
SELECT * FROM THSPAT0
   WHERE LASTNAME >= 'J';
SELECT * FROM PLAN_TABLE WHERE QUERYNO=4;
```
(a) Running the EXPLAIN

QUERYNO	QBLOCKNO	APPLNAME	PROGNAME	PLANNO	METHOD	CREATOR
4	1		DSNESM68	1	0	GELLER

TNAME	TABNO	ACCESS TYPE	MATCHCOLS	ACCESS CREATOR	ACCESS NAME	INDEXONLY
THSPAT0	1	R	0			N

NNNNCCCC UJOGUJOG	TS LOCKMODE	PREFETCH	COLUMN FN EVAL	MIXOPSEQ
NNNNNNNN	IS	S		0

(b) The contents of PLAN_TABLE

Figure 5.7. EXPLAIN for SELECT with >=.

even though many rows are to be selected, sorting them all will be costly. Since there is an index already in this order and the index is clustered, efficent access can be achieved by using this index. The data rows are going to physically be in almost the same order as the index and will have many rows on the same page. Therefore, prefetch will be used for this access path for both the index pages and the data pages.

Figure 5.8b has the EXPLAIN output that tells us that the index will be used. No sort is needed. All the columns that start with 'SORT' have a value of 'N'. This is a very useful result. Sorts of a few dozen rows are not costly, but large sorts can be. Avoiding the sort is especially useful for an online browse type of function. These are likely to need the data sorted. As described in Section 6.1, when a cursor is used and a sort is required, the entire set of data must be

```
DELETE FROM PLAN_TABLE WHERE QUERYNO=5;
EXPLAIN PLAN SET QUERYNO=5 FOR
SELECT * FROM THSPATO
   WHERE LASTNAME >= 'J'
   ORDER BY LASTNAME,FIRSTNAME;
SELECT * FROM PLAN_TABLE WHERE QUERYNO=5;
```

(a) Running the EXPLAIN

QUERYNO	QBLOCKNO	APPLNAME	PROGNAME	PLANNO	METHOD	CREATOR
5	1		DSNESM68	1	0	GELLER

TNAME	TABNO	ACCESS TYPE	MATCHCOLS	ACCESS CREATOR	ACCESS NAME	INDEXONLY
THSPATO	1	I	1	GELLER	XHSPATO1	N

NNNNCCCC UJOGUJOG	TS LOCKMODE	PREFETCH	COLUMN FN EVAL	MIXOPSEQ
NNNNNNNN	IS	S		0

(b) The contents of PLAN_TABLE - no Sort needed

Figure 5.8. EXPLAIN for SELECT with >= and ORDER BY.

retrieved and sorted before any rows are fetched into the program. However, if a sort is not needed (as in this example), then the rows will only be accessed one at a time with each fetch. A program can, therefore, quickly fetch in a screen's worth at a time, regardless of how many rows meet the search criteria. Section 6.1 has the code that a program would use to do this type of browse operation efficiently.

The name index is clustered. If it were not, then even using the ORDER BY clause may not get DB2 to use the index. It will only do so if it expects there to be only a small number of rows selected such as with:

WHERE LASTNAME BETWEEN 'JOHN' AND 'JOI'

With an unclustered index, the data rows are in a much different order than the index. It is likely that each selected row will be on a different page and a separate IO will be needed for each row. Even if there are many selected rows on the same page, but with widely separated values, separate IOs might have been needed for each row prior to Version 2.2. This would be true unless system usage was low. Then, some of the pages might still be in a buffer when needed again, and some IOs might be saved.

5.2.3.2 List Prefetch

With Version 2.2, the use of unclustered indexes has been greatly improved. Rather than reading each data row in the order of the index, DB2 may choose to first find all index entries that qualify, and sort them into RID order. Then, at most one IO per data page will be needed to read the rows—and not only that, but prefetch may also be used to read in many pages at a time. In this case, the list of rows to be read may not include all pages from the table space. DB2 will use prefetch for those parts of the table space that are needed. This process is different from the normal sequential prefetch. It is called list prefetch. The EXPLAIN output will indicate when list prefetch is going to be used. The PREFETCH column will have an 'L' in it. This is shown in Figure 5.9.

5.2.3.3 The Sort Columns

Figure 5.10 has the EXPLAIN output when a sort is needed for the ORDER BY. There are eight SORT columns to indicate different reasons for the sort. Sorts done for ORDER BY, GROUP BY, DISTINCT and UNION (SORTx_UNIQ), and for joins have different columns. There are also two sets—those for the "NEW" table (SORTN), which are for the table in the current line, and those for the "COMPOSITE" table (SORTC), which are for an intermediate table from a previous step. UNION and DISTINCT require DB2 to eliminate duplicate result rows. DB2 takes the results table produced by the selection criteria, sorts it, and then finds the unique result rows.

There are several important notes to make about this example. First, the results shown here are for DB2 Version 2. There are two steps in the process. Each step is identified by the PLANNO column. In the first step, there is a table space scan of the THSPAT0 table. In the second step, a sort is done on the rows selected by the first step. This is indicated by the 'Y' in the column SORTC_ORDERBY. In Version 1, this query had only one row in plan table with a 'Y' in SORTN_ORDERBY. Either way of interpreting the process makes sense, but apparently the DB2 developers decided to change how it is done. Unfortunately, they did not update the Version 2.1 manuals to describe the change.

In effect, the definitions of "new" and "composite" have changed. "New" currently is used for the inner table of a merge scan join. "Composite" is used for any sort applied to an intermediate results table.

We should also note that even though this example involved a table space scan,

QUERYNO	QBLOCKNO	APPLNAME	PROGNAME	PLANNO	METHOD	CREATOR
5	1		DSNESM68	1	0	GELLER

TNAME	TABNO	ACCESS TYPE	MATCHCOLS	ACCESS CREATOR	ACCESS NAME	INDEXONLY
THSPAT0	1	I	1	GELLER	XHSPAT02	N

NNNNCCCC UJOGUJOG	TS LOCKMODE	PREFETCH	COLUMN FN EVAL	MIXOPSEQ
NNNNNNNN	IS	L		0

Figure 5.9. List Prefetch.

it is certainly possible to have index access and a sort. If we want the data sorted on a different set of columns from the search criteria of the WHERE clause, DB2 might use an index to select the rows and then do a sort. Or it may use an index to avoid the sort and have more data rows to retrieve to meet the search criteria.

When we look at the EXPLAIN output, we want to check to see if any sorting is being done. In general, we want to avoid sorts, although, again, not all sorts are a problem. If only a small number of rows are being sorted, then it will not take long. A database design guideline is to have indexes on columns that are frequently needed in ORDER BY clauses as well as in WHERE clauses. A corresponding programming guideline is to try to use the same columns in both clauses. Even if the output order is not important, asking for it in order may sometimes get DB2 to use an index. However, again, index access is not always best, especially if the index is not well-clustered.

5.2.4 MATCHCOLS

At this point we will look at another index-related column of PLAN_TABLE. The MATCHCOLS column tells us how many columns of the index (for index access) are being used for matching the search criteria. In Figure 5.8b, the value in this column is 1. We are searching by LASTNAME, which is the first column of the index. If the WHERE clause read:

QUERYNO	QBLOCKNO	APPLNAME	PROGNAME	PLANNO	METHOD	CREATOR
5	1		DSNESM68	1	0	GELLER
5	1		DSNESM68	2	3	

TNAME	TABNO	ACCESS TYPE	MATCHCOLS	ACCESS CREATOR	ACCESS NAME	INDEXONLY
THSPAT0	1	R	0			N
	0		0			N

NNNNCCCC UJOGUJOG	TS LOCKMODE	PREFETCH	COLUMN FN EVAL	MIXOPSEQ
NNNNNNNN	IS	S		0
NNNNNYN				0

Figure 5.10. The Contents of PLAN_TABLE—With Sort Needed.

WHERE LASTNAME='JONES' AND FIRSTNAME LIKE 'M%'

then MATCHCOLS would equal 2. The index structure would be scanned for the first entry with a last name of JONES and a first name that begins with an M. If MATCHCOLS equals 0, then this indicates an index scan—the entire index is read looking for matching values. Figure 5.11 has an example of a query that would result in an index scan. There is no particular beginning or ending point for the index scan. We are looking for all names that end in 'SON'. Since we want them sorted by last name, it still pays for DB2 to use the index to avoid the sort. Scanning the index is quicker than scanning the table space as the index space has fewer pages. Assuming that not too many rows are going to be selected, there will not be all that much access to the data rows.

5.2.5 Other Types of Index Access

Prior to Version 2.2, the only type of index access code listed under ACCESSTYPE was 'I'. There are now a number of additional types, the most important of which involves the use of multiple indexes. The first one we will look at is the value 'N', which is used when there is a matching index lookup for a predicate with the IN keyword or with the ORing of predicates on the same

```
DELETE FROM PLAN_TABLE WHERE QUERYNO=6;
EXPLAIN PLAN SET QUERYNO=6 FOR
SELECT * FROM THSPAT0
  WHERE LASTNAME LIKE '%SON'
  ORDERBY LASTNAME,FIRSTNAME;
SELECT * FROM PLAN_TABLE WHERE QUERYNO=6;
```

QUERYNO	QBLOCKNO	APPLNAME	PROGNAME	PLANNO	METHOD	CREATOR
6	1		DSNESM68	1	0	GELLER

TNAME	TABNO	ACCESS TYPE	MATCHCOLS	ACCESS CREATOR	ACCESS NAME	INDEXONLY
THSPAT0	1	I	0	GELLER	XHSPAT01	N

NNNNCCCC UJOGUJOG	TS LOCKMODE	PREFETCH	COLUMN FN EVAL	MIXOPSEQ
NNNNNNNN	IS	S		0

Figure 5.11. The Contents of PLAN_TABLE—Index Scan.

column (which is equivalent to IN). An example of this is shown in Figure 5.12. For a matching index lookup with an equal (=) predicate, DB2 will use the index structure to directly find the matching entries. With an IN predicate, each value in the IN list can be found with a direct search of the index tree. In other words, DB2 can jump around the index to find each entry quickly. This type of processing was done in earlier releases, but is only now indicated in the EXPLAIN. It is useful information because while each entry is quickly found, the more entries in the IN list, the more accesses are necessary. Figure 5.12b has the results of the EXPLAIN. Note that it does not tell you how many values are in the IN list. MATCHCOLS has the same significance as for 'I' access.

An ACCESSTYPE of 'I1' means a "one fetch" index access. That is, only one entry of the index has to be retrieved, which is all that is necessary to satisfy the search criteria. What kind of query will this handle? It can be used for find-

```
DELETE FROM PLAN_TABLE WHERE QUERYNO=6;
EXPLAIN PLAN SET QUERYNO=6 FOR
SELECT * FROM THSPAT0
   WHERE LASTNAME IN('BAKER','COOK','TAYLOR');
SELECT * FROM PLAN_TABLE WHERE QUERYNO=6;
```
(a) The EXPLAIN

QUERYNO	QBLOCKNO	APPLNAME	PROGNAME	PLANNO	METHOD	CREATOR
6	1		DSNESM68	1	0	GELLER

TNAME	TABNO	ACCESS TYPE	MATCHCOLS	ACCESS CREATOR	ACCESS NAME	INDEXONLY
THSPAT0	1	N	1	GELLER	XHSPAT01	N

NNNNCCCC UJOGUJOG	TS LOCKMODE	PREFETCH	COLUMN FN EVAL	MIXOPSEQ
NNNNNNNN	IS			0

(b) The contents of PLAN_TABLE for IN

Figure 5.12. The Use of the IN Keyword.

ing the minimum value of a column that has a single-column index. Figure 5.13 asks for MIN(BIRTHDATE). If there is an index on BIRTHDATE (XHSPAT03), then the first entry in the index is the minimum value. Likewise, if you have a descending index on a column, then the MAX function can be satisfied by getting the first index entry.

I1 access can also be done with a composite index in some cases. In Figure 5.14, we are asking for the most recent date of admission for a patient. The index XHSADM01 is on PATIENT, ADMDATE DESC, ADMSEQ DESC. That is, for each patient, the entries are in reverse date order. In the query, the only column function is MAX and the only predicate is for a specific patient. The first entry for the patient contains the maximum admission date for him.

```
DELETE FROM PLAN_TABLE WHERE QUERYNO=6;
EXPLAIN PLAN SET QUERYNO=6 FOR
SELECT MIN(BIRTHDATE) FROM THSPAT0;
SELECT * FROM PLAN_TABLE WHERE QUERYNO=6;
```

QUERYNO	QBLOCKNO	APPLNAME	PROGNAME	PLANNO	METHOD	CREATOR
6	1		DSNESM68	1	0	GELLER

TNAME	TABNO	ACCESS TYPE	MATCHCOLS	ACCESS CREATOR	ACCESS NAME	INDEXONLY
THSPAT0	1	I1	1	GELLER	XHSPAT03	Y

NNNNCCCC UJOGUJOG	TS LOCKMODE	PREFETCH	COLUMN FN EVAL	MIXOPSEQ
NNNNNNNN	IS			0

Figure 5.13. The Contents of PLAN_TABLE—One Fetch Index Access-MIN.

```
DELETE FROM PLAN_TABLE WHERE QUERYNO=6;
EXPLAIN PLAN SET QUERYNO=6 FOR
SELECT MAX(ADMDATE) FROM THSADM0
   WHERE PATID='878787879';
SELECT * FROM PLAN_TABLE WHERE QUERYNO=6;
```
Figure 5.14. One Fetch Index Access with a Composite Index.

5.2.6 Multiple Index Access

As described in Chapter 4, Version 2.2 introduced the ability to use more than one index to access a table. This can produce tremendous improvements for queries that use AND or OR with columns that are not in the same index. It can now satisfy some of the predicates with different indexes and then combine the results by finding the intersection or union of the partial results. However, you should remember that DB2 will not always use multiple indexes for these cases. It might still choose another access path. In Figure 5.15a, we are asking for patients that have moved into WARD '1000' on February 14, 1991. The access path might involve index XHSLOC01, which has the date a patient moved into a location, and index XHSLOC02, which has the WARD. Or DB2 might choose to use only one of the indexes. It might use index XHSLOC01 to find all rows with the requested date, and then read the data rows to satisfy the rest of the criteria. It would do so if it expected to find only a few rows with a given date. Reading the data rows for these would be faster than reading the XHSLOC02 index to find the rows with WARD='1000' and then sorting the two lists and finding the intersection.

When DB2 does use multiple indexes for access, the EXPLAIN will produce several rows in PLAN_TABLE (Figure 5.15b). The first row will have ACCESSTYPE 'M'. This indicates multiple index access. Following this will be one row for each index that is accessed. Each of these rows will have ACCESSTYPE 'MX' and will list the index used under ACCESSNAME. Following these rows will be a row which indicates whether the union (OR) or intersection (AND) of the selected entries is to be found. The ACCESSTYPE for this row will be 'MU' (for OR) or 'MI' (for AND). MIXOPSEQ is a new column of PLAN_TABLE. It is used to indicate the order of the operations of a multiple index access.

There are several other fields of interest in this EXPLAIN. The first row has PREFETCH = 'L'. List prefetch is used for this type of access. Whenever multiple indexes are used, each index is searched for qualifying entries. A list of entries is produced and then sorted into RID order. This is necessary in order to merge the lists to get their union or intersection. Therefore, the resulting list is also in RID order, and list prefetch can be used. Thus, we get two benefits from this access type: the use of several indexes, as well as list prefetch. Note that since the sort of the RID entries is always done, there is no need for any indication of this sort in the EXPLAIN output.

The rows with ACCESSTYPE = 'MX' each have a 'Y' for INDEXONLY. The data rows are only read after the index criteria are resolved. The access to the indexes does not involve any data row access.

In this example, DB2 has decided that there might be many rows satisfying each of the two predicates, and that the cheapest access path is to use both location indexes and combine them to find the rows which satisfy both. The fourth row has ACCESSTYPE = 'MI', indicating the intersection of the RID lists.

5.2.7 Tracking Down a Problem—An Example

We'll now look at an example that illustrates some typical situations that can result in an unexpected access path. Figure 5.16a has a SELECT requesting locations with PATID starting with a 'J' and WARD equal to '1004'. The THSLOC0 table has two indexes. XHSLOC01 is the clustering index and is on

```
DELETE FROM PLAN_TABLE WHERE QUERYNO=6;
EXPLAIN PLAN SET QUERYNO=6 FOR
SELECT * FROM THSLOC0
  WHERE LOCDATE = '1991-02-14' AND WARD = '1000';
SELECT * FROM PLAN_TABLE WHERE QUERYNO=6;
```
(a) SELECT with AND of two predicates

QUERYNO	QBLOCKNO	APPLNAME	PROGNAME	PLANNO	METHOD	CREATOR
6	1		DSNESM68	1	0	GELLER
6	1		DSNESM68	1	0	GELLER
6	1		DSNESM68	1	0	GELLER
6	1		DSNESM68	1	0	GELLER

TNAME	TABNO	ACCESS TYPE	MATCHCOLS	ACCESS CREATOR	ACCESS NAME	INDEXONLY
THSLOC0	1	M	0	GELLER		N
THSLOC0	1	MX	0	GELLER	XHSLOC01	Y
THSLOC0	1	MX	0	GELLER	XHSLOC02	Y
THSLOC0	1	MI	0	GELLER		N

NNNNCCCC UJOGUJOG	TS LOCKMODE	PREFETCH	COLUMN FN EVAL	MIXOPSEQ
NNNNNNNN	IS	L		0
NNNNNNNN	IS	S		1
NNNNNNNN	IS	S		2
NNNNNNNN	IS			3

(b) EXPLAIN results

Figure 5.15. Multiple Index Access.

```
SELECT * FROM THSLOC0
  WHERE PATID LIKE 'J%' AND WARD = '1004'
(a) The SELECT
```

QUERYNO	QBLOCKNO	APPLNAME	PROGNAME	PLANNO	METHOD	CREATOR
20	1		DSNESM68	1	0	GELLER

TNAME	TABNO	ACCESS TYPE	MATCHCOLS	ACCESS CREATOR	ACCESS NAME	INDEXONLY
THSLOC0	1	R	0			N

NNNNCCCC UJOGUJOG	TS LOCKMODE	PREFETCH	COLUMN FN EVAL	MIXOPSEQ
NNNNNNNN	IS	S		0

(b) The plan for location access

Figure 5.16. Selecting Location Records.

PATID, LOCDATE, LOCSEQ. XHSLOC02 is on CURRENTFLAG, WARD, ROOM, PATID. There are 180,000 rows in the table.

Since the clustering index is on PATID and we are looking for a range, we would expect DB2 to use XHSLOC01. Figure 5.16b has the EXPLAIN output. A table space scan is being used ('R' in column ACCESSTYPE). Why? The first thing to do is to look at the query again to see if it appears correct. Everything seems fine. The next step is to check the DB2 catalog to see that the indexes are properly created and the statistics look right. Figure 5.17a has the SELECT statements to query the catalog and Figure 5.17b has the results of this query. However, we see from the cardinality columns that there are only 10 rows. This is in columns CARD in SYSIBM.SYSTABLES and FULLKEYCARD in SYSIBM.SYSINDEXES. If we know that there is really much more data, then the likely explanation is that a few rows were initially put into the table and RUNSTATS was run. The rest of the data was subsequently entered, but RUNSTATS was not run again. The catalog statistics are only updated when you run

```
SELECT NAME,CLUSTERED,FIRSTKEYCARD,FULLKEYCARD,NLEAF,NLEVEL,
    CLUSTERRATIO
    FROM SYSIBM.SYSINDEXES
    WHERE TBNAME='THSLOC0';
```
(a) The SELECT

NAME	CLUSTERED	FIRSTKEYCARD	FULLKEYCARD	NLEAF	NLEVELS	CLUSTER RATIO
XHSLOC01	Y	10	10	1	1	100
XHSLOC02	Y	2	10	1	1	100

(b) Output from index statistics query

Figure 5.17. Querying the Catalog for Index Statistics.

RUNSTATS. Forgetting to run it is quite common, especially if the table is initially populated with a small amount of data.

Seeing that there are only 10 rows, we can understand why DB2 decided to use a table space scan. The 10 rows all fit on 1 page (NPAGES of SYSTABLES is 1). It is quicker for DB2 to read the one data page than to use the index.

This illustrates an important point. If RUNSTATS has never been run, DB2 uses some default assumptions. It assumes that there is a reasonable amount of data (10,000 rows) and that the cardinality of each column is 25 (25 distinct values). However, if RUNSTATS is run on a tiny amount of data, it will use those statistics in its cost calculations. It is very common for a table to start with a small amount of data and for the rest to be inserted over time. When the system first goes into production, the plans will be bound. Normally, you want to run RUNSTATS before the production BIND. However, in the cases where the bulk of the data won't be entered for a while, it is better *not* to run RUNSTATS at this time at all. Wait the few months until there is a larger volume of data. Then run RUNSTATS and BIND the plans again.

Okay, we now run RUNSTATS and rerun our EXPLAIN. The output from this run is in Figure 5.18. What's going on? This time DB2 decided to use index XHSLOC02 with a nonmatching index scan (MATCHCOLS = 0); it is scanning the entire index, finding entries with WARD = '1004'. Why didn't it use XHSLOC01? After all, XHSLOC01 is the clustering index. Well, we run our query on the catalog again to see the up-to-date statistics. These are in Figure 5.19. SYSINDEXES shows that XHSLOC01 is *not* clustered, whereas XHSLOC02 is. Remember, the clustering index is not necessarily clustered. It is used for clustering on inserts and during a reorg. We now think about how we entered data into the table. It was converted from another system. We used

QUERYNO	QBLOCKNO	APPLNAME	PROGNAME	PLANNO	METHOD	CREATOR
21	1		DSNESM68	1	0	GELLER

TNAME	TABNO	ACCESS TYPE	MATCHCOLS	ACCESS CREATOR	ACCESS NAME	INDEXONLY
THSLOC0	1	I	0	GELLER	XHSLOC02	N

NNNNCCCC UJOGUJOG	TS LOCKMODE	PREFETCH	COLUMN FN EVAL	MIXOPSEQ
NNNNNNNN	IS		0	

Figure 5.18. Plan for Location Access After RUNSTATS.

NAME	CLUSTERED	FIRSTKEYCARD	FULLKEYCARD	NLEAF	NLEVELS	CLUSTER RATIO
XHSLOC01	N	100000	180000	700	3	40
XHSLOC02	Y	2	160000	700	3	99

Figure 5.19. Output from Index Statistics After RUNSTATS.

the LOAD utility to insert the rows. The file that we used for input came from the other system and the data in it was in order by CURRENTFLAG,WARD! The LOAD utility does *not* use the clustering index for inserting the data. It is physically inserted in the order of the input file! That is why the second index is clustered and the clustering index is not.

Since XHSLOC01 is not clustered, using it to find a range of values is not too efficient as the data rows will be spread out through the data pages. XHSLOC02 *is* clustered. Therefore, since DB2 expects to not find too many rows with WARD = '1004', there will be fewer IOs through this index. That explains why this access path was chosen.

We are not quite done. Our intention was for XHSLOC01 to be clustered. We can accomplish this by doing a reorg on the table space. The reorg will put the data in clustering index order. After the reorg, we must run RUNSTATS again to update the statistics. These are shown in Figure 5.20. Rerunning the EXPLAIN of our query produces the PLAN__TABLE rows of Figure 5.21.

NAME	CLUSTERED	FIRSTKEYCARD	FULLKEYCARD	NLEAF	NLEVELS	CLUSTER RATIO
XHSLOC01	Y	100000	180000	700	3	100
XHSLOC02	N	2	160000	700	3	30

Figure 5.20. Output from Index Statistics After REORG.

QUERYNO	QBLOCKNO	APPLNAME	PROGNAME	PLANNO	METHOD	CREATOR
22	1		DSNESM68	1	0	GELLER

TNAME	TABNO	ACCESS TYPE	MATCHCOLS	ACCESS CREATOR	ACCESS NAME	INDEXONLY
THSLOC0	1	I	1	GELLER	XHSLOC01	N

NNNNCCCC UJOGUJOG	TS LOCKMODE	PREFETCH	COLUMN FN EVAL	MIXOPSEQ
NNNNNNNN	IS	S		0

Figure 5.21. Plan for Location Access After REORG.

This example illustrates several important points.

The performance of an SQL statement is based on several factors:

- the statement itself
- the available indexes
- the way the data was entered into the table
- whether reorgs have been done and whether and when RUNSTATS was run

To understand and tune the performance, therefore, involves:

- looking at all this information
- possibly rewriting the statement
- possibly doing some database tuning

You cannot isolate the programming effort from the database administration effort. Both must be done together. Not only must the DBA and programmer work together, but they also must both be knowledgable in each other's tasks.

242   ACCESS PATH SELECTION

5.2.8 Index-Only Access

Most SQL statements naturally require reading data rows. However, for some SELECT statements, DB2 does not have to read any data rows at all. The query can be entirely satisfied with the information in an index. The SELECT in Figure 5.22a wants the admission dates for patient '666555444'. The XHSADM01 index is on PATID,ADMDATE,ADMSEQ. DB2 can do a direct lookup on PATID and then scan the index entries, picking up the admit date, until the PATID changes. Index-only access is desirable when it can be used. It will obviously be faster since there are no IOs for data pages. Figure 5.22b has the EXPLAIN output for this query. The column INDEXONLY will have a Y if only the index is needed to satisfy the query. Otherwise, it has an N. In this example, MATCH-

```
DELETE FROM PLAN_TABLE WHERE QUERYNO=10;

EXPLAIN PLAN SET QUERYNO=10 FOR

SELECT ADMDATE FROM THSADM0

   WHERE PATID='666555444';

SELECT * FROM PLAN_TABLE WHERE QUERYNO=10;
```

(a) Selecting the admit date

QUERYNO	QBLOCKNO	APPLNAME	PROGNAME	PLANNO	METHOD	CREATOR
10	1		DSNESM68	1	0	GELLER

TNAME	TABNO	ACCESS TYPE	MATCHCOLS	ACCESS CREATOR	ACCESS NAME	INDEXONLY
THSADM0	1	I	1	GELLER	XHSADM01	Y

NNNNCCCC	TS		COLUMN	
UJOGUJOG	LOCKMODE	PREFETCH	FN EVAL	MIXOPSEQ
NNNNNNNN	IS		0	

(b) Plan with index only access

Figure 5.22. Index Only Access.

COLS is 1 as there is a direct lookup by the first column of the index. Index scans of the entire index space (MATCHCOLS = 0) can also be index-only. To help get index-only access, programmers and QMF users should only include the columns they need in the select list. If they ask for more than they need, there is a greater chance that the data page will be needed.

5.2.9 INSERTs, UPDATEs, and DELETEs

Simple INSERT statements (those without a subselect) are always handled the same way (described in Section 4.1). The desirable page to store the row is found by doing a matching index lookup of the clustering index. Each index is updated with an entry for the row. Since there is nothing unique about the processing of a given INSERT, the EXPLAIN does not say very much. There is just one row with an ACCESSTYPE = ' ' (Figure 5.23).

UPDATEs and DELETEs have WHERE clauses to identify the rows to be af-

```
DELETE FROM PLAN_TABLE WHERE QUERYNO=10;

EXPLAIN PLAN SET QUERYNO=10 FOR

INSERT INTO FROM THSADM0
   VALUES('123456789','1990-03-15',1,'9999-12-31',1);

SELECT * FROM PLAN_TABLE WHERE QUERYNO=10;
```

QUERYNO	QBLOCKNO	APPLNAME	PROGNAME	PLANNO	METHOD	CREATOR
10	1		DSNESM68	1	0	GELLER

TNAME	TABNO	ACCESS TYPE	MATCHCOLS	ACCESS CREATOR	ACCESS NAME	INDEXONLY
THSADM0	1			GELLER		N

NNNNCCCC UJOGUJOG	TS LOCKMODE	PREFETCH	COLUMN FN EVAL	MIXOPSEQ
NNNNNNNN	IS		0	

Figure 5.23. EXPLAIN for Inserting a Row.

fected. EXPLAIN will have rows to indicate the access path to find the desired rows. There is no information about the actual updating and deleting of the rows, as the process is always the same (see Section 4.1). Figure 5.24 has an UPDATE statement and the corresponding rows in PLAN_TABLE. An UPDATE will affect some of the table indexes. It would be helpful if EXPLAIN would identify them, but it is not really essential. You can easily figure this out by checking the catalog to see which indexes contain any of the columns being changed.

As was described in Section 4.1, prior to Version 2.2, DB2 often could not use an index to find the rows to be updated if any of the index columns were being changed. In Figure 5.25, if there is an index on SALARY, this index could not be used to find the rows. For each one found, SALARY will be increased by 10%. This value is greater than the original value and, therefore, will create a new

```
DELETE FROM PLAN_TABLE WHERE QUERYNO=10;
EXPLAIN PLAN SET QUERYNO=10 FOR
UPDATE THSADM0
   SET DISDATE='1990-04-22'
   WHERE PATID='666555444' AND ADMDATE='1990-03-15' AND ADMSEQ=1;
SELECT * FROM PLAN_TABLE WHERE QUERYNO=10;
```

QUERYNO	QBLOCKNO	APPLNAME	PROGNAME	PLANNO	METHOD	CREATOR
10	1		DSNESM68	1	0	GELLER

TNAME	TABNO	ACCESS TYPE	MATCHCOLS	ACCESS CREATOR	ACCESS NAME	INDEXONLY
THSADM0	1	I	3	GELLER	XHSADM01	N

NNNNCCCC UJOGUJOG	TS LOCKMODE	PREFETCH	COLUMN FN EVAL	MIXOPSEQ
NNNNNNNN	IS		0	

Figure 5.24. EXPLAIN for an UPDATE.

```
DELETE FROM PLAN_TABLE WHERE QUERYNO=10;
EXPLAIN PLAN SET QUERYNO=10 FOR
UPDATE THSEMP0
   SET SALARY = SALARY * .10
   WHERE SALARY > 30000;
SELECT * FROM PLAN_TABLE WHERE QUERYNO=10;
```

QUERYNO	QBLOCKNO	APPLNAME	PROGNAME	PLANNO	METHOD	CREATOR
10	1		DSNESM68	1	0	GELLER

TNAME	TABNO	ACCESS TYPE	MATCHCOLS	ACCESS CREATOR	ACCESS NAME	INDEXONLY
THSEMP0	1	R	0	GELLER		N

NNNNCCCC UJOGUJOG	TS LOCKMODE	PREFETCH	COLUMN FN EVAL	MIXOPSEQ
NNNNNNNN	IS	S		0

Figure 5.25. Updates Might Not Use an Index.

index entry further down in the index. This new entry will then be found and the row will be updated again. This will repeat indefinitely. The EXPLAIN shows that, instead, DB2 will do a table space scan so that each row will only get updated once. If the table is large, it would be more efficient to delete the row and reinsert it. With Version 2.2, the affected rows may first all be found through the index. The list of RIDs will then be used to update each row (and index entry) once.

5.3 JOINS AND SUBQUERIES

5.3.1 Joins

Joins involve two or more tables. Therefore, there will be at least two rows in PLAN__TABLE for a join—one or more for each table being accessed. There may be additional rows, as additional sorts may be needed for ORDER BY, GROUP BY, etc.

As described in Section 4.2, there are several join methods—nested loop and merge scan, and (starting with Version 2.3) a hybrid join. If there are more than two tables being joined, DB2 will first pick two of them to join and then join the resulting composite table with a third, and so on. DB2 may use different join methods at each stage. With either method, one table is the outer table and the other is the inner table. You can tell which is which by looking at the PLANNO column. PLANNO indicates the steps involved in executing the plan. In a nested loop join, the outer table is accessed first, and so will have PLANNO = 1. The inner table will have a 2 in this column. If a third table is being joined, it will have a 3. An additional sort step will have the next number. If three tables are joined, the sort for the ORDER BY will have PLANNO = 4. For a merge scan join, the inner table is accessed first and will, therefore, have PLANNO = 1.

The TABNO column also lists the tables being accessed. Each table in the join will be given a unique TABNO. If a table is joined to itself, each access is as though to a different table; therefore, TABNO will be different for the two rows of PLAN_TABLE. TABNO is just assigned in the order in which the tables appear in the query. Therefore, it does not tell you anything very useful.

The way to tell which method of join is being used is with the METHOD column. A method of 1 is a nested loop join. A method of 2 is a merge scan join. The value 0 is used for steps that access a single table (or the first table in the join), and a value of 3 is for additional sort steps. The new hybrid join will have a value of 4.

A join may involve index access to a table, or a table space scan. It depends on any additional search criteria as well as the join criteria columns. The same guidelines apply to a join as for other access, the fewer IOs the better. For a nested loop join, it is especially important for the inner table to be accessed by a matching index if possible (unless the table only occupies a few pages). For each selected outer row, matching rows from the inner table must be found. If this involves a table space scan for each outer row, then the join could literally take hours. You must be careful in coding joins to try to join via indexed columns wherever possible. A nested loop join is illustrated in Figure 5.26.

DB2 "knows" that a table space scan of the inner table in a nested loop join is costly. Therefore, there is a good chance that it will do a merge scan join instead for these situations. This is especially true with Version 2. Merge scan joins involve reading the two tables in the same order. If there is no appropriate index, then a sort is needed. The SORTN_JOIN or SORTC_JOIN columns will have a Y to indicate this. The performance of sorts (especially large sorts) was greatly improved with Version 2.1 and further improved with 2.3. Even still, large sorts take time, as do table space scans, and you must look at the performance carefully. Figure 5.27b has the EXPLAIN output for a merge scan join for the query in Figure 5.27a.

Joins are not necessarily costly. It depends on several factors. Obviously, if you are joining all the rows of two large tables, it will take a long time. The fewer the rows involved (due to other selection criteria), the quicker the join. If

```
DELETE FROM PLAN_TABLE WHERE QUERYNO=11;
EXPLAIN PLAN SET QUERYNO=11 FOR
SELECT * FROM THSPAT0 PAT,THSADM0 ADM
  WHERE PATID='666555444'
    AND PAT.PATID = ADM.PATID;
SELECT * FROM PLAN_TABLE WHERE QUERYNO=11;
```

(a) The EXPLAIN

QUERYNO	QBLOCKNO	APPLNAME	PROGNAME	PLANNO	METHOD	CREATOR
11	1		DSNESM68	1	0	GELLER
11	1		DSNESM68	2	1	GELLER

TNAME	TABNO	ACCESS TYPE	MATCHCOLS	ACCESS CREATOR	ACCESS NAME	INDEXONLY
THSPAT0	1	I	1	GELLER	XHSPAT02	N
THSADM0	2	I	1	GELLER	XHSADM01	N

NNNNCCCC UJOGUJOG	TS LOCKMODE	PREFETCH	COLUMN FN EVAL	MIXOPSEQ
NNNNNNNN	IS			0
NNNNNNNN	IS			0

(b) The contents of PLAN_TABLE

Figure 5.26. EXPLAIN for a Nested Loop Join.

there are clustered indexes on the join columns of both tables, then the join can be very quick. Joining a single patient to his admissions is as simple as reading one HSPAT row and several HSADM rows. Joining all services to the admissions they are for, requires only slightly more IOs than a table space scan of both tables. For each patient admission, index access will be done to find the services. However, since the admission rows and the service rows are both clus-

248 ACCESS PATH SELECTION

```
DELETE FROM PLAN_TABLE WHERE QUERYNO=11;
EXPLAIN PLAN SET QUERYNO=11 FOR
SELECT * FROM THSPAT0 PAT,THSADM0 ADM
   WHERE YEAR(BIRTHDATE) = 1950 AND DISDATE BETWEEN '1986-01-01'
                                             AND     '1986-01-31'
     AND PAT.PATID = ADM.PATID;
SELECT * FROM PLAN_TABLE WHERE QUERYNO=11;
```

(a) The EXPLAIN

QUERYNO	QBLOCKNO	APPLNAME	PROGNAME	PLANNO	METHOD	CREATOR
11	1		DSNESM68	1	0	GELLER
11	1		DSNESM68	2	2	GELLER

TNAME	TABNO	ACCESS TYPE	MATCHCOLS	ACCESS CREATOR	ACCESS NAME	INDEXONLY
THSPAT0	1	R	0			N
THSADM0	2	R	0			N

NNNNCCCC UJOGUJOG	TS LOCKMODE	PREFETCH	COLUMN FN EVAL	MIXOPSEQ
NNNNNNNN	IS	S		0
NYNNNYNN	IS	S		0

(b) The contents of PLAN_TABLE

Figure 5.27. EXPLAIN for a Merge Scan Join.

tered in PATID order, they will all be grouped on the same or consecutive pages. Sequential prefetch will, therefore, be used for the table space pages and for the index pages.

When we look at the EXPLAIN for a join, we look to see if index access or table space access is being done for the two tables. We also see which join method is being used and whether any sorts are going to be done. If we find that sorts or table space scans are needed, then we have to try to figure out why. The most obvious reason may be that there are no (clustered) indexes on the join columns. If there aren't, we then have to decide whether or not there should be. For an infrequent report, we probably do not want to create indexes just for the one report. For a join that is used by a high volume online transaction, we do. The admissions data in our sample database is sometimes needed in date order across all patients (e.g., find patients admitted this month), but more often it is needed for a specific patient (e.g., for this patient, when was he admitted). Therefore, I have chosen to cluster the index on PATID,ADMDATE. The same is true for the other patient-related tables. This will not only facilitate direct access to these tables by patient ID, but will also facilitate joins between the tables.

The program code can also impact how a join will be done. In general, giving more information to DB2 increases the chance that it can pick the optimal path. DB2 is being improved to reduce the need for the programmer to give redundant information, so it is not as critical as with Version 1. For example, in the SELECT in Figure 5.28, the join column is PATID in the HSPAT and HSADM tables. The other selection criteria is that we only want patient '666555444' which we specify with HSADM.PATID = '666555444'. It is redundant also to say HSPAT.PATID = '666555444'. This is implicit in that we ask for the two PATID columns to be equal. Version 1, however, would not make that assumption. Therefore, it would not have the full set of qualifying predicates available to itself for calculating costs. Version 2 performs what is called "transitive closure." This means that it automatically adds in the missing predicate HSPAT.PATID = '666555444'. With the added information, DB2 can make a better decision.

While this case no longer requires extra work by the programmer (or end-user), there are many other cases where extra coding can influence DB2 to choose a different path. These apply to any type of statement, not just a join.

There are two other aspects to joins that I want to mention here, even though they are not directly performance-related. The first is that DB2 matches up rows based on join criteria (e.g., HSPAT.PATID=HSADM.PATID). The join criteria does not have to be an equal match (let alone on a unique column). You can join admission rows to locations rows where the locations record falls within the admission (Figure 5.29). The join criteria in this example involve a range predicate.

You can also join all rows of one table to all rows of another table (this is called a Cartesian product). You do this by not having any predicate that involves columns from both tables. It is not uncommon for someone to do this by mistake, especially if they are joining five or six tables. With a multitable join, there are many predicates that are needed to specify how to join each one. It is easy to

```
DELETE FROM PLAN_TABLE WHERE QUERYNO=12;

EXPLAIN PLAN SET QUERYNO=12 FOR

SELECT * FROM THSPATO PAT,THSADMO ADM
  WHERE PAT.PATID = ADM.PATID AND
      ADM.PATID = '666555444';

SELECT * FROM PLAN_TABLE WHERE QUERYNO=12;
```

Figure 5.28. A Join Without the Redundant Predicate (PAT.PATID='666555444').

leave out a predicate by accident. Remember, by default, a join will match each row of each table to every row of the other tables. There must be predicates with columns of each table to limit the matching of rows if you don't want everything to match everything. If this happens, then there are two results—you will get a lot more rows than expected, and the query will take longer to run. The EXPLAIN might help you find out that a mistake was made. If the chosen access paths are not what you expected, you will check to find out the reason. This means looking at your code as well as the catalog statistics.

There is another "unexpected" result you can get from a join. Only records that match are returned to the program. If there is a "selected" record in Table 1, but no matching record in Table 2, you do not get an output record with blanks for Table 2. You get nothing. Figure 5.30 gets the service records for patients born before 1925. If there are patients without any services, this SELECT will not show them at all. You must do the SELECT differently if you want to get all patients born before 1925 regardless of whether or not they received services. A subselect must be used to find records in a table, which do not have a matching record in another table. This example has nothing to do with the EXPLAIN function. I bring it up here simply because it is a very common mistake made with joins, and I feel it is worth mentioning with any discussion of joins.

5.3.2 Subqueries

Subquery access paths were described in Section 4.2, including the difference between correlated and noncorrelated subselects. In the EXPLAIN output, each subselect is listed. You can tell them apart with the column QBLOCKNO (query block number). The first SELECT is QBLOCKNO 1, the next (subselect) is QBLOCKNO 2, etc. This is true regardless of which table is accessed first. Remember, for a correlated subselect, the outer table is accessed first. Then, for each row selected, the inner table is scanned. The reverse is true for a noncorrelated subselect. The inner table is first scanned with an intermediate table of selected rows created. The outer table is then scanned, matching rows with this intermediate table.

Figure 5.31 has a noncorrelated subselect with the EXPLAIN output. The inner table is accessed through XHSDRG03 to find all patient IDs with the re-

```
DELETE FROM PLAN_TABLE WHERE QUERYNO=13;

EXPLAIN PLAN SET QUERYNO=13 FOR

SELECT * FROM THSADM0 ADM,THSLOC0 LOC

   WHERE ADM.PATID = LOC.PATID AND

         LOCDATE >= ADMDATE AND LOCDATE <= DISDATE;

SELECT * FROM PLAN_TABLE WHERE QUERYNO=13;
```
Figure 29. A Join of Locations with Admissions.

```
DELETE FROM PLAN_TABLE WHERE QUERYNO=14;

EXPLAIN PLAN SET QUERYNO=14 FOR

SELECT * FROM THSPAT0 PAT,THSSVC0 SVC

   WHERE PAT.PATID = SVC.PATID AND

         BIRTHDATE < '1925-01-01';

SELECT * FROM PLAN_TABLE WHERE QUERYNO=14;
```
Figure 30. Services for Selected Patients—No Record Is Returned If the Patient Had No Services.

quested DRUGCODE. Note that a table space scan is then used on the outer table, even though there is an index on PATID. For every patient, the inner result table will be scanned to see if the PATID from the patient row is there. As described in Section 4.2, a subselect with the IN predicate will prevent DB2 from using an index on the outer table. If the = predicate were used instead, an index might be used. However, = can only be used with a subselect if the subselect will return at most one row, or if ALL or ANY are used. If the subselect returns more than one row, then an error SQLCODE is returned. Therefore, you are forced in many cases to use IN for this type of subquery.

Using IN with a noncorrelated subselect will also require a sort. Note that there is a third line in the plan—METHOD = 3 and SORTC_UNIQ = Y. First, the inner table (subselect) is scanned with an intermediate table created. Then, duplicates are eliminated (sort for uniqueness). This is because we are asking for patients that have rows in THSDRG0. The patient rows, therefore, should be selected once, corresponding to one row in THSPAT0. DB2 eliminates the duplicates from THSDRG0 so that each row in the outer table matches one row of the inner table.

Figure 5.32 has a correlated subselect and the EXPLAIN output for it. Note that there is no sort in this case. The correlated query says match up a specific row of each table. As we said above, the outer table is scanned first. For each selected row (based on the other selection criteria), the inner table is searched (with an index if possible). After finding the matching rows from the inner table,

ACCESS PATH SELECTION

```
DELETE FROM PLAN_TABLE WHERE QUERYNO=15;
EXPLAIN PLAN SET QUERYNO=15 FOR
SELECT LASTNAME,FIRSTNAME,PATID FROM THSPAT0
   WHERE PATID IN
     (SELECT PATID
        FROM THSDRG0
        WHERE DRUGCODE = '012345678');
SELECT * FROM PLAN_TABLE WHERE QUERYNO=15;
```

The contents of PLAN_TABLE

QUERYNO	QBLOCKNO	APPLNAME	PROGNAME	PLANNO	METHOD	CREATOR
15	1		DSNESM68	2	0	GELLER
15	2		DSNESM68	1	0	GELLER
15	2		DSNESM68	1	3	

TNAME	TABNO	ACCESS TYPE	MATCHCOLS	ACCESS CREATOR	ACCESS NAME	INDEXONLY
THSPAT0	1	R	0			N
THSDRG0	2	I	1	GELLER	XHSDRG03	Y
	0		0			N

NNNNCCCC UJOGUJOG	TS LOCKMODE	PREFETCH	COLUMN FN EVAL	MIXOPSEQ
NNNNNNNN	IS	S		0
NNNNNNNN	IS			0
NNNNYNNN	IS			0

Figure 5.31. Noncorrelated Subquery.

EXPLAIN 253

```
DELETE FROM PLAN_TABLE WHERE QUERYNO=16;
EXPLAIN PLAN SET QUERYNO=16 FOR
SELECT * FROM THSPAT0 PAT
   WHERE BIRTHDATE >=
     (SELECT MIN(ADMDATE) - 10 YEARS
        FROM THSADM0 ADM
        WHERE ADM.PATID = PAT.PATID);
SELECT * FROM PLAN_TABLE WHERE QUERYNO=16;
```

The contents of PLAN_TABLE

QUERYNO	QBLOCKNO	APPLNAME	PROGNAME	PLANNO	METHOD	CREATOR
16	1		DSNESM68	1	0	GELLER
16	1		DSNESM68	2	0	GELLER

TNAME	TABNO	ACCESS TYPE	MATCHCOLS	ACCESS CREATOR	ACCESS NAME	INDEXONLY
THSPAT0	1	R	0			N
THSADM0	2	I	1	GELLER	XHSADM01	N

NNNNCCCC UJOGUJOG	TS LOCKMODE	PREFETCH	COLUMN FN EVAL	MIXOPSEQ
NNNNNNNN	IS	S		0
NNNNNNNN	IS			0

Figure 5.32. Correlated Subquery.

DB2 can move on to the next row of the outer table. There is no intermediate table created from the inner table, so there is no sorting required.

Which is faster? It depends. A sort of a small table is fast, whereas a large sort is not. If the subselect table is large and there is a suitable index on the subselect table, then the correlated query may be better. If it is large and there is no index, but most rows are eliminated by other criteria, then the noncorrelated query will be much better. Either way, there is a good chance that if there is an equivalent join, it will be faster.

5.4 OTHER EXPLAIN DATA

5.4.1 UNIONs

QBLOCKNO will also be greater than 1 when there is a union of SELECTs. Each SELECT is a separate query block. They are numbered in order of their appearance. Unions by default eliminate duplicate rows (UNION ALL will leave duplicates). If ALL is not used, then there will be a row in PLAN_TABLE for the sort (SORTC_UNIQ = 'Y').

5.4.2 TSLOCKMODE

Concurrent access to tables is controlled by DB2's locking mechanism, which is described in Sections 2.4 and 6.3. Table spaces can be locked, or individual pages can be locked. If a program requires page locking, then the table space receives intent mode locks. The TSLOCKMODE column of the plan table shows the locking level for the table space. S is a shared lock on the table space. IS is an intent shared lock when page level locking is used. X is an exclusive lock needed for updating. IX is an intent exclusive lock.

If a table space is created with LOCKSIZE TABLE, then any access to the tables within it will result in S or X table space locks. If LOCKSIZE PAGE or LOCKSIZE ANY was used, then TSLOCKMODE will be IS or IX if the plan is bound with cursor stability (CS). However, if repeatable read (RR) is used, then table space S locks may result, rather than locks on individual pages. RR requires that no fetched rows in an open cursor be changed by another task until the program closes the cursor. This can reduce concurrency and, therefore, is usually not recommended. RR is the default value for the bind ISOLATION parameter. TSLOCKMODE can help identify those plans that were bound with RR rather than CS.

5.4.3 The Evaluation of Column Functions

The evaluation of column functions (SUM, MAX, MIN, AVG, COUNT) has been improved in Version 2.2. These functions can be evaluated at several different points of the processing of the SELECT. If there is no GROUP BY clause (Figure 5.33), or if there is a GROUP BY but no sorting is needed (Figure 5.34), it might be done as each row is retrieved. All predicates must be stage 1 predicates and the functions must operate on a single column. If a sort is needed for the GROUP BY (Figure 5.35), then it is possible that the evaluation could be done as the

```
DELETE FROM PLAN_TABLE WHERE QUERYNO=16;
EXPLAIN PLAN SET QUERYNO=16 FOR
SELECT COUNT(*) FROM THSPATO
   WHERE ACTIVEFLAG = 'Y';
SELECT * FROM PLAN_TABLE WHERE QUERYNO=16;
```

QUERYNO	QBLOCKNO	APPLNAME	PROGNAME	PLANNO	METHOD	CREATOR
16	1		DSNESM68	1	0	GELLER

TNAME	TABNO	ACCESS TYPE	MATCHCOLS	ACCESS CREATOR	ACCESS NAME	INDEXONLY
THSPATO	1	R	0			N

NNNNCCCC UJOGUJOG	TS LOCKMODE	PREFETCH	COLUMN FN EVAL	MIXOPSEQ
NNNNNNNN	IS	S	R	0

Figure 5.33. Column Function Evaluation—No GROUP BY.

rows are being sorted. The functions must operate on a single column, but the predicates can be either stage 1 or stage 2.

The third possibility is that the functions cannot be evaluated until all the rows are retrieved and sorted. This is how they were done in earlier versions of DB2. Even if sorting is not required, the older method involves retrieving the rows and writing them to an intermediate table. Then they are read from that table and the function is evaluated. The earlier in the process, the faster the query is satisfied. The column COLUMN_FN_EVAL in PLAN_TABLE can tell you when the evaluation takes place. If it is done at data retrieval time, then it will have the value 'R'. If it is done at sort time, it will have an 'S'. Otherwise, it will be blank.

In Figure 5.33, the COUNT function is used to find the total number of active patients. The count can be done as each selected row is retrieved. Figure 5.34 has a GROUP BY. We want a count of the number of services received by each patient in June 1990. Since the clustering index for the service table is in patient

```
DELETE FROM PLAN_TABLE WHERE QUERYNO=16;
EXPLAIN PLAN SET QUERYNO=16 FOR
SELECT COUNT(*) FROM THSSVC0
   WHERE SERVDATE BETWEEN '1990-06-01' AND '1990-06-30'
   GROUP BY PATID;
SELECT * FROM PLAN_TABLE WHERE QUERYNO=16;
```

QUERYNO	QBLOCKNO	APPLNAME	PROGNAME	PLANNO	METHOD	CREATOR
16	1		DSNESM68	1	0	GELLER

TNAME	TABNO	ACCESS TYPE	MATCHCOLS	ACCESS CREATOR	ACCESS NAME	INDEXONLY
THSSVC0	1	I	0	GELLER	XHSSVC01	Y

NNNNCCCC UJOGUJOG	TS LOCKMODE	PREFETCH	COLUMN FN EVAL	MIXOPSEQ
NNNNNNNN	IS	S	R	0

Figure 5.34. Column Function Evaluation—GROUP BY.

order, no sort is needed to do the grouping. COLUMN_FN_EVAL = 'R', indicating that the count is done as each row is retrieved. Note that INDEXONLY = 'Y'. Only the index has to be scanned, no data rows are needed.

In Figure 5.35, we are asking for the number of patients with each level of education. We are grouping by EDUCATION. There is no index on EDUCATION, so a sort is necessary to do the grouping. For this query, COLUMN_FN_EVAL has 'S'.

5.4.4 Things EXPLAIN Does Not Tell You

- Prior to Version 2.2, whether prefetch would be considered.
- For UPDATE and DELETE statements, how many indexes are affected.
- How many times the statement will be issued in a program. If it is

```
DELETE FROM PLAN_TABLE WHERE QUERYNO=16;
EXPLAIN PLAN SET QUERYNO=16 FOR
SELECT COUNT(*) FROM THSCHR0
   GROUP BY EDUCATION;
SELECT * FROM PLAN_TABLE WHERE QUERYNO=16;
```

QUERYNO	QBLOCKNO	APPLNAME	PROGNAME	PLANNO	METHOD	CREATOR
16	1		DSNESM68	1	0	GELLER
16	1		DSNESM68	2	3	

TNAME	TABNO	ACCESS TYPE	MATCHCOLS	ACCESS CREATOR	ACCESS NAME	INDEXONLY
THSCHR0	1	R	0			N
	0		0			N

NNNNCCCC UJOGUJOG	TS LOCKMODE	PREFETCH	COLUMN FN EVAL	MIXOPSEQ
NNNNNNNN	IS	S	S	0
NNNNNNNY	IS			0

Figure 5.35. Column Function Evaluation—Group BY—Sort Required.

executed many times, whether the host variables used are in key value order.
- The order in which predicates are evaluated.
- What type of statement is being issued. You must tie the plan table rows back to the program code to find this out.
- Actual performance. The same access path will perform very differently depending on the values of the host variables used in the statement. It will also be hard to predict performance if the actual data statistics have changed since RUNSTATS was run. To find out just how well a plan will perform, you need to use a performance monitor.

These tools can tell you exactly how many times the statement was executed, how many IOs were needed, whether or not sequential prefetch was used, and how many pages were accessed. They can be a very valuable adjunct to EXPLAIN.

5.5 SUMMARY AND KEY GUIDELINES

Reading this section will give you the basics of how to use and interpret EXPLAIN. After running a few of your own, you will find that running EXPLAIN is easy. Understanding what it says is also easy. However, it can be more difficult sometimes to figure out why DB2 chose some particular path. Once you have that figured out, it may not always be easy to make it perform better. Not every query will run fast. If the tables are large, and many columns are needed by different queries, it is not easy to design the tables and indexes to process all requests quickly. EXPLAIN, however, is a valuable tool in helping you find out why some programs or queries are slow and in helping to figure out how to speed them up. It is also useful in many cases in eliminating the SQL code as the cause of slow response time. All DBAs and programmers should be familiar with its use and should use it on a regular basis.

EXPLAIN is essential for performance evaluation. It tells you DB2's access path for an SQL statement.

EXPLAIN should be done:

- Whenever performance is not good enough
- Routinely for all programs
- On sample queries as a tool for learning and understanding

To interpret EXPLAIN output:

- You query PLAN_TABLE to find the results.
- Investigate any access path that may not be optimal.
- Look for ACCESSTYPE = 'R'—this is a table space scan.
- For ACCESSTYPE = 'I', see which index is being used (ACCESSNAME). Check MATCHCOLS to see how many columns of the index are used to find a match. The more the better.
- With Version 2.2, ACCESSTYPE = 'N' also represents index access.
- See if any sorts are being done.
- Multiple output lines are used for joins, subqueries, sorts, multiple index access, and union operations. Check which join method is used.
- Multiple indexes can now be used to satisfy some queries. This type of access is indicated by rows with ACCESSTYPE of 'M', 'MX', 'MI', and 'MU'.
- The use of sequential prefetch is now indicated in the new PREFETCH column of PLAN_TABLE ('S'). List prefetch is a new capability and is also marked in this column ('L').

Catalog Queries are needed in conjunction with EXPLAIN. The statistics help

```
SELECT NAME,TBNAME,UNIQUERULE,CLUSTERING
  FROM SYSIBM.SYSINDEXES
  WHERE TBNAME = 'THSPAT0' AND TBCREATOR = 'GELLER'
  ORDER BY TBNAME,NAME
```
Figure 5.36. Finding the Indexes for a Table.

```
SELECT IXNAME,COLNAME,COLSEQ,ORDERING
  FROM SYSIBM.SYSKEYS K, SYSIBM.SYSINDEXES I
  WHERE K.IXNAME = I.NAME AND K.IXCREATOR = I.TBCREATOR AND
        I.TBNAME = 'THSPAT0' AND I.TBCREATOR = 'GELLER'
  ORDER BY IXNAME,COLSEQ
```
Figure 5.37. Finding the Columns in an Index.

```
SELECT BNAME,TYPE,DNAME
  FROM SYSIBM.SYSPLANDEP
  WHERE BTYPE = 'I' AND BNAME = 'XHSPAT01'
  ORDER BY DNAME
```
Figure 5.38. Finding the Plans That Use an Index.

you understand why a particular access path was chosen. Remember, the statistics are only updated when RUNSTATS is run. Queries to see the catalog statistics are given in Section 4.4. Other useful queries include finding out what indexes exist for a table (Figure 5.36), what columns are included in these indexes (Figure 5.37), and what plans use a particular index (Figure 5.38). In this figure, the PLANDEP table has all dependencies for a plan. This includes tables, table spaces, indexes, views, and synonyms. BTYPE identifies which type of object the row is for. DNAME is the plan name. BNAME is the object.

part 3

Tuning

6

Efficient Programming and Program Tuning

The previous two chapters discussed the important issues of how DB2 goes about accessing the data requested in an SQL statement. Writing efficient SQL statements is important in both programming and ad hoc query environments. This chapter will cover issues which primarily concern the programming environment, although some of the points will also apply to queries.

The primary difference between the two environments is that queries generally involve the execution of one SQL statement at a time (which may return an entire set of rows at one time). A program will generally contain a number of different SQL statements, which are processed in conjunction with each other. The results of one statement (i.e., the values returned) may control the execution of a subsequent statement. For a SELECT, only one row is returned at a time to the program, for each statement execution.

Section 6.1 covers the general issues of reducing CPU utilization and aiming for a good choice of access path. In an online transaction system, the costliest and trickiest type of processing is the browse type of transaction. There are ways to handle this efficiently, and many ways not to. I will go over several alternatives for paging through a table.

Of course, the performance of the online environment is usually the most important concern to everyone. However, in a high-volume system with extensive batch processing, it is equally important to do the batch work efficiently. Section 6.2 covers this area. In particular, the use of the LOAD utility for loading and deleting data is emphasized.

To get the most out of any file system, allowing concurrent access to the data from many users is necessary. Doing so involves understanding the concept of locking. Locking records is necessary to ensure the integrity of the data. It must be done properly to allow concurrency, but to avoid bottlenecks. These issues are covered in Section 6.3.

6.1 EFFICIENT PROGRAMMING

As a general statement, we can say that our goal is to minimize the number of IOs and the CPU utilization of our programs. As I have said before, this is *not* the primary concern of programming. It is more important for programs to work correctly, meet the users' needs, be maintainable, and be developed in a timely fashion. Programs must perform adequately, but there is usually no need to spend an excessive amount of time trying to make them perform optimally. By understanding the basic principles of efficient access, hopefully most of your programs will perform well the first time. You will then not need to spend too much time working on improving them.

Reducing IOs is especially important for online transactions. Most transactions process a small amount of data at a time. Response time of 2 seconds or less is usually needed. Therefore, it is critical that the access paths used should be matching index lookups. Table space scans of a medium-sized table may only take a few seconds, but that is too much in this case. Batch programs, on the other hand, are often processing large amounts of data. Table space scans may be unavoidable, but may also not be a problem. However, you do want to take advantage of sequential prefetch.

DB2 also uses a substantial amount of CPU time to process a request. For some requests, the CPU time might be greater than the IO time. Reducing CPU utilization can, therefore, also be important. However, "substantial" is a relative term. Today's computers are very fast. They can process tens of millions of instructions per second. If a process took 10,000 machine instructions, that would still be less than one millisecond (thousandth of a second). In a typical transaction, the addition of, say, five SELECT statements with matching index lookup will not make any noticeable impact.

The DB2 processing is also just one piece of the total transaction processing. CICS and IMS/DC use a lot of CPU time for everything they do to process a transaction. In addition, there is other program logic, file IOs, CICS temporary storage, and a host of other processing going on.

6.1.1 Using Indexes

For an online transaction, it is important for DB2 to use indexes. To do so, the application designer must work with the DBA to identify which columns are going to be used for accessing the data. The DBA must create indexes on the appropriate columns. The programmers must then be aware of which indexes exist. They should use these columns in their WHERE and ORDER BY clauses.

In Section 4.5, we covered what makes a predicate indexable. Some predicates will prevent DB2 from using an index. These include:

- LIKE a host variable
- expressions in the predicate
- ¬= value

We also discussed how, in general, joins will be more efficient than equivalent subqueries, and in many cases a correlated subquery will be much better than a noncorrelated one. Correctly specifying the join criteria is critical, both for performance and for accuracy. Sometimes, redundant predicates will influence DB2's choice of access path by affecting the cost calculation. Using an ORDER BY may also influence DB2. Even if you don't care about the order, the fact that a sort will be avoided will increase the benefit of using the index.

6.1.2 CPU Utilization

The amount of CPU time used by DB2 is dependent on the CPU model. The choice of access path is based on both the number of IOs and the amount of CPU time estimated by DB2. With a faster machine, the CPU costs go down. With a slower machine, they go up. It also takes more time for DB2 to process index entries than data row entries. Although an index scan will usually require fewer IOs than a table space scan, it may take more CPU time. The total time might be higher, too. That is why sometimes COUNT(*) may be handled with a table space scan rather than an index scan to count the entries.

6.1.2.1 Factors That Affect CPU Costs

- Each SQL statement uses a large amount of CPU time. This is true even if the data and index pages are already in buffers.
- The number of pages scanned—even if they are in buffers.
- The number of rows scanned. It takes a lot longer to check 10,000 rows than 10 rows, even if only a few are ultimately selected.
- Sorting takes time. The sort time grows at a faster rate than the number of rows to be sorted.
- The number of columns selected. Each selected column must be moved to a work area and ultimately placed into host variables. If a sort is needed, the sort will take longer with a longer select list. If the select list uses functions or expressions, this takes more time than just moving the data of a column.
- The predicates of the WHERE clause. Any functions or arithmetic in the predicates require processing. The use of stage 2 predicates is more costly than stage 1. Even an expression as simple as:

    WHERE SALARY < :CUTOFF + 200

will be stage 2. Stage 2 predicates are not indexable and require more

CPU time to evaluate. For this type of predicate, it is usually better to do the arithmetic prior to the SQL statement, and only to use the host variable in the predicate (Figure 6.1).
- The type of predicate. The algorithm that DB2 uses to process one type of predicate might be faster than for an equivalent one. But don't forget, each one may change with a new release of DB2. For example, it has often been recommended to use BETWEEN rather than > = and < =. It currently takes less time to process. However, if at some point DB2 were improved to recognize that the range checking was equivalent, it might be able to process those predicates just as well. If you use > = and < =, you should place them near each other. In Figure 6.2, there are other predicates in between the checking of the DISDATE field. If DB2 processes each predicate in order, then it would apply all of the predicates to each row that has DISDATE greater than '1980-01-01'. If, instead, it checked the upper bound right after the lower bound, all that additional checking could be skipped for most rows.
- Cursors require more processing than a single SELECT when a single row will be returned (cursors are required if you are retrieving more than one row). The cursor operation itself uses more CPU time. Plus, there is the overhead of an extra SQL call or two. There is the OPEN, FETCH, and (optionally) the CLOSE.
- Referential integrity can either increase or decrease CPU time. If you do the same checking via a program, the costs will be higher because of the need for additional SQL statements. On the other hand, if you skip some of the checking due to knowledge of the data, you can reduce some of the costs.

Remember, though, that outside of the SQL statements themselves, there are

```
CUTOFF = CUTOFF + 200;
EXEC SQL SELECT * FROM EMPLOYEE
     WHERE SALARY < :CUTOFF;
```

Figure 6.1. Remove Expressions to Make a Predicate Indexable.

```
SELECT * FROM THSADM0
  WHERE DISDATE >= '1980-01-01' AND
      DISSEQ > 1 AND
      DISDATE <= '1980-12-31'
```

Figure 6.2. Range Predicates Should Not Be Separated.

many other contributors to CPU usage. Some of them are for DB2 functions (i.e., authorization checking and thread creation), and some of them are not.

6.1.2.2 Reducing the CPU Costs

Some of the ways in which you can reduce CPU costs include:

- Limit the number of selected columns to the ones that you really need. We have already discussed that this helps isolate the program from table changes. It also helps performance. Fewer columns will mean less CPU processing to move them and quicker sorts. If the columns that are needed are in an index, then you also avoid having to read the data row. This will further reduce the CPU time, as well as saving an IO.
- Code the predicates well. Try to use indexable predicates. Sometimes, a redundant predicate might help DB2 choose to use an index. But, of course, extra predicates might increase the CPU time. Use them when necessary but don't go overboard. Also, you should put the predicates with the higher filter factor first.
- Reduce the number of SQL calls.
  — Let DB2 eliminate rows with predicates rather than returning the rows to the program and eliminating them with program logic. In Figure 6.3, both processing sequences will eliminate rows for inactive patients. In both cases, DB2 will have to look at every row. The number of IOs will be the same (table space scans will be used). However, many fewer FETCHs and data transfers are needed by the program in the second case.
  — Use a join where possible rather than two calls. In Figure 6.4a, we first read a patient, then we read his admissions (with a cursor). In Figure 6.4b, we read both together with a join (also with a cursor). The join eliminates one SQL call. I say "where possible" because the join will not always be equivalent. It will only return rows if there is a match between the two tables. In our database, every patient has at least one admission and there are no admissions without a corresponding patient row. The join will work fine. However, in Figure 6.5, if a patient has no services, then no row will be returned by the join. If we wanted to get the patient data regardless, then we should code separate SELECTs.
  — For frequently used code tables (used for validation or code expansion), substantial time can be saved if the table is kept in memory rather than in a DB2 table (or in addition to keeping it in a table). There are various ways to do so, depending on the operating environment (i.e., CICS, TSO, IMS/DC).
  — Denormalization. Sections 2.1 and 7.5 both discuss the tradeoffs of denormalizing tables. These tradeoffs go beyond performance issues. Under our current topic of reducing SQL calls, denormal-

```
EXEC SQL DECLARE PAT1 CURSOR FOR
   SELECT * FROM HSPAT;
EXEC SQL OPEN PAT1;
EXEC SQL FETCH PAT1 INTO :DCLPAT;
DO WHILE (SQLCODE = 0);
   IF DCLPAT.ACTIVEFLAG = 'Y'
      THEN CALL PROCESS_PAT;
   EXEC SQL FETCH PAT1 INTO :DCLPAT;
   END;
(a) By program logic


EXEC SQL DECLARE PAT1 CURSOR FOR
   SELECT * FROM HSPAT
      WHERE ACTIVEFLAG = 'Y';
EXEC SQL OPEN PAT1;
EXEC SQL FETCH PAT1 INTO :DCLPAT;
DO WHILE (SQLCODE = 0);
   CALL PROCESS_PAT;
   EXEC SQL FETCH PAT1 INTO :DCLPAT;
   END;
(b) By SQL predicates
```

Figure 6.3. Eliminating Inactive Patients.

ization can be effective. A display transaction that always shows the expanded values along with the code (i.e., the name of an illness along with the diagnosis code) will save a call for each row retrieved.
- Indexes can eliminate sorts as well as provide direct lookup.

Again, I want to emphasize that in most cases you should not worry too much about CPU time. It is mostly in very high volume systems or small CPUs where the CPU costs can affect response time. Even then, other factors can be more important. Tweaking every last millisecond out of a transaction is usually not worth the effort.

```
EXEC SQL SELECT * INTO :DCLPAT
   FROM HSPAT
   WHERE PATID=:PATIENT;
IF SQLCODE = 0
   THEN DO;
      EXEC SQL DECLARE ADM1 CURSOR FOR
         SELECT * FROM HSADM
            WHERE PATID = :PATIENT;
      EXEC SQL OPEN ADM1;
      EXEC SQL FETCH ADM1 INTO :DCLADM;
      DO WHILE (SQLCODE = 0);
         CALL PROCESS_ADM;
         EXEC SQL FETCH ADM1 INTO :DCLADM;
         END;
      END;
```
(a) With separate SELECTS

```
EXEC SQL DECLARE ADM1 CURSOR FOR
   SELECT PAT.PATID,LASTNAME,FIRSTNAME,ADMDATE,ADMSEQ
      FROM HSPAT PAT,HSADM ADM
      WHERE PAT.PATID = :PATIENT
           AND PAT.PATID = ADM.PATID;
EXEC SQL OPEN ADM1;
EXEC SQL FETCH ADM1 INTO :DCLPATADM;
DO WHILE (SQLCODE = 0);
   CALL PROCESS_ADM;
   EXEC SQL FETCH ADM1 INTO :DCLPATADM;
   END;
```
(b)   With a join

Figure 6.4. Reading Two Tables.

```
EXEC SQL DECLARE SVC1 CURSOR FOR
  SELECT PAT.PATID,LASTNAME,FIRSTNAME,SVCDATE,SVCSEQ,TYPE
    FROM HSPAT PAT,HSSVC SVC
    WHERE PAT.PATID = :PATIENT
        AND PAT.PATID = SVC.PATID
        AND SVCDATE BETWEEN '1990-09-01' AND '1990-09-30';
EXEC SQL OPEN SVC1;
EXEC SQL FETCH SVC1 INTO :DCLPATSVC;
DO WHILE (SQLCODE = 0);
  CALL PROCESS_SVC;
  EXEC SQL FETCH SVC1 INTO :DCLPATSVC;
END;
```

Figure 6.5. Join Will Not Return Patient Data If There Are No Services for the Patient.

6.1.3 Browse Transactions

With the proper use of indexes, most online transactions that access specific record occurrences can perform well. Matching index lookups of 5–10 related records do not take that long. There is another kind of online transaction that *can* prove troublesome—the browse transaction. This is the type of transaction where the user is presented with a screen's worth of rows with similar keys. The user can select one for further processing, or he can page forward or backward to see more rows. As is true with any other type of function, if you process a little bit of data you will get good response time no matter how you do it. If you might process hundreds or thousands of rows, you may have to be careful.

A typical example is to provide the patients whose name starts with a particular set of letters (e.g., 'K' or 'SM'). Another might be to show all services given to a particular patient. Conceptually, the process will be to read one screen's worth at a time and present the screen to the user. If he pages forward, the program reads the next set of rows. If he pages backward, the program can read the previous set of rows. There are a few basic difficulties with this idea:

- DB2 rows are not inherently ordered (but you can ask for them to be ordered).
- You cannot directly select a fixed number of rows. The SELECT will return however many rows meet the search criteria, although you can only fetch in a fixed number of the rows.
- Since there is no inherent ordering; after closing the cursor, you cannot ask for the "next" group of rows with a new cursor.
- There is no direct "read backward." You could have a cursor in which

you order the rows in descending order. Or you could save each screen somewhere (i.e., in CICS temporary storage). Then you could only allow the user to page backward through pages that they have already seen, but not before the original starting point. Storing all of the data of each screen may require a large amount of storage. Alternatively, just the key of the first row on the pages can be saved. If the user pages backward, the program can take this key and read forward through the table enough rows to fill one page.

These problems can be handled with careful coding.

Another alternative to reading one page at a time is to read in all rows that the user might page through, storing all of them in memory or temporary storage. All subsequent paging will obtain the data from there, rather than from DB2. Before we look at the pluses and minuses of each approach, let's examine the two major styles of online transaction processing: conversational and pseudo-conversational (these are the CICS terms).

A transaction will typically consist of several user interactions. On an initial screen, the user will make a request. The program will process the request, perhaps reading and writing records to the database. It will then put up a new screen on the terminal. The user will make some entries on this screen, and the cycle continues. A conversational program is one in which the program stays in place after sending a screen to the user. When the user returns the screen (by hitting ENTER or a PF key), the program continues where it left off. In this mode, the program remains in storage and maintains its positioning in the files (i.e., with DB2, the program's cursors are still open and positioned). Since the cursors are still positioned, page forwarding is easy. The program just fetches in the next screen's worth of rows.

If a commit is issued (perhaps because the program is also doing updating), all cursors are closed and positioning in the cursor is lost. The cursor will then have to be opened again, this time repositioning to the next set of rows. Techniques for repositioning are described below. With Version 2.3, there is a new option that allows a TSO or batch program to issue commits without closing the cursor and losing positioning. This cursor hold option will simplify the coding for programs that need to commit before completing the processing through a cursor.

TSO programs are generally conversational (but they do not have to be). CICS programs can be conversational, but it is usually recommended that they not be. IMS/DC programs are not. IMS/DC programs are classed as conversational and nonconversational. In IMS terms, conversational processing is equivalent to CICS pseudo-conversational processing, which is described next.

6.1.3.1 Pseudo—Conversational Programming

The alternative processing is called pseudo-conversational by CICS. In this style, after sending a screen to the terminal, the program ends. It records (somewhere) any information it needs to continue when the user hits ENTER. Included in this information is the name of a transaction (possibly the same one) that CICS should automatically invoke when the user hits ENTER.

The advantage of pseudo-conversational programming is that fewer system resources are tied up while the user is thinking. Program storage and CICS control blocks are released. This can be very important in a heavily loaded system. The drawback is that *all* resources are released. A commit point is reached, cursors are closed, and all positioning is lost. To continue with a process (including a browse operation), the program must keep track of where it was, and it must be able to reposition itself to that spot. To perform well, it must be able to reposition efficiently.

6.1.3.2 *Fetching All Possible Rows*

With pseudo-conversational programming, the SQL coding is simpler if you fetch in all rows. There is other program logic necessary to handle the storage and retrieval of the fetched rows when the user pages forward. This technique works fairly well as long as there are not too many rows to be fetched. A few dozen, or even a few hundred rows clustered on a few pages, can be read in very quickly.

To read in the rows in a particular order (which is usually the requirement), you must use an ORDER BY clause. In Figure 6.6a, we will be browsing through the patients starting with names that begin 'BR'. The clustering index is on the patient name columns and DB2 is likely to use this index. No sort will be nec-

```
STARTNAME = 'BR';
EXEC SQL DECLARE PAT1 CURSOR FOR
   SELECT PATID,LASTNAME,FIRSTNAME,BIRTHDATE
      FROM HSPAT
      WHERE LASTNAME >= :STARTNAME
      ORDER BY LASTNAME,FIRSTNAME;
(a)   Starting point only


STARTNAME = 'BR';
ENDNAME = 'BS';
EXEC SQL DECLARE PAT1 CURSOR FOR
   SELECT PATID,LASTNAME,FIRSTNAME,BIRTHDATE
      FROM HSPAT
      WHERE LASTNAME >= :STARTNAME AND LASTNAME < :ENDNAME
      ORDER BY LASTNAME,FIRSTNAME;
(b)   Starting and ending point
```

Figure 6.6. Finding Rows with a Starting Point.

essary. This query would return all names greater than or equal to 'BR'. If we want to stop at the end of the BRs, we could use the query in Figure 6.6b. Note that I use a range rather than LIKE :STARTNAME. LIKE a host variable, is not indexable even if the first character is not a wildcard.

As I said, reading in all of the possible rows is okay if there are not too many. However, many times there could be thousands or millions. Figure 6.6a returns all rows with name greater than 'BR'. That would be over 90,000 in our database. It is unlikely that the user will want to page through that many screens. The time to read in the rows also increases if the data is not clustered. In Figure 6.7, we are getting patient and characteristic data with a join. THSPAT0 is clustered by name, but THSCHR0 is clustered by PATID. Now, even if we only fetch in 200 patients, the characteristic rows are likely to be spread across many more pages.

Once the rows have been fetched into temporary storage, page forwarding becomes very quick. However, the response time for the first screen can be *very* high. Generally, it is better to provide the users with even response time. Waiting 15 seconds for the first screen will not make them happy, even if subsequent screens take less than 1 second. It is also better for system resources to do things in small chunks. Overall, DB2 performance will be better if you only read in what you need. CICS will also do better if you do not overload temporary storage.

If it is likely that the user will page through all of the pages, then by all means get the data in one shot. Usually, however, they will only go through a few pages. Preparing hundreds of pages of data is wasteful.

6.1.3.3 Fetching in One Page at a Time

There are several alternative ways to code the SQL cursor so as to be able to fetch in one screen's worth of rows at a time, and to be able to reposition at the next row. Conceptually, the simplest statement is the one shown in Figure 6.8. HIGHLAST and HIGHFIRST are host variables. The program sets them to the values of the last row on the previous screen. Essentially, we are asking DB2 to

```
STARTNAME = 'BR';
EXEC SQL DECLARE CHR1 CURSOR FOR
   SELECT PAT.PATID,LASTNAME,FIRSTNAME,EDUCATION
      FROM HSPAT PAT,HSCHR CHR
      WHERE LASTNAME >= :STARTNAME AND
            PAT.PATID = CHR.PATID
      ORDER BY LASTNAME,FIRSTNAME;
```

Figure 6.7. With the Join, the Characteristics Rows Are Not Clustered.

```
EXEC SQL DECLARE PAT1 CURSOR FOR
  SELECT PATID,LASTNAME,FIRSTNAME,BIRTHDATE
    FROM HSPAT
    WHERE (LASTNAME = :HIGHLAST AND FIRSTNAME > :HIGHFIRST)
       OR LASTNAME > :HIGHLAST
    ORDER BY LASTNAME,FIRSTNAME;
```

Figure 6.8. Repositioning to the Next Patient with OR.

pick up where it left off. The ORDER BY is necessary to create an ordering of the data. Otherwise, there is no "next" row.

If the last row of the previous screen had LASTNAME='BROWN' and FIRSTNAME='JOE', then we want people who are named BROWN with first names greater than or equal to JOE, or people with last names greater than BROWN. Note the >= operator for first name. This will cause the last row to be repeated. It is necessary in this example because name is not unique. If there are any more JOE BROWNs, they would otherwise be skipped. If the keys are unique, then > will suffice.

Before we look into whether or not this is the best way to code the SQL statement (it is not), let's look at what it takes to do this process efficiently with DB2. Remember, for each screen, the cursor must be opened, repositioning at the "next" row. We then fetch in 10–15 rows. We do not fetch in all possible rows that satisfy the SELECT.

The first requirement is that the access path to reposition to the first row be quick. We want to have index access, not a table space scan. This means that an index must exist on the columns we are using for the WHERE clause. The ORDER BY should use those same columns. This is a reasonable requirement. If we are selecting names, we would usually want them in order by name. If we are selecting the medications a patient has received, we are likely to want them in either date order or drug code order (we have indexes on both). If this is a common transaction, then it is reasonable to have an index on these columns.

The second requirement relates to how DB2 processes a cursor. The DB2 manuals say that you can think of it as though DB2, when the cursor is opened, produces a results table containing all rows that meet the search criteria. Then, for each FETCH, it will get one row from this results table and return it to the program. This is only a conceptual picture. In reality, a results table is built only when DB2 *has* to. Otherwise, DB2 will access the rows one at a time with each FETCH.

When will it *have* to? Basically, whenever it must do a sort. If a sort is needed (whether for an ORDER BY, UNION, GROUP BY, join, or for list prefetch), DB2 must get all qualifying rows and sort them before it can return any of them to the program. If a sort is not needed, then DB2 will only access the data when each FETCH is issued.

Is a results table a problem? You bet! If the operation in Figure 6.8 required DB2 to read in all names beginning with the starting value, it would have to access 90,000 rows. Even though the program will then only fetch in 10 of them, all of the work of getting the rows has already been done. *Each* page forward will be almost as costly as if we read in all of them at once.

When list prefetch was introduced (Version 2.2), it caused some unexpected problems for browse transactions. If the data is being accessed through an unclustered index, the best access path to fetch in *all* qualifying rows may be to use list prefetch. That is, find all qualifying index entries, sort by RID, and then read the data pages. As mentioned above, this may mean accessing a great many index entries even though only 10 are going to be fetched. To solve this problem, Version 2.3 has a new option on the SELECT statement—OPTIMIZE FOR n ROWS. This tells the DB2 optimizer to consider the best access path assuming that only n rows will be fetched, not the entire answer set.

Our primary goal then is to code an SQL statement that will not cause DB2 to produce a results table. We also want DB2 to be able to quickly get to the first row to be fetched. Unfortunately at present, what would seem to be the ideal method, does not result in a direct lookup.

We will now examine several alternative ways to code the SELECT to achieve repositioning. For each one, I will describe the access path that DB2 will probably use and the performance implications. In these examples, I am assuming that there is an index on the key columns LASTNAME,FIRSTNAME.

- *OR* (Figure 6.8): This is the natural way of looking at the operation. If we handled the query manually, we would say:

Find LASTNAME equal to :HIGHLAST and FIRSTNAME equal to :HIGHFIRST

Then just keep on going.

That is what we would do. It is not what DB2 does. Prior to Version 2.2, DB2 will only use an index for an OR of two predicates when the two predicates consist of a single column of the index. This was described in Section 4.5. DB2 does not recognize that the predicate LASTNAME > :HIGHLAST is a continuation of the other predicate. It will not do a matching index lookup. It might still use the index with an index scan (Figure 6.9 has the EXPLAIN results for this query), because of the ORDER BY. This will avoid the sort. However, scanning the index from the front can be time-consuming. MATCHCOLS = 0 indicates the index scan.

How well will this query perform? That depends on where the starting point (i.e., :HIGHLAST) is. If it is near the beginning of the index, then the performance will be fine. No results table is necessary and the repositioning will not take long. If the starting point is much further down in the index, then performance will depend on how big the index is. For a small table, the index will not be too many pages. For a large table, it might be thousands of pages. Version 2.2 performance will be better because of its improved prefetch algorithm. Fig-

QUERYNO	QBLOCKNO	APPLNAME	PROGNAME	PLANNO	METHOD	CREATOR
1	1		DSNESM68	1	0	GELLER

TNAME	TABNO	ACCESS TYPE	MATCHCOLS	ACCESS CREATOR	ACCESS NAME	INDEXONLY
THSPAT0	1	I	0	GELLER	XHSPAT02	N

NNNNCCCC UJOGUJOG	TS LOCKMODE	PREFETCH	COLUMN FN EVAL	MIXOPSEQ
NNNNNNNN	IS	S		0

Figure 6.9. The EXPLAIN Results for the OR Predicate.

ure 6.10 is a chart showing the results for this and the following examples. The tests were run under Version 2.1, and the results were obtained from the DB2 Performance Monitor.

- *AND* (Figure 6.11): This is a less natural query that is logically equivalent to the OR. The second predicate has been changed to LASTNAME >= :HIGHLAST. This will include all patients with the previous lastname, including some already presented to the user. The first predicate eliminates those that have already been obtained. The advantage of this query is that DB2 will do a matching index lookup with MATCHCOLS = 1 (Figure 6.12)—an exact match on LASTNAME. This eliminates scanning all prior index records.

Performance of this query will be very good, unless there are many rows with the same value for the high-order column of the key. If this were a table with millions of rows, there could be thousands of SMITHs. When positioned near the end of the SMITHs, DB2 will still scan all of these index entries to find the right starting point. Usually, though, this query will give us the best performance.

	CPU time (sec)	Data Pages	Index Pages
OR	.15	4	37
AND	.008	4	3
UNION ALL	.010	4	6
UNION	43.66	10605	680

Figure 6.10. Results of Various Predicates for Repositioning.

```
EXEC SQL DECLARE PAT1 CURSOR FOR
  SELECT PATID,LASTNAME,FIRSTNAME,BIRTHDATE
    FROM HSPAT
    WHERE NOT (LASTNAME = :HIGHLAST AND FIRSTNAME <= :HIGHFIRST)
      AND LASTNAME >= :HIGHLAST
    ORDER BY LASTNAME,FIRSTNAME;
```
Figure 6.11. Repositioning with AND.

- *UNION ALL* (Figure 6.13): Some of the early DB2 manuals recommended using UNION rather than OR so that indexes could be used. This was useful advice when you want to return all qualifying rows. For a browse operation, it is not good advice. The UNION process eliminates duplicates from the result. This is the default option for UNION. It requires doing a sort (Figure 6.14) and, therefore, a results table. UNION does not perform well here. UNION *ALL* does not eliminate duplicates. For this query we do not have to worry about them. Each of the predicates will give a disjoint set of rows. The EXPLAIN results for the UNION ALL are in Figure 6.15. There is one row in PLAN_TABLE for each SELECT (QBLOCKNO = 1 and 2). MATCHCOLS equals 2 for the first SELECT and 1 for the second.

Note that I do not have an ORDER BY clause. If I did, then DB2 would have to do a sort. The UNION operation does each SELECT separately. It does not know that the rows will be accessed through the same index. In order to get the rows in the correct order, I had to put the predicates in this particular order. For the OR and AND queries, the order of the predicates did not matter. The performance of this query is very good. It is longer than the AND because the index is accessed twice, once for each SELECT (if there are fewer than a screen's worth of rows returned by the first SELECT). In the case of many rows with the same high-order key, then it might perform better than the AND.

278   TUNING

QUERYNO	QBLOCKNO	APPLNAME	PROGNAME	PLANNO	METHOD	CREATOR
1	1		DSNESM68	1	0	GELLER

TNAME	TABNO	ACCESS TYPE	MATCHCOLS	ACCESS CREATOR	ACCESS NAME	INDEXONLY
THSPAT0	1	I	1	GELLER	XHSPAT02	N

NNNNCCCC UJOGUJOG	TS LOCKMODE	PREFETCH	COLUMN FN EVAL	MIXOPSEQ
NNNNNNNN	IS	S		0

Figure 6.12. The EXPLAIN Results for the AND Predicate.

```
EXEC SQL DECLARE PAT1 CURSOR FOR
    SELECT PATID,LASTNAME,FIRSTNAME,BIRTHDATE
       FROM HSPAT
         WHERE (LASTNAME = :HIGHLAST AND FIRSTNAME > :HIGHFIRST)
    UNION ALL
    SELECT PATID,LASTNAME,FIRSTNAME,BIRTHDATE
       FROM HSPAT
         WHERE LASTNAME > :HIGHLAST;
```
Figure 6.13. Repositioning with UNION ALL.

EFFICIENT PROGRAMMING AND PROGRAM TUNING

QUERYNO	QBLOCKNO	APPLNAME	PROGNAME	PLANNO	METHOD	CREATOR
1	1		DSNESM68	1	0	GELLER
1	1		DSNESM68	2	3	
1	2		DSNESM68	1	0	GELLER

TNAME	TABNO	ACCESS TYPE	MATCHCOLS	ACCESS CREATOR	ACCESS NAME	INDEXONLY
THSPAT0	1	I	2	GELLER	XHSPAT02	N
	0		0			N
TSHPAT0	1	I	1	GELLER	XHSPAT02	N

NNNNCCCC UJOGUJOG	TS LOCKMODE	PREFETCH	COLUMN FN EVAL	MIXOPSEQ
NNNNNNNN	IS	S		0
NNNNYNYN				0
NNNNNNNN	IS	S		0

Figure 6.14. The EXPLAIN Results for UNION Without ALL.

- *Separate SELECTS* (Figure 6.16): A similar process to the UNION ALL would be for the program to have several cursors. When it runs out of rows in the first one, it will open the second and start fetching. ORDER BY can be used to help influence DB2 to use the index. This will be efficient as with the UNION ALL, but requires more program coding.

It should also be pointed out that if these queries are used with constants rather than host variables, a table space scan might be chosen for the predicate LAST-NAME > 'BR'. This would not be good. With the host variable, DB2 assumes half of the rows will be returned, with 'BR' it assumes a large majority. Note

QUERYNO	QBLOCKNO	APPLNAME	PROGNAME	PLANNO	METHOD	CREATOR
1	1		DSNESM68	1	0	GELLER
1	2		DSNESM68	1	0	GELLER

TNAME	TABNO	ACCESS TYPE	MATCHCOLS	ACCESS CREATOR	ACCESS NAME	INDEXONLY
THSPAT0	1	I	2	GELLER	XHSPAT02	N
TSHPAT0	1	I	1	GELLER	XHSPAT02	N

NNNNCCCC UJOGUJOG	TS LOCKMODE	PREFETCH	COLUMN FN EVAL	MIXOPSEQ
NNNNNNNN	IS	S		0
NNNNNNNN	IS	S		0

Figure 6.15. The EXPLAIN Results for UNION ALL.

```
EXEC SQL DECLARE PAT1 CURSOR FOR
    SELECT PATID,LASTNAME,FIRSTNAME,BIRTHDATE
       FROM HSPAT
          WHERE (LASTNAME = :HIGHLAST AND FIRSTNAME > :HIGHFIRST)
          ORDER BY LASTNAME,FIRSTNAME;
EXEC SQL DECLARE PAT2 CURSOR FOR
    SELECT PATID,LASTNAME,FIRSTNAME,BIRTHDATE
       FROM HSPAT
          WHERE LASTNAME > :HIGHLAST
          ORDER BY LASTNAME,FIRSTNAME;
```
Figure 6.16. Repositioning with Separate SELECTs.

that in an application generator, such as CSP, you will get different results depending on whether you use dynamic or static SQL.

6.1.3.4 Test Results

The results shown in Figure 6.10 are not actually from these queries. They are from similar queries on a different set of data. Therefore, you should look at them as representative of this type of process. The exact results for a given query are very dependent on the size of the table and indexes, and the starting value for the browse. The CPU times, of course, depend on the particular machine being used. These tests were run on a 3090 300S. All of the tests fetched in 10 rows through the cursor. In all cases, the data and index pages were already in the buffer pool.

The OR test required getting many more index pages than the AND or UNION ALL. This is due to the index scan. UNION ALL accessed twice the number of index pages as the AND because it went to the index twice, once for each SELECT. The CPU times of these three tests reflect the difference in the index lookups. Notice that the UNION took 43 seconds. This is not acceptable for an online transaction. The UNION forced DB2 to produce a results table before any FETCHs. This meant reading in all qualifying rows.

6.1.3.5 Summary

As you can see, it is not difficult to code a cursor to fetch in a screen of data at a time. This can perform much better than fetching in all possible rows at one time. Reading backward can be done by using predicates with reversed operators (Figure 6.17). For this to be efficient requires indexes that are descending on the key columns. A simpler and more efficient alternative is to store each screen of data after it is displayed. Page backward would then be restricted to previously read pages. If the user wants to go further back, he can request a new starting position.

```
EXEC SQL DECLARE PAT1 CURSOR FOR
   SELECT PATID,LASTNAME,FIRSTNAME,BIRTHDATE
     FROM HSPAT
     WHERE NOT (LASTNAME = :HIGHLAST AND FIRSTNAME >= :HIGHFIRST)
       AND LASTNAME <= :HIGHLAST
     ORDER BY LASTNAME DESC, FIRSTNAME DESC;
```
Figure 6.17. Repositioning to Read Backward.

6.2 LOADING AND PROCESSING LARGE VOLUMES OF DATA

There are two basic ways in which data can be put into a table. These are through INSERT SQL statements, and through the LOAD utility. INSERTs are normal SQL processing and can be used at any time—with a program or through SPUFI or QMF. DB2 tables do not require an initialization through a special load process as do VSAM files and IMS databases. The first row can be inserted by itself with a regular transaction program.

The LOAD utility is an alternate way to insert data into a table. It takes its input from a sequential file and can be used to add rows to an already populated table, or to an empty table. It can also replace the existing data in a table. Although not perfect, the LOAD utility is a very nice feature of DB2. It does a number of nice things for you without any programming. It is particularly beneficial in the area of performance.

These are the basic ways of inserting rows. Data can also be inserted in QMF with the SAVE DATA and IMPORT DATA commands. Several utilities (such as DSN1COPY) can copy datasets and, therefore, can copy an entire table space.

6.2.1 Deleting All Data from a Table

Even though this is primarily a section about inserting data, the first aspect we'll look at is the deletion of data. There are several situations in which you want to delete *all* rows of a table. Some tables are used for reporting purposes and are refreshed on a periodic basis from another source. The old data must first be removed. Test data is another example where you may want to start over with a new set of data.

There are several ways to delete all rows of a table. The most straightforward approach is with the DELETE statement:

DELETE FROM THSADM0;

will delete all rows from the table (there is no WHERE clause to limit the selection of rows to be deleted). This works fine for very small tables but is not ideal for larger amounts of data. Each row of the table will be deleted one at a time. A table space scan is needed to find the rows. In addition, every index entry pointing to each row must also be deleted. Moreover, log records must be written for each change (data and index). This can all be quite time-consuming. There is actually an exception to all this processing. For a segmented table space (introduced in Version 2), the above DELETE statement (with no WHERE clause) will be processed very efficiently. DB2 will not go through and delete each individual row. It will instead mark the space map for this table as being empty and it will reset the indexes to empty. Simple table spaces and Partitioned table spaces are not processed this efficiently, even with only one table in the table space.

The second way to empty out a table is by dropping the table. This is faster, but has two drawbacks: the space is not made immediately available (except for a segmented table space), and a reorg is needed to reclaim the space; the other drawback is that when a table is dropped, DB2 will also drop all dependent information. All indexes, views, synonyms, referential constraints, and authorizations are also dropped and must be recreated when the table is recreated. This is practical in the early development stages when tables are frequently dropped to make changes to them (adding, removing, and changing columns), as at this stage there are only a few users (programmers) of the table. For a production table, this is not too practical. There are third-party products that help automate this process. If a command is given to drop and recreate a table, these products will build the needed CREATE and GRANT statements.

Dropping the table space has an advantage over dropping the table in that the space will be reclaimed immediately and no reorg will be needed; however, this procedure still requires recreating all other objects and will also drop all tables in the table space, not just one. The space reclamation makes dropping the table space better than dropping the table. The space is not actually directly "reclaimed." If the table space is defined in a storage group (see Section 2.4), the underlying VSAM cluster is deleted (with the DROP) and then redefined (with the CREATE). This is how the space is reclaimed.

There is one more very simple way to delete all the rows. As I said in the first paragraph, the LOAD utility can replace all existing rows of a table space (for *all* tables in the table space). It will do this simply and quickly for any type of table space. It will reclaim the space immediately and does not require any logging for the deleted rows. When running it, you can reload the table space with many rows or with none—emptying it out. For nonsegmented table spaces, there is no better way.

There is one situation where LOAD is not good for deleting. LOAD can add data to more than one table (in the same or different table spaces) in one run. However, the REPLACE option (deleting the existing data) will replace an entire table space—all tables in the table space—regardless of whether you have data for all of the tables. This is true for any kind of table space, including a segmented one. Therefore, if you are going to use the LOAD utility with REPLACE, the table you are loading should reside in its own table space. If you need to periodically refresh a table through a program and are not going to use the LOAD utility, then the table should be in a segmented table space (even if it is the only table there). This will enable efficient delete with the DELETE SQL statement.

6.2.2 Running the LOAD Utility

Now we've covered why LOAD is good for deletion. Before we look at why it is good for insertion, let's see how to run LOAD and what some of the options are. Figure 6.18 has the JCL for running LOAD. DSNUPROC is the DB2 utilities procedure that is supplied with DB2. There are several parameters that are specified on the EXEC statement. SYSTEM is the name of the DB2 subsystem being used. If the installation is only running one subsystem, then the proc will probably default to that subsystem. If there is more than one, then you have to be

```
//LOAD   EXEC DSNUPROC,SYSTEM=DB2T,UID=LOADPAT,UTPROC='',
//            LIB='DB2T.DSN.DSNLOAD'
//SYSREC DD DSN=PAT.INPUT.DATA,DISP=SHR
//SYSUT1 DD UNIT=SYSDA,SPACE=(CYL,(20,20))
//SORTOUT DD UNIT=SYSDA,SPACE=(CYL,(20,20))
//SORTWK01 DD UNIT=SYSDA,SPACE=(CYL,(20,20))
//SORTWK02 DD UNIT=SYSDA,SPACE=(CYL,(20,20))
//SORTWK03 DD UNIT=SYSDA,SPACE=(CYL,(20,20))
//SYSERR DD UNIT=SYSDA,SPACE=(CYL,(1,1)),DSN=PAT.ERR,
//            DISP=(NEW,DELETE)
//SYSMAP DD UNIT=SYSDA,SPACE=(CYL,(1,1)),DSN=PAT.MAP,
//            DISP=(NEW,DELETE)
//SYSDISC DD UNIT=SYSDA,SPACE=(CYL,(1,1)),DSN=PAT.DISC,
//            DISP=(NEW,CATLG)
//SYSIN  DD *
LOAD DATA REPLACE LOG NO INDD SYSREC
INTO TABLE THSPAT0
(PATID       POSITION(10:19) CHAR,
 LASTNAME    POSITION(20:34) CHAR,
 FIRSTNAME   POSITION(35:44) CHAR)
```

Figure 6.18. JCL for the LOAD Utility.

careful to specify the right one. UID is an ID that you give to this run of the job. DB2 records in its directory the execution of all utilities (in the SYS-IBM.SYSUTIL table). When a utility has been successfully completed, it removes the entry from the directory. Otherwise, it remains there. DB2 does this to try to ensure the integrity of the database. If a utility fails, action may be necessary to keep the database intact. A recovery may be needed. Or you may want to rerun this utility either from the beginning or from an intermediate step. Some utilities can pick up from the middle.

By uniquely identifying a utility run, DB2 can keep track of what is running and what needs action, and can force you to do something in case of a failure. For some utilities, you may just want to rerun the job. To do so, you must first have DB2 remove its entry by using the Terminate Utility command (Figure

6.19). The UID identifies which job you want to terminate. This command can be issued through JCL or through DB2I.

There is also a parameter for specifying a restart at an intermediate step. We will not be looking at the details of all the load steps and from where you can rerun. This information can be found in the Command and Utility Reference manual and in the DB2 Utilities Guide and the Version 2 Presentation Guide.

The SYSREC DD statement identifies the input file. The LOAD control statement (bottom of Figure 6.19) can name a different DDname to use instead. The SYSDISC DD statement is the discard file where LOAD will place input records that have errors and cannot be loaded. The other DD statements are various workfiles.

The control statement in Figure 6.19 is one that loads data into one table. The JCL procedure is used by many utilities. The keyword 'LOAD' tells DB2 that this is a run of the LOAD utility. REPLACE tells DB2 to replace the existing data in the table space. The alternative is RESUME YES. That tells DB2 to add the data in, not deleting anything. The list of columns and positions is discussed below.

6.2.3 LOG NO

The LOG parameter represents another very nice feature of LOAD. DB2 provides very good recovery facilities for its databases. All updates done through programs are logged by DB2 to its log datasets. This is done automatically for you. The programmer does not have to worry about creating logs, nor about identifying them for update or for recovery. DB2 will automatically do backout when either a program or the system fails. If forward recovery is needed, DB2 knows which logs to use as input. There is one drawback. There is no way to turn off logging for a program, even if the program will be running by itself (no concurrent update) and even if you do not require any recovery (a table that can easily be refreshed). For adding data to a table, the only exception to this rule

```
//TERM EXEC PGM=IKJEFT01
//         LIB='DB2T.DSN.DSNLOAD'
//SYSPRINT DD SYSOUT=*
//SYSTSPRT DD SYSOUT=*
//SYSOUT   DD SYSOUT=*
//SYSTSIN DD *
DSN S(DB2T)
-TERM UTILITY(LOADPAT)
```

Figure 6.19. JCL for the TERM UTILITY Command.

is the LOAD utility. You can run LOAD without logging by specifying LOG NO (the default is LOG YES).

Using LOG NO has several advantages (and one drawback). It can make the LOAD run much faster, simply by eliminating the logging. This will also improve the performance of everything else using DB2. The log dataset is shared by all DB2 activity. Since a load is doing a lot of insertions, there will be a lot of update activity on the log. This will compete with the log activity from other tasks and will increase the overhead of the system. Any load run of more than a few hundred rows should be run with LOG NO, especially if there is other activity in the DB2 system.

The other advantage of not logging is the saving of space. Each log record contains any changed data. For an insert, this is the entire row. The amount of logging, therefore, will be at least the size of the table being loaded. Thus, the log datasets can easily fill up from a large table load. This is no real problem in that DB2 will automatically archive a full log and switch to another active log. However, if the archived logs are on tape, more tapes will be used. If they are on DASD, then more DASD space will be used up. To get a feel for how much of an impact this is, let's look at a simple example.

The log datasets are created when DB2 is installed (they can be changed later by the systems programmer). The default is three active logs (to rotate as one fills up) of 57 cylinders each (there are also two copies of each active log). Although 57 cylinders is a good size, it is not that large. If we have a table with 200 byte rows, there are:

- 20 rows per page
- 200 per track on a 3380
- 3000 per cylinder

Therefore, 57 cylinders can hold about 170,000 rows worth of data. There are many tables that are much bigger than this. A 1 million row table of 200 bytes would fill up 6 of these log datasets in one load run.

As I said, there is a drawback to LOG NO. If you don't log udpates, DB2 cannot do recovery. DB2 will not allow that, so it turns on a flag in its catalog and gives a message in the LOAD output that tells you that a COPY is required. The table space is marked as having COPYPENDING. Before you can do any other updating of this table space, you must remove the COPYPENDING condition. This is done by backing up the table space with the COPY utility. Until then, the table space is available for reading (or for a LOAD REPLACE) but not for updating. This is not really that bad. The COPY utility runs very quickly. It uses sequential prefetch to do the IO and can back up a table of 100,000 rows in a couple of minutes. For a large table, it is more efficient overall to run LOG NO and then do a COPY than to use LOG YES. If you are adding in a small number of rows (RESUME YES) then LOG YES is preferable. For large tables that are only being loaded for queries and are only updated with the periodic LOAD REPLACE, there is no need to even bother with a COPY. If there is no updating, backout will never be needed. If the file is physically damaged, it can be recreated by rerunning the LOAD.

There are alternative ways to remove the COPYPENDING condition. The REPAIR utility can be used to turn off the condition. Or, the -START DATABASE(...) SPACENAM(...) ACCESS (FORCE) command can do the same. You might want to do this if you have no need for DB2's automatic recovery. For example, a test table often can be recreated in case of disaster, and may not need backups.

Eliminating logging is one way that LOAD can be faster than INSERTs. It also has the advantage that it is a DB2 utility and, therefore, does not involve the normal call sequence between a program and DB2. A program can insert one row at a time, or can insert a whole set of rows that it takes from another table with a subselect. With the first method, there is one call for each inserted row. With the second method, there is only one call. Each row is extracted from the other table. Either way, LOAD can avoid a lot of the overhead.

6.2.4 Replacing a Partition

Partitioned table spaces are often used for tables that have separate categories of data that are cyclical. For example, a table may keep a year's worth of data with each month's data in a separate partition. The LOAD utility allows you to replace one partition at a time. You use RESUME YES for the table space and the PARTnn REPLACE option (Figure 6.20). This will replace all the rows in the one partition, but will leave the other partitions intact.

6.2.5 Building of Indexes

The biggest performance gain of using LOAD can come with the building of indexes when a REPLACE is done. Whenever a row is inserted into a table, all indexes must be updated to include an entry pointing to the new row. When a LOAD with RESUME YES is done, the same is true. In general, the indexes are not in the same order as the data (some are, some aren't). Building up an index out of order can be very time-consuming. This is true of any index file including VSAM KSDSs. When the index entries are in order, a whole block's worth can be accumulated at a time before the IO to write out the block. When the entries are out of order, each block is likely to be written many times. DB2 will also do 32 output blocks in one IO when they are consecutive, thereby saving many

```
LOAD DATA RESUME YES LOG NO INDD SYSREC

INTO TABLE THSPAT0 PART 2 REPLACE

(PATID       POSITION(10:19) CHAR,

 LASTNAME    POSITION(20:34) CHAR,

 FIRSTNAME   POSITION(35:44) CHAR)
```

Figure 6.20. LOAD Control Statement to Replace a Partition.

more IOs. In addition, when out of order, there is much more splitting of index pages. Section 4.1 describes this process.

However, when REPLACE on a LOAD is specified, DB2 knows that the entire table space and all indexes are going to be replaced. Instead of inserting index entries one at a time as each row is loaded, it writes out records for each index to a work file. This work file is then sorted in order for each index. The index can then be built very efficiently. For tables with nonclustering indexes, there is a tremendous improvement in performance.

The DB2 world is not perfect. There is an option that LOAD does not have that I would really like to see. When REPLACE is used, the indexes are built from scratch with a sort of the data. When RESUME YES is used, the indexes are updated one row at a time. This is true regardless of how many rows are being added. In particular, it is also true for partitioned table spaces where you are replacing one partition. In this case, RESUME YES is used for the table space as a whole. The partitioning index is updated efficiently. The one partition being replaced has that partition of the clustering index rebuilt. However, all other indexes are updated, as they are not being completely replaced and they span all partitions. This means, for example, that if the replaced partition had 100,000 rows and is being replaced with a new set of 100,000 rows, there will be 100,000 entries deleted from each index and 100,000 entries added to each index. Performance will not be good.

There are currently two possible alternatives. One is to unload the entire table except for the partition being replaced. Then you add the new rows to the unloaded rows and LOAD REPLACE the entire table space. This is not a great solution because there is a lot of extra work being done. Another choice is to drop the nonclustering indexes, load the partition, and then recreate the indexes. This is also not ideal, as the CREATE INDEX of Version 2 is not as fast as it should be (but much faster than in Version 1) and it invalidates all application plans. These would then need rebinding.

A much simpler solution would be for LOAD to have an option that requests DB2 not to update the indexes, but instead to unload the entire table, sort the index work records, and rebuild the indexes as with the REPLACE option (or the way the RECOVER utility works). Of course, this has to be an option. When RESUME is used to load a small number of rows to a large table, updating the indexes would be much faster than rebuilding them. However, when adding many rows, unloading and rebuilding can be much, much faster. Hopefully, in a future release of DB2, this option will be available.

6.2.6 LOAD Reduces the Need for Programs

Inserting data from an input file is a very common function. LOAD can reduce the need to code a program for each table or each input file. Of course, a program to read a file, move the data to a host structure, and issue an SQL INSERT statement is a very simple program; but any reduction in programming can be worthwhile. The LOAD utility can do some things for you beyond just associating an input field with a column. It can do some data conversion [e.g., a decimal column can be loaded from a packed decimal field, a zoned decimal field (e.g.,

PIC '9999'), or from an external decimal field (with leading or trailing blanks)]. There can also be conditional loading based on field values. Different input records can be loaded to different tables (or skipped), depending on the value in a field. The order of the input fields does not have to match the order of the columns. When listing the columns to be loaded, you can specify the format, length, and position of the input field (Figure 6.21).

There are, of course, limitations to what LOAD can do. The input file must be a sequential file. It cannot be a VSAM file or another DB2 table. These must first be copied or unloaded to a sequential format before being used by LOAD. There is no interfield or interrecord editing, no calculations done on columns, and there are many types of conversion that cannot be done. For example, decimal external can have leading and trailing blanks, but it cannot be all blank. DB2 will not automatically treat this as zero or as null. It will be a conversion error and the record will be rejected if there is a discard file (if there is no discard file, the LOAD run will abend). There is an alternative, however, where you can tell DB2, that if it finds blanks (or other control value) in a field, to use the field's default value (if defined as NOT NULL WITH DEFAULT) or to give the field a null value if nulls are allowed. These options are illustrated in Figure 6.21. However, if the field is defined as NOT NULL, then all blanks is no good for a numeric field, and there is no way around that.

Date fields must also be a valid DB2 date format. If not, the date cannot be loaded. This includes the format YYMMDD, a very common date format for files coming from another data system, but not recognized by DB2. For any of these conversion or editing requirements, a program will be necessary. If you still want to use LOAD for its other benefits (e.g., performance), then you could have a conversion program that writes out the converted records to another sequential file to be input to LOAD.

6.2.7 Duplicate Index Records

When a unique index exists, any INSERT or UPDATE statement that would create a duplicate entry is rejected by DB2. The program that issues this statement will get back an error SQLCODE (−803). The LOAD utility processes the

```
LOAD DATA REPLACE LOG NO INDD SYSREC00
INTO TABLE THSPAT0
(PATID       POSITION(10:19)  CHAR,
 LASTNAME    POSITION(20:34)  CHAR,
 FIRSTNAME   POSITION(35:44)  CHAR,
 SEX         POSITION(1)      CHAR NULLIF(SEX=' '),
 BIRTHDATE   POSITION(45:54)  DATE EXTERNAL)
```

Figure 6.21. LOAD Control Statement with Selected Columns.

updates in stages. First, the data rows are put into the table, then the indexes are udpated. Prior to Version 2, there was a serious flaw in the operation of LOAD. When it came upon a duplicate index entry, it wrote out an error message and did not update the index. However, it left the duplicate data row. It was up to the DBA to manually correct the situation (using the REPAIR utility to eliminate the duplicate). This was abominable and unreasonable. Fortunately, Version 2 corrected the situation. When a duplicate is found, the corresponding data row is also removed (and placed in the discard file if specified in the JCL). Neither row is loaded into the table. Therefore, it is no longer as critical (but still desirable) to ensure that the input file does not violate the unique rule for any indexes.

6.2.8 Referential Integrity Considerations

If a table has referential constraints, then each inserted row requires a parent row to exist. LOAD will do this checking.Any row that does not have a parent will be written to the discard file. However, if the database has a cycle of referential constraints, it is impossible to load each table in turn with checking of the constraints. Thus, there is an option to tell LOAD not to check the constraints—ENFORCE NO (the opposite is ENFORCE CONSTRAINTS). If this option is used, the table space is given the CHECKPENDING status. No access to the table space is allowed until the CHECK utility is run on the set of related table spaces. Another alternative is to use the REPAIR utility or the -START DATABASE command with ACCESS(FORCE) to remove the CHECKPENDING condition.

6.2.9 Using LOAD to Aid in Making Changes to Tables

When a column has to be added, deleted, or changed, the usual procedure is to save the data, drop the table space, change the DDL statements on the CREATE TABLE, and recreate everything. The data can then be put back into the table. Note that ALTER TABLE can be used to add a column, but not for other changes to the columns. There are several ways to accomplish the saving and restoring of the data. One is to create a new table and use INSERT with a subselect to copy the data from the original to the new table. Then do the reverse to copy it to make the recreated table. In doing so, specific columns can be selected for each part of the move. This works fine for small tables but can be costly for large tables with several indexes.

6.2.9.1 DSNTIAUL

Another alternative is to unload the data (either with a user-written program or with the DSNTIAUL sample program) to a sequential file and then use LOAD to reload it after the table is recreated. LOAD can also load selected columns. There are, of course, some changes that may require a user program, such as if the format of a column is being changed from one data type to another, or some other combination of data manipulation is required.

The DSNTIAUL approach is nice in that it can unload any table and will also write out LOAD control statements to reload the table. You can edit this control statement dataset to correspond to any changes you are making to the table, such as dropping a column. Figure 6.22 has the JCL to run DSNTIAUL. The input statement to DSNTIAUL names the table to be unloaded. You can also add on selection criteria (any WHERE clause) to extract a subset of the data. There are, however, several potential problems with DSNTIAUL.

- As a sample program, there is no guarantee that the system administrator has made it available to you and that it will continue to be available (unless you talk to him about it).
- The plan name is changed by IBM for every new release of DB2. If the system administrator uses this convention, then you must change your JCL to match.
- The program was not thoroughly thought out for user friendliness. DCBs for the output files are hardcoded into the program. The control card dataset (DDname SYSPUNCH) is 80 bytes in length, with a

```
// EXEC PGM=IKJEFT01,REGION=1M
//STEPLIB DD DSN=DB2T.DSN.DSNLOAD   DB2 load library
//SYSPRINT DD SYSOUT=*
//SYSTSPRT DD SYSOUT=*
//SYSPUNCH DD DSN=GELLER.PAT.LOADCARD,DISP=(NEW,CATLG),
//            UNIT=SYSDA,DCB=(RECFM=FB,LRECL=80,BLKSIZE=800),
//            SPACE=(TRK,(1,1))
//SYSREC00 DD DSN=GELLER.PAT.UNLOAD,DISP=(NEW,CATLG),
//            UNIT=SYSDA,SPACE=(CYL,(10,10),RLSE)
//SYSTSIN DD *
DSN SYSTEM(DB2T)
RUN PROGRAM(DSNTIAUL) LIB('DSN220.RUNLIB.LOAD') PLAN(DSNTIB22)
/*
//SYSIN DD *
  THSPAT0
/*
```

Figure 6.22. JCL to Run DSNTIAUL Sample Program.

blocksize of 800. If you try to specify an existing library to contain this file as a member, the DCB of the library will be overwritten to a blocksize of 800. This will prevent you from accessing any other existing members. You should, therefore, create a new file for this dataset—don't use an existing one unless it happens to have a blocksize of 800.
- It calculates the record length (LRECL) and blocksize for the unload file (DDname SYSREC00). Unfortunately, it uses a blocking factor that is much too small for good performance. The blocking factor will depend on the row length, but even for medium-sized rows (e.g., 50 bytes) it will use a blocking factor of 10—giving a blocksize of 500 for a 50-byte row. Considering that the reading of the DB2 table will use sequential prefetch, each IO to read the data will read up to 32 4K pages. That's an effective blocksize of 128,000. You can clearly see that many more IOs will be needed to write out the unload file than to read the table. Since the DCB is recorded in the program, it cannot be overridden in the JCL. There is a fairly easy solution if you have a good assembler language programmer. I changed the program to still calculate the LRECL and blocksize, but not put it into the DCB. Instead, it writes out the information. I run the program once for a given table to get the LRECL, then put a DCB into my JCL to do the actual run. This way I can use a much larger blocksize and get better output performance.

Even though DSNTIAUL is not very efficient for large tables, it is available and easy to use. This makes it a handy tool.

6.2.10 Summary

Even with its limitations, the LOAD utility is one of the nicest features of DB2. Some guidelines in using it are:

- Use LOG NO
- Sort the input file into clustering index order before the load
- LOAD REPLACE will replace all tables in the table space

6.2.11 Updating Large Batches

So far, we have covered how initially to load a large batch of data and how to empty out a table. For large systems, it is also common to have batch updates of existing data. These updates might include insertion, update, and deletion of records based on an input transaction file. With this type of process, there are several techniques which can improve the performance of the job. Essentially, the idea is to process all rows on a page together, rather than having to jump back and forth through the table. Ideally, we would also like to get DB2 to use sequential prefetch.

The first thing to do is to sort the input file by clustering key. Sorting sequential files is very fast. This will allow us to process the table with only one read per page. The most straightforward processing of the file would be to:

- read a transaction record
- read the DB2 row with the corresponding key
- insert, update, or delete the row as appropriate

The only problem with this approach is that sequential prefetch will not be used. When separate SELECTs are issued for each row, DB2 does not know if they will be for rows on the same or nearby pages. The use of sequential prefetch is decided on at BIND time, not during execution.

An alternative method is to use one cursor and fetch in every row in the table. Program logic wil be used to bypass records that are not needed. This is essentially a standard merge of two files. Now, prefetch will be used. Of course, there is a little more overhead in the extra FETCH statement executions and program logic to skip the rows. It is a tradeoff depending on what percentage of the table is updated with each batch run. If it is only 1%, then you can just do the individual reads. If it is 10% or more, using prefetch will be of benefit.

Another factor to consider is what type of DASD and DASD controller the table space is on. If a cache controller is used, then the DASD subsystem will do some of the things that prefetch does. It will read ahead one track of data. This will improve the IO performance of the individual SELECT process. One track of a 3380 has 10 4K pages. A 3390 track has 12 4K pages. This is still less than the prefetch amount.

If the table being updated has several unclustered indexes, then the updating of the indexes will still involve a lot of jumping around no matter how the input file is sorted. If a large percentage of the table is being updated, then there is another approach to the problem. You could:

- read all rows of the table and transaction file
- write out a new sequential file containing an updated image of the table
- replace the table with LOAD REPLACE

This approach will also take care of rebuilding the indexes efficiently. It also eliminates the overhead of logging the updates (if LOG NO is specified).

6.2.11.1 Locking and Committing

Whenever you are doing a large number of updates, you must consider the locking requirements of the job. If too much locking is done, then you might exceed the locking limits (see Section 2.4). Page locks for updated records remain until a commit point is reached. This can reduce concurrency. There are two basic approaches you can take.

- If there will be no concurrent update, the program should issue the SQL LOCK TABLE statement. This will avoid individual page locks and so will be more efficient. For a simple or partitioned table space, the entire table space is locked. For a segmented table space, only the table is locked. You can lock the table in EXCLUSIVE or SHARE mode, depending on whether or not you need to allow read access to the table:

EXEC SQL LOCK TABLE HSPAT IN SHARE MODE;
EXEC SQL LOCK TABLE HSPAT IN EXCLUSIVE MODE;

- If there will be concurrent update, then the program must commit frequently. If not, then the locks will be held a much longer time. When a commit is taken during the run, all cursors are closed and positioning is lost. The program must reposition itself afterward. With commits during the run, the program must also be written to be able to restart at any commit point. In case of system failure, DB2 will back out to the last commit point. A control table could be set up to keep track of where the program is. Right before issuing the commit, the program could update the control table. It will be in sync with the rest of the processing.

All programmers should be aware of these issues when writing batch update programs. One of these methods should be utilized.

6.3 DB2 LOCKING AND CONCURRENCY

One of the aspects of DB2 that make it a productive system is that it allows concurrent access by many tasks, both for read and update access. DB2 takes care of all of the housekeeping functions, such as logging and recovery. Programmers do not have to worry too much about these things. To allow concurrent access, there is another function DB2 must do. This is called locking of the data.

6.3.1 What Is Locking, and Why Is It Needed?

Essentially, the problem is that we do not want two transactions to be updating the same record at the same time. More specifically, there are a few potential problems.

- If a transaction has read a record in preparation for updating it, another transaction should not be allowed to update it, too. For many applications, the updating of a record is based on the existing value. If a withdrawal is to be made from a bank account, the balance should not be changed by another task. The withdrawal amount must be less than the current balance. If two separate tasks each need to withdraw $300 from an account with a $500 balance, the first transaction should be able to subtract the $300, leaving a $200 balance. The second transaction should then disallow the other withdrawal. If both transactions read the $500 balance and each does the subtraction with pro-

gram logic, you would end up with a $200 balance after both updates. If both read $500 as the balance and did the subtraction in the SQL UPDATE statement (SET BALANCE=BALANCE−300), the balance would become $−100.
- Once a record has been updated, the new value does not really exist until the transaction has been completed successfully. No other transaction should be allowed to read the record until it is committed.
- If a program wants to reread a record it had looked at previously, it should be possible to prevent the record from being changed in between.

To accomplish these goals, DB2 locks the data in various ways. A (very) simplified conceptual picture is that:

- If a record is read, it is locked until the task moves on to another record. Two tasks may both read the same record if there is no update intent, but not otherwise.
- If a record is updated, it is locked until a commit point is reached. No other task can even read the record until that time.

There is a lot more to it than that, but this gives you the basic concepts and reasoning behind locking.

6.3.1.1 Why Do You Need to Know About Locking?

You do not need to know every detail about DB2's locks for most programming and design work. However, it helps to know somewhat about how it affects several areas.

- Data Protection—What is and isn't protected. Locks are only maintained within a task. In between tasks, the locks are dropped. Therefore, the protection is not complete (but sometimes adequate).
- Programming—How often and when a program issues a commit affects the locking and data protection. At a commit point, all locks are dropped and any updates are committed. They will not be backed out if there is a subsequent failure. It may be important to group all related updates together within one unit of work (i.e., between commit points). The issuing of commits also affects performance and how the program must be coded. Also, the BIND ISOLATION parameter (CS or RR) is set by the programmer. He or she, therefore, needs an understanding of how this parameter affects locking.
- Performance
  - DB2 has several types of locks. Which ones are used, and how often, has an affect on performance.
  - Concurrency is also affected by the type of lock DB2 uses.
  - If concurrent access is allowed, there can be contention for resources due to the locking. Performance will be degraded if there is too much contention. There is also the danger of timeouts and

deadlocks. DBAs and programmers need to be aware of what can contribute to these and how to avoid them.

6.3.2 The Types of Locks

There are several attributes of locks. These are the size, object, duration, and mode. Don't worry about these terms, the individual concepts are simple enough and do not really need labels.

6.3.2.1 Lock Size

In the simplified picture I described the locking of records. I purposely did not use the word "row" because DB2 does not (at present) lock individual rows. The smallest sized lock is a data page (or index subpage). Whenever a row needs a lock (e.g., it has been updated), it is the page that is locked. This effectively locks all rows on the page. An alternative to page locking is table space locking. In this case, the read or update lock is taken on the entire table space. For segmented table spaces, an individual table can be locked rather than the entire table space.

The tradeoffs between page and table space locking are fairly simple. Page locking allows more concurrency; table space locking is more efficient. If a program udpates rows on many different pages, then each page requires a lock. Locks take up storage space, and the locking process takes up CPU time. One table space lock is much more efficient. However, locking out all other access to the table space is often unacceptable.

Row locking is not done by DB2 because of the extra overhead it would entail. Of course, as machines get faster and more memory becomes available, don't be surprised if one day DB2 includes row locking as an option.

The lock size is primarily controlled by the LOCKSIZE parameter of the CREATE TABLESPACE. It can also be set by the LOCK TABLE statement. For a table space which will be read only or will only have one updater (with no readers) at a time, then LOCKSIZE TABLESPACE (or TABLE) should be used. If there are to be multiple updaters and readers, then LOCKSIZE ANY (or PAGE) should be used. These choices are described in Section 2.4. LOCK TABLE can be used by a program to temporarily cause the locking to be at the table level for a segmented table space (or the table space level for a nonsegmented one).

6.3.2.2 Object of a Lock

The object is simply that item which is locked. It might be a particular table space or a particular page. Both the data and the indexes receive locks.

6.3.2.3 Duration

The duration of a lock relates to when it is acquired and how long it is held. The possibilities depend on whether the lock is a page or table space lock. A table space lock that is needed for dynamic SQL is acquired when the table space is first referenced and released at a commit. For static SQL, the ACQUIRE and RELEASE parameters of BIND control the duration. These were described in Section 3.3. ACQUIRE(USE) RELEASE(COMMIT) work as with dynamic SQL. ACQUIRE(ALLOCATE) obtains all table space locks when the plan is allocated. RELEASE(DEALLOCATE) releases them when the plan is deallocated (regardless of how many commits occur during the task).

Page locks are acquired when the page is accessed. They are released either at commit time or earlier, depending on the ISOLATION parameter of the BIND. Update locks are always held until commit time. Read locks are held to commit if RR is used. With CS, they are released when the cursor moves to a row on a different page.

6.3.2.4 Mode

The mode of a lock basically indicates whether it is a read or update lock. The types of modes are different for page locks and table space locks.

6.3.2.5 Page Locks

- S—read lock. If one task has an S lock on a page, other tasks cannot obtain X locks.
- U—update intent. A U lock is taken when finding data to update or delete. One case is a cursor with the FOR UPDATE OF clause. When the row is fetched, a U lock will be taken for the page. For a direct DELETE or UPDATE, DB2 will take a U lock when it finds the row. Then, when there are no other locks on that page held by any other task, an X lock will be taken (the lock is promoted).
- X—Exclusive. This is the lock that is used when data is actually updated. It will prevent any other task from having *any* access against the page.

6.3.2.6 Table Space Locks

Locks on table spaces come in two flavors. When page locks are used by a task, they also cause a type of table space lock called intent locks. These are needed to govern concurrent access by tasks that are using page locks and those that are strictly using table space locks. The regular locks are:

- S—If one task has an S lock, then only concurrent readers are allowed.
- U—This task can read and change data. Others can only read. If any data in the table space is changed, then this lock is promoted to an X lock.
- X—No other task can access the table space.

The intent locks are:

- IS—This task can read data, others can update the table space.
- IX—This task and others can update data.
- SIX—This task can read or change data, others can only read.

The DB2 Administration Guide, Volume III, has more details about these locks. It also has charts showing the compatibility of tasks trying to obtain locks of different modes. The basic rules are that X locks are exclusive and U and S locks are not. A task cannot take an X lock if any other lock exists on the object. Two U locks cannot be taken on the same object, but one U and many S locks are allowed. If a task needs a lock that is not compatible with the existing locks, the task waits until it can have it. This is called contention for the data. It is discussed below.

To summarize the lock modes, we can make the generalization that the different DML statements cause particular locks:

SELECT—S
DELETE,UPDATE,cursor with FOR UPDATE OF—U
UPDATE,INSERT,DELETE—X

6.3.2.7 Lock Promotion and Escalation

When repeatable read is used, all pages accessed through a cursor are locked until the commit. This enables a program to reread a row and be guaranteed of getting the same data. In order to do this, the BIND process may decide that a table space lock should be taken instead of page locks. This is called lock promotion. You will get a warning from BIND.

Lock escalation occurs if the number of page locks on a table space (including the locks on the index pages) exceeds the installation limit on table space locks (NUMLKTS). At this point, a table space lock is taken and all page locks are released. This occurs only for table spaces created with LOCKSIZE ANY. Its purpose is to prevent an excessive amount of locking. Section 2.4 discusses this parameter in more detail. The DB2 Performance Monitor can tell you if lock escalation occurred for a program. If LOCKSIZE PAGE is used for a table space, then lock escalation will not occur. However, in this case there is a good chance that NUMLKUS will be exceeded. This installation parameter sets an upper limit on the total number of locks a task can hold.

6.3.2.8 Locks on Other Objects

In addition to locking user data in table spaces and indexes, DB2 also locks other objects. These include parts of the application plans, the catalog table spaces, and the DBDs (Data Base Descriptors). DBDs are execution time control blocks representing all objects within a database, including tables, views, and indexes.

Dynamic SQL (e.g., QMF queries) take S locks on the DBD. CREATE DDL statements take X locks on the DBD. Therefore, a CREATE of a table will contend with both CREATEs of other tables in the same database, and with QMF queries on any table in the database. For production, this is not too much of a problem. It is a problem for developers or QMF users who create their own tables. For these groups, there should be separate databases for each person. Having many databases is no problem.

6.3.2.9 Finding Out What Locks Have Been Taken

- EXPLAIN—The TSLOCKMODE column of PLAN__TABLE will tell you the table space lock mode for the plan. The possibilities are IS,IX,S,X.
- Performance trace will trace the execution of a task, including the locks taken.
- −DISPLAY DATABASE command will show all locks currently held for any table space in the database. This can be used when there are contention problems to see what task is accessing the data.
- DB2 Performance Monitor will give statistics on the number of locks taken, timeouts, deadlocks, and lock escalations. This is good tuning information.
- Online performance monitors—IBM's monitor is primarily a batch-oriented reporter. There is also an online component. Other vendors offer monitors which can provide real-time data on the tasks that are executing.

6.3.3 Contention

Contention occurs when more than one task wants to access the same resource with incompatible modes. When this happens, one task will wait for the other to finish with the object. A little bit of contention does not cause any problems with performance. A lot of contention can cause several problems:

- Response time will be longer if resources are held for a long period of time.
- Timeouts: A limit is set when DB2 is installed on the length of time a task should wait for a resource. If the limit is exceeded, the task is timed-out. In IMS/DC, a −911 SQLCODE is returned to the program. In CICS, if ROLBE=YES is specified in the RCT (the default), a −911 is returned and the unit of work is rolled back. If ROLBE=NO is used (not generally recommended), a −913 is returned and no rollback is done. An occasional timeout is inconvenient, but not too serious. Of course, it would be best for the programs to issue an appropriate error message to let the user know that he should reenter the transaction. When I say "not too serious," I am assuming the simple case of a program that is only updating resources that are all backed out in sync, and that the user is notified. If other data is updated and not rolled back, problems can occur.

The default timeout parameter is 60 seconds. For BMPs, the pro-

gram gets four times this amount before timing out. Fast Path non-message regions get six times the limit.
- Deadlock: A deadlock occurs if two (or more) tasks have resources locked that the other task needs. They would wait forever if left alone. Instead, DB2 will recognize this situation and abend one of the tasks. In IMS, the transaction will automatically be rescheduled. In CICS, the results are the same as for a timeout.

Timeouts and deadlocks are monitored by the IRLM (IMS Resource Lock Manager). The IRLM handles all of DB2's locking. It is discussed in Section 8.4.

6.3.3.1 Avoiding Timeouts and Deadlocks

To get greater concurrency, there are several things that can be done by the database designers and programmers:

- Table spaces should have LOCKSIZE ANY with a high value of NUMLKTS, or LOCKSIZE PAGE. If lock escalation occurs, there is a greater chance for a deadlock.
- Programs should commit frequently so that locks are not held for long periods of time.
- CS should be used rather than RR for most plans.
- Timeouts and deadlocks occur more often with high-volume systems, which are accessing data that reside in a few pages. Therefore, you should try to avoid small tables used for update, or other hot spots.
  - A single control row that is updated by each transaction will increase contention and slow transactions down. If possible, this control record should be updated and a commit issued before any other processing. If the control record is a system-generated sequence number, then gaps might occur. But that may not be a problem. Using a TIMESTAMP instead of a sequential number avoids the hot spot.
  - If a table containing a small number of rows is heavily updated, then both contention and deadlocks are more likely. If any row is updated, the entire page is locked, effectively locking out many other rows. One solution is to spread the rows onto different pages. This could be done by using a very high free space percentage before a LOAD or REORG. Another way is to make each row bigger than a half page. Then only one row can fit on each page. Now, only one row will be locked at a time. There are, of course, more pages in the table space now, but if there aren't too many rows, the table space size will still be small.
- Access data in the same sequence in every program. If several tables are updated, try to do them in the same order. If several rows in one table are updated, try to do them in key order. These suggestions are not always easy to implement. Do not worry about it unless you've got a high-volume system with a potential problem.

- Even when accessing data in the same order, deadlocks can still occur if DB2 uses different access paths. If a table has several indexes, each program might be accessing the data through a different one. When a row is inserted or updated, you have no control over the order in which DB2 will update the indexes. This is also true for statements that update or delete many rows.
- Use FOR UPDATE OF on cursors rather than a read-only cursor followed by a direct UPDATE. Also use FOR UPDATE OF if you are planning to issue a DELETE WHERE CURRENT OF cursor. In this way, a U lock will be taken on the page until the update occurs. This might reduce the chances of a deadlock.
- QMF F parameter: When a query is issued, QMF does not necessarily fetch in all the rows for the query. A limit is set by the F parameter used when invoking QMF. If more rows are needed, the cursor being used will stay open until the user pages forward far enough. It will be closed when there are no more rows or if the user RESETs the query or data. If DB2 has not produced an intermediate results table for the query, then whichever row the cursor is positioned on will have its page locked the entire time the user is thinking. No transaction can update any data on the same page.

 The default value for F is 100. It is sometimes suggested that it be made high enough that most queries will be fully fetched the first time. Unfortunately, you cannot make it high enough to do so for every table, nor is it desirable to do so. QMF users often issue SELECT * FROM table, when they only want to see a few rows (this query is easier to type in). For a large table, fetching all of the rows will take a very long time, and will fill up the buffer pools, thus affecting overall system performance. It is better to keep F at a reasonable value.

 There are two possible solutions if you are experiencing contention due to QMF usage. One is not to allow direct QMF access to tables with high update volumes. Instead, make a copy each night and let the users see the data as of a day ago.

 If this is not acceptable, then the QMF Governor can be used to limit the number of rows an online query can see. You could set F to 1000 and the upper limit of rows to 800. If the user wants a query that will return more than 800 rows, he must do so in batch. This way, the F limit will never be reached and the cursors will be closed.

If you have a high-volume system, you should take these suggestions into consideration when planning the system. If deadlocks and timeouts are occurring, use a performance monitor or trace to track down the programs involved.

6.3.4 Locking Across Transactions

Repeatable read assures the stability of a row during the execution of a task. However, with pseudo-conversational programming, data may be read in one task (for presentation to the user) and then updated in a subsequent task. DB2 cannot help you here. In many applications, there is no need to worry. The nature of the data is such that two users will not be concurrently accessing the same rows. In other cases, you do have to worry.

There are two basic solutions. One is to reread the row before updating it. If the data has changed, issue an error message to the user and let them try again. This is adequate if the frequency of occurrence is fairly low. For example, in a bank account system, you have to handle concurrent deposits or withdrawals carefully to keep the balance accurate and nonnegative, although concurrent access to an account is not very frequent. However, in a ticket reservation system, you cannot tell a customer that the seats he has been considering are no longer available. This will keep happening repeatedly.

For highly concurrent systems, it is necessary for the application to devise its own locking mechanism. The possible ways are beyond the scope of this book. Basically, you need a place to record the locks and a consistent way of identifying records to be locked. An installation should develop a scheme that is easy for all of its programmers to use with those applications that may require it.

6.3.5 Summary and Key Guidelines

For DBAs, the important points are to:

- Use LOCKSIZE ANY on most table spaces.
- Ensure that the NUMLKTS parameter has been set at a high enough value by the systems programmer.
- Avoid designs that will result in update hot spots. In particular, small tables with extensive updating can cause contention problems.

Programmers should:

- Use CS rather than RR for most plans. CS should also be used in SPUFI.
- Know what value to which NUMLKTS has been set. Large batch update programs should commit frequently or use the LOCK TABLE statement, depending on whether or not concurrent access is needed.

7

Database Tuning

7.1 DETERMINING THE NEED FOR TUNING

The previous chapters were on program tuning—how to improve the performance of individual SQL statements. This chapter discusses database tuning—how to tune the whole database (the set of tables) to improve the performance of a whole class of queries and programs. We will cover why databases need tuning, how to recognize the need, and how to tune the databases.

In general, there is less tuning to be done with DB2 than with other DBMSs, and it is easier. Other DBMSs have many more options for controlling the placement and access of data. Therefore, in some ways you have more control with the others than with DB2, but it takes more effort to get everything just right. Yet, in other ways, you have more control of the DB2 database. With DB2, it is much easier to create new indexes, separate high-volume data, and make changes to the design.

7.1.1 Types of Tuning

This chapter will cover several different types of tuning and methodologies, including:

- Data placement
  - controlling the clustering of data (using REORG)
  - the amount of freespace (ALTER and REORG)
  - improving the organization of indexes (REORG INDEX)

- the amount of space allocated and the number of file extents (ALTER and REORG or RECOVER)
- Data access
  - index design and modification
- Access path selection
  - DB2 uses the catalog statistics to choose the best path. The DBA sets the statistics (RUNSTATS) and can also manually change them
- Redesign
  - Does it pay to denormalize the tables? Or should they always be normalized?
  - a column might be better located in a different table, or maybe there should be some duplicate data (which would require program control)
  - we might want a different clustering index
  - other indexes may need changes, and they might benefit from additional columns or having the columns in a different sequence
- Too much data
  - as tables grow, performance goes down; it often is beneficial to archive (have a history file) for the older data
- Locksize
  - the type of locking (page or table space) specified for a table greatly impacts the concurrency of access
- Utilities
  - we will look at the utilities which are used to make changes to the tables, and which tune the tables

7.1.2 How to Tell When a Database Needs Tuning

In general, the catalog statistics tell you the most about database organization. These are covered in Section 4.4. Figures 4.45, 4.46, and 4.48–4.51 illustrate the catalog queries at which to look. In addition, there are other indicators of the need to tune:

1. Performance is not good. Either it was never satisfactory, or it used to be satisfactory but has been getting worse.
   a. Always bad. This assumes that volume testing has been done. Small test tables will almost always perform well. You need a realistic volume to properly judge performance. If performance has always been poor, there are several possible reasons.
      —RUNSTATS was never run, or it was run on a small set of data (which is even worse). To see if this is the case, you can check the DB2 catalog. If the statistics columns have a -1 as their value, then RUNSTATS was not run (see Section 4.4 for more details).

—The data was loaded in nonclustering order. The LOAD utility loads the rows in the order they appear in the input file. You should sort the data in clustering order before running LOAD. If the data was inserted with SQL INSERTs, it is quite possible that the table is not in clustering order. A REORG can be run to reorder the rows.

—Poor design. This covers many things. The indexes could be inadequate—either not on the right columns or not in the right order. The wrong index may have been chosen to be the clustering index. Poor design often results from a lack of communication between the DBAs and the programmers and analysts. The choice of indexes is very dependent on what columns are going to be used for selection and ordering by the transactions. If the transactions need columns from many tables or need many rows from several tables, it is likely that these tables may not all be in the same clustering order. This can be costly. Perhaps the tables are too normalized or too unnormalized.

If design problems are found early during development, then they can be changed easily. If they are not found until later (i.e., after the system is in production), then it is harder to make changes. Some changes (e.g., moving columns to other tables) may affect some of the programs that access the tables.

b. Getting worse. The system used to perform well, but it has been steadily worsening. There are some simple reasons for this.

—Volume increase. This will certainly affect table space scans. If there is twice as much data in a table, a table space scan will take twice as long. An increase in volume will also affect nonmatching index scans because the indexes will be bigger. Direct index access will mostly be affected if more rows meet the selection criteria and are returned to the programs. Otherwise, there will not be too much impact. Having a history file to store older data is a good way to limit the growth of the tables.

—Disorganized tables and indexes. As data is inserted into the database, the tables become less clustered and the indexes become less well-organized. Both of these factors affect performance. REORGs help solve these problems.

2. Look at the catalog statistics.

a. When performance problems occur you can look at the statistics to try to find the cause. You don't, however, have to wait for a problem. It is a good idea to look at the statistics on a regular basis so that you can monitor trends and anticipate potential problems. There are several things that you will be looking for.

—Growth. When checked regularly, the cardinality columns tell you how much data is being added to the database. For data volumes you look at

FULLKEYCARD and NLEAF (of SYSINDEXES)
CARD (of SYSINDEXPART)
CARD and NPAGES (of SYSTABLES)
COLCARD (of SYSCOLUMNS)
CARD (of SYSTABLEPART)
SPACE AND NACTIVE (of SYSTABLESPACE)

—Changes in clustering indicators, index organization, percent of space used. They indicate the need for a REORG or for changes to the amount of freespace. To check these you look at

CLUSTERRATIO, NLEVELS and NLEAF (of SYSINDEXES)
NEAROFFPOS and FAROFFPOS (of SYSINDEXPART).

—Changes in the distribution of indexed columns. Version 2.2 can record (through RUNSTATS) the 10 most frequent values of the first column of each index. The number of occurrences of each value are stored in SYSIBM.SYSFIELDS.

—See if the automatic statistics (of RUNSTATS) are adequate for your data distributions and queries. You *can* change some of them manually.

3. EXPLAIN
   a. As described in Chapter 5, EXPLAIN tells you the access path chosen by DB2 for each SQL statement. If an inadequate path has been chosen, there are several possible causes. The SQL statement itself may not be coded well. The statistics in the catalog may be old and may not reflect the current status of the tables. The database design as a whole may not be good for this particular statement. You may not have created the best set of indexes. You may want to add new ones, change some existing ones, or get rid of some. Finally, the locksize may not be right. Table space locks may result in contention for resources. EXPLAIN will tell you what kind of locks are being used. Table space locks could have been defined for the table space, or repeatable read might have been used for the BIND instead of cursor stability.

4. VTOC/LISTCAT
   a. The quickest ways to monitor space utilization and growth are to look at the VTOC of the disk packs and execute VSAM LISTCAT commands to find the space usage of the datasets. These reports will tell you the amount of space being used and the number of disk extents used. If there are many secondary extents, then you have not allocated a big enough primary extent. Many small extents will especially impact the performance of table space and index scans.

5. Performance monitors
   a. There are performance monitors available from IBM and many other vendors. They help pinpoint concurrency problems and slow

transactions, and help you find out why they are slow. They report on buffer utilization—one of the major factors in overall system performance.

The remaining sections of this chapter will provide more details on the topics of database tuning.

7.2 CHANGING DB2 CATALOG STATISTICS MANUALLY

7.2.1 Why RUNSTATS Is Not Enough

In Section 4.4, we looked at the statistics that DB2 keeps on the tables and indexes. These statistics are used by DB2 in its access path selection. They are used by the DBA to tune the databases. Furthermore, they are used by programmers to tune their SQL statements. DB2 does a good job of picking access paths, but it is not perfect. The statistics do not tell everything about the data and the queries that will be run.

There are several ways in which the statistics are not complete. The cardinality columns tell how many different values there are, but until Version 2.2 they did not indicate the distribution. Therefore, DB2 would always assume a uniform distribution. Even with 2.2, only the 10 most frequent values are recorded, and only for columns which are the first column of an index. Column cardinality was also originally only available for columns that are the high-order column of an index. With Version 2.1, you can ask for statistics on all columns. This is an option, and under 2.1 made RUNSTATS take longer to run and so may not always be used by the DBA. This option is faster under 2.2 and should be used. DB2 also does not find an exact value for each column. That would involve sorting each column to find distinct values. Instead, it uses sampling techniques. The results may be close enough, but they may not.

Another problem with the statistics is that they are based on the actual data present. If you only have a small set of test data, but want to know what access paths will be chosen in production, you may not be able to, if you are limited to using the statistics produced by RUNSTATS.

7.2.2 The Statistics That Can Be Updated

To solve these problems, Version 2 introduced the ability for an installation to manually update some of the statistics columns of the catalog. This is done with normal SQL UPDATE statements. There are 13 columns which can be updated (as of Version 2.2)—mostly ones that are used for access path selection. You can change the values to put in more accurate column cardinalities, to make a test table look like a production table, or just to fool DB2 to get it to use a different access path when there is an uneven distribution of data.

The columns that can be updated are:

TABLE	COLUMN
SYSCOLUMNS	COLCARD
	HIGH2KEY
	LOW2KEY
	FOREIGNKEY
SYSINDEXES	FIRSTKEYCARD
	FULLKEYCARD
	NLEAF
	NLEVELS
	CLUSTERRATIO
SYSTABLES	CARD
	NPAGES
	PCTPAGES
SYSTABLESPACE	NACTIVE

7.2.3 Production-Sized Volumes

To get the most accurate analysis of the performance of a system prior to its being in production, you need a production-sized volume of data, loaded in the same manner as it will be in production. There is no complete substitute for volume testing. The manner in which the data is loaded can be significant because the LOAD utility loads data in the same order as the input file. If the data is loaded by random updates, the distribution may be different than if it is mass-loaded. It is sometimes not practical to have a full volume of data available for testing early on. If so, then the access path selection may not be anywhere near the same as for high volumes. As we saw in Section 5.2, you are actually better off not running RUNSTATS at all if there are only a dozen rows. If RUNSTATS is not run, DB2 will use some default values that include 10,000 rows and 25 different values for each column. This is likely to be more representative of production than a dozen rows.

If you have run RUNSTATS on test data and would now like to change the statistics, you can do so. The cardinality columns can be updated to simulate the expected number of rows and values. NPAGES in SYSTABLES tells DB2 how many pages have rows for this table. NACTIVE in SYSTABLESPACE tells how big the table space is. PCTPAGES in SYSTABLES gives the percentage of the pages of a table space containing rows for this table. NLEAF in SYSINDEXES tells DB2 how many pages there are in the index. These are needed for IO calculation. NACTIVE is used for simple table spaces and NPAGES is used for segmented table spaces. CLUSTERRATIO is an important value in that clustered indexes are much preferred for access when more than a few rows will be selected. A cluster ratio of 95% or greater indicates that the index is clustered.

By putting in your own statistics you can increase the chance of DB2 using the same access path and plan as it will for production. This will give you a chance early on to evaluate your SQL statements and your database design. It is not perfect, however, and I still recommend using production volumes for testing. Any 12-row table will perform well no matter what access path is chosen and no matter what joins or subselects are done with it. DB2 may choose an access path that looks good to you on paper (i.e., with EXPLAIN), but this still does not tell you whether the statement will be executed in 1 vs. 5 seconds. It does not tell you whether the batch program will run in 45 minutes (acceptable) or 4 hours (unacceptable). Will the actual distribution of data be as uniform as DB2 assumes, or should it have picked a different path? Updating the statistics for this purpose is useful, but it is not a replacement for real volume testing.

7.2.4 Nonuniform Data

Nonuniformity of data distribution can play havoc on DB2 performance. Let's look at some simple examples. Let's say we have a table with 100,000 rows. There is a column that contains a flag indicating exception processing. There are five different values—0 through 4. Most rows have a zero, there are only on average 100 rows with nonzero values. The DBA created an index on this column to enable quick access to the nonzero rows. The index should actually have this column as the high-order column, but there should be additional columns in the index, too. The reasons for this are explained in Section 7.4—they do not affect the current discussion.

We know that there are very few rows with each of the nonzero values. DB2 (prior to Version 2.2) does not know this. It assumes an equal distribution of 20,000 rows for each value. For the SELECT statement in Figure 7.1, DB2 will not use the index, it will do a table space scan. After all, it thinks it must select 20% of the table. What do we do?

If we update the cardinality columns to pretend that there are 10,000 distinct values for this column, then DB2 will assume that there are 10 occurrences of each and will use the index. We would change COLCARD in SYSCOLUMNS, and FIRSTKEYCARD and FULLKEYCARD in SYSINDEXES.

There is a potential drawback to doing this. Presumably, no one will ever query this table to find rows with a 0 value for the flag. Why bother since it is most rows? However, if it were done, DB2 might use this index to find them. The resulting processing (assuming that the index is not clustered) will be much worse than a table space scan. Actually, this might occur. The SELECT in Figure 7.2 has several predicates, one of which is for a zero value in this column.

```
SELECT * FROM THSXYZ0
   WHERE EXCEPTION_FLAG = 4;
```

Figure 7.1. DB2 Assumes a Uniform Distribution of Values.

```
SELECT * FROM THSXYZ0
   WHERE TRANDATE = '1989-04-17' AND QUANTITY > 7 AND
       EXCEPTION_FLAG = 0;
```

Figure 7.2. A Predicate on the Most Frequent Value Is Not Unusual.

This is a reasonable query—finding rows that meet other criteria but do not have an exception recorded. If only 10 rows will be selected with this index (as DB2 is assuming), the access path through this index may be the best based on these statistics. This, of course, depends on what other indexes exist and the other search criteria. The point, though, is that it is quite feasable that such a situation might arise. The DBA and programmers must carefully evaluate the types of access that will be used.

Now that DB2 can keep some statistics on the distribution of values, the situation has been improved. DB2 will record that 99,900 rows have a 0 value and that there will be a couple of dozen rows for each of the other values.

Let's look at another case where modifying the statistics was of benefit. I had a table with two indexes, both of which were fairly well-clustered (they had similar although not identical columns). The queries I would be using require an index scan. One of the indexes was a much better choice. It was slightly better clustered and my queries used a partial key that was better satisfied by this index. However, this index had more columns than the other and, therefore, it was physically bigger (more pages and a higher NLEAF value). Thus, DB2 chose the smaller index to do the index scan, figuring on fewer IOs of the index. My solution was to update NLEAF after I ran RUNSTATS. The UPDATE statement is shown in Figure 7.3. I multiplied NLEAF of the smaller index by 2. This increased its value to make it larger than my preferred index (but not so large as to make it totally ignored by DB2). I did not have to worry about the exact volume of data or growth because I did not use a fixed value but rather an adjustment to the real value. After this change, DB2 used the index I wanted it to.

7.2.5 How to Update the Statistics

There are restrictions on who can update the catalog statistics. Initially, only someone with SYSADM authority may do so. However, people with SYSADM authority may grant catalog UPDATE authority to other IDs. Figure 7.4 has the GRANT statement to give GELLER the authority to update the NLEAF column

```
UPDATE SYSIBM.SYSINDEXES
   SET NLEAF = NLEAF * 2
   WHERE NAME = 'XHSABC01' AND CREATOR='GELLER';
```
Figure 7.3. Updating the Catalog Statistics.

```
GRANT UPDATE(NLEAF)
   ON TABLE SYSIBM.SYSINDEXES
   TO GELLER;
```
Figure 7.4. Granting Authority to Update the Catalog Statistics.

of SYSIBM.SYSINDEXES for all indexes. If I wanted to restrict this ability to only certain indexes, I could create a view on SYSINDEXES and grant UPDATE on the view (Figure 7.5). You can also imbed the UPDATE statements in a program (bound by someone with the necessary authority) and then grant EXECUTE authority on the plan to other IDs.

The statistics are always updated when RUNSTATS is run. If you changed them manually, you must do so again each time you run RUNSTATS. Version 2.3 of DB2 introduces a new option where you can choose which catalog tables should be updated by RUNSTATS. Therefore, you might be able to update some of the statistics while leaving alone those that were manually updated.

There is one more important thing to note about updating these columns. The HIGH2KEY and LOW2KEY columns must have values if COLCARD has a value. If RUNSTATS were run with COL(ALL), then they will have values. If RUNSTATS is run without using the COL option, then only columns that are the high-order column of an index have values. HIGH2KEY and LOW2KEY have character data types. For noncharacter columns which they represent, the data is stored in DB2's internal format. For example, decimal data is stored in a packed decimal format with special encoding. The internal format of columns is described in the Administration Guide. You must use the hexadecimal value for this internal format when you update these columns.

7.2.6 Summary

The ability to manually adjust the catalog statistics can be a powerful tool. However, it must be used carefully. You must remember to redo it each time RUNSTATS is run. It is also very easy to make changes incorrectly. Selection criteria must be used to ensure that only the intended rows of the catalog are updated. For example, if you want to update a particular column's cardinality, you have to identify the right column, table, and creator to limit the update to that one column.

```
CREATE VIEW GELLER.HSNLEAF
   (NAME,TBNAME,NLEAF)
  AS
  SELECT NAME,TBNAME,NLEAF FROM SYSIBM.SYSINDEXES
    WHERE TBNAME LIKE 'THS%' AND CREATOR='GELLER';


GRANT UPDATE(NLEAF)
  ON TABLE GELLER.HSNLEAF
  TO GELLER;
```

Figure 7.5. Using a View to Control Catalog Updating.

7.3 TABLE SPACE REORGANIZATION

7.3.1 What the REORG Utility Does

One of the tools for keeping a database well-tuned is the REORG utility. It reorganizes the physical storage of table spaces and indexes. The indexes for a table can be reorganized at the same time as the table space or they can be done separately. In general, DB2 requires less tuning effort than other DBMSs because there are fewer parameters to specify. Most of the row placement is not under the control of the DBA. The things that can be specified and which REORG will affect are the clustering of the rows (in clustering index order), the amount of freespace for the table space and indexes, and the space allocations.

7.3.1.1 Clustering Index Order

The primary reason for reorganizing a table space is to store the data rows in clustering order. There are several reasons why a table space might not be in this order. When a table is initially loaded with the LOAD utility, the data is stored in the order of the input file. It is a good idea to sort the input file into the order of the clustering index before running the load.

7.3.1.2 Freespace

Each row is stored in the next available place in the page. The page is not filled completely on a load or a reorg. A certain amount is left free. This is the amount specified in the PCTFREE parameter of the CREATE TABLESPACE statement. The same is true for the index space. The default for table spaces is 5%, and for indexes it is 10%. The FREEPAGE parameter is used to indicate that some whole pages are to be left free during the load. It defaults to 0.

The reason for freespace is to allow room for rows which are inserted later on, to be stored in pages that contain nearby rows. Nearby means similar values for the clustering index columns. When an SQL INSERT statement is issued, DB2 will use the clustering index to find a desirable page to store the row. The INSERT will use the freespace or any space made available from a delete of an existing row. If there is no room on this page, then the inserted row cannot be stored there and will go elsewhere (see Section 4.1). If LOAD was not used, then no space will be reserved in each page and it will all be used by subsequent INSERTs.

As more and more insertions occur, the freespace will get used up and more rows will be stored out of clustering order. The clustering level will go down. This affects performance. When retrieving rows in clustering order (e.g., patients whose names start with a 'J'; all services for patient '987654321'), more pages will need to be read. In fact, the same page may be needed several times, as DB2 may have to jump back and forth between pages.

7.3.1.3 Disorganized Indexes

Freespace in indexes is important, too. Freespace is left during a LOAD or a CREATE INDEX for a populated table. Index entries are always logically stored in index order. When an index page is full and a new entry must be stored, DB2 must create a new index page and move some of the entries to the new page to make room for the new entry. The new page may not be in physical sequence with the preceeding page. This makes for a disorganized index which will be more costly to scan.

The REORG utility puts the rows back into clustering order. It will also re-establish the freespace. This will allow more inserted rows to go into the best page and will greatly improve access through the clustering index. Reorging the index will also reestablish the freespace and will place consecutive entries into physical sequence.

When a table is built up with insertions (rather than a LOAD), indexes will get disorganized very quickly. The index will start with one page. The rows will be inserted with (probably) widely separated index values. Many page splits will result as more and more entries are stored. This process is not just true of DB2 indexes. It also happens with VSAM KSDSs and other indexes. These indexes are likely to need a reorg early on. After time, reorgs will be needed less often, as the existing entries after a reorg will be spread over many index pages rather than an initial few. The indicators of a need to reorg an index are an increase in NLEVELS and NLEAF of SYSINDEXES and LEAFDIST of SYSINDEX-PART. LEAFDIST is the best indication. It represents the average distance (number of pages * 100) between logically successive leaf pages. A perfectly organized index will have LEAFDIST=0 (unless the FREEPAGE parameter is greater than 0). Section 4.4 discusses LEAFDIST in more detail.

The amount of freespace can be changed with the ALTER statement (Figure 7.6). The new values will take effect with the next REORG (or LOAD).

Space allocations can also be changed with the ALTER statements, and also can take effect with the next run of either the REORG or the RECOVER utilities.

7.3.2 The Reorganization Process

The basic process to reorg a table is to unload the data and then reload it in clustering order. One way to do this would be to unload the rows by accessing them through the clustering index. This can be very slow if the clustering index is very unclustered. DB2 would have to jump around from page to page and may have to reaccess the same page many times. Up through Version 2.2, this is how

```
ALTER TABLESPACE DHSHOSO.SHSPATO
   PCTFREE 25;
```

Figure 7.6. Changing the Freespace of a Table Space.

the REORG utility works. Another alternative would be for DB2 to read through the rows in physical sequence, sort them, and then reload them. The sorting done with the operating system sort utility is very quick. The performance of this method would be much better in some cases. In fact, this method will be an option with Version 2.3 of DB2. It is used if you include the SORTDATA keyword on the Reorg control statement.

When you reorganize a table space, the indexes must also be rebuilt, as the data rows have been moved to new locations. As REORG reloads each row, it writes out work file records for the indexes. This work file is sorted and then the indexes are rebuilt very efficiently. The indexes are, therefore, reorganized as part of the table space reorganization.

Figure 7.7 illustrates the process. It is fairly similar to the LOAD utility process. The JCL and some of the options are similar. See Section 6.2 for a description of LOAD. The JCL for a reorg is in Figure 7.8. UID is used to uniquely identify this utility run. SYSTEM identifies the DB2 subsystem that this table space is part of. The SORT DD statements are sort work files for the sorting of the index records. The SYSUT1 DD statement is for the index work file. The DBA has to ensure that the space allocations for these files are large enough for the table being reorged. Not enough work space is one of the leading causes of failure in reorg jobs. The other leading cause is not specifying enough CPU time for a job which is reorging a large table space.

The control statement for reorging a table space is shown in Figure 7.9. In this example, we are reorganizing the admission table THSADM0. Note that it is actually the table space which is reorganized (SHSADM0). LOG NO has the same meaning as for the LOAD utility. By default, REORG will write out log records for every row. This can cause a lot of contention for the log dataset. It is

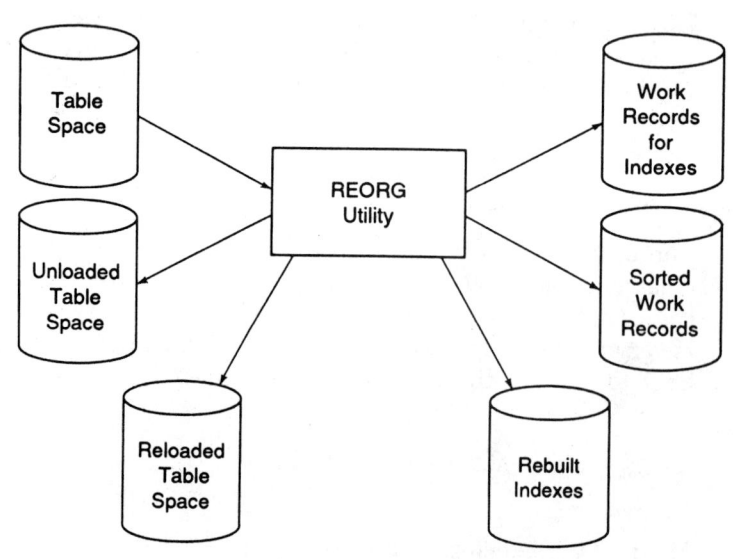

Figure 7.7. Reorganizing a Table Space.

```
//REORG    EXEC DSNUPROC,SYSTEM=DB2T,UID=REORGPAT,UTPROC='',
//              LIB='DB2T.DSN.DSNLOAD'
//SYSREC   DD UNIT=SYSDA,SPACE=(CYL,(20,20)),    unload dataset
//         DSN=GELLER.REORGPAT.SYSREC,DISP=(MOD,DELETE,CATLG)
//SYSUT1   DD UNIT=SYSDA,SPACE=(CYL,(20,20)),    index work dataset
//         DSN=GELLER.REORGPAT.SYSUT1,DISP=(MOD,DELETE,CATLG)
//SORTOUT  DD UNIT=SYSDA,SPACE=(CYL,(20,20)),
//         DSN=GELLER.REORGPAT.SORTOUT,DISP=(MOD,DELETE,CATLG)
//SORTWK01 DD UNIT=SYSDA,SPACE=(CYL,(20,20)),
//         DSN=GELLER.REORGPAT.SWK01,DISP=(MOD,DELETE,CATLG)
//SORTWK02 DD UNIT=SYSDA,SPACE=(CYL,(20,20)),
//         DSN=GELLER.REORGPAT.SWK02,DISP=(MOD,DELETE,CATLG)
//SORTWK03 DD UNIT=SYSDA,SPACE=(CYL,(20,20)),
//         DSN=GELLER.REORGPAT.SWK03,DISP=(MOD,DELETE,CATLG)
//SYSIN    DD *
REORG TABLESPACE DHSHOS0.SHSPAT0
```
Figure 7.8. JCL for the REORG Utility.

```
REORG TABLESPACE DHSHOS0.SHSADM0 LOG NO
```
Figure 7.9. Control Statement for a Reorg.

generally much faster to skip logging (LOG NO) and then run a COPY after the reorg. If logging is not done, the COPY will be required before further updating of the table can take place.

Another parameter of the REORG control statement is UNLOAD. The default value (CONTINUE) is used most of the time. This means that after unloading the table space, the utility should continue running, reloading the table space and building the indexes. There are two other choices. UNLOAD PAUSE tells the utility to pause after the unload until an operator tells it to continue. This option is useful when you are managing the table space datasets yourself (with IDCAMS DEFINEs), rather than letting DB2 manage them (with storage groups). In order to make some changes to the datasets, you might have to delete and redefine them after unloading the data, but before reloading it.

The third choice for this parameter is UNLOAD ONLY. This creates an unload dataset, but does not reload the table space. The table space is not reorganized. The obvious use for this option is to create a backup of the data. It is not, however, as useful as you might think or hope. This backup can be used as input to the LOAD utility, but only for reloading into the same table space. It cannot be used to load a copy of the tables, either on the same DB2 subsystem, or on another. Every DB2 object (i.e., database, table space, etc.) is assigned an internal identifier by DB2. This identifier is stored in each page of a table space, and is on the unload dataset. The unload cannot be reloaded into another table space that is logically the same as the original, but has a different internal identifier. Therefore, the only use of this option is to have a copy of the data to be used as a stable point to go back to if necessary. The most likely situation would be in a test environment where you want to repeat a test several times with the same starting point. This method can be a little bit simpler than using the COPY and RECOVER utilities (see Section 7.6).

DB2 tries to ensure the integrity of the tables. If a utility run fails, DB2 prevents further updating (or utility runs) against the table space until you have told DB2 that the problem has been cleared up. For any utility run, it records in the catalog the running of that utility. The UID parameter is used to identify a particular run. If the utility fails for any reason, this catalog record is still there. If you wish to simply rerun the REORG and not restart it at some intermediate step, then you have to execute the Terminate Utility command. This command is described in Section 6.2 (Figure 6.19).

7.3.3 Performance and Concurrency

The performance of the reorg can be improved with a larger blocksize for the output datasets (SYSREC, SYSUT1, and SORTOUT). If no blocksize is given in the JCL, DB2 will pick one. For the index work datasets (SYSUT1 and SORTOUT), the blocksize must be a multiple of the record length, which is 12 plus the length of the longest index key (as of Version 2). In general, DB2 will pick a large blocksize for 3380 devices but a smaller one for older devices. Moreover, for each new release of DB2, there has been an increase in the default. For Version 2.1, a 16K blocksize was used. For 2.2, it is now 20K.

For Version 2.3, you should test out the new SORTDATA option. For highly unclustered table spaces, performance can be significantly improved.

During the unload portion of the reorg, the table space is available for read access. It is not available at all during the other phases. For a very large table space that takes over an hour to reorg, read access for a portion of the time might be useful.

Partitioned table spaces are often used for very large tables. One of the benefits of using partitioned table spaces is that many utilities can be run for a single partition at a time. This includes REORG. You cannot reorg two partitions concurrently because an exclusive lock on the table space is taken during several of the REORG phases. However, you can schedule each partition for a different night if time does not allow you to do the entire table space at once. There is one drawback, though, to doing one partition only. For regular table spaces, all indexes are rebuilt during a reorg. When a single partition is reorged, only the corresponding partition of the clustering index is rebuilt. All other indexes must be updated. The entries that point to rows in the one partition are deleted and reinserted. This is less efficient and may leave the index disorganized. A reorg of the index may then be needed.

7.3.3.1 Restarting a Reorg

A REORG can fail part way through for several reasons. The most common causes include work datasets which do not have enough space allocated for them and not enough CPU time specified for the job. Having to rerun a large REORG from the beginning might take up more time than is available. Fortunately, DB2 allows most utilities to be restarted at the point of failure, or at the beginning of the phase that the utility was in. Each of the processes of the REORG is a separate phase. DB2 writes checkpoint information periodically to the log so that a restart does not even have to redo an entire phase. These restart checkpoints are written whether or not LOG YES has been specified.

A basic requirement to enable a utility restart is to correctly specify the dataset dispositions. In Figure 7.8, each of the output datasets has a (nontemporary) dataset name and a disposition of (MOD,DELETE,CATLG). This means that if the job goes to normal completion (with or without an error return code), the dataset will be deleted at the end. However, if there is an abnormal termination (abend), the datasets will be retained. They can then be used to continue processing during a restart. To specify a restart you change the UTPROC parameter of the EXEC statement to either:

UTPROC='RESTART(PHASE)' or
UTPROC='RESTART(CURRENT)'

If a reorg of a large table space was almost finished with the RELOAD phase, restarting at the current checkpoint would save all of the time needed for the unload of the table space as well as most of the reload time.

There is another advantage to restarting rather than rerunning from the beginning. The course of action for rerunning will depend on the phase during which the job failed. If it was during the UNLOAD, then the REORG can simply be rerun (after terminating the utility with the TERM command). However, if the failure was during the RELOAD, the table space would be incomplete. You would first have to RECOVER the table space before you could rerun the REORG. Therefore, the operational procedures are a little simpler with a restart.

On the other hand, some operator thought and action is still required. The JCL must be changed to indicate a restart. Furthermore, if the failure is due to insufficient space allocations, then some action will be needed to allocate new datasets with more space and copy in the partially built data so that restart can continue where it left off.

Either way, handling a REORG failure is not trivial and requires good operational procedures to be established.

7.3.4 Reorganizing Indexes

Whenever a table space is reorganized (except for a single partition reorg), the indexes are also reorganized. There may also be times when an index could benefit from a reorg even if the table space doesn't need one. For example, if there are many insertions into a table with adequate freespace, the clustering index and the data will remain well-organized. However, since it is unlikely that the order of inserts is in the order of all the other indexes, they may become disorganized. Indexes can be reorganized in three ways.

- Reorganizing the table space
- Reorganizing the index alone (Figure 7.10)
- RECOVER INDEX

Reorging an index involves unloading the index pages, sorting the entries, and rebuilding the index. The table space does not have to be accessed, as the data rows are not moved. Unloading in physical sequence and sorting the entries is much faster than unloading in index order. This is because an index that needs reorging has its pages out of physical order. Therefore, accessing them is slowed down.

Recovering an index involves unloading the table space (with a table space

```
//REORG   EXEC DSNUPROC,SYSTEM=DB2T,UID=REORGIDX,UTPROC='',
//             LIB='DB2T.DSN.DSNLOAD'
//SYSREC  DD UNIT=SYSDA,SPACE=(CYL,(20,20)),    unload dataset
//    DSN=GELLER.REORGIDX.SYSREC,DISP=(MOD,DELETE,CATLG)
//SYSUT1  DD UNIT=SYSDA,SPACE=(CYL,(20,20)),    index work dataset
//    DSN=GELLER.REORGIDX.SYSUT1,DISP=(MOD,DELETE,CATLG)
//SORTOUT DD UNIT=SYSDA,SPACE=(CYL,(20,20)),
//    DSN=GELLER.REORGIDX.SORTOUT,DISP=(MOD,DELETE,CATLG)
//SORTWK01 DD UNIT=SYSDA,SPACE=(CYL,(20,20)),
//    DSN=GELLER.REORGIDX.SWK01,DISP=(MOD,DELETE,CATLG)
//SORTWK02 DD UNIT=SYSDA,SPACE=(CYL,(20,20)),
//    DSN=GELLER.REORGIDX.SWK02,DISP=(MOD,DELETE,CATLG)
//SORTWK03 DD UNIT=SYSDA,SPACE=(CYL,(20,20)),
//    DSN=GELLER.REORGIDX.SWK03,DISP=(MOD,DELETE,CATLG)
//SYSIN DD *

REORG INDEX GELLER.XHSPAT01
```

Figure 7.10. Reorganizing an Index.

scan), sorting the rows in index order, and rebuilding the index. This is just as good as a REORG INDEX. It is almost as fast. The index scan of the REORG will be a little faster as there are fewer index pages than data pages.

7.3.5 Running RUNSTATS Again

DB2's choice of access path is dependent on the statistics in the catalog. Since a REORG may substantially rearrange the data and index entries, the statistics will no longer reflect the actual data distribution. It is, therefore, a good idea to always run RUNSTATS right after a REORG. You might also want to REBIND some plans if their access path might be changed due to the new statistics.

7.4 ADDING AND DROPPING INDEXES

One of the great benefits of DB2 is that you can have indexes on any combination of columns, and it is fairly easy to change them at any time. DB2 indexes are used to enforce uniqueness of column values and are required for primary keys, but they are primarily created for performance. We design the indexes, with performance in mind, to meet the requirements of the programs and anticipated queries and reports. Since requirements change frequently (both during initial development and during later enhancements), it may be necessary to frequently make changes to the indexes. Fortunately, this is something which can be done easily with DB2.

7.4.1 Reasons for Not Having Indexes

Indexes can be on any column, or columns, of a table. However, not every column should be indexed. There is overhead in maintaining each index, so it only pays to have indexes which will be useful. Useful means that the columns are frequently used in WHERE and ORDER BY clauses. It also means that DB2 will choose to use this index for those SQL statements. Not every index will be used even for queries that involve the columns of the index. We'll look at some examples below.

For small tables, there is just no need to have indexes for performance. A 100-row table of 40 bytes per row will be stored in one data page. To access any row in the table will take just one IO. To use an index will take at least one IO for the index plus one IO for the data row. Therefore, it will take longer to use the index. There is some extra processing in scanning the 100 rows, but this comes to less time than an IO. Even if the table occupies several pages, it probably doesn't pay to have indexes.

7.4.1.1 Too Many Indexes Add Overhead

For larger tables, to judge the benefit of having an index, you must weigh the cost of maintaining the index. To insert a row in a table requires one write to the table space. Each index will also require one write. If a table has 10 indexes, inserting a row will take 11 IOs (not counting reading the higher levels of the indexes) as opposed to 2 IOs if there were only one index. This is more than five times as much.

For large batch updates, the increase can be even more. Let's say we were inserting 10,000 rows with the data in the order of the clustering index. If there is no available space in the table, they will all be written to the end of the table space. 80 byte rows would fit 50 per page. Therefore, 200 pages would be written. DB2 will write 32 consecutive pages with one IO. The number of IOs will, therefore, be very few. The clustering index will also require only a few IOs, as many index entries will be written to the same index pages. The other indexes, however, are likely to be unclustered. The index entries will be spread far apart. Thus, 10,000 rows might take up to 10,000 IOs for each index (some index pages may be in buffers, so there may be fewer actual IOs). This is much more than five times the IO activity of a similar table with just one index.

Even when using the LOAD utility, which can be more efficient for loading large amounts of data, too many indexes can be a problem. LOAD is often used for tables that are being populated from another source and which will be used mainly for retrieval. There is the temptation to have many indexes for this situation. If RESUME YES is used, the indexes are still updated as with insert statements, and performance will be similar. With REPLACE, the table and the indexes are built efficiently, but 10 indexes will still take 10 times as long as one index. For a large table, the LOAD run could take longer than the batch window will allow.

7.4.1.2 Some Indexes May Rarely Be Used

Some indexes are not too useful because they will not be used much by DB2. Since you can have any combination of columns, you may have several which are similar to each other. Prior to Version 2.2, nonclustered indexes are also not used by DB2 except when only a few rows are expected to be returned. An = predicate may result in the index being used, but ranges (e.g., > predicate) are not too likely to make use of a nonclustered index. The use of nonclustered indexes has now been improved and they may be chosen more often than in the past. The improvements are described in Sections 4.1, 4.3, and 5.3.

When you have many different indexes, DB2 will also sometimes not use the best one for each query. It may be fooled due to nonuniformity of data distribution or by other factors. One index may be smaller (lower NLEAF) than another because it has fewer or shorter columns, but in other aspects may be less useful for a given query.

Figures 7.11–7.14 have an example of an index that is not too useful unless we manually change some of the statistics. The table has information on telephone calls. The most common access is by phone extension or by department. The clustering index is, therefore, on department, phone (Figure 7.11). There is an index on phone by itself for quick access to the calls made from a particular extension. There are also requirements for access by various other fields. In particular, there will be a query to find long calls—those with a duration greater

```
CREATE TABLE GELLER.TTECAL0
(DEPARTMENT   CHAR(5)       NOT NULL WITH DEFAULT,
 PHONE        CHAR(4)       NOT NULL WITH DEFAULT,
 AREACODE     CHAR(3)       NOT NULL WITH DEFAULT,
 EXCHANGE     CHAR(3)       NOT NULL WITH DEFAULT,
 LINE         CHAR(4)       NOT NULL WITH DEFAULT,
 CALLDATE     DATE          NOT NULL WITH DEFAULT,
 DURATION     DECIMAL(7,2)  NOT NULL WITH DEFAULT,
 COST         DECIMAL(7,2)  NOT NULL WITH DEFAULT)
IN DTETEL0.STECAL0;


CREATE INDEX GELLER.XTECAL01 ON GELLER.TTECAL0
 (DEPARTMENT,
  PHONE)
 CLUSTER
 USING STOGROUP STG1 PRIQTY 1000 SECQTY 200
 SUBPAGES 4 CLOSE NO;


CREATE INDEX GELLER.XTECAL02 ON GELLER.TTECAL0
 (PHONE)
 USING STOGROUP STG1 PRIQTY 1000 SECQTY 200
 SUBPAGES 4 CLOSE NO;
```

Figure 7.11. A Table for Telephone Calls.

than some threshold. Therefore, initial design had the index in Figure 7.12 on DURATION.

A typical query would be that in Figure 7.13. This query will not use index XTECAL03. The reason is that there are many different values of DURATION. Figure 7.14 has some statistics on this table and the indexes. DB2 (prior to Version 2.2) assumed a uniform distribution of data values. It now knows the distribution of the 10 most frequent values of any column that is the high-order

```
CREATE INDEX GELLER.XTECAL03 ON GELLER.TTECAL0
(DURATION)
USING STOGROUP STG1 PRIQTY 1000 SECQTY 200
SUBPAGES 4 CLOSE NO;
```
Figure 7.12. An Index on Call Duration.

```
SELECT * FROM TTECAL0
  WHERE DURATION > 60;
```
Figure 7.13. Selecting Calls Greater Than 60 Minutes.

```
TABLE CARDINALITY = 1,000,000


COLNAME        CARD       LOW2KEY        HIGH2KEY


PHONE          2000       1001           9523

DURATION       4000        .03           120
```
Figure 7.14. Catalog Statistics for the Telephone Table.

column of an index. This is not enough information to help with a field like DURATION, which has many values with a few occurrences of each. For a range operator (such as >=) DB2 takes the HIGH2KEY and LOW2KEY values and the operand of the WHERE clause (60 in this example) and estimates what the percentage of rows returned will be. In our example, HIGH2KEY is 120 minutes (actually HIGH2KEY would not *show* as 120 because it is a character field containing the internal representation of a decimal 120). Therefore, DB2 will assume that 1/2 of all the rows will have durations greater than 60 minutes. Since the index is not clustered, using the index would result in reading over half the data rows in a random order. Based on this asssumption it would be much faster to do a table space scan. For a nonclustered index, Version 2.2 will sort the index entries by RID (row ID) of the data rows. However, even with this improvement, it would still choose a table space scan if it expects to select half the rows. The statistics that the DB2 optimizer uses are described in Section 4.4.

Using an = predicate (DURATION = 33) might make use of this index, but the queries that are needed require a > operator. In this case, DB2 will probably only consider using this index if the operand were greater than HIGH2KEY. As it stands, this index will rarely be used and is, therefore, of little use.

7.4.1.3 Improving the Usefullness of an Index

There are some solutions to get DB2 to utilize this index. You can change some of the statistics in the catalog (as described in Section 7.2) after RUNSTATS has been run. Changing the cardinality columns would not be of much use because there are already a large enough number of different values. We could change HIGH2KEY. If the query asks for a DURATION > the HIGH2KEY value, DB2 assumes there is only one value higher and, therefore, not too many rows will be returned. If we set HIGH2KEY to some lower value (e.g., 30), then any query requesting higher durations will make use of the index. Before picking a value, we must carefully analyze the data and understand the distribution of values as well as the user requirements. If there are only 30 or so rows with DURATION > 30, then accessing them via the index will be quick enough. If, however, there are 1000 rows with DURATION > 30, then using the index may be costly. Therefore, we would want to pick a value that will give good performance. Another danger of changing the statistics is that we have to remember to change them each time RUNSTATS is run.

Before Version 2, we couldn't change the statistics. Another alternative that would have a similar affect would be to introduce a new column to the table. This column will be under program control and will serve as a "high duration" flag. Whenever a program inserts a row, it will set this column to either the duration itself, if it is less than a threshold value (e.g., 30 minutes), or to a flag value (e.g., 9999), if the duration is higher than the threshold. The duration index will be on this new column plus the actual duration. The queries will look like Figure 7.15. If a particular query only wants longer calls, you could also have a predicate with the DURATION column. DURAFLAG will have a high cardinality because most of the rows have small durations of different values. Since the high-order column of the index is used with an = predicate, DB2 will assume that a reasonably small number of rows will be returned and will use the index. In fact, with Version 2.2, DB2 will know how many rows do have a flag value of 9999 and can make a better decision on the access path.

Either of these methods will work. Without them, though, the index will be of little use and, therefore, is not worth having.

7.4.2 Choosing the Columns to Index

Any column can be in an index. In fact, a column can be in any number of indexes along with any combination of other columns, in any order. A table with 20 columns could have 20 indexes, one for each column, plus many more with several columns each. This would not, however, be practical, even for a "read

```
SELECT * FROM TTECALO
  WHERE DURAFLAG = 9999;
```

Figure 7.15. Selecting Long Calls with a Flag Column.

only" table. As mentioned above, even a table without online updates must still be loaded, and there may be a limit to the available load time. Many possible indexes are also not very useful (as shown in the preceeding example). Moreover, indexes take up space. If each column appeared in one index, the total amount of space taken up by the indexes would probably exceed that of the data rows themselves (each entry of a unique index has the index value plus a pointer to the data row). DASD storage is not that expensive and is not the primary concern in database design, but the person who pays the bills (whether it is the user or the data center) may not want to acquire additional devices for the application. Indexes that improve the performance of the system will be cost-effective, but excessive indexes are not.

Since we want to limit the number of indexes, choosing the right combination of columns to index can sometimes be tricky. The following examples will illustrate this. There are often several possibilities that can make sense, and we must pick the right ones.

If we have columns COLA and COLB and we have an index on COLA,COLB, do we need or want an index on just COLA? Conversely, if we have an index on COLA, then is there any benefit in there being one on COLA,COLB? What about an index on COLB,COLA?

Performance wise, if you have queries based on COLA alone, there is not that much difference between using an index on COLA or one on COLA,COLB. The first is obviously smaller, so queries that scan the index will be faster (e.g., COLA > ...). However, a query with predicate COLA = ... (where there are not too many rows meeting this criteria) will be fairly similar either way. By having COLB in the index you do not lose much for these queries, but you gain the advantage of much faster processing of queries with both COLA *and* COLB in the predicates.

Let's look at the admission table, THSADM0. The index XHSADM01 is in PATID, ADMDATE DESC, ADMSEQ DESC order. Queries to retrieve admissions for a patient, such as in Figure 7.16, can be satisfied with the use of XHSADM01 with a matching index scan. If we had an index on just PATID, that index could be used, but there would be no real advantage. There is a side benefit to using XHSADM01. The rows will be retrieved in descending admit date order for the patient. Without an ORDER BY clause, we are not guaranteed a particular order, but for ad hoc queries it is nice to get them in order when the simple query of this figure is used.

For the patient table, THSPAT0, there is an index on PATID (XHSPAT02). Even though there may occassionally be queries that also have predicates on

```
SELECT * FROM THSADM0
  WHERE PATID = '998877665';
```

Figure 7.16. Selecting Admissions for a Patient.

SEX or BIRTHDATE as well as PATID, there is no benefit to adding either of these columns to the index. Most queries of this type would return only at most a few rows so a separate index of this type will not be used often. If we only want one index with PATID, then we cannot have it on PATID,BIRTHDATE. The PATID must be unique in the patient table. The way to achieve this is by having a UNIQUE index on the PATID field alone. Therefore, we must have XHSPAT02 as it is.

As you can see from these examples, there are times when you would need indexes on COLA and on COLA,COLB. The COLA index would be for uniqueness, and the other index might also be needed for ordering and selection.

For the admission table, we also have index XHSADM02 on ADMDATE. Sometimes, we need to find all patients who have been admitted in some time period. For batch access, this index would not be critical. The time required to do an index scan or table space scan would not be too much. For online access, this index would be of use. XHSADM02 is not clustered. Therefore, it is good for short date ranges, but not for long ranges. For a long range, DB2 will probably decide to use a table space scan. Even for short ranges some queries could have a performance problem. In Figure 7.17, we ask for admissions between July 4 and 5, 1989. This is only two days and the index is likely to be used. If for some reason there are an abnormally high number of admissions on these days, the index access could be very high. However, for most queries, the appropriate choice will be made.

In Section 7.2, we had an example of an index on a column with many duplicate values. Most rows had a zero value for a flag, while a small number of rows had nonzero values. An index might be useful (with Version 2.2) for quick access to these rows. I mentioned that it would be better to have additional columns in the index (with the flag as the high-order). Queries with selection criteria on the flag will be processed almost as quickly even if the index entries are larger. Having the extra columns will increase the cardinality of the index and greatly reduce the number of duplicate entries.

The problem with many duplicate entries is the performance of delete processing. When a row is deleted, all indexes on the table must also be updated. The index entries pointing to the rows must be deleted from the index. For non-unique indexes, the duplicate entries are just chained together. To find the entry to be deleted, DB2 must search through the entire chain until it finds one with the RID (row ID) of the data row. If there are a dozen duplicate values, this presents no problem. If there are 90,000 entries with zero as the index value, then performance will definitely suffer. On average, half of the entries must be searched.

```
SELECT * FROM THSADM0
    WHERE ADMDATE BETWEEN '1989-07-04' AND '1989-07-05';
```

Figure 7.17. Admissions for Specific Dates.

The simplest solution is to add on other fields to the index. Using the primary key is a possibility. You do not have to make the index unique, but it should not have so many duplicates.

So, to summarize, we can certainly have many different combinations of columns in indexes and more than one combination can be useful.

7.4.3 Unique Indexes

Some index choices are straightforward. Unique indexes are created on any combination of columns that must be unique. If three columns together are unique, the index will still be unique if any additional columns are added to the end. Unique indexes are not required just because some columns happen to have unique values, but are needed where it is important for the application to *ensure* uniqueness. If a primary key is defined for a table, then you *must* create a unique index on the primary key columns.

7.4.4 Choosing the Clustering Index

Choosing the *clustering* index is one of the most important decisions to be made. Only one index can be the clustering index and, therefore, only one index can be guaranteed to be in clustering order (and only after a reorg). You choose as the clustering index the one for which the application most often needs the rows grouped or ordered by. If a number of rows are accessed with each SQL statement, then performance will be greatly improved if they are clustered on the same page. For the patient table, I chose the name index as the clustering index rather than the patient ID index. Most online transactions are by PATID, but only require a single patient row at a time. Clustering by PATID would be useful for occasional queries or reports that want the data sorted by PATID. On the other hand, many queries and reports want the data in name order. The selection criteria may also be for a range of names. Even more important is an online browse function based on name. Sometimes, a patient record needs to be accessed when the PATID is not known and the name is only partially known (e.g., LIKE 'JOHN%'). The browse function will put up a screen's worth of names starting with some value. The user can then page forward or backward until he finds the one he wants. Since each SQL SELECT will retrieve a set of rows with similar names, it is much quicker if they are in physical order in the table. Therefore, even though more access is through PATID, overall performance may be better if the name index is the clustering index.

The other tables in the hospital database have records of various types for each patient. Admissions are keyed by PATID and date. I have made this index (XHSADM01) the clustering index because access by this key is much more common than access by just admit date. Each patient may have several admissions, and we often want to retrieve all of them together. By clustering on this index we can usually get all admissions for a patient with one IO to the table space. The same holds true for patient locations and services.

Occasionally, it is difficult to pick one clustering order that will always be best.

There is another type of access to the patient table that would benefit from clustering on PATID. A join with one of the other tables (which are clustered on PATID) will be a common type of query. If the selection criteria result in records selected from many patients, it would be better if the joined tables were all clustered on the same field. Clustering the patient table by name is not the best solution for *these* queries. The DBA and systems analysts must determine which types of access are most frequent and require better response time.

7.4.5 Changing the Indexes

One of the most common changes to the database is to make changes to the indexes. Why? For many reasons. Queries may be running too slowly. EXPLAIN may show that an index is not being used, or is being used when it is *not* the best access path. There may be new requirements (new programs) that access the data through different columns than the original specifications called for. DB2 makes it fairly easy to add and drop indexes.

7.4.5.1 Dropping an Index

When it turns out that an index is not of much use, it pays to get rid of it. Why pay the overhead of maintaining it? Dropping an index is simple. Figure 7.18 has the DDL statement to drop one of the indexes of the location table. Dropping the index is simple, but there are some implications that the DBA must be aware of. Any application plan which used that index will be affected. A new access path for the plan must be used in the future. This new path may provide adequate performance, or it may perform slower. Before dropping the index, the DBA can query the catalog to find all plans that use the index (Figure 7.19 asks for all plans that use index XHSLOC02). After dropping the index, EXPLAIN can be run on all affected plans to see what access path will now be used. It is also a good idea to test the programs that use these plans ahead of time in the test environment, to see how performance will be affected.

7.4.5.2 Creating a New Index

Adding new indexes to a DB2 table is also fairly easy. The CREATE INDEX statement can be executed at any time (but there will be some contention for catalog resources and concurrency will be affected). Any combination of columns

```
DROP INDEX GELLER.XHSLOC02;
```

Figure 7.18. Dropping an Index.

```
SELECT * FROM SYSIBM.SYSPLANDEP
  WHERE BNAME = 'XHSLOC02' AND BTYPE = 'I';
```

Figure 7.19. Checking the Catalog to Find Plans Using Index XHSLOC02.

can be used (unlike VSAM alternate indexes where the indexed fields must be consecutive). However, the time it takes to create the index may be a problem. If the table is not yet populated, the CREATE runs in seconds. The DB2 catalog is updated to record the existence of the index, and the index dataset is allocated and initialized. On the other hand, if the table has many rows, the index must be built at this time. CREATE INDEX has been greatly improved in Version 2, and is much faster than it used to be (as described in Section 2.4). It is improved further in Version 2.3 (especially on the newer processors). However, it still takes time for a large table.

There is another problem with creating indexes for large tables. The performance speedup in Version 2 was achieved by first sorting the index entries and then loading the index. The sort is done using DB2's sort, which uses the DB2 temporary table spaces. If the application system has large tables, then large temporary table spaces *may* have previously been created to handle complex queries. But they may not have been. The default size is not very large. Without a large enough temporary table space, the CREATE INDEX cannot work. The system administrator will first have to enlarge these table spaces (during off hours). Then the index can be created. The administrator may then want to reduce the size again if it is not needed for other work.

When a new index is added to a table, any dynamic SQL (e.g., QMF) will take advantage of it immediately. For static SQL (e.g., most programs), a REBIND will be needed. Otherwise, the access paths of the plan will not change on their own. Before rebinding these plans, RUNSTATS should be run. The CREATE INDEX will build the index but it will not update the DB2 catalog to put in statistics on the index. So, first create the index, then run RUNSTATS, then REBIND any plan that you expect will use the new index. When you REBIND, you should run EXPLAIN on the plan to see if it *is* using the index. There may be something you didn't think of.

7.4.6 Summary

The ease with which you can change the indexes of DB2 tables is one of the key advantages of DB2 over other access methods and DBMSs. Index design and creation still requires analysis and performance evaluation by the DBA, but the tasks to do the job are simpler.

- It is quicker to create an index on an empty table.
- Indexes can be created on populated tables. A large temporary table space is needed to create a new index on a large table.
- The clustering index does not have to be unique or to be the index on the primary key. It should be on the columns where groups of rows are needed together.
- A table does not need a unique index unless there is a primary key or a requirement for uniqueness.
- Columns can appear in more than one index.
- Nonclustered indexes are more useful with Version 2.2.

- Indexes with thousands of duplicate values will have poor delete performance.

7.5 TABLE CHANGES

This section discusses changes that a DBA might want to make to the table design—to the tables themselves, not the indexes. Those are discussed in Section 7.4. Table changes are very common. Most often, they are made because of changing application requirements, but they are often made for performance reasons, too. We'll look at what some of these reasons are, and we'll look at how to go about making the changes.

7.5.1 Reducing IOs

Performance is not a problem for all systems or for every table. It depends on the volume of data, the transaction volume, the number of rows accessed per transaction, whether the access is online or batch, and the size of the machine. So, database design should *not* have performance as its main goal. However, performance certainly is important in many cases.

In general, the main performance goal in designing a system is to reduce the number of IOs. To access a single row through an index will probably use 2 IOs. It may need more IOs for the higher index levels if they are not in a buffer, and it may need less than two if the index or data page is already in a bufffer. A transaction that reads 5 rows (either from 5 tables or from different pages of one table) will need 10 IOs. 3380 disk drives can do 40 random IOs per second, so this adds up to 1/4 second (depending on other contention for the device). This is not bad at all for most systems. For browse-type screens, even longer response time is generally acceptable. This is true for most systems. An exception is for very high transaction rates. In these cases, every IO may be critical. For some of these systems, DB2 may not be able to handle the load if 10 IOs are needed for each transaction. However, for a typical load, 2–10 IOs per transaction is good.

The above example talks about transactions that need a handful of rows from a few tables. Many transactions need more than that. An online transaction may need several dozen or hundreds of rows. A QMF query or batch program may need thousands, and it may need them in a particular order. These are the requirements that demand careful attention.

7.5.2 Clustering the Data—The Need for Several Clustering Orders

With DB2, any SQL statement can access any set of columns in the tables regardless of any indexes that are present. Indexes are primarily there to speed things up. One of the biggest limitations to DB2, and one of the biggest problems in table and index design, is that there can only be *one* clustering order to a table. This is also a problem with just about any other DBMS or access method. Sometimes, you need sets of data in *several* orders. An example was given in the previous section.

Many tables have one primary order. In our hospital database, the majority of the access is by patient. Occasionally, though, we need the data in some other order. The patient table may be needed in birthdate order; we may need admissions by date (regardless of patient). If these requests are only issued occasionally, they can be handled with QMF or batch or a long-running online transaction. It may be okay to make the user wait a minute for a seldom-used query. However, if these alternate orders are needed frequently, then we may have a problem.

A good example is that of a database for customer orders for parts. Figure 7.20 has some representative tables and indexes. We most frequently need the data by customer number and/or order number. Occasionally, though, we also need the order information by part number (to find all orders for a particular part). The inventory table, although most often needed by part number, contains some columns that are also needed when looking at a particular order. Each of the two tables can have one clustering order. The order table is clustered by customer number, order number. All the parts for an order are likely to be on one or two data pages (assuming at most a few hundred parts per order). However, all the order rows for a particular part are going to be spread wide apart. Similarly, the inventory table is clustered by part number. If data from this table is needed for the parts from a single order, the rows are not likely to be on the same page. Let's look at a few possible scenarios.

If there are usually only a few parts per order, then things aren't bad. If a browse-type screen needs to retrieve 5 inventory rows for an order, then there will be about 10 IOs for the inventory table access (index + data for each part), in addition to the couple of IOs for the order table. This is quite reasonable. If, instead, there are typically thousands of parts per order, then there is a good chance that this type of query would be done in batch anyway (the user wouldn't be scanning a thousand lines on a screen). DB2 might use a table space scan and sort the selected rows (sorting is pretty fast in Version 2).

The biggest problems arise when there are a hundred or so rows. This may very well be done with an online transaction and might require hundreds of IOs to satisfy. This will have slower response time and may not be acceptable. Accessing either the order table by part number or the inventory table for an order can require many rows that are on widely separated pages—therefore, each row requiring an IO. Version 2.2's list prefetch might help a bit, but not if the table is large and the rows are far apart. If we clustered the order table by part number instead of order number, then the rows for a single order would be on different pages. How do you design the tables and indexes for good performance for all transactions?

The first thing to do is to weigh the transaction frequencies. It is most important to optimize the performance of the most frequently occurring transactions. The response time requirements for each must be determined. For each access order, you need to know the number of rows that will be accessed, both on average and the worst case (i.e., most transactions may need 5 order rows, but a

```
CREATE TABLE TINODR0
    (ORDERNUM    CHAR(7)     NOT NULL WITH DEFAULT,
     CUSTNUM     CHAR(9)     NOT NULL WITH DEFAULT,
     ORDERDATE   DATE        NOT NULL WITH DEFAULT,
     PARTNUM     CHAR(5)     NOT NULL WITH DEFAULT,
     PARTQTY     DECIMAL(4)  NOT NULL WITH DEFAULT)
IN DININV0.S1NODR0;
CREATE UNIQUE INDEX XINODR01 ON TINODR0
(ORDERNUM,
 PARTNUM)
USING STOGROUP STG1 CLOSE NO;
CREATE UNIQUE INDEX XINODR02 ON TINODR0
(CUSTNUM,
 ORDERNUM,
 PARTNUM)
CLUSTER
USING STOGROUP STG1 CLOSE NO;
CREATE UNIQUE INDEX XINODR03 ON TINODR0
(PARTNUM,
 ORDERNUM)
USING STOGROUP STG1 CLOSE NO;
CREATE TABLE TININV0
    (PARTNUM     CHAR(5)        NOT NULL WITH DEFAULT,
     PARTQTY     DECIMAL(4)     NOT NULL WITH DEFAULT,
     PRICE       DECIMAL(6,2)   NOT NULL WITH DEFAULT,
     ITEMTYPE    CHAR(3)        NOT NULL WITH DEFAULT,
     LOCATION    CHAR(3)        NOT NULL WITH DEFAULT)
IN DININV0.SININV0;
CREATE UNIQUE INDEX XININV01 ON TININV0
(PARTNUM)
CLUSTER
USING STOGROUP STG1 CLOSE NO;
```

Figure 7.20. Order and Inventory Tables.

few may need 200 rows). The analysis of these items gives you the basis for the table and index design.

7.5.2.1 Deciding in Which Table to Place a Column

In addition to picking which columns should make up the clustering index, there may be choices as to which table to put some of the columns into. The inventory table may be generic for a type of part (as in Figure 7.20 above). In this case, most of the information about a part would belong in the inventory table. On the other hand, if the inventory table is for large products, each row may be for a specific item, identified by a unique serial number (see Figure 7.21 for the table definition). In this case, each inventory row contains data for a specific item. As such, there is one row in the inventory table for the item and one row in the

```
CREATE TABLE TININV0
(PARTNUM     CHAR(5)      NOT NULL WITH DEFAULT,
 SERIALNUM   CHAR(7)      NOT NULL WITH DEFAULT,
 SOLDFLAG    CHAR(1)      NOT NULL WITH DEFAULT,
 CUSTOMER    CHAR(9)      NOT NULL WITH DEFAULT,
 PRICE       DECIMAL(6,2) NOT NULL WITH DEFAULT,
 ITEMTYPE    CHAR(3)      NOT NULL WITH DEFAULT,
 LOCATION    CHAR(3)      NOT NULL WITH DEFAULT)
IN DININV0.SININV0;


CREATE UNIQUE INDEX XININV01 ON TININV0
(PARTNUM,
 SERIALNUM)
CLUSTER
USING STOGROUP STG1 CLOSE NO;


CREATE UNIQUE INDEX XININV02 ON TININV0
(SERIALNUM)
USING STOGROUP STG1 CLOSE NO;
```

Figure 7.21. Inventory Table for Individual Items.

order table, once the item has been sold. Therefore, some of the item information could be stored with the order data instead of being in the inventory table. You would do so if those columns were more frequently needed with the order inquiry transactions. Some examples might include the date the item was sold and the date it was shipped.

It may not be that easy to pick one table to best store a column. The data may be needed both when accessing order information and when accessing inventory information. As I said before, in many cases it doesn't matter. When only a few rows are needed, then going to several tables is no problem.

There are other considerations as to which columns go in which tables. Separating rarely used columns into another table is a good means of reducing the row size. Larger rows mean longer table space scans. If some of the columns are usually not needed with the other data, there is little performance penalty in accessing them, but a gain in accessing the other data. Extremely short or long rows also lead to wasted space. A maximum of 127 rows can be stored in a page. A 10-byte row (plus 8 bytes of overhead) will only occupy 2286 (127 * 18) bytes out of the 4K page. Likewise, a large row that does not divide fairly evenly into 4K will waste space. For example, four 900-byte rows can fit on a page, but they only take up 3600 bytes.

7.5.2.2 Redundant Data

In the cases where many rows are needed, an alternative solution is to store duplicate data. For example, the location within the warehouse is certainly needed for inventory functions. However, it is also needed when preparing an order for shipping. When the item is sold, the location information can be copied to the order table. Then when the order is looked at, the location is readily available without needing to read the inventory table. Conversely, after items are sold, it may be required to keep a record of which customer bought the item. The customer information and order number is stored as part of the order information, but it could also be stored in the inventory row.

This duplicate data is maintained by the application programs. That has some disadvantages.

- Since the data is maintained by a program, the system is more error-prone. There will probably be rules for the existence of data in one table or both, and consistency will have to be maintained for several different columns. If only one program is involved, then it will not be too difficult to maintain this consistency. However, if several programs update the data, one to insert a row, one to place an order, one to handle the shipping, and one for corrections, each must be programmed to handle the same rules.
- There is a greater chance for future changes being needed to the programs and tables. If it turns out that additional columns are needed by one of the transactions, new columns will have to be added to one of the tables. Not only will the retrieval programs need modification, but the insert and update programs will, too.

- The update functions will be more costly. More tables may need updating, and certainly more columns will need updating.

Weighed against these problems is the advantage that you now have in effect created two clustering orders for the information. If you need to find out which customers bought a certain type of item, you can get this by reading the inventory table (Figure 7.22). There is no need to access the order table for this query. Similarly, if you need the locations for the items of an order, only the order table needs to be accessed, not the inventory table.

In designing this type of system, you have to carefully look at all the transaction requirements. It is always best to avoid duplicate data. It keeps the programs much simpler and makes the system more flexible. However, there may be a few occasions where the performance benefit can be important.

7.5.3 Normalization — Denormalization

The topic of how normalization affects performance is a bit controversial. There are some people who feel that "overnormalization" leads to more IOs and is detrimental to good performance. In reality, there is no such thing as overnormalization. A database may be normalized or it may be *under*normalized—that is, not fully normalized. As far as the affect on performance, the answer is—it depends! There are some cases where performance will be better by denormalizing some tables and there are cases where it will be worse.

In determining whether or not a set of tables are normalized or not, you have to understand the rules of normalization (Section 2.1). It is possible to have a design with extra unnecessary tables that have nothing to do with normalization.

A one-to-many relationship between two entities does not usually require a "relationship" table. The patient and drug order entities have such a relationship. One patient can have many drug orders and one drug order is for a single patient. To represent this relationship, the drug order table has the patient ID as part of the key. However, I have seen database designs that would create an additional table to represent the relationship. Such a table would have the same keys as the drug order table (PATID,DRUGCODE,DRUGDATE). Any "intersection" data (i.e., data which are attributes of the patient/drug order occurrence) could just as well have been placed directly in the drug order table. At first glance, you might say that this design is overnormalized. It *is* unnecessary, and should be eliminated. However, this extra table has nothing to do with normalization.

```
SELECT CUSTNUM FROM TININVO
    WHERE ITEMTYPE = 'XYZ';
```

Figure 7.22. Finding Customers Who Bought Items Only Requires the Inventory Table.

If all SELECT statements of a system always retrieve one row from each of two tables and the access is via an index, then performance will be slightly better if the two tables are combined into one. Figure 7.23a shows two tables and the SELECT statement to retrieve a patient and the patient's sex (in words, rather than the 1-byte code). The statement is a join of the two tables. Figure 7.23b has a denormalized table in which the sex expansion is combined into the patient table. The SELECT statement now only has to access one table. With the join, there would be an additional access to the second table. In this example, *this* SELECT statement will perform better with the denormalized table.

On the other hand, when you denormalize a table, you are generally storing much more data in each row of the base table. The sex field is 6 bytes long. Each row of the patient table will be that much bigger if the expanded sex column is stored in the patient table. That means that all table space scans will take longer, regardless of which columns are referenced. Any access that looks at a group of rows will also generally need more data pages as the required rows will be spread over more pages. Therefore, denormalizing tables will result in greater cost for many types of access. This is in addition to the other disadvantages of unnormalized tables. These include the need to maintain duplicate data (resulting in greater maintenance costs and additional program complexity). See Section 2.1 for more details.

In order to get an idea of the costs of normalizing or denormalizing tables, you have to weigh the type and frequency of access. Are table space scans going to be used? How often? Will the elimination of one access to a second table cause any noticeable impact on transaction response time?

Always start will normalized tables. Then consider denormalizing, but only if it is necessary. If it is not necessary, then don't even think about it. Bear in mind the increased storage space and table space scan time.

It should be mentioned that there is one more benefit to denormalizing some tables. Some of the program code to read the data will be a little simpler (whereas updating will be a little more complex). Joins are harder for end-users to code (especially if more than two tables must be joined). If the only access is via programs, then it is no big deal. The programmers can take the extra time to get the SQL statements working. However, if there is much ad hoc access by end-users, then some consideration must be given to their ease of use.

On the other hand, some coding is more difficult with denormalized tables. Some reference data will now be stored in multiple rows in the base table instead of just once in the reference table. Denormalization can also make DB2-controlled referential integrity difficult to implement effectively.

Another design issue is similar in concept to denormalization. One-to-one relationships are usually kept as two tables. Some people like to combine them into one huge table. However, as described in Section 2.1, there are many problems with doing so. Performance might be improved if you always need the data from both tables, but will be much worse if you often need only one set (especially via a table space scan). You also eliminate the possibility of the second table having multiple occurrences for the common key. If the address information were stored in the patient table, then there would be no way at a later point

```
CREATE TABLE THSPAT0
(PATID      CHAR(9)   NOT NULL WITH DEFAULT,
 NAME       CHAR(25)  NOT NULL WITH DEFAULT,
 SEX        CHAR(1)   NOT NULL WITH DEFAULT,
 BIRTHDATE  DATE      NOT NULL WITH DEFAULT)
IN DHSHOS0.SHSPAT0;


CREATE TABLE THSSEX0
(SEX        CHAR(1)   NOT NULL WITH DEFAULT,
 SEXPANSION CHAR(6)   NOT NULL WITH DEFAULT)
IN DHSHOS0.SHSSEX0;


SELECT PATID,NAME,BIRTHDATE,SEXPANSION
  FROM THSPAT0 P,THSSEX0 S
  WHERE PATID='324354657' AND
        P.SEX = S.SEX;
```
(a) Joining a Patient table with a Sex Expansion table

```
CREATE TABLE THSPAT0
(PATID      CHAR(9)   NOT NULL WITH DEFAULT,
 NAME       CHAR(25)  NOT NULL WITH DEFAULT,
 SEX        CHAR(6)   NOT NULL WITH DEFAULT,
 BIRTHDATE  DATE      NOT NULL WITH DEFAULT)
IN DHSHOS0.SHSPAT0;


SELECT PATID,NAME,BIRTHDATE,SEX
  FROM THSPAT0
  WHERE PATID='324354657';
```
(b) An unnormalized table eliminates the need for a join

Figure 7.23. Finding a Patient's Sex.

in time to keep a history of patient addresses. Only one occurrence per patient would be possible. As a separate table, it is easy to do so. The only requirement would be a flag indicating which is the current address.

7.5.4 How to Make Changes to Tables

There are a number of changes that can be made to tables. You can:

- add columns
- delete columns
- change the attributes
- change the data content
- change the names of the columns

Only one of these changes can be done easily, without unloading and reloading the data. That is adding a new column to the end of the table. This is done with the ALTER TABLE statement. Figure 7.24 adds a column to the THSADM0 table. There are some disadvantages to using this statement.

- It can only add a column, and only to the end. If you want to put the new one near related columns, you cannot use this method.
- The new column is not filled in immediately. New rows will have it filled in. Old rows will have it filled in only when data is put into the column with an UPDATE statement. When this happens, the row will now be larger than it was before. If there is no room in the page for this expansion, then the row will be moved to another page. However, the index entries are not updated. Instead, a pointer is left in the original spot. This pointer contains the new address of the row. This results in poorer performance because an extra IO is needed to access the row. If the row is expanded yet again (i.e., if data is later entered into another new column), and relocated to another page, no additional marker is created. Rather, the original one is updated to point to the new RID location.
- It is very useful for the DBA to keep the source for the CREATE TABLE in one place. This makes it easier to move a system to production, or to make similar tables for testing. If you have a source for the CREATE and separate ALTER statements for each time you have added columns, then it becomes much more difficult to keep track of things.

Because of these problems I find it better to use the same methodology for all table changes and I do not use ALTER to add columns.

```
ALTER TABLE GELLER.THSADM0
   ADD ADMDIAG  CHAR(10);
```

Figure 7.24. Adding a Column to a Table with ALTER TABLE.

7.5.4.1 The Change Process

The basic method is to:

- copy the data out of the table
- drop the table
- recreate it with the new definition
- copy back in the appropriate columns

There are several side effects of dropping a table:

- For a segmented table space, dropping the table will work well. For other table spaces, it is better to drop the table space; otherwise, the space from the table will not be reclaimed. Of course, if you have more than one table in a table space, dropping the table space will drop all the tables.
- Whenever a table or table space is dropped, all indexes, views, synonyms, referential constraints, and privileges are also dropped automatically. You must then recreate them yourself after the table is recreated. Referential constraints, in particular, can cause confusion. Index definitions are usually kept with the table definition, but referential constraints are defined with the dependent table, not the parent. It is common for a new DBA not to realize that the dependent's constraints have disappeared when the parent table is dropped. Version 2.3 introduces a new feature which allows you to preview the affect of dropping an object or revoking a privilege. If you use it, you will at least be aware of which objects will need recreation.
- Plans are affected whenever any resource used by the plan has been dropped. This includes indexes and tables. DB2 needs to keep track of which plans need to find a new access path due to changes in the database. In the catalog table SYSIBM.SYSPLAN, there are two flags called VALID and OPERATIVE. Whenever any resource that a plan uses (such as an index or a table) is dropped, the plan is marked as being invalid (an 'N' in column VALID of SYSPLAN). VALID = 'N' means that a REBIND is necessary before the plan can be used. This REBIND will be done automatically by DB2 the next time the plan is accessed. However, if any resource needed by the plan is unavailable (i.e., doesn't exist) at the time the REBIND is attempted, then the plan will be marked inoperative (an 'N' in the OPERATIVE column). An inoperative plan requires an explicit BIND to be performed. Until this BIND is done, the plan is unavailable for use (a -923 SQLCODE is returned to any program on the first SQL call). This will usually not occur for a dropped index. The DBA is also likely to recreate the table before anyone uses it (but only if the change is done on off hours or all users and programmers are instructed not to use the system). As described in Section 3.2, it is most likely to occur in a development environment when tables are dropped along with the

SYNONYMs of the programmers who last did the BIND on the plans. The synonym is one of the resources needed by the REBIND. The recreation of the synonym is in the hands of each programmer. It is not a bad idea to query the catalog to find all plans that use the table before dropping it. The appropriate synonyms can be recreated, and the REBIND can then be explicitly done by the DBA at the same time.

There are many third-party products that can ease this effort by automatically building CREATE and GRANT statements for the dependencies.

There are two straightforward methods for making table changes when you are adding, dropping, renaming, or changing the order of columns. Other changes, such as changing the data type of a column, might require a program to be written to convert the data. The first method is good for fairly small tables. It consists of the following steps:

1. Create a temporary table with the new columns (no indexes are needed for this table).
2. Copy the rows to this temporary table (Figure 7.25). Only the columns that are going to be in the new table are selected for the copy operation.
3. Drop the old table and recreate it with the new definition. Note that DB2 does not allow you to rename a table. We cannot simply rename the temporary one, we must copy the rows back.
4. Copy the rows back (Figure 7.26).
5. Drop the temporary table (to clean things up).

There are some disadvantages to using this method for large tables. The SQL INSERT will require quite a bit of processing. The INSERT will also log every inserted row. This can add a lot of time and can cause contention for the DB2

```
INSERT INTO GELLER.THSADMX
(PATID,ADMDATE,ADMSEQ,DISDATE,...... others)
SELECT PATID,ADMDATE,ADMSEQ,DISDATE.....
  FROM GELLER.THSADM0;
```
Figure 7.25. Copy the Rows to a Temporary Table.

```
INSERT INTO GELLER.THSADM0
(PATID,ADMDATE,ADMSEQ,DISDATE,...... others)
SELECT *
  FROM GELLER.THSADMX;
```
Figure 7.26. Copy the Rows Back to the Original Table.

log if the operation is done while other activity is occurring. When copying the rows back to the real table, the indexes have to be built. If there are nonclustering indexes this can be very costly, as each index record will likely be on a different page from the preceding one. You must also clean up the temporary table if you don't want things to get cluttered over time.

The second method involves unloading the data to a sequential file. The table is dropped and recreated. Finally, the data is loaded into the new table with the LOAD utility. The unload can be performed with the DSNTIAUL sample program (see Section 6.2 for performance issues related to this program). Figure 6.22 has the JCL and control statements needed to run DSNTIAUL.

There are several advantages of this method over the use of a temporary table:

- No logging. With the LOAD utility, you have the option of not logging any updates. The COPY that is required after the load will be less costly overall than logging all the inserts for a large table with several indexes (and the table would actually be inserted twice with the other method).
- LOAD is much faster than INSERTs.
- Building the indexes is much, much faster than building them one row at a time, especially for the nonclustered indexes.
- There is no temporary table to create and clean up.
- DSNTIAUL will also create the LOAD control statements for you. These statements will have to be edited to eliminate any old columns that you are not retaining and to change the names of any columns you are renaming. You also want to put in LOG NO.

You might think that you could use the REORG utility with the UNLOAD ONLY option to create the unload file. However, this file can only be used to load the exact same table space. Once the table space has been dropped and recreated, the file can no longer be used as input to the LOAD utility.

If you are making changes to columns, such as changing the data type from numeric to character, then you will probably need a custom program for the unload. This program can issue SQL SELECTs to read all of the rows, and can reformat the fields. It can then either write out the records to a file or INSERT the rows to a temporary table. More extensive changes, such as moving some columns from one table to another, will also need a program. This program could read the rows from both tables (possibly with a join) and then write out records to one or more sequential files for subsequent loading.

7.5.5 Data Compression

There is one other type of database change which might be a tremendous help to performance. This is data compression. Many types of data can be compressed to save a lot of storage space. Textual data, for example, often has many consecutive blanks. These can be compressed down to a single blank plus a count of the number of spaces. Data compression is achieved by having an EDIT procedure (EDITPROC) defined for the table. This routine (written in assembler language) is automatically invoked by DB2 every time a row is inserted or updated (to compress the data), and every time a row is retrieved (to expand it back to its full size). The process is transparent to the programmer or end-user. There are compression packages available to buy, so there is no need for you to have to write your own. In fact, Version 2.3 will come with a sample compression exit that you can use as is, or modify. This way, you may not even need to spend money to obtain a package.

How beneficial is it to compress the data? The answer depends on the volume of data (number of rows), the amount of compression that can be achieved (50–75% is possible for some data), and the type of access that the table has. Data that is inserted but rarely read does not benefit much. It also only pays to bother doing it for large tables.

The savings is in IOs. With smaller data rows, you can fit more rows on a page (and, therefore, have fewer pages in the table space). Thus, table space scans will benefit the most. The other type of access that will benefit is when you are accessing many rows that are clustered together (such as reading all services for a patient). Let's say a patient has 200 service rows. If uncompressed, and each one is 80 bytes, then there are 50 per page and it will take four IOs to read all the services for the patient (assuming they are clustered together). If after compression the rows take up only 40 bytes, then they will all fit on two pages and can all be read with fewer IOs. All utilities will also run faster if there are fewer pages in the table space. This includes the COPY and REORG utilities.

The type of access that will not benefit is the reading of a single row through an index. The indexes are not compressed and, therefore, the index access does not change. A single row will require a read of one page, regardless of whether or not the row is compressed.

There are some costs involved in doing compression. There is CPU processing to compress or expand the row. Generally, the savings in IO (and the CPU costs of doing an IO) will outweigh the CPU costs of the compression and expansion, but only if there are the types of access outlined above. The other cost is due to each row now occupying a different amount of storage. The layout of the rows on the pages is similar to that for rows with varying length columns. In general, DB2 will process fixed-length rows somewhat faster than variable-length rows. With these costs in mind, I will repeat myself and say that it is cost-effective to use compression for high-volume tables that often require table space scans or are just so large as to benefit from the savings in DASD storage and utility run times.

One final note about compression. For those of you who have used compression successfully for IMS databases, you will find that the benefit for DB2 is not quite as great. In IMS, many different segment types are stored in the same physical blocks. Large segments, therefore, affect the performance of accessing other segment types. In DB2, each different data type is in a different table and, therefore, is physically separated from the other data types. Thus, large-sized rows of one table do not impact the performance of other tables.

7.6 RECOVERY

DB2 has very extensive backup and recovery facilities. They are much more thorough than many previous DBMSs and file systems. There are several reasons why files need a recovery mechanism. If a job abends (abnormally terminates) or the operating system fails, the file may be damaged. This was more true of older file access methods. A more likely cause arises because updates often consist of several parts. An indexed file has a data portion and an index portion. If a power failure occurs before an update is complete, the index may not match the data. An application may also be making several related updates in the same transaction. One may be complete as far as the individual file is concerned, but the related data may not have been updated at the time of failure. Even more damaging than just a program failure is the possibility of damage to the physical storage medium. The disk pack itself may be damaged, making the file completely unusable.

7.6.1 Recovery Schemes—Other File Systems

VSAM files, for example, do not have any automatic recovery mechanism of their own. When used in a batch job, the most direct recovery is to create a backup of the file before the batch updates and then restore that file if there is a failure during the update jobs. This is a manual procedure. It will bring the file back to the point in time before the batch updates. If there are five batch jobs in a row and the backup is only done at the beginning, then a failure in the fourth job will require restoring the file (and any other updated files) and rerunning all of the jobs.

When VSAM is used with CICS, CICS will provide logging of the updates to the file. The log records contain images of the physical records from before the updates. This way, if there is a transaction abend or CICS failure, the transactions that have not completed can be backed out. The file itself is not damaged, and no other transactions are affected. The user does not have to reenter any work other than the current transaction. If, however, the file is damaged, then you have to restore to the last backup and reenter all transactions from that point. Actually, there are utilities available, which would allow you to apply log records (images of the physical block after the update) to the restored file in order to recover the file back to the point of failure. This way the user does not have to reenter everything. This process is not automatic. It must be done manually, and very carefully.

Some DBMSs, such as IMS, improve on this mechanism by providing the means to log updates in batch so that batch jobs can also be backed out if necessary. There are several different options. Batch jobs can be run stand-alone, or as a Batch Message Program (BMP). A BMP runs in conjunction with an IMS control region. The databases and logging are handled by the control region. Logging and backout will be automatic.

A regular IMS batch program runs in its own region. As such, it must do its own logging. The logging is not required, it must be put into each job. There is an option to request automatic backout for a program abend. If not requested, or for any system failure, the backout process is still manual and it must be performed before any other batch jobs are run. Forward recoveries of online databases also require the careful and proper use of the correct log datasets. IMS does have an (optional) control facility (DBRC) to help ensure the correct recovery process.

7.6.2 DB2's Recovery Scheme

DB2 greatly simplifies the entire recovery scheme. There can be any number of concurrent updates of a DB2 table, yet DB2 will take care of most of the tasks necessary to ensure the integrity of the datasets. It does this automatically.

DB2 has the standard type of utilities for backup (COPY) and recovery (RECOVER). However, for most developers, there is rarely a need to run a recovery, as we will see below. It is still advised, though, for them to run backups of their table spaces and to be familiar with how to recover them, just in case. DB2 runs in a separate region (actually several regions) from the application programs that use DB2. This allows many concurrent jobs to run, all using the same set of tables. There is no problem of one job affecting the recovery and integrity of any other. The DB2 region does the logging of updates for you. There is nothing for the programmer to set up and keep track of. The relationship between the regions is illustrated in Figure 7.27.

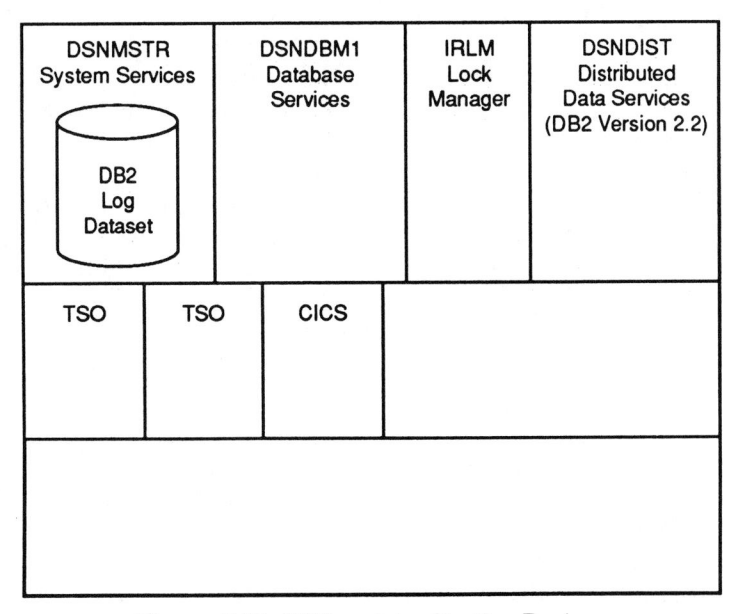

Figure 7.27. DB2 and Application Regions.

7.6.2.1 Backout for a Program Failure

There are several different recovery scenarios to look at. The first case is when an application program fails (abends). In this case, DB2 will back out any updates, bringing the tables back to the point of the last commit (or to the beginning if there were no commits issued). There is no fuss, no bother. The programmer does not have to do anything to invoke this backout. The only thing the programmer has to be concerned with is handling the restart of a program that issues commits. Any updates made before the commit will not be backed out. The program must take this into consideration (see Section 6.1).

The above scenario is for any type of abend, including system abends, such as timing out, and program abends. However, it does not apply to program failures which do not abend. There is no automatic backout, for example, in the case of a severe error in the data for which the program puts out an error message and then terminates. The programmer must decide in this case whether he wants to back out the updates made so far, or to leave them. If he wants to back them out, then the program must force a rollback. For CICS, it could issue an EXEC CICS ABEND statement, or the EXEC CICS SYNCHPOINT ROLLBACK statement. In batch, it could issue an SQL rollback statement:

EXEC SQL ROLLBACK WORK;

7.6.2.2 Backout for a System Failure

The next scenario is when the whole system crashes (such as from a power failure) or the DB2 region abends for some reason. No problem. If the system crashes, all applications will also fail. If just DB2 abends, then the programs will also abend. First, they will be returned a −923 SQLCODE. When the program tries to terminate, an abend will occur, because there is no DB2 subsystem to handle the termination (commit). Either way, when DB2 comes back up, it backs out everything that was in-flight.

So, when do you need recovery? When the file (table space or index space) is damaged. The disk pack could be clobbered, or some other IO error could have corrupted the dataset. This is fairly rare, but it can happen. A recovery may also be needed if a REORG fails during the RELOAD phase and you cannot restart it (i.e., you have not saved the work datasets). Then, there is no longer a table space, and it must be recovered.

7.6.2.3 RECOVER Utility

What do you do? You run the RECOVER utility with the RECOVER TS control statement (see Figure 7.28 for the JCL and the control statement). If the indexes are also gone, then you must also recover them (RECOVER INDEX). Figure 7.29 has the control statement for an index recovery. You can either recover a specific index (the first control statement), or recover all of the indexes for a table space (the second control statement). That's all you have to do. DB2

```
//RECOVER EXEC DSNUPROC,SYSTEM=DB2T,UID=RECOVERGPAT,UTPROC='',
//          LIB='DB2T.DSN.DSNLOAD'
//SYSUT1 DD UNIT=SYSDA,SPACE=(CYL,(20,20)),   index work dataset
//     DSN=GELLER.RECPAT.SYSUT1,DISP=(MOD,DELETE,CATLG)
//SORTWK01 DD UNIT=SYSDA,SPACE=(CYL,(20,20)),
//     DSN=GELLER.RECPAT.SWK01,DISP=(MOD,DELETE,CATLG)
//SORTWK02 DD UNIT=SYSDA,SPACE=(CYL,(20,20)),
//     DSN=GELLER.RECPAT.SWK02,DISP=(MOD,DELETE,CATLG)
//SORTWK03 DD UNIT=SYSDA,SPACE=(CYL,(20,20)),
//     DSN=GELLER.RECPAT.SWK03,DISP=(MOD,DELETE,CATLG)
//SYSIN DD *
RECOVER TABLESPACE DHSHOS0.SHSPAT0
```

Figure 7.28. JCL and Control Statements for the RECOVER Utility.

```
RECOVER INDEX(GELLER.XHSADM01)
RECOVER INDEX(ALL)  TABLESPACE DHSHOS0.SHSPAT0
```

Figure 7.29. Control Statements for Index Recovery.

takes care of the rest. You don't have to worry about which backup (copy) and log files to use. DB2 recovers the files to the last good commit point. It starts with the last COPY that has been run. The SYSUT1 and SORTWK datasets are required for index recovery, but are not needed for a table space recovery.

7.6.2.4 COPY Utility

The name of the backup dataset is recorded in the DB2 catalog. The location of the backup (i.e., disk pack or tape VOLSER) is also recorded there, unless this information is in the MVS system catalog. A dataset created with

DISP=(NEW,CATLG)

is catalogued in the system catalog. If it is created with

DISP=(NEW,KEEP)

then it is not. In this case, DB2 will record the VOLSER information. It is always possible that the last COPY no longer exists. The dataset on disk or tape may have been deleted. If so, DB2 will use its catalog to find the previous backup and will use that one instead. From this backup, all logs from that point on are used to roll forward. That is, the updates are applied to the file to bring it up to date. This is all automatic. The process is illustrated in Figure 7.30. The COPY control statement is shown in Figure 7.31. Under Version 2.3 you can create two copies at the same time. This gives you added protection in case one copy dataset is damaged. Actually, you can create four copies at once. Two will be recorded in the DB2 catalog. The other two are for a recovery DB2 subsystem at a remote site (for disaster recovery).

If there is no good backup, the recovery process will start with the beginning of the log records—those from the CREATE TABLESPACE. If the table space was created a long time ago, then many logs may have to be scanned. This takes much longer. Besides the extra time it takes, there is another problem with this. Periodically, the logs get full and are archived. The person responsible for the system (usually a systems programmer) may not have set things up to save the archived logs (or maybe only for some period of time). If the table space was created prior to the oldest saved log records, then the table space cannot be recovered at all. So, be sure to COPY all table spaces, even test ones, periodically. This holds unless you don't need to recover the test tables. If you can recreate the test data, then you do not need to bother backing it up. However, without RECOVER you will have to drop and create the table space, and recreate all dependencies (authorizations, indexes, synonyms, etc.) before recreating the test data.

With all this in mind, it is very important that the system administrator (or systems programmer) save the archived logs as long as possible (say, for one year). This is especially true for production systems.

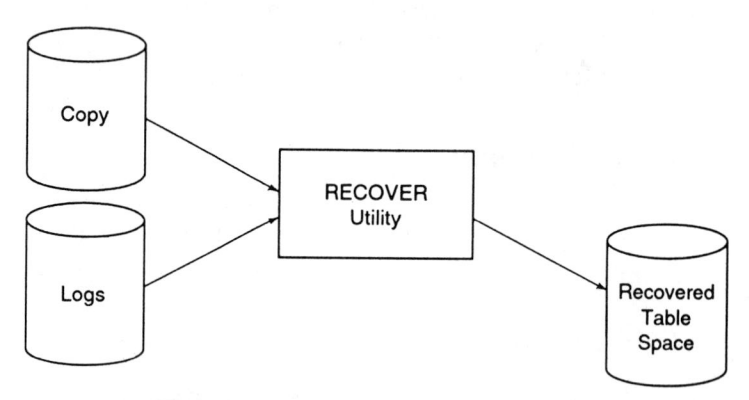

Figure 7.30. Recovering a Table Space.

```
COPY TABLESPACE DHSHOSO.SHSPATO DEVT SYSDA
     FULL YES SHRLEVEL REFERENCE
```
Figure 7.31. Control Statement for COPY.

7.6.3 Copy Dataset Names

Any valid MVS dataset name can be used for the backup dataset. You also have the option of either cataloging it in the MVS catalog, or just saving it without cataloging it, as described above.

MVS lets you use the same name several times if the dataset is not catalogued. However, only one dataset with a given name can be catalogued by MVS. Normally, an MVS output dataset can be reused by specifying DISP=OLD on the DD statement. However, DB2 does *not* allow you to reuse a copy dataset. This can be a pain in the neck. To allow you to reuse one, DB2 would not only have to store a new row in the SYSCOPY table, but would also have to find the old row and delete it or mark it no longer valid. So what? When you are running backups, especially for the test environment, it is often convenient only to keep one backup, reusing the same JCL and, therefore, the same dataset name. Assuming that you don't want to keep changing the name in the JCL, or putting it on a different volume (disk or tape) each time, the best solution is to use generation dataset groups (GDGs). This is also a very good idea for the production environment.

7.6.3.1 Generation Datasets

GDGs are a way to have several generations of a dataset. You can refer to it with a single dataset name. Each time you create one, a new dataset is created. A new generation is created as (+1):

//SYSCOPY DD DSN=TEST.THSPAT0.COPY(+1),DISP=(NEW,CATLG)

After creation, you can refer to the current generation as (0), the previous one as (−1), etc. Each generation is also given a specific individual dataset name by MVS of the format:

TEST.THSPAT0.COPY.G0001V00

This is the name recorded in the DB2 catalog. Since each copy dataset has a different name as far as DB2 is concerned, there is no problem. The COPY JCL does not have to be changed each time. Everybody is happy.

There is one potential problem. When a GDG is defined to MVS (with the IDCAMS DEFINE GDG statement), you tell the system how many generations to keep. For example, you can retain seven copies. When the eighth is created, the earliest one is automatically removed from the catalog (and optionally deleted). The eighth generation will have a name ending in G0008V00. This is fine. However, if the datasets are manually deleted at some other time, then the MVS catalog does not know about their existence and the next available number may be one that was used previously. For example, if five datasets are created and then deleted, the next one will be given a name ending in G0001V00. This is okay as far as the MVS catalog is concerned, but not okay with DB2. It already has G0001V00 in *its* catalog.

7.6.3.2 MODIFY Utility

What do you do? First, you try to avoid this situation. If that is not possible, then you can use the DB2 MODIFY utility to delete entries from SYSCOPY. Over time, there will be many old entries in SYSCOPY that correspond to backups that were done a long time ago and are no longer retained or needed for recovery purposes. To keep SYSCOPY from getting too full of useless old data, the MODIFY utility is used. It can delete any rows for a table space backup that are older than a given date or number of days. It can also be used in situations where you need to remove an entry so that the name can be reused. Figure 7.32 has the control card for MODIFY. It will delete any rows for the table space SHSPAT0 that are from before today (AGE(0)). Despite the possible need to run MODIFY when doing occasional test backups to DASD, GDGs are still a very good way of setting up COPY JCL that does not need constant modification.

7.6.4 Index Recovery

As mentioned above, indexes may also need recovery. Indexes point to (have the address of) the data row. When a clobbered table space dataset is recovered, its rows are back in the same place they were before. The COPY is an image of the data pages and the log records have the address of the rows. Therefore, the indexes do not need recovery just because the table space does. There are other cases, however, where an index does need recovery. One index dataset may get damaged. That one index will then need to be recovered. If there is a failure during the running of a REORG and it cannot be restarted, then the indexes may have all been wiped out and need recovery. If the failure occurs passed the RELOAD phase, the table space is okay and it will not have to be recovered, only the indexes.

Indexes are recovered with the RECOVER INDEX control statement (Figure 7.29). The process (illustrated in Figure 7.33) consists of unloading the table space, sorting the work records into index order, and building the index. This is very fast, as sequential prefetch is used to read the table space and up to 32 pages can be written out at a time to the index file. This process also produces a reorganized index just like REORG INDEX does. Any changes that had been done with ALTER INDEX (such as a change in the space allocations) will take effect.

7.6.5 Timestamp Recovery

There is another scenario that will require a table space and its indexes to be recovered together. Normally, we recover a table space up to the last commit point. We may, however, want to recovery it to some earlier point in time. This

```
MODIFY RECOVERY TABLESPACE DHSHOS0.SHSPAT0 DELETE AGE(0)
```
Figure 7.32. Control Statement for MODIFY.

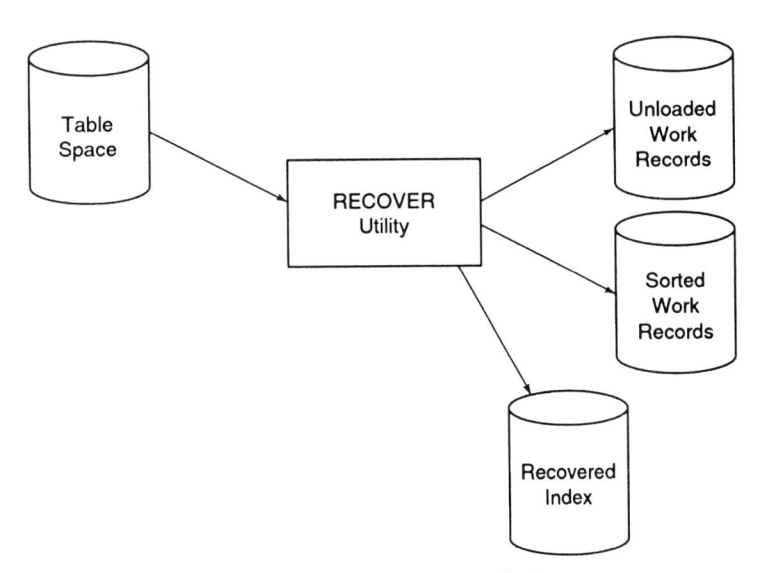

Figure 7.33. Recovering an Index.

is called a timestamp recovery. For example, we may have a point where there was stable test data and we want to recreate that situation. One way to do this is to have unloaded the table with the stable data (perhaps with DSNTIAUL) and then use LOAD REPLACE to recreate it. Another way is to COPY the table space when there are no updates going on, to get a stable image. Then you can RECOVER it to that time period. In production, you might also need to recover to a previous point if you discover an error in a new version of a program that just went into production a few days ago. If bad data has been put into the database, you might be able to fix it using QMF or a program. SQL's set processing capabilities are very powerful. If you have a column in each table containing the date of last update, it is fairly easy to identify records in question. However, sometimes bad data cannot be fixed this easily. In these cases, you have no choice but to go back to before the errors were introduced. You lose all processing that occurred after this point. The users may hate you for it, but there may be no other choice. When you do the recovery, you must recover all related tables to the same time. This means all tables that are related in the application, not just those that are related through referential constraints. Since the indexes have had updates as well, you must recover all the table spaces and all the indexes to the same time. Just doing the table space will not work. The indexes will be out of sync. The control statements to do a timestamp recovery are shown in Figure 7.34.

The TOCOPY or the TORBA parameters are used for the timestamp recovery. TOCOPY names a copy dataset that marks the endpoint for the recovery. Alternatively, you can use the TORBA parameter. This specifies a log RBA to which the recovery should go. You would use this if the point in time you want does not coincide with a backup. TOCOPY names a specific dataset. If generation

```
RECOVERY TABLESPACE DHSHOS0.SHSPAT0

   TOCOPY TEST.COPY.SHSPAT0.G0005V00

RECOVER INDEX(ALL) TABLESPACE DHSHOS0.SHSPAT0
```

Figure 7.34. Control Statement for Timestamp Recovery.

datasets (GDGs) are used for the backups, you must give the specific GDG name (e.g., DB2T.THSPAT0.COPY.G0007V00) rather than a relative generation number [e.g., DB2T.THSPAT0.COPY(-2)]. After a timestamp recovery, you must run another image copy (DB2 marks the table space as needing one). The requirement to always use unique image copy datasets (i.e., different names if catalogued, different VOLSERs if not) makes it somewhat cumbersome for application development purposes. It is often necessary to have a stable point in time to go back to. This is needed in case the programs you are testing put garbage into the tables, or you want the same starting point for several test runs. Unfortunately, you cannot have simple backup and recovery jobs that never need changing. A better solution for the development environment is to use DSNTIAUL to unload the stable data, and LOAD REPLACE to put the table spaces back to where they were.

7.6.6 COPY/RECOVER Performance

Both of these utilities run very fast. They do multiple pages per IO, using sequential prefetch to read the pages. For most systems, there is no need to use any other backup/recovery programs (e.g., full pack backups). However, for large systems you might want a combination of utilities. Perhaps a full pack backup daily for emergencies and COPY once a week on each table space. When you use COPY for the backup, recovery is easy. When you use a full pack backup (or any other utility), recovery is harder. Recovery is not needed often, so if you use COPY once a week, that is good enough. DB2 will use the logs to go forward when necessary. The "Operation and Recovery" chapter of the Administration Guide describes the use of other backup products, including DSN1COPY and dump/restore utilities. One useful feature of using one of these products is that they run when DB2 is down, whereas COPY requires DB2 to be operational.

A nice feature of the DB2 backup scheme is that the COPY utility does not require exclusive access to the table spaces it is copying. Other processes can concurrently access the data, either for read-only or for update. The SHRLEVEL parameter of the COPY statement indicates what level of sharing is allowed. SHRLEVEL REFERENCE is the default. This issues a share lock for the table space, thus permitting read access to any part of the table space, but no updates. SHRLEVEL CHANGE will allow updates. Locks are taken for each page that is being copied. Other pages can be updated in the meantime. If a recovery is needed that uses this copy dataset, the log records from the same time period will also be used to get the table space back in sync.

The performance of COPY and RECOVER can be improved by using a large blocksize for the backup dataset. The reading and writing of the table space is fast due to the reading and writing of multiple pages per IO. For the sequential backup file, a large blocksize will reduce the number of IOs to access that file.

Very large tables may consist of more than one dataset. If the table space exceeds the maximum size of a VSAM dataset, then additional VSAM datasets are automatically allocated by DB2. If a table is stored in a partitioned table space, then each partition is a separate dataset. Either way, it is possible to copy one dataset at a time, or several datasets in parallel. Doing them separately gives you the flexibility to schedule each dataset for a different day. Doing them in parallel can backup the entire table space at once, but in less time then it would take if they were done consecutively. To backup the datasets in parallel, you must specify SHRLEVEL CHANGE. To prevent actual updating, the table space could be started (with the DB2 −START command) for utility access only.

Up through Version 2.2, indexes for a table space had to be recovered one at a time. The table space would be unloaded once, but the build of the indexes would be sequential. Version 2.3 allows you to run more than one recovery utility job in parallel against the same table space. This will enable the indexes to be recovered in parallel. For large tables with several indexes, this can greatly speed up the recovery time.

7.6.6.1 Incremental Copies

There is another feature which can save backup time and storage space. This is an incremental copy of the table space. FULL YES on the COPY statement is a regular (full) copy. FULL NO is an incremental copy. In this case, only pages which have been updated since the last COPY are copied to the backup dataset. Each page in the table space has a timestamp indicating when it was last updated. This timestamp is used to determine whether to copy the page. This feature is very useful for large tables that have low update volumes. Only a small percentage of the pages will be updated between backups. Therefore, the backup cost can be greatly reduced.

When a recovery is needed, DB2 will start with the last full copy, then apply any subsequent incremental copies, and finally any logs since the most recent copy. It pays to periodically run a full backup so as to reduce the number of datasets needed for a recovery. Another choice is to run the MERGECOPY utility, which will take a full copy and a set of incremental copies and produce a new full copy.

7.7 ARCHIVING—CREATING A HISTORY TABLE

Archiving old data is a neglected area of database design. It is rarely thought of during initial design and implementation, but is worried about and retro-fitted much later. Most data files grow over time. As the files (tables) get bigger, more space is occupied and performance generally suffers. Therefore, it is quite beneficial (and sometimes necessary) to remove old data. The meaning of what is old depends on the application, but generally it means that the data is not usually needed for online transactions or most batch reports. For a hospital database, it could be records for patients who were discharged over a year ago. For customer orders, it might be those that have been delivered or are from the previous fiscal year. For bank accounts, it might be those accounts that have been closed.

7.7.1 The Importance of Archiving

In each of the above examples, the data may still be needed on occasion. The archiving process must, therefore, place the data in some form where it is still available, but where it is not part of the main database. This way there may be savings in DASD space and in the costs of processing the current data.

There are several ways in which archiving provides benefit.

- If the data is not kept on DASD, then there is a cost savings for this resource.
- There is substantial time saved in the processing of table backups, recoveries, and reorgs.
  - Smaller tables take less time to run utilities against. This saves a lot of money. There is a reduction in CPU and IO time (and charges for them) and fewer backup tapes are needed.
  - If utility runs take less time, there is less likelihood of running out of time in the batch window to get all the batch work done.
  - Quicker utility runs (especially recoveries) also mean greater availability of the system. This has substantial cost benefit, although these costs are hard to quantify.
- Normal transaction and query processing also benefits from the reduced tables. This is true of any type of file but is especially true for DB2 because with DB2's flexibility the user can access any data easily. With index access to a row, there is not that much difference whether the files are large or small. However, for table space scans, there can be a tremendous difference in time. A table space scan grows linearly with the size of the table space. If you have 6 years of data when you could get by with only one year's, then all table space scans (as well as backups and reorgs), will take six times as long as would otherwise be possible. The table in Figure 7.35 gives a feel for the difference. A simple query that takes 4 seconds with 1 year of data will take 24 seconds with 6 years of data. For the user at a QMF terminal, this is a difference between a quick response versus sitting and twiddling her thumbs. A 10-minute report can be run in batch and come back quickly enough to respond to a request. A 60-minute report is much less timely. There is a cost to the business with these differences.

It is easy to see that there is a need for archiving. We will see below why it is

```
1 Year         3 Years         6 Years
_____

  4 secs        12 secs         24 secs
 10 secs        30 secs         60 secs
 10 mins        30 mins         60 mins
```
Figure 7.35. Table Space Scans Grow Over Time.

useful to do the planning up front. In general, it is important because it is often necessary to plan the table layout to simplify the archiving process and to plan for ways to do the archiving and store the history data to make it still available for access. There are also systems where archiving is needed for other reasons besides size. Let's say we had a database for a used car lot. There is a row for each car on the lot. The primary key to the table is the vehicle registration number. When the car is sold, information about the sale is put into this row. This includes the sale price, the date of the sale, and the name of the customer. This appears to be a nice simple system. What happens, though, when 3 months later a customer sells the car back to the used car dealer? It is the same car as was there previously. There is already a row with the same registration number. If the system was built to support one row per car (probably with a unique index), then there is no way to keep track of the old sale information and the fact that the car is once again available for sale.

There are other database designs to handle this type of situation. It is not difficult to do, but it is much better to plan for it up front. A separate table could be used to store the information about cars that have been sold. If this is thought of originally, then the programs to support the system can be written to handle the possible situations and will not need modification later on.

7.7.2 Archiving Criteria

The first step in planning for archiving is to determine the needs of the system. Even old data is needed sometimes and you have to know when and how it will be needed. If old data is needed online by the same programs and transactions that use the current data, and it must always be available, then it might not be possible to archive this data. In this case, you probably do not think of it as "old" data.

Perhaps the data is needed as an alternate. If the patient is not in the active file, then check to see if he was in the hospital at some prior point of time. In this case, it might be a separate program that does the checking for prior records.

Another possibility is that the data is not needed by the regular transactions at all, but is needed for QMF reports, either online or maybe just in batch. If needed for reports, then is it needed together with the active data, or are separate reports adequate? The data may only be needed occasionally. In this case, it could be kept on tape and loaded to a table when needed. Or, it could be kept on nonelectronic media, such as microfiche.

Different sets of data in a system may have different criteria for archiving. In the patient database, services could be archived for inactive patients or when over a year old. They are likely to be needed for statistical reports but not for online query. Location data may not be needed at all for older records, and certainly not online. On the other hand, admission and diagnosis data may be needed longer. When a person is admitted, it is useful to have access to data about previous admissions.

7.7.3 Where to Keep the Archived Data

There are several different choices for where to archive to, and when to do it. The simplest is to unload the rows to a sequential dataset that could be kept on tape. A program can read through the table(s), selecting records based on some history criteria. It could do some formatting of the data, write it to the sequential file, and delete the row from the table. Another choice is to store the data in another DB2 table. The same program as above could be used. Instead of writing to a sequential file, it could insert the row into the history table. Over time, there could be a problem with duplicate key values being assigned to new records (unless the application is written to avoid this). If the history table is created without unique indexes, then you do not have to worry about inserting the rows. If there are unique indexes, then you have to make sure you can handle the situation.

An advantage to keeping the history in a DB2 table is that the data is still readily available to programs and to QMF. For QMF, the same reports can be used for archived data as for the current data if synonyms are used. The user can change his synonym to reference the table he wants to report on. To combine history with current data requires doing a UNION of two selects, one on the old, one on the new. With this approach, the data is still available, but not *as* available as the main table. The online transactions will probably be written just to access the table with the current data.

The obvious approaches for history files involve separate tables or files for the history data. Another alternative is to use a partitioned table space, with one partition for the active data and a second partition for the archived data. There will be a flag to indicate whether a given row is active or not. The clustering (partitioning) index will be on this flag plus the other columns that you would normally cluster on. The partitioning will be based on just the flag. Figure 7.36 shows how this might be coded for the admissions table.

There are several nice features of this design. The partitions are separate datasets so you get the advantages of separating out the older data. The COPY and RECOVER utilities can be run on single partitions so you do not have to backup the archived data as frequently. Transactions and queries that want to access only current data can use the flag to restrict the selection to active rows. When used this way, scans will only go against the active partition. A disadvan-

```
CREATE TABLE GELLER.THSADM0
(PATID      CHAR(9)         NOT NULL WITH DEFAULT,
 ADMDATE    DATE            NOT NULL WITH DEFAULT,
 ADMSEQ     SMALL INTEGER   NOT NULL WITH DEFAULT,
 ACTIVE     CHAR(1)         NOT NULL,
 DISDATE    DATE            NOT NULL WITH DEFAULT,
 DISSEQ     SMALL INTEGER   NOT NULL WITH DEFAULT,
 PROCESSED  TIMESTAMP       NOT NULL WITH DEFAULT)
IN DHSHOS0.SHSADM0;



CREATE INDEX GELLER.XHSADM01 ON GELLER.THSADM0
 (ACTIVE,
  PATID,
  ADMDATE DESC,
  ADMSEQ DESC)
 CLUSTER
 (PART 1 VALUES('N'),
  PART 2 VALUES('Y'),
  )
 UNIQUE
 USING STOGROUP STG1 PRIQTY 1000 SECQTY 200
 SUBPAGES 2 CLOSE NO;



CREATE INDEX GELLER.XHSADM02 ON GELLER.THSADM0
 (ADMDATE)
 USING STOGROUP STG1 PRIQTY 800 SECQTY 200
 SUBPAGES 2 CLOSE NO;
```

Figure 7.36. Partitioning the Admission Table for Archive Data.

tage compared to a completely separate archive table is that DB2 will not do a table space scan of the "active" partition only. Instead, nonmatching index scans through the clustering index will be used in situations that do not use matching index lookup. This will be a bit more costly than a table space scan would be. Also, the nonpartitioning indexes will contain entries for active and archive rows. Nonmatching index scans of these indexes will take longer.

Reports that need both active and inactive data can do so easily by leaving out the active flag from the selection criteria. This makes it possible to archive inactive data as soon as it becomes inactive, even if it is still needed for reports for the current year. Online transactions can easily be coded to get either only active rows or all rows. Using the active flag can restrict the access to active records. Not using it will make all rows available.

To archive a row with this scheme, a program must delete the row from the table and reinsert it with the flag set to the inactive value. It cannot just update the active flag because the columns that set the partition cannot be updated to a value that belongs to a different partition. The archiving can be done periodically as in the other schemes, or it can be done as part of the transaction that makes a record inactive.

Obviously, this type of scheme should be considered and should be built into the design of the tables, the programs, and any queries and reports. It can be retro-fitted afterward, but that involves program changes as well as table changes.

7.7.4 When to Archive

Archiving can be an ongoing activity. When a record is deactivated, it can be archived. This could be a closed bank account, a discharged patient, or a car that is sold. The alternative is to do the archiving periodically in batch. It could be done once a year, once a week, or daily. The frequency will depend on the nature of the data and how the archived data will be stored. It is very common for data from the same fiscal year to be needed together. This may govern where and when it is archived.

You may also need a reactivating transaction to bring an archived data record back to an active status. This may be needed because the record was closed in error. Or it may be a requirement that if an entity is active, all older data related to the entity must also be accessible. For example, previous diagnosis data might need to be available for active patients. When different types of data have different archiving criteria, it becomes a little more difficult to make the right choices for archiving and reactivating. The programs also have to be coded carefully to handle a mixture of situations. We might want to keep all admission rows in the active file but delete the location rows for discharged patients. However, some programs may expect a location for each admission. These programs must be written to handle admissions that have no locations due to archiving.

The patient database has data with several different requirements for archiving. For simplicity, I have not designed in any archiving features in the tables of Appendix A. In practice, I would have done so. The patient table (THSPAT0) *has* an active flag but it is not used for archiving with this table. I would probably keep the patient record for all patients. This table is not too large as there is only one row per patient. It is useful to know who has been in the hospital, especially when admitting a patient. If the rows were archived after discharge, they would have to be reinserted if the patient is readmitted. Most lookup to this table is by patient ID. Since the lookup is direct through the index, there is not much gain in removing the older records. The most common function which scans large parts of the table is lookup by name. This is often needed to find people who have been in the hospital, not just those who are currently there. For all these reasons, I would not do any archiving of this table.

While the patient table is one of the smallest in our database, the services (THSSVC0) table is the largest. Each patient receives many services, and there is one row for each service. Direct lookup by patient is usually only needed for relatively recent services on active patients. Other access is primarily statistical reports and batch processing. Therefore, we can remove older rows based on two criteria: those for discharged patients, and those who are over a year old, even if the patient is still active. These criteria can be handled easily by a simple batch program that is run periodically. Access to the older data is not very frequent. This data will take up a lot of space. The most cost-effective approach, therefore, is to store the archive on tape rather than DASD. As a sequential tape file, the data can be used by other report writers and statistical packages. In addition, if we create an archive DB2 table, we can load parts of the service data to it when it is needed for QMF reports. This way we do not need to keep a full history in the archive table on DASD.

The admission table (THSADM0) presents us with some choices to make. Even for discharged patients, it might be useful to have a row for their prior admissions (especially the most recent). It would be easy to code an archive program that removes older admissions, leaving the most recent. However, there are many queries that need the older data along with the more current data. Splitting them up will complicate this access. The best choice might be to use a partitioned table space. The current admission row for active patients will be in one partition and the other rows will be in the other partition. When looking up a patient, all of his admissions are readily available. When looking at patients currently in the hospital, the older admissions do not have to be scanned. The discharge transaction can take care of the archiving on the spot.

There is one thing to note about using a partitioned table space for the archiving. It changes our clustering scheme a bit. The admission table is clustered by PATID, ADMDATE, ADMSEQ—the clustering index (XHSADM01). If we have an active flag, then the clustering index will be ACTIVEFLAG, PATID, ADMDATE, ADMSEQ. The partitioning will be by ACTIVEFLAG. Since one admission row will be active and the rest inactive, we will no longer have all rows for a patient clustered on the same page. The most recent admission will be in one partition, the others will be clustered in the other partition. This should be acceptable for our needs.

Instead of having an active flag, we could have used a logical flag—the discharge date column of this table. This column is filled in with a valid date when this column, those rows with the default value could be in one partition and the others in the inactive partition. The drawback with using this approach is that the partitioning index is the clustering index. The high-order column is always used as part of the partitioning. We would, therefore, have the rows clustered in discharge date order, not by patient. Thus, I would not use this column for the partitioning.

Location data (THSLOC0) is mostly needed for active patients. As soon as a patient is discharged, the location rows can be archived. They may be needed occasionally for special reports or queries that need information about certain wards of the hospital, but not often. Keeping the data on tape seems reasonable. Again, having an archive table around may be useful so that the data can be loaded when needed for QMF reports. The archiving can be done on a periodic basis.

Whichever method is chosen for doing archiving, the plans for it should be part of the initial database design. Sooner or later most systems will benefit from removing the older data. You might as well plan for it from the beginning.

7.8 SUMMARY AND KEY GUIDELINES

If the database is not well-designed or well-tuned, then performance can suffer. Access paths are based on the statistics in the DB2 catalog. These are updated when RUNSTATS is run. If EXPLAINs of important queries and programs indicate an inadequate access path, the first step is to examine the catalog statistics. These statistics provide guidelines to the tuning effort. There are several simple tuning steps that can be done short of a total redesign of the tables.

- Some of the statistics in the catalog can be updated manually by the DBA. This provides a means of influencing DB2's choice of access path.
- If the table space is out of clustering order, or the indexes are disorganized, a reorg can be very helpful.
- Indexes can be added fairly easily to a DB2 table. This can enable a system to keep up with changing requirements.
- Denormalizing tables can help the performance of some queries, but might hurt others. Careful thought must be given to the performance tradeoffs, as well as to the programming requirements of handling unnormalized tables.
- The DB2 backup utility (COPY) runs very quickly because of the use of sequential prefetch. Since recovery is simpler when COPY is used as the backup mechanism, this is the recommended approach. The performance of COPY can be improved by
  —Using a large blocksize for the backup file.
  —Running incremental copies.

—Using SHRLEVEL CHANGE allows concurrent update access by applications. While not speeding up COPY, this does allow the online system to continue running.
- Substantial processing time can be saved if older data is removed from the operational tables. The benefits are usually worth the effort of developing an archiving process.

8

System Tuning

There are many interacting factors that affect the performance of DB2 programs. We've looked at how the design of the tables and indexes play an important role in these regards, and how the individual DML statements can be coded efficiently or inefficiently. There are also factors that influence the performance of the entire DB2 system. You may think that system parameters fall strictly into the systems programmer's area of concern, but many of them are also of concern to the DBA and programmer. In this chapter, we will look at how:

- The setup of buffer pools affects the DDL statements used by the DBA.
- The size and number of log datasets and the handling of archive logs affect recovery procedures.
- Performance monitors can be used by the DBA, the programmer, and the systems programmer, working together to analyze and solve performance problems.

This book has emphasized how the DBA and programmer must work together and understand each other's tasks to develop effficient systems. Sometimes, the systems programmer must also be involved. This involvement is at both the DB2 subsystem and the MVS operating system level. A poorly running operating system will result in individual applications running poorly as well. IO bottlenecks may be identified by long transaction wait times, but may require investigation on the system's level to resolve.

There are a number of DB2 parameters specified when DB2 is installed that can affect both DB2 application and system performance. The larger the DB2 workload, and the more concurrent DB2 users there are, the greater the interaction at the system level, and the greater attention must be paid to these issues.

8.1 BUFFER POOLS

8.1.1 How Buffer Pools Are Used

When DB2 reads a data or index page, it does an IO and places the page into a storage area in memory. This storage area is called a buffer. Once a page is in storage, it can stay there until the space is needed by something else. When DB2 needs to read a page, before doing the IO it checks the buffers to see if the page is already there. If it is, the IO can be skipped. Access to a page in a buffer is much faster than access to the disk.

DB2 maintains more than one buffer for IO operations. The set of buffers is called a buffer pool. There are many buffers in the pool. If a desired page is not found in the pool, then it is read from disk and placed in the next available buffer. If all the buffers are in use, then DB2 will take the least recently used one for the new page. The buffer pool is shared by all of the concurrent transactions. One buffer pool may be shared by all of the table spaces and indexes, or there can be several pools.

It is quite common for an accessed page to be needed again a short while later. It may be needed by a different transaction accessing a row on the same page, or it may be needed by the same transaction. Often, the page is needed again in a fraction of a second. Other times, it is reaccessed a minute late. A transaction may fetch several rows from the same page, or after reading a row it may then update or delete it. In these cases, the second access may be a fraction of a second after the first. Another common situation is for a transaction to read a row and send a screen to the user. When the user responds, the row may then get updated. In this case, the second access to the page may be after 10 seconds or more. In each of these instances, response time will be much faster if the page is still in memory. That is why buffer pools are so useful.

8.1.2 DB2 Can Take Advantage of Very Large Buffer Pools

How many buffers should there be in a buffer pool? Generally, the more buffers, the greater the chance of the page still being in memory, but there are some other factors. With older database or file systems it wasn't always good to use too many buffers. Even with 100 buffers, there was an increase in CPU time for the searching of the buffer pool. IBM has now developed very efficient search algorithms and DB2 can support very large buffer pools. The default for Version 2 is 1000 buffers (for Version 1 it was 256). Much larger pools than that can easily be supported. However, there are still other limiting factors, such as the amount of available main memory. This is discussed below.

The buffer pool is used for both random access and for table space scans using sequential prefetch (including utility processing). DB2 keeps separate areas of the buffer pool for each type. Table space scans can quickly fill up the available buffers because many pages will be read in a very short time. If not separated, this could impact normal transaction processing, where a smaller number of pages are accessed at a time, but are often needed repeatedly. It is fairly clear that random access is benefited by the use of buffers. They are also very useful for table space scans. This is especially true for small- and medium-sized tables that do not completely fill the buffer pool. A QMF user, for example, may repeatedly issue the same or a slightly modified query. If the pages are still in memory, the subsequent queries will run much faster. To give an idea of size, let's look at a quick example. An 80-byte row will fit 50 rows per page. Therefore, 100 pages will hold 5000 rows. A table space scan of a table of this size will occupy only a small part of a typical buffer pool. The entire table may stay in memory for a little while.

Sequential prefetch will only be used if there are enough available pages in the buffer pool. Otherwise, a table space scan will be handled with synchronous IOs of each page. A large pool, therefore, enables more concurrent table space scans with prefetch.

A larger buffer pool also helps sort performance. DB2 maintains a sort work area based on the size of the buffer pool. It is based on 10% of the buffer pool, with a minimum of 60 pages and a maximum of 2500.

8.1.2.1 Available Memory Is the Limiting Factor

The CPU search time is no longer a factor, but available memory is. If a computer system does not have enough memory for its needs, too much paging would result as each of the tasks would be competing for the available real memory. For 4K data pages, each buffer is 4K bytes. 256 buffers would take 1 megabyte of memory. 1000 buffers use 4Mb. The computer may also have more than one DB2 subsystem, each with its own buffer pools. Today, large systems have much real and expanded memory under MVS/ESA. 128 Mb of each is not unusual, and these systems can support much larger buffer pools. However, smaller systems have much less memory. Some may have 32 Mb or less. Besides the buffer pools, the DB2 regions have heavy memory requirements, as do CICS regions, TSO users, VTAM, JES, and everything else running in the system. 4 Mb for buffers may be pushing it for a small shop. With excess paging, overall system performance (and DB2 performance) will suffer.

If you are a small shop with low DB2 volume or few concurrent users, then 256 may be an adequate buffer pool size and it would be better for system utilization. This is especially true for a separate test subsystem. You could get by with even less for very low-volume testing. On the other hand, a large system with several hundred megabytes of memory can benefit from larger buffer pools. You can have a maximum of 500,000 buffers. This is a total of 2 gigabytes (2 billion bytes). The bigger the buffer pool for large systems, the better—up to what memory can support.

8.1.3 Buffer Pool Specification

Each DB2 subsystem can actually have several buffer pools. Up to four can be defined. They are called BP0, BP1, BP2, and BP32K. The first three have 4K buffers. BP32K has 32K buffers. It is required if you have any tables with 32K pages (the CREATE TABLESPACE statement will have BUFFERPOOL BP32K). Obviously, a 32K page needs a 32K buffer. Even if you do not have any large tables, you may still need a BP32K buffer pool. Some SQL statements will create work records that are over 4K. If you join several tables, the columns selected from them may total over 4K. Therefore, 32K buffers should always be defined. If you expect little use of them, you can go with the default of 12 buffers. This will handle any requests that arise.

BP1 and BP2 are usually not used by most shops. With one buffer pool (BP0) all table spaces and indexes share the same pool. It would seem that you might get better performance if you split them up among three different pools. This would be true if each pool were as large as one single pool. Three pools with 256 buffers each would be better than one pool of 256 buffers. However, usually you decide how much memory you want to use for buffer space. It can then all be given to BP0. If you want to use 3 Mb of memory, having 750 buffers for BP0 will generally perform better than having three pools of 250 buffers each. DB2 will manage the one large pool better.

If you know your data requirements well, you might come up with some situations where using the other pools might be useful. If you have one small table that is used by many transactions, assigning it to its own (small pool) might allow the entire table space to remain in memory. It would not contend with any other tables. For a sales system, the prices of each item would be needed by every transaction. One thousand 80-byte items would only take up 20 pages. A 20-page buffer pool for just this table would keep the entire table in the buffers. Even for a much larger price table, a small buffer pool would suffice as only a subset of the items would have frequent access.

Using several pools might be useful for analyzing system performance. For example, you could place all table spaces in one pool and the indexes in another pool. Then, performance monitor reports could more readily show you the table space and index buffer utilizations. You would not get better performance, but you would get some useful tuning information.

Normally, you should start out with just using BP0 (and a small BP32K). Only define the others if you find a real need for them.

8.2 CATALOG MAINTENANCE

8.2.1 Catalog and Directory Table Spaces

This section is of primary importance to system administrators, but it is useful information for programmers and DBAs, too. Most of the DB2 catalog is made up of ordinary DB2 tables and indexes which are in database DSNDB06. There is another part of the catalog which is called the directory. This is database

DSNDB01. The objects here are not in the format of tables and cannot be accessed with SQL statements. The four objects in the directory are:

SYSIBM.DBD01—the database descriptors
SYSIBM.SCT02—the skeleton cursor tables for plans
SYSIBM.SYSUTIL—records the execution of all utilities
SYSIBM.SYSLGRNG—the starting and ending log RBAs for all table spaces that have had update activity

These objects are used at run time by DB2 to control the execution of the system. Therefore, they are in an internal format which DB2 can use very efficiently. The catalog tables, while consisting of table spaces and indexes, also contain pointers (called hashes) between different objects. These hashes are used by DB2 for efficient access to related objects. When a user issues SELECT statements to access the catalog, DB2 uses the indexes.

8.2.2 Backups of Catalog Table Spaces

Since the catalog consists of datasets (table spaces), the same types of maintenance apply to it as to application tables. Updates to the catalog (from DDL statements and utility runs) are logged to the DB2 log. The catalog table spaces can also be backed up with the COPY utility. This should be done on a regular basis. When you COPY a catalog table space, the backup information is written to SYSIBM.SYSCOPY, just as for a user table space. There are two exceptions to this. The information about backups of SYSCOPY itself are recorded on the DB2 log. Otherwise, if SYSCOPY were damaged, there would be no record of its backups. The other exception is SYSIBM.SYSUTIL. This, too, is recorded on the log.

8.2.3 Reorgs of Catalog Indexes

As DB2 objects (table spaces, indexes, etc.) are created, the catalog tables can become unclustered and the indexes disorganized. Therefore, it might be desirable to reorganize parts of the catalog occasionally. However, the catalog table spaces cannot be reorganized, only the indexes. This does not create as much of a performance problem as might be expected. Since DB2 uses its hashes to access the catalog, it is not much affected by the physical layout of the data. User access, however, might be affected. Figure 8.1 has the SELECT to check the indexes that are part of the catalog.

For a high-volume system, placement of files can be important. Datasets whose performance is important should not be placed on the same disk packs as other high-access datasets. This is true of the DB2 catalog as well. For best performance, it should not be on a pack with high-volume DB2 tables, the DB2 log datasets, or any other frequently accessed file.

```
SELECT NAME,TBNAME,CLUSTERING,CLUSTERED,FIRSTKEYCARD,FULLKEYCARD,
   NLEAF,NLEVELS,CLUSTERRATIO
   FROM SYSIBM.SYSINDEXES
   WHERE CREATOR = 'SYSIBM'



SELECT IXNAME,CARD,NEAROFFPOS,FAROFFPOS,LEAFDIST
   FROM SYSIBM.SYSINDEXPART
   WHERE IXCREATOR = 'SYSIBM'
```
Figure 8.1. Checking the Catalog Indexes.

8.2.4 Removing Old Entries from the Catalog

Another performance consideration is the cleaning up of unused data from the catalog. For production systems, there is usually not much unused data (such as no longer needed entries for tables, indexes, synonyms, etc). For test systems, these are sometimes left over when a programmer or DBA leaves the company, or is finished working with the objects. While there may not be a lot of these, dropping them is beneficial in terms of catalog performance. It also makes it easier for people to look at the catalog. The less garbage, the better.

8.2.5 MODIFY Utility

There is one high-volume (relatively speaking) item in the catalog that does need cleaning out. In order for DB2 to keep track of all recovery requirements, it records every COPY run. A row is inserted into SYSIBM.SYSCOPY for each COPY, REORG, and LOAD (which also affect recovery). These rows stay there forever unless manually deleted. If the backup dataset may still be needed, then you want to keep the row in SYSCOPY. However, if the backup is no longer around (e.g., a cycle of five backups on tape are kept), then there is no need for the catalog entry. Old rows in SYSCOPY are deleted with a DB2 utility—the MODIFY utility. The corresponding old records from SYSIBM.SYSLGRNG are also removed.

Figure 8.2 shows the JCL and control statements for it. You can delete entries that are of a specified age, either a number of days or a specific date. In this example, any records older than 7 days for SHSPAT0 will be removed. If you retain backups on a regular basis, then the backup job can also have a MODIFY step to remove the older entries. You cannot tell DB2 to keep five entries, but if you know that you run the backup weekly and keep five copies, then you can use an AGE of 35 days.

```
//MODIFY   EXEC  DSNUPROC,SYSTEM='DB2T',UID='MODIFY',UTPROC=''

//DSNUPROC.SYSIN DD *

MODIFY RECOVERY TABLESPACE DHSHOS0.SHSPAT0 DELETE AGE(7)

//
```

Figure 8.2. The MODIFY Utility.

8.3 LOG DATASET MAINTENANCE

8.3.1 Active and Archive Logs

DB2 manages the log datasets. The programmers do not need to specify logs in their jobs, but they do need to know some things about them. Each DB2 subsystem has its own set of log datasets. There are active logs and archive logs. Whenever any update activity takes place, DB2 writes out log records. These are written to the active logs, which are online to the DB2 system. When an active log is full, it is automatically copied to an archive log dataset which can be on tape or disk. A subsystem can have anywhere from 2–53 active log datasets defined for it. You need more than one so that when each one fills up, the system can switch to another one and continue processing while the archiving takes place. The default is for three active logs. The systems programmer also has the choice of defining one copy or two of each active (and archive) log. Two copies (the default) provide added protection in case of an IO error that affects the log.

8.3.1.1 Retention of Archive Logs

Although full active logs get copied to an archive log, you should not think of these archive logs as something that is no longer needed. They very well may be used by DB2 for recoveries or restarts of programs. These processes are described in Section 7.6. If a program is running when the system crashes, or if a program abends, all uncommitted updates are backed out. DB2 uses the logs to find the records to back out. In a very high-volume system that does not have large enough active logs, some of the updates may have already been archived. Then, DB2 would have to access the archive log (which may be on tape) to do the backout. Hopefully, long-running jobs will issue commits frequently so that this will not be necessary. If a table space needs a recovery, the RECOVER utility finds the most recent COPY dataset, restores the table space from the backup, and applies all subsequent updates from the log records. If backups are not done frequently, it is quite possible for the COPY to be old enough that some of those log records will be on the archive logs.

There are two important points:

1. Copy all table spaces as often as possible so as to shorten recovery time and reduce the need for accessing the archive logs.
2. *Keep* the archive logs. Do not throw them away. It is important to set up operational procedures whereby the archive logs are kept (whether

on disk or on tape) at least as long as the backups are kept. It does little good to have a 2-week-old COPY but be missing the log records that are 1 week old.

8.3.2 The Size of the Active Logs

When defining each DB2 subsystem, the systems programmer can choose how many active logs to use, whether to have one or two copies, and the size of each log. The size is not actually specified directly. Instead, the installer gives an expected update rate and desired archive frequency. The system then calculates how much space to use. There is always a strong desire on the part of systems programmers to save space and there is, therefore, a temptation to use fewer and smaller logs if possible, especially for a test subsystem. My recommendations are as follows:

- Do not make the logs smaller than the default for either the production or test subsystems. If there is a third subsystem for systems programming testing, this one can have smaller logs.
- The production subsystem should have two copies of the logs, but it is probably okay to have only one copy for the test subsystems.
- Use at least three active logs for production, but two may be enough for test.

8.3.3 Log Data

To explain these guidelines, we will look at how big the defaults are and what goes into the logs. For the default values, each log will be 57 cylinders on a 3380 disk drive. If there are three active logs and two copies of each, then there are a total of six log datasets. That represents almost 300 cylinders for each subsystem. If you only have one subsystem, that is not too bad. If you have three or more, the space starts adding up. That is why I recommend only one copy for the test subsystems and possibly only two active datasets.

The reason I don't recommend reducing the size of each dataset is that 57 cylinders is not really that much. It gets filled up very quickly. Each time an active log is filled up, it is archived. You don't want to have zillions of archive logs being created. Therefore, you want the active log to be big enough so that it does not fill up too frequently. Generally, you might want to archive about once a day. Of course, a very high-volume system might need to archive more often than that even with bigger logs. A low-volume system might go a week without archiving.

Log records consist of everything DB2 needs in order to do backout or recovery. For an INSERT, this means the entire row. For an UPDATE, DB2 logs every field from the first changed one to the last changed one, even if those in between were not changed. It is clear from this why the logs fill up quickly. Essentially, for a newly created table, the log records will be as big as the table and its indexes. If you insert 100,000 rows of 200 bytes each, the rows will take up about

20 million bytes or 5000 4K blocks (not counting the indexes). At 150 blocks per cylinder (on a 3380), this is over 33 cylinders. The log records will take up the same amount of space. If the log dataset were only 10 cylinders, then three log datasets would be filled by this one process.

The above example is meant to discourage systems programmers from making the logs too small. It is also meant to give some advice to programmers. Whenever you have to insert a large number of rows, you should consider using the LOAD utility with the LOG NO option (see Section 6.2). INSERT statements will always write log records. LOAD with LOG NO will not. This will make the insertion much faster, will avoid filling up the logs, and will reduce contention with other programs for the log. REORGS of large table spaces should also use LOG NO for the same reasons. Batch programs that insert or update many rows should also commit frequently. This way, in case of system failure, backout can proceed much more quickly, and there is less likelihood of archive logs being needed for the system restart. If DB2 restart needs an archive log on tape, the restart process will take much longer, and all DB2 users will wait for the system to come back up.

8.3.4 Other Log Parameters

8.3.4.1 Number of Log Copies

Having two copies of the active log is a good safety measure. If one dataset is damaged, the system will still run with no loss of data. There is very little overhead to having a second copy. The second log is updated asynchronously. The applications do not have to wait at all for it to be updated. For the first log copy, the applications only wait at a commit point. Log records are buffered by DB2 and only written out when DB2 requires it. However, at a program commit point, all log records for that program must be written out.

8.3.4.2 Write Threshold

This is the number of log buffers for DB2 to fill before actually writing to the log dataset. It can be specified as 1–256. The default is 20. The more buffers, the fewer the number of IOs that are necessary. However, since each application commit forces a write to the log, the DB2 system may not be able to take advantage of a larger threshold.

8.3.4.3 Output Buffer

This is the size of the log buffer. It can range from 40K–4000K, with a default of 400K. When DB2 needs to read a log record for backout, it will first check the output buffer. If not found there, it will read the active log and if necessary the archive log. The larger the output buffer, the greater the chance that the record will be found there. This will save an IO and improve backout performance. However, a larger buffer will increase the virtual storage requirements for DB2 and could affect overall system performance. Since there is usually no need to optimize the system for backout performance, it is better not to make this value too high.

8.3.4.4 Recording Max

I have already recommended that the archive logs be retained for a long enough time period (at least as long as the table space backups). DB2 keeps track of these archive logs in its boot strap data set (BSDS). This value tells DB2 how many archive logs to record there. The default is 500 but it can range from 10–1000. Make sure that the number is sufficient to match your retention period.

8.4 OTHER SYSTEM PARAMETERS

8.4.1 DB2 Installation

There are two parts to the installation of DB2. The first part involves the systems programmer tasks of loading the DB2 libraries onto the system disks. The installation is controlled and recorded using IBM's SMP package. These tasks are similar to those used to install other IBM software. On the surface, there is very little here that requires specific DB2 knowledge. However, all software contains many bugs. Fixes to these bugs are continually being supplied by IBM. Part of the installation process includes researching outstanding problems and understanding which ones are critical to the running of the system. This task is helped by a strong knowledge of the product.

The second part of the installation is very DB2-specific. It is the running of a TSO CLIST to set a number of DB2 parameters to customize the installation. Some of these parameters directly affect the DBA and programmer. This installation CLIST is often run by a systems programmer with no DB2 knowledge. Instead, it should be run under the direction of the DB2 system administrator. Section 8.1 covered buffer pool specifications, and Section 8.3 covered the log datasets. This section will look at several other parameters.

8.4.2 NUMLKTS and NUMLKUS

These parameters are described in Sections 2.4 and 6.3. Briefly, NUMLKTS is a limit on the number of concurrent page locks a task may have on any table space (and its indexes) which has LOCKSIZE ANY, before the locks are escalated to a table space lock. There is no limit if the table space has LOCKSIZE PAGE. NUMLKUS is the total number of concurrent locks that any task may have before further processing is prevented (with a negative SQLCODE). System's programmers are often wary of applications programmers "abusing" resources, and they have a desire to place a limit on what a programmer can do. They see these two values as something they should reduce to prevent excess locking, but they often do so without an understanding of how they affect the DBA and programmer. The default values (NUMLKTS=1000 and NUMLKUS=10,000) are not that high, and there is probably no reason why they should be reduced without some detailed analysis.

Whatever values they are set to, the DBAs and programmers should know what they are. Most table spaces should be given LOCKSIZE ANY. If LOCKSIZE PAGE is used, then there is no limit on the number of page locks for each table space, but there is a much greater chance that NUMLKUS will be exceeded. Programmers should know what these limits are. For programs that will cause many locks, they can use the LOCK statement to lock the table space instead of the pages. Alternatively, they should issue commits frequently. This requires restart logic to be written into the program.

Without some thought into these matters, batch programs are likely to run into problems.

8.4.3 IRLM

The IRLM (IMS Resource Lock Manager) is the locking manager that DB2 uses. It runs in its own region. If you have several DB2 subsystems or an IMS/DC system, they can each have their own copy of the IRLM, or they can share one. It is recommended that they each have their own for performance reasons. If several subsystems are sharing an IRLM, then that IRLM will be processing more locks at a time, with an increase in overhead.

Another choice for the installer to make is where in memory the locks should be kept. The choices are either ECSA (extended common storage area), or within the IRLM address space. USING ECSA (the Cross Memory install parameter is set to NO), will be more efficient. However, it is necssary that a large enough ECSA has been defined by the MVS systems programmer.

The time period for timing out a task that is contending for a DB2 resource and the time period for detecting deadlocks (see Section 6.3) are also parameters related to the IRLM. The default values set the timeout period as four times the deadlock detection period (60 seconds vs. 15 seconds). This ratio is a good general guideline. Otherwise, tasks would time out before a deadlock was detected and the real problem would be masked.

8.4.4 Database Size Parameters

Part of the installation requires estimating the number of databases, tables per database, columns per table, etc. When first installing DB2, it is very hard to know just what the eventual totals will be. Don't worry about it. The values that are entered are used by DB2 to set the size of the DB2 catalog, directory, and EDMPOOL. However, they do not place an actual limit on the size of any of these. If the estimates are exceeded, the system may be slightly less efficient (e.g., secondary extents may be needed for the catalog datasets). If the estimates are too large, there may be some wasted space and extra memory needed.

The best bet is to go with the defaults until you have gained more experience (unless you know your requirements will be much larger than the defaults). For a test subsystem, you could use lower values.

The sizes of the temporary table spaces are initially defined when installing DB2. They may be changed later on. The temporary table spaces are used by DB2 for sorting and for creating indexes on populated tables. Give as much space as you can, and use multiple temporary table spaces. The extra space and table spaces will increase DB2's capacity for doing multiple concurrent sorts.

8.4.5 Application Programming Defaults

These installation parameters set default values to be used by the SQL preprocessor and for DB2I defaults. You should set the language to the one most frequently used by your installation.

The other parameters which you are most likely to consider changing are the date and time defaults. The date data type has one internal representation, but several possible external formats (i.e., formats in which dates can be entered and returned). Any of the possible formats can be used for input, but only one can be the default for output. The default for output is YYYY-MM-DD. Some shops might prefer the default to be MM/DD/YYYY or one of the other possibilities.

A shop may also create their own LOCAL format by writing an exit routine. If they do so, then they must change the parameter for LOCAL DATE length (or TIME length) to the length of dates (or times) in the local format. The default value of 0 indicates that no exit is to be used (i.e., there is no local format).

8.4.6 System Security

Access to DB2 objects is controlled with DB2's authorization mechanism. There is another aspect to security which is controlled by the systems programmers. That is access to the DB2 libraries, datasets, utilities, and the performance monitor. Some shops automatically prevent any access to anything by anybody. This is going overboard. Resources can be protected while still providing useful information and knowledge to the DBAs and programmers. Let's look at a few situations.

The next section covers how a performance monitor can be very useful to all DB2 users. If the systems staff is reluctant to allow general access to the SMF datasets, or to allow access to all performance data, the solution is to extract the relevant information on a daily basis. This extracted data can then be made available to the staff.

Several of the installation parameters are of importance to DBAs and programmers. This information should be readily available. Some performance monitors or other tools extract this information and produce a report or online display. Alternatively, the programmer can browse the DSNSAMP library. However, he would have to know which member is the current one in use, and would have to look up the names of each parameter in the Administration Guide.

The DSN1COPY and DSN1PRNT programs are examples of several utilities that run outside of DB2. They are used for copying table spaces and dumping (printing) the pages of table spaces. DSN1PRNT is useful for resolving problems with the files. However, this output is also useful for helping a programmer or DBA understand how DB2 stores its data and for relating some of it to the DB2 catalog and log files. Yet, since it is run outside of DB2, its use cannot be controlled by normal DB2 grants. Some shops, therefore, disallow general use of these utilities. Or they use a high-order node for all DB2 table spaces that are controlled by RACF and not accessible to most programmers.

There is a simple solution that will protect the DB2 datasets, but allow programmers to use these utilities on the test table spaces. The high-order node for a table space is defined for the storage group being used. Rather than just using one high-order node for all test table spaces, different nodes could be used for different programming groups. For example, if one group creates all of its (non-DB2) files under the node XYZ, then they should also use a storage group that uses XYZ. Typically, a shop does not assign that many high-order nodes, so there will not be an excessive number of storage groups needed. The RACF protection can then allow people in this group to have read-only access to datasets that begin XYZ.DSNDBC. These are the dataset names for their table spaces. They will now be able to use DSN1PRNT on their table spaces only. Moreover, they will not be able to write to these datasets except through DB2.

It is important to provide the programming and DBA staff with knowledge, not hide it from them. The more they know about DB2, the better they can do their job.

8.5 PERFORMANCE MONITORS

There are many software tools made by IBM and other vendors to work with DB2. Most of these tools are intended for the DBA with the expressed purpose of making the DBA's job easier. I have found that if you understand DB2 and do your work carefully, most of these tools are not essential. However, for a shop with inexperienced personnel, some of them might be helpful. It is beyond the scope of this book to describe any specific products, but it is certainly worthwhile to investigate and evaluate them.

One class of DB2 product is the performance monitors. I do highly recommend obtaining one of these for any high-volume shop and even for the small, low-volume installation. They really help in finding performance problems and in monitoring DB2 usage and growth. The reason they are more important for a large shop is that concurrency problems (see Section 6.3) occur more often when there is a high volume of concurrent DB2 usage. A monitor is the best means of pinpointing these problems.

Since I have given such a strong recommendation, I will now describe what a performance monitor can do for you. Monitors are available from IBM (the DB2 Performance Monitor) and from many other vendors. Most of these have both online monitoring capabilities as well as batch reports (IBM's was originally strictly batch, but now has an online component as well). There are certainly

8.5.1 Application Performance

As we saw in Chapter 5, EXPLAIN (together with queries on the catalog statistics) tells you a lot about how an SQL statement will be processed, although it does not tell you about the actual performance. Some of the things it cannot tell you include:

- How many times an SQL statement in a program is executed. A matching index lookup seems like a good choice of access path, but if the statement is executed 200 times in an online transaction, it might be responsible for slow response time.
- The performance of an imbedded statement is dependent on the particular values of the host variables.
- EXPLAIN (as of Version 2.2) will now tell you whether or not prefetch is being considered, but not if it is actually used. Prior to 2.2, you did not even know if it was a possibility.
- The number of IOs that are actually needed to process a statement.
- The actual time the program takes to run. The access path chosen by DB2 may be the "best" possible, but it may not be good enough. Is slow response time due to DB2 activity, or does the problem lie elsewhere?

You can estimate many of these things by looking at the EXPLAIN output, and manually calculating IOs based on the catalog statistics. However, the statistics may not be up to date. Any calculations you make will not be completely accurate. A performance monitor can give you accurate information on all of this. It can report on the CPU and elapsed time spent by DB2 and outside of DB2 for each transaction (or even for individual statements if additional DB2 traces are set). This reporting can be done for each execution, as well as providing averages and totals by plan or authorization ID.

For an individual plan, a monitor can report on how many SQL statements of each type were issued, how many pages were accessed, how many IOs were needed (synchronous or through prefetch), and the number of locks taken. This information can help in analyzing the performance of a specific program.

8.5.2 System Statistics

On the overall system level, a monitor can be used to keep track of DB2 utilization. It can show who is using DB2, and how much. Heavy QMF users can be easily identified. Heavy use does not necessarily mean misuse. It might just mean that the data is being effectively utilized. If so, the monitor information can be used to plan for growth. On the other hand, heavy use by a particular user might mean inefficient use of SQL. This user might need additional training (or the use of the governor to control his use).

Overall patterns of use can be determined—transaction vs. ad hoc query, retrieval vs. update, number of SQL statements per commit or per thread, etc.

Transactions that are running slower than expected can be spotted. It can be determined whether they always run slowly, or if the response time is very variable. For the slow transactions, a monitor will help pinpoint the cause. Perhaps it is DB2 CPU time, DB2 IO time, or other processing outside of DB2.

One of the key system-wide components is the buffer pool. A buffer pool which is too large for the amount of main memory may result in excess system paging. A pool which is too small for the workload will result in many more IOs than desirable. If the size of the buffer pool is going to be adjusted, there must be some way of determining the affect of the change. Performance monitors can report on the buffer pool utilization, either overall for the system, or for each individual transaction.

Accessing a data or index page is called a getpage. There is CPU processing required for each getpage, whether or not an IO is needed. Of course, if the page is found in a buffer, the cost is much cheaper than if an IO is necessary. The monitor will show the total number of getpages for each transaction, for each buffer pool. It will also show the number of IOs (both synchronous, and those obtained asynchronously through prefetch). These statistics show how well the pool is being utilized (as well as being useful for tuning the application). The affect of changes to the buffer pool can readily be determined.

The EDMPOOL is a memory area where DB2 loads the DBDs for databases in use, and the skeleton cursor tables to be used by application plans. Every open table space requires some control blocks in memory. Remember that if a table space is created with CLOSE NO, it will stay open even when not in use. The size of the EDMPOOL is set at DB2 installation time based on the estimated number of objects to be created in the subsystem. If the pool is too small for all control blocks that have been opened, DB2 will have to remove the control blocks (and close the table spaces) of any ones not currently in use. This does not prevent further use of these table spaces, but will slow down the next transaction to use them. The datasets will have to be reopened, and the control blocks reloaded into the EDMPOOL, with another inactive one removed. A performance monitor can quickly tell you whether this problem is occurring.

Figure 8.3 is an excerpt from a performance monitor report for an execution of a batch program. The program was run on a 3090/300J. The buffer pools had 9000 buffers in BP0 and 2000 in BP1. All indexes used BP1, and the tables spaces used BP0. This division was done just for monitoring purposes—to easily see how much index activity there was.

Elapsed and CPU times are given for both the application as a whole (actually starting from the first SQL statement) and the time spent by DB2. In this example, you can see that there is a very high DB2 CPU utilization—60 minutes out of a total of 65 minutes of DB2 elapsed time. The non-DB2 time is only a few minutes. The program issued a total of 800,000 SQL statements. Of these, 54,000

```
                Application    DB2
             Times (min:sec)
Elapsed      68:11          65:10       I/O   1:59
CPU          61:13          59:30


Total SQL DML Statements   816,020


SQL Activity
SELECT        53960
INSERT            0
UPDATE            0
DELETE            0
OPEN         213230
FETCH        336036
CLOSE        213230


Buffer Manager          Pool0      Pool1        Total
Getpage                548,000  2,002,100    2,550,100
Sequential Prefetch       1043          2         1045
Synchronous Reads        10968       2336        13304


Locking
Timeouts              0
Deadlocks             0
Lock Requests   1,189,320
```

Figure 8.3. Sample Performance Monitor Report.

were SELECTS. Most of the statements were related to cursors—OPENs, FETCHes, and CLOSEs.

The buffer pool statistics show 550,000 getpages for data pages and over 2 million for index pages. These are much higher than the actual number of rows read in. At most there were 54,000 + 336,000 = 390,000 rows found. There are really fewer found. Many of the FETCHes returned a −100 SQLCODE—no record found. The fact that the number of sequential prefetch requests (1000) is not zero indicates that some of the statements resulted in table space scans, rather than matching index lookups. Therefore, for those statements, DB2 had to read in many more data pages than actually contained selected rows. The reason that the index getpages is so high is that for every direct index lookup, the higher level index pages must be examined. Even if these pages are already in the buffer pool (which is likely in this case), looking at the page still entails a getpage and CPU processing.

There are relatively few synchronous IOs compared to the number of pages looked at. This means that most of the pages were in buffers. It also means that IO time should not be significant for this run. Indeed, DB2 IO time was less than 2 minutes.

What all of this shows is that DB2 CPU time can be a big factor in overall performance. IOs are not the only concern. Every getpage takes CPU time, and every SQL statement takes time to process. This program had a large number of both.

Once it had been determined that CPU time was the largest component of the run time, the next thing to do was to examine the program code to see if there were any inefficiencies in the use of SQL. In fact, two problems were found. One was a bug. A join of several tables included one where the join criteria were not unique. This resulted in duplicates returned, and twice as many subsequent OPENs and FETCHes.

The other problem involved the searching of a particular table. This table had four record subtypes based on the value in a particular column. For every key value, the program opened four cursors—one for each subtype. Most of the records were of one type only; therefore, for three of the cursors, no row was returned. The alternative processing was to open one cursor for the table. As the program fetched in each row, it checked the subtype and performed the appropriate action. This reduced the number of OPENs and CLOSEs to a quarter of the original number. The number of FETCHes also went down because only one "not found" was returned per key value, rather than four.

Not only did the number of SQL statements reduce dramatically, but so did the number of index getpages (with the original scheme, the higher level index entries were searched more often). Overall CPU time was reduced from 1 hour to 20 minutes. The performance monitor helped confirm the reductions in each of these categories.

8.5.3 Problem-Solving: Contention and Deadlock Detection

The performance of individual transactions can be analyzed and improved even without a performance monitor. To be sure, a monitor can help pinpoint the problem areas and possible causes. However, careful analysis of the code and the EXPLAIN output can help determine most of the processing issues. The place where a performance monitor is most useful is in determining the way in which multiple concurrent transactions interact. A stand-alone program may make effective use of the buffer pool. Several programs together may require a larger pool.

The area of which it is most difficult to do a static analysis is that of contention and deadlock (see Section 6.3). These problems can occur when two or more tasks access the same resources. Of course, there are always several programs accessing the same data types. The same program will also be executed by many different users. The questions are:

- Whether or not these executions will require data on the same pages?
- Which order the pages will be accessed by each program?
- Will the executions of the programs be simultaneous (i.e., are they concurrent)?

Whether or not two transactions are run concurrently, and whether or not they will access the same data or index pages does not have a simple answer. It may never happen, it may happen once or twice, or it may happen frequently. A performance monitor (especially an online, real-time monitor) is an essential tool for handling this type of problem.

When contention occurs, a transaction will wait for a fairly long time for the resource to become available. When this degraded response time occurs, an online monitor can be used to see what other tasks are running, and what resources they are accessing. This can help identify those transactions that are competing for resources. Then, the programs can be analyzed to see if they are coded in such a way as to foster such contention.

A batch-oriented monitor can also be used for this purpose, but it requires more effort. Detailed trace reports can show each transaction that was executed, and when. However, to obtain detailed information on which resources were being accessed, additional DB2 traces must be started. These traces add overhead to DB2. If the contention or deadlock problem is intermittent, then it is hard to decide when to enable these traces.

8.5.4 Using Monitors

DB2 captures, and writes out to a file, many types of information which are useful for performance monitoring or accounting. This information includes buffer pool, IO, and locking data, and the elapsed and CPU times of tasks. It also includes data on the SQL statements that are used—how many of each type, and against which resources. For each piece of data, the authorization ID and plan name are recorded, as well as a task number, to allow the data to be properly correlated.

Capturing all of the possible types of data adds a lot of overhead to DB2. Therefore, the amount of performance data to be collected is determined by the installation. When DB2 is installed, the system administrator sets particular trace classes to be collected. Other classes can be turned on as needed. The manuals for the various performance monitors give guidance as to which data is needed for different types of reports and for solving different types of problems.

There are several choices of where the performance data can be directed. The usual choice for batch-oriented reports is the SMF files. These are the datasets used by MVS for collection of system statistics from MVS itself, as well as various subsystems, such as DB2. The data can also be directed to destinations that directly feed online monitors for real-time reporting.

8.5.4.1 Types of Reports

There are several different ways in which the data can be reported. Some of the terminology I am using here is that of IBM's performance monitor—DB2PM. A Report accumulates the individual performance records into a meaningful grouping, such as a plan name or an authorization ID, or a combination of the two. There are a number of different types of DB2PM reports, including accounting data, statistics, audit information (i.e., which authorization IDs are accessing which resources), IO, and locking.

A Trace report prints detailed information in time order, showing a detailed sequence of events. These are the reports you would use to see each event as it occurred. For each SQL statement, you would see the access path used by DB2, the occurrence of IOs, and the pages accessed. The volume of output can be very high. This makes reading a trace a time-consuming task. A trace would normally be used after one of the other reports has indicated that a problem exists, but has not provided enough information to pinpoint the cause.

Another way to see the output is through a graph. Most monitors provide some type of graphing capability. Graphs are a very effective way to look at overall system usage and performance. The data can be grouped by time periods or by other categories, such as plan names or authorization IDs.

Especially useful is the ability to save the data and produce historical reports. Performance data can be saved in DB2 tables. This enables the use of SQL to analyze the information. You are then not limited to the reports that the particular monitor provides.

Each of the above are different ways to see a report of performance data *after* the transactions have occurred. Online monitors enable you to see what is happening in the system as it is occurring. You can see which transactions and programs begin and end, how long they run, and which SQL statements they are executing. A long-running task can be displayed repeatedly. If one particular statement continuously appears as the active statement, you get a fair indication that this statement is the one to investigate. When a task is waiting for resources, you can see which other tasks are concurrently running. You get a feel for the running of the system that is not possible with after-the-fact reports.

8.5.4.2 Who Should Use a Performance Monitor

Some shops think of any performance monitor as a tool for the systems programmer. Certainly, a systems programmer may be needed to help analyze wait-time problems that may be caused by other system activity. However, the systems programmers often do not have an in-depth knowledge of what DB2 does and how it processes SQL statements. A monitor is a tool which should be used by the DB2 system administrator, the DBAs and the project leaders, and lead programmers. You cannot analyze the performance of a program without knowing what that program does. You cannot analyze the effectiveness of the indexes of a table without knowing how they are defined, how the data is clustered, and how the data is accessed by the programs and users.

A performance monitor can be beneficial to each of these groups. The only requirement is that the person should know DB2 well, in order to understand the reports. Nor are all of the reports that easy to generate or read. Of course, the ease of use will vary among the various products available. Regardless of which product is used, it takes practice to learn how to produce the reports you need, which traces need to be set, and how to interpret the output. For IBM's monitor (DB2PM), the manual DB2 Performance Monitor Usage Guide (GG24-3413) is a valuable aid. But whichever monitor you are using, don't wait for a problem before learning how to use the tool.

8.6 CONTROLLING SQL USAGE: THE RESOURCE LIMIT FACILITY (RLF) AND THE QMF GOVERNOR

8.6.1 The Need to Control Usage

The wonderful thing about DB2 and QMF is that they have enabled end-users to easily access their own data. They no longer have to rely on a programming staff to code a COBOL or PL/I program. In fact, the programming staff no longer has to code a program for every report that they are assigned to create. On the other hand, in the past only a relatively small number of programs went into production without verification that they performed well enough (or accurately enough). Now, with so many reports being developed directly against the production data, there will be a great many of the following:

- inefficient queries
- incorrectly coded queries
- correct, efficient queries that process a very large amount of data

Most of these queries will be run during the prime shifts, in an online environment (either TSO or—starting with QMF 3.1—CICS). In addition to training and monitoring, it may also be necessary to control the usage of the DB2 system. It is not that we want to restrict the information that users may obtain from their data. It is that the growth in use of the DB2 data may exceed the growth in computer capacity that the organization has.

There are two facilities that can control the resources used by DB2 users. They do not prevent access (normal DB2 GRANTs control that). Rather, they limit the amount of processing that may be done by a query. The first facility available was the QMF governor. It sets limits for online access (long-running queries may still be run in batch). Version 2 of DB2 introduced the Resource Limit Facility (RLF) which controls processing of dynamic SQL statements. Therefore, it is especially of use to shops that have report writers other than QMF.

8.6.2 The Governor and the RLF

The governor is a QMF facility. It controls usage of online QMF commands. RLF is a DB2 facility. It controls dynamic SQL DML statements (i.e., not CREATEs, GRANTs, etc.). It applies to any environment (TSO, batch, CICS) where a dynamic SQL statement is issued. The two facilities control different things with some overlap. You may want to use both.

The governor controls the execution of QMF commands. It can place limits on the number of rows returned by a query, or the CPU time used. The CPU time includes the entire QMF command, including the time spent by QMF for interpreting the query and formatting the report. It only goes up to the first page presented. Any rows that are fetched during a page forward are considered part of the page forward command, not the original query. RLF, on the other hand, monitors CPU time only, and is for each individual DML statement. A cursor-controlled SELECT will include all FETCHes as part of the total for that statement. When the RLF time limit is exceeded, an SQLCODE of -905 is returned.

The governor has two limits—a prompt and a cancel limit. When the prompt limit is reached (either CPU or number of rows), the query is interrupted, the user is presented with a panel that shows the usage so far, and the user is asked if she wishes to continue. When the cancel limit is reached, the query is canceled. The user may then run the query in batch. QMF provides a batch submission panel and skeleton job. Your installation may have modified this panel, or it may not be set up to work in your shop.

8.6.3 The RLST Table

The governor and RLF also differ in the specification of who or what should be monitored. RLF can monitor users (authorization IDs) or plans. A table is created by the system administrator listing combinations of user IDs and plans with a CPU limit. This table is called the resource limit specification table (RLST). Figure 8.4 has a sample RLST table. If there is an entry for a specific user and plan, then that entry will be used. The next priority will be the specific user with a null plan entry. Then an entry for the plan with no user. Finally, if there is an entry with both user ID and plan name null, this will be used.

AUTHID	PLANNAME	ASUTIME
		500
	QMF230	1500
	HSSVC03	2000
GELLER	QMF230	2500
JONES		NULL

Figure 8.4. Sample RLST Table.

The CPU time limit is not given in CPU seconds, but in service units. This is a means of making the table independent of a change in computer model. Service units are dependent on the particular model and are the same units as are used by the MVS SRM (system resource manager). A faster CPU will have fewer seconds per service unit. Since the machine is faster, a given function will take less time.

In this example, the default is 500 units. User GELLER is allowed 2500 units when using QMF, 2000 units when using plan HSSVC03, and 500 units for anything else. User JONES has no limit on any plan. All other QMF users will be allowed 1500 units.

8.6.4 The Governor Resource Table

The governor only controls users. It does this indirectly. A table (Figure 8.5) is created, associating a group name with a set of limits. Individual users are associated with a group through the QMF Profile table, which is maintained by the QMF administrator. You can have many users within a group or you can have separate groups with different limits for each user.

Another feature of the governor is that it can be modified by an installation. The one that is supplied with QMF monitors CPU utilization and row counts. You could write one that monitors total CPU time for the QMF session (not just on each command), has different limits for different times of day, or that can prevent specific users from using certain QMF commands. There are many possibilities, but the coding of your own governor will not be trivial.

Figure 8.5 is a sample resource table for use with the supplied governor. There

RESOURCE_GROUP	RESOURCE_OPTION	INTVAL	FLOATVAL	CHARVAL
HOSPTEST	SCOPE	1		
HOSPTEST	TIMEPROMPT	100		
HOSPTEST	TIMELIMIT	1000		
HOSPTEST	ROWPROMPT	2000		
HOSPTEST	ROWLIMIT	10000		
HOSPPROD	SCOPE	1		
HOSPPROD	TIMEPROMPT	200		
HOSPPROD	TIMELIMIT	2500		
HOSPPROD	ROWPROMPT	2000		
HOSPPROD	ROWLIMIT	20000		

Figure 8.5. Sample QMF Governor Resource Table.

are two groups defined—HOSPTEST and HOSPPROD. Any QMF user with these entries in their profile record will use this table. The column RESOURCE_OPTION indicates the type of checking. INTVAL provides a value for this governor. SCOPE with a nonzero INTVAL turns on governing. TIMEPROMPT has the number of CPU seconds (100 for HOSPTEST) allowed before prompting the user. TIMELIMIT sets a limit before the command is canceled. ROWPROMPT and ROWLIMIT do the same for the number of rows returned by the command.

There is a good chance that one or the other form of resource control will be needed by most shops. Equally (or more) important is the need to set up procedures (and assign staff) to train the users and to monitor the usage. This is the best means of effectively utilizing the system. It will also help you plan how to set up the resource tables—who should be controlled and what limits to use. Good planning is essential to controlling the system resources without undue limitations.

9

Application Interfaces

Section 3.4 described in general the DB2 attachment facilities that must be used from the different execution environments (e.g., TSO, CICS, and IMS/DC). This chapter will discuss these in more detail. This information is needed by the DB2 systems programmer and the DBA, and is an important adjunct to the programming process.

9.1 CALL ATTACHMENT FACILITY

9.1.1 CAF vs. the DSN Attachment

For programs that are going to run under CICS or IMS/DC, you must use the attachment facilities for those products. For batch or TSO, you can use the TSO attachment (under the DSN command) or you can use the call attachment. When using the call attachment facility, there are several tasks to perform. The program must connect to DB2, open threads, close the threads, and disconnect from DB2. It must also handle error codes returned from DB2, and provide error messages for them.

Since DSN does several of these things for you, there is no point in bothering to use CAF for most programs. Certainly not for batch jobs. There are two situations where CAF can be useful. If you are developing an application to run under TSO (perhaps with ISPF panels), CAF can provide a more efficient system. An application will usually have several screens and programs. It is possible to do the whole system with one program, executing under DSN, which uses ISPF functions to display each of the screens. This approach has some drawbacks. The program can get very large and cumbersome, and the plan can also get very large since it would have the SQL calls for the entire application. Very large plans create problems:

- The bind can take a long time.
- The plan must be bound every time any part of the program is changed.
- During this long-running bind, parts of the DB2 catalog are locked.
- There could be contention with other plans being bound.

The alternative approach is to have separate programs for each function in the process. After each panel is displayed and the user enters data, a different program can be executed for the different subapplications. This has the advantage of modularizing the programs and keeping the size of things manageable. The drawback, however, is that each program that uses DB2 would be invoked by first invoking DSN and then issuing the RUN subcommand. This creates extra overhead. The first source of overhead is that a TSO CLIST (i.e., the TSO commands you are executing) is interpreted. That means extra time for TSO to translate the DSN and RUN commands to determine what to execute. The other source of overhead is that for each program the connection to DB2 must be established, the thread opened, and at the end, the thread closed and the program disconnected from DB2.

With CAF, it is possible to leave the connection open between screen interactions. It is also possible for a single program to change plans. It can close a thread and then open another one using a different plan. This gives added flexibility to the application. A larger program can still have several smaller plans which it executes at different times. It can also decide at execution time which plan to use. DB2 comes with a sample CAF application which does this. It is a demo application that has a COBOL version and a PL/I version. A menu allows you to choose which one to execute. The main routine will open a thread specifying the plan that was created for the appropriate program (the PL/I or COBOL version). The corresponding program is then executed. It is also possible for parts of the application to be available even if DB2 or some databases are not. Under DSN, DB2 must be available before the program can begin. Under CAF, the program starts first, then connects to DB2. Therefore, it can take appropriate action if parts of the system are unavailable.

Although more coding is needed to do the initial interaction with DB2, CAF can simplify the overall application for a TSO-based system.

The other area where CAF may be useful is if you are setting up your own multitasking region. DSN only supports single tasking, which is adequate for most TSO and batch use. CICS is a multitasking region, but it requires using the CICS attachment facility. If you need multitasking for other environments, then you would need to use CAF.

9.1.2 Using CAF

To use call attach prior to Version 2.3, your program must be link-edited with DSNALI, and you need an assembler language routine to call DSNALI to connect to DB2, to open threads, close the threads, and disconnect from DB2. Version 2.3 has a high level language interface to CAF to simplify its use. If there is an error opening the thread (e.g., a database is not available) a return code and a reason code are returned. Your assembler routine can call DSNALI to translate this into an error message. The TSO attachment (DSN) does this for you. For the TSO environment, you may also want to code an attention-handling routine. This will enable the user to interrupt an executing program with customized handling of the interruption. DSN also does this.

9.2 CICS INTERFACE

9.2.1 The RCT

In order to use DB2 with CICS, an interface table must be set up. This table reflects the relationship between CICS transactions and the DB2 plans that will be used with them. There are items in the table that affect performance, DB2 authorizations, and plan organization. These issues concern the programmers, DBAs, and systems programmers. The concerns of these three groups are interrelated.

The interface table is called the RCT (Resource Control Table). It lists every DB2 plan that will be used with CICS, and the transactions that will use each plan. Only one table is used with a CICS region at one time. Different tables may be used at different times. Since every plan and transaction is listed, the programmers must understand the relationship between plans and CICS transactions. They must know how this relationship is affected by whether the transactions are conversational or pseudo-conversational. This is described in Section 3.3.

Since there is one table per CICS region, it is often maintained by a systems programmer. However, since most of the data in it is related to the programmer or DBA, these groups must be aware of what goes into the RCT. The systems programmer cannot guess what is needed or when it is needed. The programmers must tell him in advance, and the further in advance the better. Adding an entry to the RCT is not difficult, but it involves reassembling the RCT, and stopping and starting the connection to DB2. Therefore, most shops will only make changes to production systems overnight. Even for development systems, it is not desirable to stop the connection during the day because all developers will be affected by the outage. In addition, many shops have standard periods for making changes to any CICS tables. They may want several days or a week's notice.

Now let's look at the RCT. Figure 9.1 has a sample RCT. We will start with

```
       DSNRCT TYPE=INIT,SUBID=DB2T,SUFFIX=1,THRDMAX=100,
           SIGNID=CICST
       DSNRCT TYPE=POOL,
           AUTH=(CICSTEST),THRDM=50,THRDA=20,THRDS=0,TWAIT=YES
       DSNRCT TYPE=ENTRY,AUTH=(CICSTEST),
           PLAN=PG01,TXID=(PG00,PG01),
           THRDM=3,THRDA=3,THRDS=3,TWAIT=POOL
       DSNRCT TYPE=ENTRY,AUTH=(CICSTEST),
           PLAN=PG02,TXID=(PG02),
           THRDM=3,THRDA=3,THRDS=0,TWAIT=YES
       DSNRCT TYPE=ENTRY,AUTH=(USERID,TERM,TXID),
           PLAN=PG04,TXID=(PG04),
           THRDM=3,THRDA=3,THRDS=3,TWAIT=POOL
       DSNRCT TYPE=ENTRY,AUTH=(CICSTEST),
           PLNEXIT=YES,PLNPGME=PG03XIT,TXID=(PG03),
           THRDM=0,THRDA=0,THRDS=0,TWAIT=POOL
       DSNRCT TYPE=FINAL
```
Figure 9.1. The CICS RCT Table.

the basic parameters for plan entries. Then we will look at the more esoteric parameters.

9.2.1.1 Entries for Plans

There are four occurrences with TYPE=ENTRY. The first three list the plan name (PLAN=) and one or more transaction IDs (TXID=). Let's review the relationship between plans and transactions. A plan must include all DBRMs from modules that might get executed as part of the same transaction. A CICS transaction consists of all programs that are executed from the initial program until control is returned to CICS. This includes subroutines that are called, modules that are linked to (EXEC CICS LINK), and modules that are transferred control to (EXEC CICS XCTL). Parts or all of a program may be executed in different transactions. For any modules that issue SQL calls as part of a transaction execution, their DBRM must be in a plan for that transaction. Of course, more than one transaction may execute the same programs. Therefore, more than one transaction may be associated with the same plan (as for plan PG01).

The basic requirement is that all plans that might get executed must have an entry in the RCT. The programmer should remember to request this in advance. By the same token, if the shop has naming conventions for plans, the programmers must be informed of this.

As described in Section 3.3, the original (and still most common) way to handle CICS/DB2 plans is that a transaction can only be associated with one plan. This plan must have all DBRMs that might ever be needed by the transaction. DB2 Version 2 introduced the ability to have dynamic plan selection. With this option, the plan can be changed in the middle of the transaction. It can be changed when a program issues a syncpoint and links or transfers control to another module. In order to use this capability, the installation must use a DB2 user exit. A sample exit (DSNCUEXT) is supplied with DB2. Instead of an RCT entry for each plan, there will be an entry for the exit program (PLNPGME=) as in the fourth entry of our sample RCT. In this case, the parameter PLNEXIT=YES must also be given. Several transactions may all use the same exit program, or there may be different programs for different transactions.

9.2.2 Authorization

For dynamic SQL (such as through QMF), access must be granted to the tables. For static SQL (most programs), you grant authority to execute the plan. With TSO and batch programs, these authorities are granted to the person who will be executing the programs. For production systems, you usually do not grant this authority to PUBLIC.

With CICS programs, there are several choices as to who (or what) is granted authority. The authorization scheme is specified in the RCT. The AUTH parameter is used. The choices are:

- a character string
- GROUP
- SIGNID
- TERM
- TXID
- USER
- USERID

USERID means that the user ID is used for authorization. This is similar to what is done in TSO and batch. It does require the use of the CICS Signon transaction, so that CICS can obtain the user ID. Not every shop requires users to sign on to CICS. The USER option is similar. There is a three-character CICS code called the OPID. This, too, comes from the sign on.

Although using the user ID seems like a likely choice, in practice it is often neither necessary nor desirable for CICS/DB2 security. Many application systems have their own security system built into them. The user must sign on to the application. The application security controls which functions the user may access. This security may not only control particular transactions and programs, but may also control options within the transaction. If the application system has such a security feature, then there is no need for additional DB2 security.

There is a distinct advantage to having the application control security. DB2 authorization is at the plan level. A user might be able to invoke the transaction and get the initial screen. Only when the first SQL call is issued will authorization be checked. This is much sloppier than preventing the user from accessing the transaction at all. If the user ID is used for DB2 security, then every user of the transaction will have to be granted authority to execute the plan. This can be a maintenance headache, as the user community undergoes frequent changes.

With application security in place, DB2 authorization (which must still be specified in the RCT) can be granted to a fixed value. For example, the "character string" option can be used (see PG01 — AUTH=(CICSTEST)). Then, the creator of the plan will grant execute authority to either CICSTEST or to PUBLIC. Granting execute to PUBLIC means in theory that anyone could use the plan. In practice, it is safe. If accessed in batch or TSO, the programs that use that plan would not work, and when accessed through CICS, the real security checking will be done by the application. If you are worried, grant it to CICSTEST. Version 2.3 has a new BIND option to limit which environment (i.e., TSO or CICS) a plan can be executed in.

Instead of a character string, another option which has the same affect is SIGNID. This is the applid of the CICS region. Each CICS region has an associated applid. Therefore, it is constant for all transactions in that region. Using this option, you could distinguish different regions that use the same DB2 subsystem. Of course, "constant" is a relative term. The systems programmers who set the applid may not be the same people who maintain the RCT. They might change it without knowing how it would affect the DB2 connection. Instead of the applid, the SIGNID can be overridden with a parameter on the TYPE=INIT record of the RCT (e.g., SIGNID=CICST). This way, the value is coded in the RCT and is less likely to be inadvertently changed without understanding the consequences.

Another option is TXID—the transaction ID. If your shop uses security at the transaction level, then this might be useful. Effectively, it says that a particular transaction can use a particular plan.

When dedicated terminals are used for an application, the TERM option restricts access to the plan to the specific terminals. This option also requires a lot of DB2 security administration. Every terminal using each of these transactions must be granted access to each of the plans. If new terminals are added, they too must be granted execute authority.

Many MVS shops use a system security package such as IBM's RACF. With RACF, each user's ID is registered with the system. Groups of users may be defined, with a user assigned to one or more groups. The GROUP option can be used when RACF groups are defined in the system (see Section 3.2). This option also requires the user to sign on to CICS, but requires less DB2 maintenance than the USERID option. Access to the plans does not have to be granted to each user, just the appropriate groups. When users leave a user group or new users come in, only the RACF security has to be updated, not the DB2 security. This, of course, requires good control of RACF security.

There is another factor affecting a shop's choice of authorization ID. That is their accounting procedures. The authorization ID is what shows up in the DB2 accounting records. A shop may want to identify DB2 usage by user or group or transaction, etc. That requirement may influence its choice.

9.2.2.1 Authorization Checking: Performance Implications

The most efficient checking is when plan EXECUTE authority is granted to PUBLIC, even when AUTH=constant is used. DB2 always checks for PUBLIC authorization before looking for a specific value. If a plan does allow PUBLIC access, this will get marked in storage when the plan is brought into the EDM pool. For a high-use plan, it is likely to stay in storage. Each time it is used, it is obviously quicker to check main storage than to reread the catalog table.

With Version 2.2, the checking of other constant authorizations has also been sped up quite a bit. DB2 will now set aside part of its storage for a cache of recently used authorization ID/plan combinations. Frequently used combinations are also likely to stay in storage. When a constant value is used in the RCT, there are fewer combinations, and each one is used more often. Again, the checking of the catalog will often be skipped. If USERID is used, then most invocations of the transactions will be for different authid/plan combinations.

9.2.2.2 Other AUTH Parameters

Notice that plan PG04 of Figure 9.1 has three subparameters of AUTH:

AUTH=(USERID,TERM,TXID)

Normally, only one option is used for authorization. However, it is possible to give the CICS attachment facility a choice of up to three. In this example, the USERID option is first. This means that if the user is signed on to CICS, USERID will be used. If the user is not signed on, then the terminal ID will be used if the transaction is associated with a terminal (not all CICS transactions are). If not, then the transaction ID will be used.

The setting of the the AUTH parameter is usually based on shop standards. The programmer must be aware of what it is being set to, because it is the programmer (or whoever binds the plan) who must grant authority to use the plan. Therefore, he must know who (or what) to grant this authority to. The programmer must also know what SQL code is returned when the correct authorization has not been granted. The program will get a −922 SQLCODE. This code is also returned for other reasons, but he should certainly check the authorizations as a likely cause, especially for a new plan.

Remember, for static SQL it is EXECUTE authority on the plan that must be granted. However, if the programs use dynamic SQL, then access to each table must be granted to the appropriate IDs. Normally, there is a clear distinction, but not always. IBM's CSP (Cross System Product) is a high-level application development system. It gives you the option of executing the same code either with dynamic or static SQL. This choice can be made at execution time. The programmer must understand this distinction.

9.2.3 Threads

The communication between a program and DB2 is done through threads. In effect, a thread is a set of control blocks that hold information about the interaction between an execution of a program and DB2. This information includes such things as the authorization ID, the SQL calls, and the returned results. With TSO, there is one thread for each TSO user who is connected to DB2 through the DSN processor. Since CICS handles many concurrent transactions, the CICS attachment facility must support multiple threads. In this section, we will look at such terms as active threads, maximum number of threads, protected threads, and thread reuse.

In our sample RCT, there are lines with TYPE=ENTRY, one line with TYPE=INIT, and one with TYPE=POOL. Each plan or plan exit program has a TYPE=ENTRY record. On these you specify values for thread usage. The pool entry is for a pool of threads, threads which can be used for the individual plans under certain circumstances. The TYPE=INIT record is used for defining default values and other parameters.

You may start by asking why we would need a maximum number of threads. Why not just have plenty around to support all the users who might want to access DB2? The reason is that threads use system resources (even unused threads), and there is a limit to those system resources. The main type of resource that is limited is main memory. Every thread, as well as every active transaction, requires system memory. If more memory is needed than is available, then the operating system must juggle things around. The juggling of real memory is called paging. A limited amount of paging is okay, but too much can lead to poor system performance. It may be better for a few transactions to wait a little while than to have too many competing at the same time. The other limited resource is the CPU itself.

Maximum threads is specified on the TYPE=INIT record with the THRDMAX parameter and on TYPE=ENTRY records with THRDM. There is a difference in their meaning. THRDMAX is the upper limit of all threads that may be used by the attachment facility with this RCT. It must be larger than the sum of the values of all the other thread parameters of the other entries in the RCT. In determining THRDMAX, there are two other values that the systems programmer should bear in mind. When DB2 is installed, there is a parameter for maximum number of connected users. There is no point in THRDMAX exceeding that. The other values are the CICS maximum tasks parameters. On the one hand, there is no benefit in exceeding that. On the other hand, you might choose to control overall usage of the system with the CICS parameters, and not limit DB2 access once the CICS transaction is started. Therefore, you might allow the CICS task limits to be lower than the DB2 limits.

Each of the individual entries have parameters THRDM and THRDA. THRDA is the number of active threads that can be used for this plan under normal conditions. The CICS operator can change this value dynamically up to a limit of THRDM (which obviously must be at least equal to THRDA). This allows you to adjust the system for different work loads at different times of day. Certain transactions may be used more frequently at one time of the day.

Before we go any further explaining how you decide on these values, we must first answer another important question. What happens when a transaction starts and the limit on the number of threads has already been reached? The answer depends on the TWAIT parameter for that entry. The choices are TWAIT=YES, NO, or POOL. YES says that the transaction should wait until there is an available thread. NO says that the transaction should be abended. POOL says that the transaction can use a thread from the pool. Let's look at how each of these can be used.

Under most circumstances, you want to limit the total number of concurrent threads because of limited system resources. Therefore, you keep the THRDA values fairly low. If each of 50 different plans had 10 threads dedicated to them, then at peak times there could be a very large number of concurrent transactions accessing DB2. If you only want a maximum of 100 threads, you might limit THRDA to two for each of them. However, most of the time, the transaction usage fluctuates. At one moment there might be four transactions wanting PLAN1 and none for PLAN2. At other times, the reverse might be true. Therefore, the pool provides a solution. Each entry might have THRDA=1 and TWAIT=POOL. The POOL entry might have THRDA=50. This way there are still 100 threads altogether. The second concurrent transaction for a plan will use a pool thread instead of one of the dedicated threads. TWAIT=POOL is the default for individual entries.

A value of THRDA=0 makes sense. An entry is needed to identify the transactions that will use a plan. THRDA=0,TWAIT=POOL means there are no dedicated threads for this plan. Instead, the transactions will use pool threads.

TWAIT=YES is useful when you want to limit the number of concurrent users of a plan. Perhaps the program uses a lot of resources and you just do not want more than one or two at a time. Or the program might have to run by itself. It may update some control information and requires serialization. THRDA=1,TWAIT=YES will only allow one at a time. The POOL entry defaults to TWAIT=YES.

TWAIT=NO might be useful when you want to limit concurrency, but do not want the next transaction to sit and wait. In some cases (such as with a long-running transaction), it might be better to abend the transaction, so as to inform the user immediately.

9.2.3.1 Thread Reuse

Inactive threads are not left sitting around forever. Even inactive ones use memory. On the other hand, it takes time to allocate a thread. Therefore, it would be beneficial if a thread could be reused by another transaction when the previous transaction is finished with it. This is only important in high-volume systems. Otherwise, there is no need to be concerned. There are some circumstances where a thread can be reused. However, there are some requirements for this to happen and for it to be effective.

The first requirement for thread reuse is that the application plan be the same. It is not that likely that a pool thread will be requested by a transaction using the same plan. So, more often it will be with dedicated (THRDA>0) threads. Under normal circumstances, the thread is removed when the transaction ends. A dedicated thread can be reused if there is a transaction queued up waiting for a thread. This might happen with a high-volume transaction, especially if TWAIT=YES was specified. There are situations where you know there are going to be a lot of transactions of one kind, but not necessarily queued up. You would like the threads to stay around a little while after each transaction is completed. This can be done by defining protected threads. The THRDS parameter is used for this (e.g., THRDS=3). A protected thread is not terminated for an average of 45 seconds after the transaction has ended. If another transaction for the same plan is initiated, it may reuse the thread.

The default for THRDS is 0 for individual entries. The default for the pool is 3. With a general mix of many different application plans, it is unlikely that the pool threads will be reused. Some shops, however, combine all the DBRMs for an application system into one big plan. There are a number of drawbacks to this (as described in Section 3.3), but the one advantage is a greater chance of thread reuse.

The creation of a thread involves a number of operations. These include the allocation of DB2 resources for the plan. Section 3.3 described the BIND parameters ACQUIRE and RELEASE. For transactions that usually use only part of the SQL statements of the plan during one execution, ACQUIRE(USE) RELEASE(COMMIT) is better. For ones that use all of the SQL statements each time, ACQUIRE(ALLOCATE) RELEASE(DEALLOCATE) may be better. If you want to make use of thread reuse, the latter set of options is much better. With RELEASE(DEALLOCATE), the table space locks are not released when the transaction ends, but rather when the thread is finally terminated. If the thread is reused, then the resource allocation is not needed for the next transaction. If USE and COMMIT are used, the resources will be released and will have to be reallocated.

Another function performed during thread creation is authorization checking. If a thread is reused and the authorization ID is the same as the prior transaction, then this checking can be skipped. This is much more likely if the AUTH options of SIGNID, a constant, or TXID are used. If the others (such as USERID) are used, then it is likely that the next transaction for the same plan will have a different user ID and, therefore, a different authorization ID. The checking will have to be done for the new ID.

In general, you might want to use the following guidelines:

- high-volume transactions: THRDA > 0 THRDS > 0 TWAIT=POOL or YES
- to control concurrency: THRDA > 0 THRDS=0 TWAIT=YES
- high priority, low volume: THDRA > 0 THRDS=0 TWAIT=POOL
- the rest of the transactions: THRDA=0, THRDS=0 TWAIT=POOL

9.2.4 The CICS/DB2 Connection

We know that the RCT describes the connection between a CICS region and DB2. What we need to know now is how do you tell CICS which RCT to use? And how do you tell which DB2 subsystem to connect to?

The second question we can answer right away. It is a parameter in the RCT. The TYPE=INIT entry has a parameter SUBID=... . In Figure 9.1, it is set to DB2T. This is the DB2 subsystem identifier. Clearly, one RCT can only be used with one DB2 subsystem. You need a separate one for different subsystems. This is true even if the plans and transactions are identical for the two systems. Of course, maintenance can be simplified by using the assembler COPY function to include the common definitions and only having the different parts (such as the TYPE=INIT entry) coded in the different RCT sources.

As mentioned above, a CICS region can use one RCT at a time. This tells us a few things. First, a CICS region can only be connected to one DB2 subsystem at a time (although several regions may be connected to the same DB2 subsystem). Second, at different times, different RCTs can be used. This means that there must be ways to easily change which RCT is going to be used. In fact, you have a few choices of how to specify the RCT. It can be connected when CICS comes up or it can be connected through an operator command. After it is connected, it may later be disconnected. The same or a different RCT may then be connected. One reason for connecting and disconnecting the RCT is that any changes require a reassembly of the RCT and require the connection to be stopped and restarted.

Different RCTs are identified with a parameter on the TYPE=INIT entry. SUFFIX=x is used to distinguish them. The default is 0. The full RCT name is DSNRCTx. If you want CICS to connect to DB2 when it comes up, you must put entries into several CICS tables—in particular the PLT. This table contains programs that CICS should execute when it is initialized. The details can be found in the DB2 Administration Guide. By default, it will use DSNRCT0. If you want a different one (e.g., you have several regions, each using different RCTs), you can tell CICS which one to use on the PARM parameter of the EXEC statement:

// EXEC PGM=DFHSIP,PARM=(DSNRCT1,.....)   DFHSIP is the CICS pgm.

Once the connection is started, you can start and stop it with the DSNC STOP and STRT commands (Figure 9.2). The STOP command tells CICS to stop the attachment facility. STRT tells it to start the attachment. The default RCT will be DSNRCT0. In Figure 9.2, we are starting DSNRCT3.

Knowing which RCT is being used is mostly the concern of the person in charge

```
-DSNC STOP

-DSNC STRT 3
```

Figure 9.2. Starting and Stopping the Attachment.

of the RCT. However, programmers should know which one is used and where the source for it is. This way they can check it to see if their entries are in it and are correct. Working in the dark makes it much more difficult to track down problems.

9.3 IMS INTERFACE

The TSO environment is not designed as a transaction processing system (although there are many installations that use it for that purpose). IBM has two teleprocessing systems that are specifically designed for high-volume online transactions. The previous section described the DB2 connection through CICS. The other major teleprocessing system is IMS/DC. While CICS is intended as a general-purpose transaction system, IMS/DC was orignally intended to provide these functions for systems using IMS databases. Since it was developed with databases in mind, there are many shops that use IMS/DC rather than (or in addition to) CICS. As these shops add in or move to DB2, they continue to use IMS/DC as their teleprocessing monitor.

The structure of IMS/DC is very different from CICS. CICS consists of one MVS region. All transactions are subtasks of this region. IMS/DC consists of a control region and separate dependent regions for each executing transaction. Batch jobs can also run under control of the IMS system, thus sharing the databases and other resources. The dependent regions can remain active, processing transactions as they come in. Alternatively, they can be started when a transaction arrives. Online regions are called MPPs (message processing programs) or IFPs (Fast Path regions). Batch regions are called BMPs (batch message processing).

9.3.1 Defining the Connection to DB2

Whereas a CICS region can only be connected to one DB2 subsystem at a time, an IMS system can be connected to more than one. Each dependent region (i.e., each transaction) can only be connected to one at a time, but subsequent transactions handled by the same dependent region may use a different DB2. To identify the DB2 subsystems that the control region and the dependent regions are allowed to connect to, you create a subsystem member (SSM). This member is stored in a PROCLIB and identified on the EXEC statement that starts the region.

9.3.1.1 Subsystem Member

The subsystem member is a set of control cards. There can be one SSM member in PROCLIB that all regions can point to, or there can be separate members for different regions. There will be one control card to define the connection to each subsystem. It consists of positional parameters and is in the following format:

SSN,LIT,ESMT,RTT,REO,CRC

Each of these parameters will be described below. The first parameter, SSN, names the DB2 subsystem (e.g., DSN, DB2T). If the IMS system can connect to multiple DB2s, then the SSM for the control region will name each of them. The SSM is specified with the SSM parameter on the JCL EXEC statement. For each dependent region, there are three possibilities:

- No SSM is specified for the region. It defaults to the SSM of the control region and can connect to any of the subsystems of the control region.
- An SSM is specified for the region. This SSM can name all of the DB2 subsystems, or a subset of them.
- If the region will not be used for DB2 processing, then an empty SSM should be specified.

9.3.1.2 Language Interface

A dependent region may be allowed to connect to one of several DB2 subsystems, but it can only connect to one at a time. There must be a means of identifying which one. There are two parts to achieving this. The LIT (language interface token) parameter of the SSM is used to identify a language interface module, which in turn is link-edited with the application program. There is a default interface module DFSLI000, which uses an LIT equal to SYS1. If you only plan to use one DB2 with each IMS system, then this is the only interface module you need. All programs will include it with their link-edit. For the test system, you might code an SSM with a control card that looks like:

DB2T,SYS1

For the production IMS, you would have an SSM with:

DB2P,SYS1

On the other hand, if you wanted the production IMS to be able to connect to either test or production DB2, then you would need two language interface modules. A new one can be produced with the DFSLI macro:

DFSLI TYPE=DB2,LIT=SYS2

The new interface module would be assembled and link-edited as DFSLI001 (or any other name). The SSM for the control region would have two records:

DB2P,SYS2
DB2T,SYS1

Programs that are to connect to DB2P would include DFSLI001 in their link-edit; those which are to connect to DB2T would include DFSLI000. An application program can only be linked with one interface module (and, therefore, be associated with one LIT). However, if you needed to temporarily run the program against another DB2 subsystem, you could change the SSM member (e.g., SYS2 – >DB2S).

9.3.1.3 ESMT Parameter

ESMT is the External Subsystem Module Table. It identifies a table that IMS will load into the region. For DB2, it is always the value DSNMIN10.

9.3.1.4 Resource Translation Table

The RTT is the Resource Translation Table. It is optional. There are two circumstances where it may be needed. One is if the plan names do not follow the IMS default. The other is if you want to use a region error option (REO) that differs from the default. These are described below.

9.3.1.5 Plan Names

The plan that a program will be using must be identified to IMS. The default is to give the plans the same name as the application program. If you do so, then there is no need for an RTT. You will not have to explicitly associate a plan with an application as you do with CICS. IMS transactions also have a PSB (program specification block) associated with them. The PSB name is also the same as the program name. If you want to use different names for the plans, then you must define a resource translation table. You do this with the DSNMAPN macro. The table is then assembled and link-edited into a load library available to IMS.

Figure 9.3 has an example of an RTT. There will be one DSNMAPN macro for each application that uses a different plan name. The first line has a label. This label becomes the name of the module and is used in the RTT parameter of the SSM. The last line has the parameter END=YES.

The APN parameter names the application program. PLAN gives the associated plan name. The OPTION parameter is for the recovery error option (REO) and is described below. The entries must be in ascending order by application name.

Since the name of the RTT is given in the SSM member for each dependent region, different RTTs can be used by different regions. This gives much more

```
RTTT1    DSNMAPN APN=HSADM01,PLAN=HSADM01T
         DSNMAPN APN=HSADM02,PLAN=HSADM02T
         DSNMAPN APN=HSDIS01,PLAN=HSDIS01T,OPTION=Q
         DSNMAPN APN=HSSVC01,PLAN=HSSVC01T,END=YES
```
Figure 9.3. An IMS RTT Table.

flexibility than with CICS. Only one RCT can be used by a CICS system at one time. With IMS, you could create more than one plan for an application and use them at the same time within different dependent regions. This might be especially useful for testing the effect of different BIND parameters.

9.3.1.6 Region Error Option

IMS gives you a choice of action to be taken by the system if DB2 is not up or a resource is not available when a region tries to connect to DB2. The choices are:

- R—An error SQLCODE is returned to the application. This is the default.
- Q—The transaction abends with a U3051 abend code. IMS requeues the input message so that it can be reprocessed.
- A—The transaction receives a U3047 abend and the message is discarded.

If you want a particular application to have an action other than the default, then you need to code an RTT. The entry for the application can override the error option with the OPTION parameter of the DSNMAPN macro (entry 3 of Figure 9.3).

9.3.1.7 Command Recognition Character

The last parameter of the SSM is the CRC (command recognition character). This is needed if the IMS system might connect to more than one DB2 subsystem. Applications identify the DB2 system with the LIT. The CRC is used to identify the DB2 system when DB2 commands are issued from an IMS terminal. DB2 commands are issued with the /SSR command. The default CRC is a −. If it is associated with DB2T, then you could display active threads to DB2T with the command:

/SSR −DISPLAY THREAD

9.3.2 Threads

The specification of threads for IMS transactions is much simpler than for CICS. There are fewer options. There is one thread for the control region (to each connected DB2) and one for each dependent region which is connected to a DB2. The maximum number of threads is the number of dependent regions.

IMS dependent regions can continue executing when there is no current transaction. This is called wait for input (WFI). Or they can terminate when the application terminates and be reinitiated when a new message arrives. Using WFI regions will result in thread reuse. Otherwise, the threads are not reused. Reusing threads can save some DB2 time for the creation of the thread and the checking of authorization. However, there are some drawbacks to using WFI. Since the region remains even if there is no waiting message, system resources may be wasted. WFI should be used if the region will be occupied at least 75% of the time.

WFI might also require some application redesign. If there are several interactions with the user to process a request, the usual design might involve an IMS program to program switch to invoke a new function. Instead, you might have to combine the subfunctions into one program using subroutine calls.

Fast Path (IFP) regions are also online transaction regions that are used for simple high-priority transactions. These regions always reuse the thread.

9.3.3 Authorization

The authorization scheme of IMS also has fewer choices than CICS. For message-driven regions (MPP, IFP), the possibilities are:

- If RACF is being used—the signon ID.
- If RACF is not being used—the LTERM (logical terminal) name, if there is one, otherwise the PSBNAME.

For nonmessage-driven regions, the possibilities are:

- If RACF—ASXBUSER
- If no RACF—the PSBNAME

As with CICS, it is best if security is controlled by an application security system.

9.3.4 DB2 Data Propagator

A new program product is being released by IBM to allow updates to IMS databases to automatically update a corresponding DB2 table. This product requires the use of IMS 3.1 (IMS/ESA) through the use of a new Data Capture Exit of IMS. The DBA defines which IMS data is to be passed through the exit and which DB2 tables and columns correspond to the IMS data. This process will allow data to be entered one time, yet will update both the IMS and DB2 databases together. The data can be immediately available to DB2.

The data propagation can be either synchronous or asynchronous. Synchronous updating means that the data will immediately be passed to the Data Propagator and the DB2 tables will be updated as part of the unit of work. There are no programming changes required. The two databases are always in sync, and recovery is coordinated by IMS and DB2. The drawback is that the existing IMS transactions will take longer to execute because there is more work being done.

With asynchronous updating, the data is fed to a program which must save it somewhere. At a later time, it can be processed by the Data Propagator. This process does not affect transaction response time, but requires a shop to write special recovery procedures and programs to keep the data consistent in case of failure. Also, the DB2 tables are not in sync with the IMS databases at all times.

Either way, this is an important new capability for large IMS shops which wish to utilize both IMS and DB2 for their processing.

9.3.5 The IRLM

The IRLM (IMS Resource Lock Manager) is the locking mechanism used by DB2 to enable concurrent access to the DB2 tables from many regions. As the name implies, it is also a lock manager used by IMS (and was originally written for IMS). An IMS system does not have to use an IRLM. Instead, it can use a system called PI (Program Isolation). This was the original IMS locking system.

If the IMS system is using the IRLM, you have the choice of using one IRLM for both IMS and DB2, or separate ones for each. It is generally recommended to use separate ones. The more locks that are active at a time in one IRLM, the more overhead there is in processing the locks. There is also a limit on the number of locks that an IRLM region can hold at one time. Therefore, it is better to separate the IMS and DB2 locking.

9.4 SUMMARY AND KEY GUIDELINES

- The call attachment facility can be useful in TSO Dialog Manager environments. With CAF, a more efficient modular system with small application plans can be set up.
- CAF requires more difficult coding than the TSO attachment. A sample application is supplied with DB2.
- Application plans that are to be used under CICS must be entered into the RCT table. This table is usually maintained by a systems programmer and requires an assembly and link-edit. The systems programmers often require several days' (or more) notice to make any changes—so plan ahead. Procedures should be established so that it does not take a week for updates to be made to the RCT.
- There are several possible schemes for determining the authorization ID for CICS/DB2 transactions. The programmers must know which scheme is being used so that they can issue the correct grants for the plans.
- If an application security system is being used to control access to the CICS transactions, then the DB2 plan authorization can be kept simple. Execute authority can either be granted to PUBLIC, or to a fixed character string assigned in the RCT.
- Threads are associated with each plan in the RCT. Each concurrently executing task requires a thread. High-volume plans or those that require serialization can have threads dedicated to them. Others can share a pool of threads.
- Thread reuse is desirable for very high-volume transactions. There are specifications in the RCT that can facilitate the reuse of a thread.

- A CICS region can be connected to one DB2 subsystem at a time.
- An IMS/DC control region can be connected to several DB2 subsystems. Each dependent region can connect to one DB2 at a time.
- If more than one DB2 will be connected to an IMS system, then additional language interface modules (the default is DFSLI000) will be needed.

Appendix A

Sample Tables

```
CREATE TABLE GELLER.THSPAT0                  CARDINALITY - 100,000
  (PATID       CHAR(9)     NOT NULL WITH DEFAULT,
   LASTNAME    CHAR(15)    NOT NULL WITH DEFAULT,
   FIRSTNAME   CHAR(10)    NOT NULL WITH DEFAULT,
   SEX         CHAR(1)     NOT NULL WITH DEFAULT,
   BIRTHDATE   DATE        NOT NULL WITH DEFAULT,
   ACTIVEFLAG  CHAR(1)     NOT NULL WITH DEFAULT)
IN DHSHOS0.SHSPAT0;


CREATE INDEX GELLER.XHSPAT01 ON GELLER.THSPAT0
  (LASTNAME,
   FIRSTNAME)
  CLUSTER
  USING STOGROUP STG1 PRIQTY 1000 SECQTY 200
  SUBPAGES 4 CLOSE NO;
```

```
CREATE INDEX GELLER.XHSPAT02 ON GELLER.THSPAT0
  (PATID)
  UNIQUE
  USING STOGROUP STG1 PRIQTY 800 SECQTY 200
  SUBPAGES 4 CLOSE NO;


CREATE TABLE GELLER.THSCHR0                    CARDINALITY - 100,000
 (PATID       CHAR(9)       NOT NULL WITH DEFAULT,
  EDUCATION   SMALL INTEGER NOT NULL WITH DEFAULT,
  PARENT1     CHAR(25)      NOT NULL WITH DEFAULT,
  PARENT2     CHAR(25)      NOT NULL WITH DEFAULT,
  NOTIFYNAME  CHAR(25)      NOT NULL WITH DEFAULT,
  NOTIFYRELAT CHAR(1)       NOT NULL WITH DEFAULT)
 IN DHSHOS0.SHSCHR0;


CREATE INDEX GELLER.XHSCHR01 ON GELLER.THSCHR0
  (PATID)
  CLUSTER
  UNIQUE
  USING STOGROUP STG1 PRIQTY 800 SECQTY 200
  SUBPAGES 4 CLOSE NO;


CREATE TABLE GELLER.THSADM0                    CARDINALITY - 150,000
 (PATID       CHAR(9)       NOT NULL WITH DEFAULT,
  ADMDATE     DATE          NOT NULL WITH DEFAULT,
  ADMSEQ      SMALL INTEGER NOT NULL WITH DEFAULT,
  DISDATE     DATE                        ,
  DISSEQ      SMALL INTEGER ,
  PROCESSED   TIMESTAMP     NOT NULL WITH DEFAULT)
 IN DHSHOS0.SHSADM0;
```

```
CREATE INDEX GELLER.XHSADM01 ON GELLER.THSADM0
  (PATID,
   ADMDATE DESC,
   ADMSEQ DESC)
  CLUSTER
  UNIQUE
  USING STOGROUP STG1 PRIQTY 1000 SECQTY 200
  SUBPAGES 2 CLOSE NO;

CREATE INDEX GELLER.XHSADM02 ON GELLER.THSADM0
  (ADMDATE)
  USING STOGROUP STG1 PRIQTY 800 SECQTY 200
  SUBPAGES 2 CLOSE NO;

CREATE TABLE GELLER.THSDIS0                CARDINALITY - 140,000
  (PATID      CHAR(9)       NOT NULL WITH DEFAULT,
   DISDATE    DATE          NOT NULL WITH DEFAULT,
   DISSEQ     SMALL INTEGER NOT NULL WITH DEFAULT,
   CONDITION  CHAR(4)       NOT NULL WITH DEFAULT,
   REFERRAL   SMALL INTEGER NOT NULL WITH DEFAULT,
   PROCESSED  TIMESTAMP     NOT NULL WITH DEFAULT)
  IN DHSHOS0.SHSDIS0;

CREATE INDEX GELLER.XHSDIS01 ON GELLER.THSDIS0
  (PATID,
   DISDATE DESC,
   DISSEQ DESC)
  CLUSTER
  UNIQUE
  USING STOGROUP STG1 PRIQTY 1000 SECQTY 200
  SUBPAGES 2 CLOSE NO;
```

APPENDIX A

```
CREATE TABLE GELLER.THSLOC0                    CARDINALITY - 280,000
 (PATID       CHAR(9)       NOT NULL WITH DEFAULT,
  LOCDATE     DATE          NOT NULL WITH DEFAULT,
  LOCSEQ      SMALL INTEGER NOT NULL WITH DEFAULT,
  WARD        CHAR(4)       NOT NULL WITH DEFAULT,
  ROOM        CHAR(4)       NOT NULL WITH DEFAULT,
  CURRENTFLAG CHAR(1)       NOT NULL WITH DEFAULT,
  PROCESSED   TIMESTAMP     NOT NULL WITH DEFAULT)
IN DHSHOS0.SHSLOC0;


CREATE INDEX GELLER.XHSLOC01 ON GELLER.THSLOC0
  (PATID,
   LOCDATE DESC,
   LOCSEQ DESC)
  CLUSTER
  UNIQUE
  USING STOGROUP STG1 PRIQTY 1000 SECQTY 200
  SUBPAGES 2 CLOSE NO;


CREATE INDEX GELLER.XHSLOC02 ON GELLER.THSLOC0
  (CURRENTFLAG,
   WARD,
   ROOM,
   PATID)
  USING STOGROUP STG1 PRIQTY 800 SECQTY 200
  SUBPAGES 8 CLOSE NO;
```

SAMPLE TABLES   407

```
CREATE TABLE GELLER.THSDRG0                CARDINALITY - 500,000
   (PATID       CHAR(9)     NOT NULL WITH DEFAULT,
    DRUGDATE    DATE        NOT NULL WITH DEFAULT,
    DRUGCODE    CHAR(9)     NOT NULL WITH DEFAULT,
    ORDERNUM    CHAR(7)     NOT NULL WITH DEFAULT,
    PROCESSED   TIMESTAMP   NOT NULL WITH DEFAULT)
   IN DHSHOS0.SHSDRG0;


CREATE INDEX GELLER.XHSDRG01 ON GELLER.THSDRG0
   (PATID,
    DRUGDATE DESC)
   CLUSTER
   UNIQUE
   USING STOGROUP STG1 PRIQTY 1000 SECQTY 200
   SUBPAGES 2 CLOSE NO;


CREATE INDEX GELLER.XHSDRG02 ON GELLER.THSDRG0
   (PATID,
    DRUGCODE,
    DRUGDATE DESC)
   USING STOGROUP STG1 PRIQTY 800 SECQTY 200
   SUBPAGES 2 CLOSE NO;


CREATE INDEX GELLER.XHSDRG03 ON GELLER.THSDRG0
   (DRUGCODE,
    PATID,
    DRUGDATE DESC)
   USING STOGROUP STG1 PRIQTY 800 SECQTY 200
   SUBPAGES 2 CLOSE NO;
```

```
CREATE TABLE GELLER.THSSVC0                 CARDINALITY - 2,500,000
  (PATID       CHAR(9)        NOT NULL WITH DEFAULT,
   SERVDATE    DATE           NOT NULL WITH DEFAULT,
   SVCSEQ      SMALL INTEGER  NOT NULL WITH DEFAULT,
   TYPE        CHAR(4)        NOT NULL WITH DEFAULT,
   CLINICIAN   CHAR(7)        NOT NULL WITH DEFAULT,
   PROCESSED   TIMESTAMP      NOT NULL WITH DEFAULT)
  IN DHSHOS0.SHSSVC0;


CREATE INDEX GELLER.XHSSVC01 ON GELLER.THSSVC0
  (PATID,
   SERVDATE DESC,
   SVCSEQ DESC)
  CLUSTER
  UNIQUE
  USING STOGROUP STG1 PRIQTY 2000 SECQTY 400
  SUBPAGES 1 CLOSE NO;


CREATE INDEX GELLER.XHSSVC02 ON GELLER.THSSVC0
  (CLINCIAN,
   SERVDATE DESC)
  USING STOGROUP STG1 PRIQTY 2000 SECQTY 400
  SUBPAGES 1 CLOSE NO;


CREATE INDEX GELLER.XHSSVC03 ON GELLER.THSSVC0
  (TYPE,
   PATID)
  USING STOGROUP STG1 PRIQTY 1600 SECQTY 400
  SUBPAGES 1 CLOSE NO;
```

```
CREATE TABLE GELLER.THSADD0                    CARDINALITY - 100,000
  (PATID       CHAR(9)     NOT NULL WITH DEFAULT,
   STREET      CHAR(50)    NOT NULL WITH DEFAULT,
   CITY        CHAR(20)    NOT NULL WITH DEFAULT,
   STATE       CHAR(2)     NOT NULL WITH DEFAULT,
   ZIP         CHAR(5)     NOT NULL WITH DEFAULT,
   PROCESSED   TIMESTAMP   NOT NULL WITH DEFAULT)
IN DHSHOS0.SHSADD0;

CREATE INDEX GELLER.XHSADD01 ON GELLER.THSADD0
  (PATID)
  CLUSTER
  UNIQUE
  USING STOGROUP STG1 PRIQTY 800 SECQTY 200
  SUBPAGES 4 CLOSE NO;
```

Appendix B

DASD Considerations

For years, the 3380 disk drive has been the mainstay of large MVS shops. The space calculation examples in this book have used this device. Recently, a new disk drive, the 3390, has been introduced by IBM. The new device is somewhat faster and has a larger capacity. Estimating the amount of DASD needed by an application system is an important task for the DBA and the system designer. Therefore, they must know the basic characteristics of the devices.

In terms of creating table spaces and indexes, there is nothing new that a DBA must do. DB2 will still use either 4K or 32K pages, based on the bufferpool specification. The PRIQTY and SECQTY parameters are still in units of 1024 bytes (1K). What changes is the number of pages that can fit on a track and on a cylinder. These are the space allocation units that DASD administrators use for planning and monitoring dataset size.

Both the 3380 and 3390 disk drives have 15 tracks on a cylinder. The 3380 has 47,476 bytes on a track, whereas the 3390 has 56,664 bytes per track. It is important to note that not all of this space will be used on each track. The amount used depends on the block size (page size). There are two reasons why the full capacity is not used. First, the block size may not divide evenly into the track size. Therefore, some space will be wasted. The other reason is that these devices require a fairly large interblock gap between each physical block. The smaller the blocksize, the more blocks per track there will be, but also the more interblock gaps.

On a 3380, a 4K (4096) block can have 10 blocks per track. This adds up to only 40,960 bytes per track. For a 3380, once you know how many pages a table space has, you can translate this into tracks by dividing by 10, and into cylinders by dividing by 150 (10 * 15).

A 3390 has a track size of 56,664 bytes. A track can hold 12 4K pages. This is a total of 49,152 bytes. The amount of unused space is similar on the two devices. Since a 3390 also has 15 tracks per cylinder, a cylinder has 180 4K pages.

From a space allocation point of view, this difference in track capacity is the major concern of the DBAs and analysts. The total number of cylinders on the device also differs, but that also depends on the particular model of 3380 or 3390. The 3390 comes in single or dual density (1113 vs. 2226 cylinders). The 3380 comes in single, dual, or triple density (885, 1770, or 2655 cylinders).

B.1 CACHE CONTROLLERS

DASD units are controlled by a DASD control unit (either a 3880 or the newer 3990). These control units might have a cache. A cache is volatile memory (similar to the processor's main memory). It is used to hold on to some of the data from the disk after it has been read. If a subsequent read request needs the same data, the information may still be in the cache, and the actual IO does not have to take place.

There are several ways to use the cache. In one mode, whenever a read is issued for a block, the control unit will read in the entire track, not just the one block. This is beneficial for sequential processing, where the subsequent blocks are likely to be requested, too. This sounds a bit like DB2's sequential prefetch. In fact, it is similar. DB2's prefetch is more effective in that it can read much more than one track's worth of data at a time and is selective, based on the access path chosen by DB2.

There is one situation where the cache can be of particular benefit. Prefetch is only used if a single SQL statement will require the reading of many rows on many pages. Some programs read through a table by repeatedly issuing an SQL statement, each time with a new value for a host variable in the WHERE clause. For example, the program might be driven by a transaction file which is sorted into the same order as the clustering index of the table. Each row read from the table will be either on the same page as the preceeding row or on the next page. Each page will only be read once, but sequential prefetch will not be used. The program does not get the benefit of the asynchronous reading ahead of the pages. With a cache controller, this program will gain some benefit, as the whole track will be read at once.

Obviously, not all table spaces can benefit from a DASD cache. If the access is not of this type, there will be no benefit. Much analysis must be done to find the datasets that can best make use of this feature.

Appendix C

Remote Database Access

Distributed data processing has been a concern to many shops for a number of years. An enterprise's application systems and data may be spread across several computers either in one site, or physically separated across the country. If the data is truly separate and is only needed at the local site, then there is no problem. However, if the data is needed both locally and at other sites, there are many problems.

The problem can be summed up as follows: How do you get up-to-date, accurate information to the other sites? If the data will be stored strictly at one site, but needs to be read at others, the problems are ones of communication and the programming needed to obtain the data. If any of the data needs to be stored in more than one site, then the problems are ensuring the accurate updating (and if necessary) backout of the data at multiple sites.

Some installations have worked hard at writing software to accomplish these tasks. For most shops, this type of effort, and the expertise required, is not feasible. For them, the only practical solution is for the DBMS and the operating system to provide the necessary functions.

DB2 Version 2.2 introduced IBM's first distributed database capability for MVS. It is just an introduction, providing limited capabilities, although these capabilities are provided with full data integrity. Version 2.3 introduces a different implementation based on IBM's Distributed Relational Database Architecture (DRDA).

This appendix will present an overview of the remote database access of Versions 2.2 and 2.3, and some performance considerations. In DB2 terms, a remote database is one which resides in another subsystem. This other subsystem may be on the same CPU (as with test and production subsystems), or it may be on another CPU. Version 2.2's implementation only supports remote DB2 subsystems. Version 2.3's capabilities can be used to access any remote DB2 or SQL/DS subsystems. When other IBM database systems also implement DRDA, they will also be accessible from a DB2 subsystem.

C.1 TYPES OF REMOTE ACCESS

There are three types of distributed processing that I want to define. DB2 does not implement each of these. The term, unit of work, should be understood by the reader. It consists of all processing between commit points.

Remote Unit of Work—The SQL statements within the unit of work are all processed at one other site (i.e., database subsystem). This is not implemented by Version 2.2, but is the basis for the DRDA implementation of Version 2.3.

Distributed Unit of Work—Within the unit of work, each SQL statement may access data at a different subsystem. This is partially implemented by 2.2, but is not part of the DRDA functions.

Distributed Request—A single SQL statement may reference several tables located at different sites. This would be truly transparent distributed processing. It is not implemented by DB2.

The DRDA architecture is different from the 2.2 implementation. With 2.3, both types of remote access are available. The original functions of 2.2 are still supported, but the future direction is based on the DRDA functionality.

Version 2.2 implements distributed unit of work with several limitations. There can be multiple-site read (i.e., each SQL SELECT statement could reference a different DB2 subsystem). However, there is only single-site update (i.e., only one DB2 subsystem may be updated within the unit of work). For TSO, this can be any site, although, for IMS and CICS, only the local site may be updated. The reason for these limitations is that it is not easy to coordinate the update and recovery of multiple systems.

With Version 2.3's remote unit of work, remote update is still limited to the TSO environment. CICS and IMS may only update the local site. From any of the environments, only single-site read may be done within a unit of work. After issuing a commit, the program may then issue a CONNECT SQL statement to connect to a different site. It is, therefore, possible to access multiple sites within a program, but only one at a time between commits.

C.2 IMPLEMENTATION

In order to have remote access, the system administrator or systems programmers must identify to each DB2 subsystem the other subsystems. This involves two major pieces. VTAM is the communications access method used to control telecommunications between CPUs (as well as to terminals and other devices). VTAM definitions must be specified to identify, to the operating system, the various DB2 subsystems.

Once VTAM knows about the DB2 systems, then definitions must be created to let DB2 know about each of the other systems. This is done by inserting rows into the Communications Database. This is a new set of DB2 system tables. Each DB2 subsystem has a location name as well as a VTAM LUNAME. The location name is used by applications to identify where the data resides. Information on the Communications Database can be found in the DB2 Administration Guide and in the DB2 Distributed Database Application Implementation and Installation Primer (GG24-3400).

C.3 THREE-PART NAMES AND ALIASES

Prior to Version 2.2, DB2 tables had two-part names—creator.tablename. Now, they have three-part names—location.creator.tablename. This does not obsolete all existing code. If a two-part name is given, it defaults to the local DB2. If a one-part name is given, it defaults to the local site, and the creator ID defaults to the authorization ID of the task. This is the same as always. However, if you give a three-part name, you have explicitly identified a particular site.

Of course, programs should be written to be independent of the location of the data. This enables tables to be moved. To accomplish this, Version 2.2 introduced Aliases. These are described in Section 3.2. An alias is similar to a synonym, with two major differences. It can represent a three-part name, whereas a synonym cannot. It can also be shared by any user, whereas a synonym is unique to its creator. Using aliases enables a program to be independent of table location.

In Version 2.2, the location of each remote table must be identified. With the remote unit of work of Version 2.3, only one site can be accessed at a time. Therefore, each SQL statement does not have to identify the locations of the tables. The CONNECT statement identifies the location. Or, if only one site will be accessed in the program, there is no need for a CONNECT. The BIND can identify the location.

C.4 STATIC AND DYNAMIC SQL

For Version 2.2, all remote access is processed using dynamic SQL. The program is written using standard DML statements; however, at bind time, these statements are only seen at the local site. At run time, they are shipped by DB2 to the remote site, where they are executed as dynamic SQL statements. This, of course, has performance implications. Only DML statements may be executed on the remote site. The program cannot issue DDL or DCL statements.

For Version 2.3's remote unit of work, either static or dynamic SQL may be used. Moreover, any type of SQL - DML, DDL, or DCL statements can be issued. Version 2.3's Package BIND (see Section 3.3) is an important part of this implementation. If a program is to access a remote subsystem, the BIND of the package (i.e., the DBRM of the one program) will be done at the local site, but the package will be stored in the catalog of the remote subsystem. The plan at the local site will reference the remote package. This enables the use of static SQL at the remote site.

C.4.1 SQL Return Codes

If all of the subsystems being accessed are DB2 subsystems, then the SQLCODEs returned from any statement will be standard DB2 values. However, other DBMSs, such as SQL/DS, have different return codes. To allow a shop to write programs that can work with data at any type of subsystem, there is a new data area called SQLSTATE. This area will be filled with a return code which will be standardized across IBM's relational DBMSs.

C.5 PERFORMANCE

There are several basic considerations in designing a distributed DB2 application system. Of course, there is transmission overhead. The SQL statement is first processed by the local DB2 and transmitted to the remote DB2. There, it is executed by the remote DB2. Any results (i.e., the SQLCA and any rows returned) are transmitted back to the originating DB2. The transmitting of the SQL statement and the SQLCA are approximately the same for any statement. However, the more rows returned, the more transmission of data there will be.

The most efficient utilization will occur if there are many rows processed by each SQL statement, but few returned. For example, an UPDATE statement that updates 1000 rows and returns no data back to the local subsystem. The time to do the processing will be much greater than the transmission overhead. On the other hand, 1000 SELECT statements (or one SELECT with 1000 FETCHes) will return one row per statement. Now, the transmission time is a significant part of the overall time.

Another factor is that, for the distributed unit of work, at the remote site the SQL statements are always executed as dynamic SQL. The performance implications of this were discussed in Chapter 3.

Once it has been decided to use remote databases, there is one programming technique that should be used to improve performance. When a cursor is used to fetch many rows, transmission overhead can be minimized if the rows are collected at the remote site and then transmitted in a block, rather than transmitted one at a time with each FETCH. This is called Block Fetch. It is used by DB2 when the cursor is read-only. Cursor SELECTs with ORDER BY or with joins are read-only. You can include a new parameter FOR FETCH ONLY on the DECLARE CURSOR statement to tell DB2 that the cursor will be used for reading only. When Block Fetch is used, up to 32K bytes of data will be fetched at the remote site before it is transmitted.

It will take some thought and planning to determine if distributed processing can be beneficial to an installation. Certainly, Version 2.2 does not provide everything that might be useful. Version 2.3 adds new capabilities, but still has limitations. Thought has to be given to which functions to use—distributed unit of work, or remote unit of work. However, it is worth investigating the benefits of distributed processing, and to gain some experience with the functions.

Index

ACCESS_CREATOR. *See* PLAN_TABLE
ACCESS_NAME. *See* PLAN_TABLE
Access paths, 9, 10, 116, 159–198, 220–221. *See also* EXPLAIN
   joins, 178–184, 246
   matching index lookup, 161–162, 167–168, 201–202
   multiple index. *See* Multiple index access
   non-matching index lookup, 165–167, 202
   one-fetch, 234–235
   subselects, 187–189
   table space scan. *See* Table space scan
ACCESS_TYPE. *See* PLAN_TABLE
ACQUIRE, 126–127, 297, 394
Active logs, 286, 367–368
Alias, 115–116, 415
ALL, 186, 188, 251

ALTER
   INDEX, 348
   TABLE, 54–55, 176, 208, 290, 337
   TABLESPACE, 64
AND, 170–172, 236, 276, 281
ANY, 186, 188, 251
Application plan. *See* Plans
APPLNAME. *See* PLAN_TABLE
Archive logs, 286, 367–368
Archiving, 39, 351–358
Attachment facilities, 128–132. *See also* CAF, CICS, DSN, IMS
AUTH. *See* RCT
Authorization, 21–25. See also GRANT, REVOKE
   accessing objects, 21, 114, 135
   catalog tables, 310–311
   creating objects, 22, 23, 114
   for DBAs, 22, 23
   for programmers, 23, 24, 114

   for users, 24, 134, 389–391, 400
   performance, 24, 391
Authorization ids, 22, 114–115, 135
AVG, 12

Backout, 344. *See also* COPY, RECOVER, Logs
Backups. *See* COPY
Backwards selection of rows, 270–271, 281
BETWEEN, 134–135, 266
BIND, 117–118, 120–121, 124–127
   authorization, 23, 24, 126
   BINDADD authority, 23, 24, 126
   BIND REPLACE, 120–121
   catalog tables, 117, 119, 125
   CICS, 121–125
   DBRM. *See* DBRMs
   EXECUTE authority, 24, 126

419

(*continued*)
   JCL, 117–120, 125
   parameters, 125–127
      ACQUIRE, 126–127, 297, 394
      ACTION, 126
      ISOLATION, 126, 254, 295, 297
      LIBRARY, 125
      MEMBER, 125
      OWNER, 114, 126
      PKLIST, 125
      PLAN, 125
      QUALIFIER, 113, 126
      RELEASE, 126–127, 297, 394
      REPLACE, 120–121, 126
      RETAIN, 126
      VALIDATE, 126
   packages. *See* Packages
   performance, 124
   plans. *See* Plans
   REBIND, 111, 113, 120–121, 338
BINDADD, 23, 24
Block fetch, 416
Browse transactions, 270–281
Buffer pools, 23, 65–66, 162, 164–165, 192–193, 205, 362–364
   BP0, 65–66, 364
   BP32K, 65–66, 364
   choosing, 65–66, 164–165, 364
   default sizes, 362
   size (number of buffers), 162, 164–165, 362–364
   sorts, 363
   specifying, 23, 65–66, 364

CAF. *See* Call attachment facility
Call attachment facility, 128–130, 385–387
   connecting, 386
   vs. DSN, 386
CARD, 201, 204, 206, 207, 238
Cardinality, 201–202, 204, 206, 207

Cartesian product, 14–15, 180, 249
CASCADE, 54
Catalog, 19–21. *See also* RUNSTATS
   maintainence, 364–366
   queries, 20, 21, 200, 206–209, 238–239, 258–259, 365–366
   tables, 20, 117, 119, 200–210
Catalog statistics, 20, 198–212, 305–311. *See also* Access Paths, RUNSTATS
   cardinality, 201–202, 204, 206, 207
   changing manually, 307–311
   data distribution, 203–204, 211–212, 307, 309–310
   defaults, 198–199, 239, 308
   production sized values, 198–199, 307–309
Character data type, 43–44, 67
   long, 43–44
   varying, 43–44
Check pending, 290
CHECK utility, 290
CICS, 121–125, 387–396. *See also* RCT, Plans: CICS
   attachment facility, 128–129, 132, 387–396
   authorization, 135, 389–391
   conversational, 122, 271
   DB2 connection, 395
      starting the connection, 395
   dynamic plan selection, 124–125, 389
   link edit, 121, 124, 129–130
   pseudo conversational, 122, 271–272
   RCT, 387–391
      AUTH, 389–391
      plans, 388–389
      plan exit, 389
      specifying, 395
      threads, 392–394

   threads, 392–394
      dedicated, 392–394
      entry, 392–393
      pool, 392–393
      protected, 394
      thread reuse, 393–394
CLOSE, 59, 71, 77
CLOSE cursor, 99–100
CLUSTER, 77, 192
CLUSTERED, 201
Clustered indexes, 9, 77, 166, 168, 191–198, 200–201, 204–205, 249. *See also* List prefetch
CLUSTERING, 201
Clustering index, 70, 77, 172–173, 192, 238–239, 312, 326–327
CLUSTERRATIO, 201, 308
COBOL, 43–44, 93, 98, 99, 108, 136, 137
Code tables, 37–38, 267
COLCARD, 208, 209, 309
COL_FN_EVAL. *See* PLAN_TABLE
Column functions, 8, 12, 177–178, 234–235, 254–256
   description, 12
   evaluation, 177–178, 254–256
   EXPLAIN, 254–256
   performance, 254–256
Columns, 7, 43–48, 67
   data types, 43–46
   inserting, 107
   names, 41–42, 96–97
   select list, 9, 10, 103–107
   views, 83–84
Communications database, 415
Compression, 48–49, 340–341
COMMIT, 73
Commiting, 73, 101–102, 126–127, 293–294, 344
   cursors, 102
   frequency, 294
   locking, 73, 102, 293–295, 297
   positioning, 271–272
   restart logic, 274–280, 294
   syncpoints, 73

INDEX

Composite table. *See*
 EXPLAIN, sort
 columns
Concurrency, 77–78, 174, 293–
 302, 377–378
CONNECT, 116, 414
Conversational transactions,
 122, 271
COPYPENDING condition,
 286–287
COPY utility, 286, 345–347,
 350–351. *See also*
 Backout, MODIFY
 utility, RECOVER
 utility
 copy datasets, 345, 347
 GDGs, 347
 incremental copies, 351
 JCL, 345–347
 MERGECOPY, 351
 performance, 350–351
Correlated subselect, 185–191,
 250–251, 253–254
Correlation name, 15, 96, 97.
 See also Join, Subselect
COUNT, 12, 177, 213
CPU utilization, 106, 140, 154,
 264–270, 281, 377
CREATE,
 ALIAS, 115
 DATABASE, 65
 INDEX, 76, 80–82, 173, 288,
 327–328
 STOGROUP, 64
 SYNONYM, 113
 TABLE, 23, 51–54
 TABLESPACE, 23, 58, 59,
 65, 72, 296
 VIEW, 83–86
CREATETAB authority, 23
CREATETS authority, 23
CREATOR. *See*
 PLAN_TABLE
Creator id, 41, 111–115
CS. *See* Cursor stability
CSP, 135, 391
CURRENT DATE, 46
CURRENT SQLID, 114
Cursors, 98–103, 110, 228–229
 CLOSE, 99–100
 cursor hold, 102, 271

DECLARE, 99–100
FETCH, 99–102, 273–280
FOR UPDATE OF, 102
 locking, 101–102, 297, 301
OPEN, 99–101
OPTIMIZE FOR, 275
performance, 99, 101, 266,
 274–275
repositioning, 272–281
results table, 99, 101, 274–
 275
Cursor stability, 101–102, 126,
 147, 254, 297

DASD, 63, 82, 160, 163, 293,
 329, 411–412
 space allocation, 63, 66, 68–
 69, 411–412
 3380, 66, 69, 160, 163, 293,
 411–412
 3390, 293, 411–412
Database descriptor, 298
Database design,
 logical, 27–40
 physical, 40–82, 319–337
Databases, 73, 89
Data compression. *See*
 Compression
Data manager (DM), 213
Data models, 29–38
Data propagator, 400
Dataset names, 62–64
Data types, 43–46
 char, 43–44, 67
 date, 43, 45–46, 67, 372
 decimal, 43–45, 67, 289
 integer, 43–45, 67
 time, 43, 67
 timestamp, 43, 67, 300
 varying character, 43–44, 67
Dates, 45–46, 67
 formats, 46, 372
 ISO, 46
 Local, 46, 372
 USA, 46
DBADM, 22, 23
DBD. *See* Database descriptor
DBRMs, 110, 116, 117, 120–
 125. *See also* Bind,
 Plans

DB2I, 129, 140–147
 defaults, 129
DB2PM, 373, 379–380
DCL. *See* GRANT, REVOKE
DCLGEN, 94–95, 98, 107, 144
DDL. *See* ALTER, CREATE,
 DROP
Deadlock, 300–301, 371, 377–
 378
DECIMAL, 45–46, 107, 289
DECLARE CURSOR, 99–100
DECLARE TABLE, 94–95,
 107
Default values, 17, 46, 106,
 289
DELETE, 19, 177
 index maintenance, 19, 177,
 325
 performance, 177, 282, 325
 processing, 58, 59, 177, 244,
 282, 325
 syntax, 19
 with a cursor, 102, 301
Delete rule, 54
Denormalization, 37–38, 163,
 334–335
 code tables, 37–38
 disadvantages, 38, 163, 335
 performance, 38, 163, 267–
 268, 335
 redundant data, 37
Dependent row, 50–51, 52, 54–
 57
Dependent table, 30, 50–53, 55
DESCRIBE, 138
DFSLI000, 129–130, 397
Directory, 284, 364–365. *See
 also* Catalog
Discard file. *See* LOAD utility
DISTINCT, 16, 168–169, 189,
 230
Distributed database, 115–
 116, 413–417
DML. *See* SQL
Domain integrity, 54–55
DROP,
 INDEX, 327
 TABLE, 58, 59, 113, 282–
 283
 TABLESPACE, 283
DSN, 120, 129–132, 385–387

DSNALI, 129–130, 387
 –DSNC, 395
DSNCLI, 129–130
DSNDB01, 365. *See also*
 Catalog, maintenance
DSNDB06, 364. *See also*
 Catalog, maintenance
DSNDB07, 64. *See also*
 Temporary table space
DSNELI, 129–130
DSNTEP2, 136, 146
DSNTIAD, 132, 136, 144, 146
DSNTIAUL, 136, 290–292
DSNUPROC, 283
DSN1COPY, 282, 350, 372–373
DSN1PRNT, 372–373
Dynamic plan selection, 124–125
Dynamic SQL, 132–142
 authorization, 135
 coding, 135–142
 controlling usage, 139–140, 380–383. *See also* Governor, RLF
 performance, 133–135, 140

EDITPROC, 48–49, 341
 data compression, 48–49, 341
EDMPOOL, 126, 371, 375
ENFORCE CONSTRAINTS, 290
Entity/relationship model, 29–31, 36–37
 mapping to normalized relations, 36–37
EXECUTE, 136–137
EXECUTE authority, 24, 126, 134
EXECUTE IMMEDIATE, 137
Execution JCL, 119–120, 130–131
EXISTS, 16, 186–187, 189. *See also* Subselects
EXITPARM, 204. *See also* SYSFIELDS
EXITPARML, 204
EXPLAIN, 146, 160, 219–259. *See also* Access paths,

PLAN_TABLE, RUNSTATS
 bind parameter, 127, 220–222
 running, 146–147, 220–222

FARINDREF, 208
FAROFFPOS, 204–205
Fast path, 396, 400
FETCH, 99–102, 138, 273–280
 limiting the number of rows, 274–275
FIELDPROC, 48
Filter factors, 214
FIRSTKEYCARD, 201–202, 309
Foreign key, 52–56, 110
 defining, 52–53
 rules, 53–54
FOR FETCH ONLY, 416
FOR UPDATE OF, 103, 297, 301
Forms. *See* QMF
F-parameter, 301
FREEPAGE, 70–71, 173, 198, 205–206, 312–313
Freespace, 67, 70–71, 78, 173, 300, 312–313
FROM clause, 9, 13
FULLKEYCARD, 201–202, 238, 309
Functions. *See also* Column functions
 performance, 217, 265
 AVG, 12
 COUNT, 12
 MAX, 12, 184, 188, 234–235
 MIN, 12, 188, 234–235
 SUBSTR, 217
 SUM, 12
 YEAR, 12, 217

Generation datasets (GDGs), 347
GETPAGE, 375–377
Governor, 140, 154–155, 380–383. *See also* QMF, RLF
GRANT, 22–24, 126

GROUP BY, 13, 168, 177–178, 254–256

HAVING, 13, 178, 184
HIGH2KEY, 134, 208, 210, 214, 311, 322
History files. *See* Archiving
Host variables, 92–93, 95–98
Hybrid join, 181–182, 246

IDCAMS. *See* VSAM
Identifiers, 40–41
IKJEFT01, 118–119, 131
Image copy. *See* Copy
IMS,
 attachment facility, 128–129, 132, 396–401
 authorization, 400
 data propagator, 400
 language interface module, 397
 link edit, 129–130, 397
 plan names, 398–399
 regions, 396, 399–400
 RTT, 398–399
 SSM, 396–397
 threads, 399–400
IN,
 CREATE TABLESPACE, 73
 SELECTS, 95, 232–233
 subselects, 17, 185–186, 188–189, 251
Indexable predicates, 213, 216–217, 265
Indexes, 9, 10, 74–82
 access paths, 161–162, 165–172
 choosing columns, 55–56, 323–326
 CLOSE, 77
 clustered, 9, 77, 161, 166, 168, 191–198, 200–201, 204–205, 249
 clustering, 77, 172–173, 192, 238–239, 312, 326–327
 creating, 76–78, 80–82, 327–328
 design, 227, 230, 319–327
 dropping, 327

duplicates, 78–80, 325
freespace, 78, 173, 198, 313
how used, 10, 11, 74, 161–162, 165–172, 201–202
index scan, 165–168, 202, 232
inserting data, 80–81, 172–175, 197, 287–288
layout, 77–80, 174
LOAD utility, 77, 80–81, 287–289
matching index lookup, 161–162, 167–168, 201–202, 232
multiple index access, 170–172, 196, 235–237
non-matching lookup, 165–167
ordering data, 11, 74, 168–169, 177, 268
page splits, 78, 173–175, 197, 313
primary key, 51, 76, 326
recovering, 348
reorganizing, 80–81, 198, 313, 314, 318–319
SUBPAGES, 77–78, 82, 197
unclustered, 166, 193–195, 197, 205, 230, 320–325
unique, 76, 78–80, 175, 289, 326
updating, 78, 175–177, 325
INDEXONLY. *See* PLAN_TABLE
Index only access, 168, 242
Index scan,
matching, 161–162, 167–168, 232
non-matching, 165–167, 232
Indicator variables, 98
INSERT, 16–18
column list, 16–18, 106, 107
duplicates, 110
page splits, 78, 313
processing, 81–82, 172–175, 243, 312
SUBPAGES, 77–78, 82
subselect, 18
syntax, 16–17, 106
INTEGER, 45–46
INTO clause, 93, 95, 99

IO, 160, 162–165, 193–195, 197, 201, 204–205, 329
getpage, 375–377
reducing, 264
IRLM, 72, 300, 371
IMS, 401
ISOLATION, 126, 254, 295, 297

Join, 6, 7, 13–15, 178–184
cartesian product, 14, 15, 180, 249
criteria, 7, 13–15, 178–180, 181, 249
equijoin, 179
EXPLAIN, 245–250
hybrid, 181–182, 246
inner table, 181–182, 246
merge scan, 182–184, 246
methods, 181–184, 246
nested loop, 181–182, 246
non-equijoin, 14, 180
outer join, 15, 250
outer table, 181–182, 246
performance, 181–184, 246–250

Language Access. *See* SAA Language Access
LEAFDIST, 205–206, 313
LIKE, 95, 133–134, 216
performance, 133–134, 216, 265, 273
syntax, 133
wildcards, 133–134, 216, 273
Limits,
datasets, 58
names, 40–41
NUMLKTS. *See* NUMLKTS
NUMLKUS. *See* NUMLKUS
Link edit, 116–118, 124, 129–130, 397
List prefetch, 166, 197, 230, 236, 275
LOAD, 282–292
authorization, 24
control statements, 285–287

discard file, 289, 290
duplicate index entries, 290
ENFORCE, 290
index building, 80–81, 287–289
input file, 240, 288–289
JCL, 283–285
LOG NO, 285–287
partitions, 287–288
performance, 283, 285–288
referential integrity, 290
REPLACE, 77, 192, 283
RESUME, 285
row order, 240
Load modules, 118, 120–121, 124
plans, 120–121, 124
timestamp, 120
Local dates and times, 46, 372
Locking, 77–78, 294–302
bind parameters, 102, 295, 297
commits, 101–102, 293–295, 297
contention, 174, 299–301, 377–378
CS, 102, 254, 295
cursors, 101–102, 297, 301
deadlocks, 300–301, 377–378
duration, 296–297
escalation, 298
index page splits, 78, 174
index subpages, 77–78
intent locks, 297–298
IRLM, 300, 371
locksize, 71–73, 254, 296, 298
mode, 297
NUMLKTS, 72–73, 298, 300, 302, 370–371
NUMLKUS, 72–73, 298, 370–371
page locks, 102, 296, 297
promotion, 298
RR, 102, 254, 295
table space locks, 58, 296–298
timeouts, 299–300
LOCKSIZE, 71–72, 254, 296, 298, 300, 302, 370–371

LOCK TABLE, 71, 293–294, 196
LOG NO, 285–287, 314
Logging, 282, 283, 285–287, 343, 368–369
Logs, 367–370
  active, 286, 367–368
  archive, 286, 367–368
  archiving, 367
  backout, 344
  defining, 367–370
  saving, 367–368
  size, 286, 367–369
  table space recovery, 346
LOW2KEY, 134, 208, 210, 214, 311, 322

Manuals (IBM), 20, 21, 55, 95, 109, 144, 285, 380, 415
MATCHCOLS. See PLAN_TABLE
Matching index scan, 161–162, 167–168, 201–202, 232
MAX, 12, 184, 188, 234–235
Merge scan join, 182–184, 246
METHOD. See PLAN_TABLE
MIN, 12, 188, 234–235
MIXOPSEQ. See PLAN_TABLE
MODIFY utility, 348, 366
Multiple index access, 170–172, 196, 235–237

NACTIVE, 207, 308
Naming conventions, 40–42, 112, 115
NEARINDREF, 208
NEAROFFPOS, 204–205
Nested loop join, 181–182, 246
New table. See EXPLAIN, sort columns
NLEAF, 201, 308
NLEVELS, 161, 201
Non-correlated subquery, 185–191, 250–252, 254
Non-matching index scan, 165–167

Non-sargable predicates. See Stage 2 predicates
Normalization, 33–38, 334–335
  denormalization, 37–38, 163, 334–335
  1st normal form, 33–34
  2nd normal form, 34–35
  3rd normal form, 35–36
Normalized relations, 31–38
NOT EXISTS, 185, 189
NOT NULL, 17, 46, 106, 107
NOT NULL WITH DEFAULT, 17, 46, 106
NPAGES, 206–207, 239, 308
NULLS, 17, 46, 57, 98, 111. See also Indicator variables
  inserting, 17, 98, 106
  retrieving, 98, 111
  vs. default values, 17, 46, 106
NUMPARTS, 60–61. See also Table spaces, partitioned
NUMLKTS, 72–73, 298, 300, 302, 370–371
NUMLKUS, 72–73, 298, 370–371

OPEN, 99–101
OPTIMIZE FOR, 275
Optimizer, 160, 167, 168, 220. See also Access paths
OR, 171–172, 216, 232, 236, 274–275, 281
  index use, 171–172, 216, 236, 274–275
ORDER BY, 11, 101, 227, 230–231
Ordering, 5, 11, 101, 168
Outer join, 15, 250
OWNER, 114, 126

Packages, 116–117, 120, 121, 124–126, 415
  collections, 125

Pages, 65–68, 70, 172–175. See also IO, Locking, USING
  buffer pools, 65–66, 192, 362, 364
  index, 77–80, 173–175, 197
  layout, 67–68, 70, 77–80, 174, 333
  pagesize, 65–66, 333, 364
  splits, 78, 173–175, 197, 313
Parameter markers, 138–139
Parent row, 50–51, 53–56
Parent table, 30, 50–53, 55, 56
Partitioned table space, 60–62, 287–288, 351
Partitioning index, 60–61, 288
PCTFREE, 70–71, 312
PCTPAGES, 207, 308
PERCACTIVE, 207
PERCDROP, 208
Performance, 9, 38, 133–134
  access paths, 133–134, 159–198, 220–221
  authorization checking, 24, 391
  buffer pools, 162, 164–165, 362–363
  contention, 295–296, 367–368
  CPU utilization, 106, 140, 154, 264–270, 281, 377
  denormalization, 38, 163, 267–268, 335
  distributed databases, 416
  EXPLAIN. See EXPLAIN
  indexes, 75, 161–162, 165–172, 201–202
  number of rows, 266, 267, 352–353
  referential integrity, 56, 266
  row size, 163
  table space scans. See Table space scans
Performance monitors, 373–380
Plans, 112–113, 116–127
  authority, 23, 24, 126
  BIND, 116, 125
  catalog tables, 117, 119, 125

CICS, 121–125
  RCT, 388–389
  dynamic plan selection, 124–125, 389
  dbrm, 110, 116–117, 120–125
  execution JCL, 119–120
  IMS, 398–399
  OPERATIVE, 111, 338
  ownership, 113, 126
  packages, 116–117, 120, 124, 125
  timestamp, 110, 117, 120, 124
  VALID, 338
PLAN_TABLE, 146–147, 222–259. *See also* EXPLAIN
  creating, 222–224
  querying, 147, 222, 224
  ACCESS_NAME, 227, 258
  ACCESS_TYPE, 225–227, 232–234, 236, 243, 258
  APPLNAME, 224
  COL_FN_EVAL, 255–256
  INDEXONLY, 236, 242
  MATCHCOLS, 231–232, 258
  METHOD, 246, 251
  MIXOPSEQ, 236
  PLANNO, 246
  PREFETCH, 227, 230, 236, 258
  PROGNAME, 224
  QBLOCKNO, 250, 254
  QUERYNO, 222, 225
  TABNO, 246
  SORT columns, 227–231, 246, 251, 254
  TSLOCKMODE, 254, 299
PLANNO. *See* PLAN_TABLE
PL/I, 43–44, 93, 98, 108, 136
Predicates, 213–218
  indexable, 213, 216–217, 265
  non-indexable, 216
  redundant, 212, 220
  stage 1, 213, 215, 217–218, 265–266
  stage 2, 213, 215, 217–218, 265–266
Prefetch. *See* Sequential prefetch, List prefetch
PREFETCH. *See* PLAN_TABLE
PREPARE, 136–139
Preprocessor. *See* SQL preprocessor
Primary allocation, 65–66, 68–69, 74
Primary authorization id, 22, 114
Primary key, 33, 51–54, 56–57, 76
  defining, 51–52, 76
  index needed, 51, 76, 326
  referential integrity, 51–54, 56
  updating, 53–54, 56, 57
PRIQTY, 65–66, 68–69, 74. *See also* CREATE: INDEX, TABLESPACE
Processing date, 39–40
Production implementation, 113–115, 121, 198–199, 239
PROGNAME. *See* PLAN_TABLE
Prompted query, 150, 152–153
Pseudo conversational, 122, 271–272
PUBLIC, 22–24, 391

Qualified reference, 15, 96–97
QBE, 150–152
QBLOCKNO. *See* PLAN_TABLE
QMF, 4, 146, 147, 150–155
  CICS, 147, 150
  default table space, 59
  forms, 153
  F-parameter, 301
  governor, 140, 154–155, 380–383
  proc, 153–154
  prompted query, 150, 152–153
  QBE, 150–152
  query, 150
  report, 153
  SAA Language Access, 4, 150, 153
  SAVE DATA, 59, 60
QUERYNO. *See* PLAN_TABLE

RACF, 114–115, 373, 390
RCT (Resource Control Table). *See* CICS: RCT. *See also* Threads
RDS (relational data system), 213
REBIND, 111, 113, 120–121, 338. *See also* Bind, replace
RECOVER utility, 81, 343–345, 348–351
  backups, 345–347
  JCL, 344–345
  logs, 346
  performance, 350–351
  timestamp recovery, 348–350
Redundant predicates, 212, 220
Referential constraints, 52–55
Referential integrity, 49–57, 110
  defining, 51–53
  performance, 55–57, 266
  rules, 52–55
Region error option. *See* REO
Relational databases, 4–8
Relational database design, 29–38
Relational data system. *See* RDS
Relations, 31–36
Relationships, 6, 7, 30, 49–50
  many to many, 30, 36
  one to many, 30, 36, 335
  one to one, 30, 36–37
RELEASE, 297, 394
Remote database, 115, 413–417

Remote unit of work, 116, 414
REO, 399
REORG utility, 58, 77, 80–81, 173, 198, 201, 312–319
   JCL, 314–316, 318
   performance, 316
REPAIR utility, 287, 290
Repeatable read (RR), 101, 126, 147, 254, 297
Resource control table. *See* RCT
Resource limit facility. *See* RLF. *See also* Dynamic SQL, Governor
Resource translation table, 398–399
Restart, 274–280, 294
   utilities, 317
RESTRICT, 54
Results table, 86–87, 274–275
RETAIN, 126
REVOKE, 24, 25
RID, 78–80, 166, 182
RID sorting, 166, 193–197, 230, 236
RLF, 140, 154–155, 380–382
RLST. *See* RLF
Rollback, 344
RR. *See* Repeatable read
RTT, 398–399
RUNSTATS, 127, 198–200, 208–210, 212, 238–240, 307. *See also* Catalog, statistics
   bind, 127, 198, 210
   catalog columns, 198–210
   catalog tables updated, 198–210
   JCL, 198–199
   manual updating of statistics, 307–311
   when to run, 127, 198–199

SAA language access, 4, 150, 153
Sample programs,
   DSNTEP2, 136, 146
   DSNTIAD, 132, 136, 144, 146
   DSNTIAUL, 136, 290–292

Sargable predicates. *See* Stage 1 predicates
Search criteria. *See* Selection criteria, WHERE clause
Secondary allocation, 65, 68–69, 74, 173
Secondary SQL ids, 112, 114–115
SECQTY, 65, 68–69, 74
Security, *See* Authorization, RACF
Segmented table space, 59–60, 173, 282
SEGSIZE, 59
SELECT,
   column list, 9, 10, 12–13, 103–107, 265, 267
   dynamic, 138–139
   GROUP BY, 13
   HAVING, 13
   host variables, 92–93, 95–98
   INTO, 93, 95, 99
   join, 13–15, 178–184, 245–250
   select *, 9, 10, 103–107
   subselect, 15–16, 184–191, 250–254
   syntax, 9–16
Selection criteria, 10–12, 14, 191, 213. *See also* Predicates
Sequential prefetch, 162–165, 166, 227, 228, 293, 363. *See also* List prefetch, Table space scan
SET CURRENT SQLID, 114
SET NULL, 54
Simple table space, 57–59, 173, 282
SMALLINT, 43, 45
SOME, 186, 188
Sorting, 9, 11, 101, 106, 168–169, 227–231
   DISTINCT, 168–169, 230
   GROUP BY, 13, 168, 177–178, 230
   joins, 182, 246
   list prefetch, 197, 230
   ORDER BY, 11, 74, 168–169, 227, 230–231

temporary table spaces, 81, 372
UNION, 168, 230, 277
using indexes, 11, 74, 168–169, 268
utilities, 314, 316
Space allocation, 65–71, 74
   default, 65, 69
   primary, 65, 66, 68–69, 74
   secondary, 65, 68–69, 74
Space map, 173
SPUFI, 92, 102, 144–147, 221
   defaults, 102, 147
   vs. QMF, 146, 221
SQL, 8–19, 21–25
   DCL, 8, 21–25
   DDL, 8
   DML, 8
   dynamic, 92, 116, 132–142
   embedded, 92–112
   static, 92–98, 112–113, 116, 133
SQLCA, 93, 108, 110
SQLCODE, 93, 108–111
SQLDA, 138–142
SQLERRD, 93
SQLIDS,
   CURRENT, 114
   primary, 22, 114
   secondary, 112, 114–115
SQL preprocessor, 94–95, 116
SQLSTATE, 416
SQLWARN, 93, 111
SSM. *See* Subsystem member
Stage 1 predicates, 213, 215, 217–218, 265–266
Stage 2 predicates, 213, 215, 217–218, 265–266
START DB command, 287, 290
Statistics. *See* Catalog statistics, RUNSTATS
STOGROUP, 23, 63–65
Storage groups, 23, 64–65
   creating, 64
STOSPACE utility, 63
Subpages, 77–78, 197
Subselects, 15–18, 184–191
   access paths, 187–191, 250–254
   correlated, 185–191, 250–251, 253–254

EXISTS, 16, 185–187, 189
EXPLAIN, 250–254
   non-correlated, 185–191, 250–252, 254
   performance, 187–191
Subsystems, 112, 120, 121, 128–129, 283
Subsystem member, 396–397
SUM, 12
Syncpoint, 125
SYNONYMs, 112–113, 115, 126. *See also* Aliases, Secondary SQLIDs
   creating, 113
   use in programs, 111–113
SYSADM, 22–23, 115, 126
SYSCOLUMNS, 20, 134, 208–210, 306
SYSCOPY, 347, 348, 365, 366
SYSDBRM, 117
SYSFIELDS, 204, 306
SYSINDEXES, 20, 200–202, 238–240, 259, 306
SYSINDEXPART, 200, 204–206, 306
SYSKEYS, 259
SYSLGRNG, 365, 366
SYSPLAN, 20, 117, 125, 338
SYSPLANAUTH, 20, 119
SYSPLANDEP, 119, 259
SYSSTMT, 119
SYSTABAUTH, 20
SYSTABLEPART, 207–208, 306
SYSTABLES, 20, 201, 206–207, 238–240, 306
SYSTABLESPACE, 20, 207, 306
SYSTEM, 120, 129, 283
System administrator, 22, 114, 115
SYSUSERAUTH, 20
SYSUTIL, 284, 365

TABNO. See PLAN_TABLE
Tables, 4, 40–49. *See also* Normalization, Denormalization
   changing, 337–340
   creating, 51–54
   design, 40–49, 329–337
   loading data, 282–292
   naming, 40–42, 112–113, 115
   redundant data, 333–334
Table spaces, 57–74
   altering, 64
   authorization, 23
   creating, 58
   datasets, 62–64
   layout, 59, 65, 333
   LOAD REPLACE, 58, 60, 283
   naming conventions, 41
   partitioned, 60–62, 287–288, 351
   segmented, 59–60, 173, 282
   simple, 57–59, 173, 282
   space allocation, 65–71
Table space scan, 9, 58, 59, 162–165, 225, 227. *See also* Access paths, Sequential prefetch
Temporary table spaces, 64, 81–82, 372
   CREATE INDEX, 81–82, 328, 372
   creating, 64, 372
   size, 82, 328, 372
   sorting, 81, 372
TERM utility command, 144, 284–285
Threads, 128. *See also* CICS, threads, IMS, threads
   reuse, 127, 393–394, 399–400
TIME data type, 43, 372
Timeout, 299–300, 371
TIMESTAMP data type, 43, 67, 300
Timestamp,
   load modules, 120
   plans, 110, 117, 120, 124
Timestamp recovery, 348–350
TNAME. *See* PLAN_TABLE
TOCOPY. *See* Timestamp recovery
TORBA. *See* Timestamp recovery
Transitive closure, 249

TSLOCKMODE. *See* PLAN_TABLE
TSO, 116–119, 121, 128–132, 135, 385–387
Tuning, *See also* Performance
   catalog statistics, 198–212, 305–311
   database, 303–359
   monitoring, 373–380
   program, 236–241, 267–269, 375–377
   system, 361–383

UID, 284, 285
UNION, 168, 230, 254, 277, 281
UNION ALL, 254, 277, 281
UNIQUE, 76
Unique indexes, 76, 78–80, 110, 175, 201, 289
UNLOAD, 315
UPDATE, 18
Updating, 78, 175–177
   access paths, 175–177, 243–245
   index columns, 176, 177
   index maintenance, 17, 78, 176
   performance, 175–177, 292–293
   primary key, 53–54, 56–57
   with a cursor, 102–103
USING,
   in CREATE TABLESPACE, 64, 69
   in dynamic SQL, 137
Utilities. *See* COPY, LOAD, MODIFY, RECOVER, REORG, REPAIR

VALIDATE, 126
VALIDPROC, 49, 54
VARCHAR, 43–44
Varying length string, 43–44
VCAT, 63–64
Version 2.3, 102, 115–116, 117, 120, 121, 124–126, 164, 181, 199–200, 271, 275, 314, 351, 387, 390, 413–417

Views, 55, 83–88
   creating, 83–86
   performance, 87–88
   select *, 84, 106
   view materialization, 87
VSAM, 5, 62–64, 65, 77. *See also* CREATE TABLESPACE, Storage groups
   defining table space datasets, 62–64
   linear datasets, 62

WHENEVER, 109
WHERE, 10, 13, 15, 93, 178, 184, 191. *See also* Predicates, Selection criteria
WHERE CURRENT OF, 103, 104, 225, 301
WITH CHECK OPTION, 55, 86

YEAR, 12